Cyber-Bullying

Issues and solutions for the school, the classroom and the home

Shaheen Shariff

Routledge
Taylor & Francis Group

LONDON AND NEW YORK

First published 2008
by Routledge
2 Park Square, Milton Park, Abingdon, Oxon OX14 4RN

Simultaneously published in the USA and Canada
by Routledge
270 Madison Ave, New York, NY 10016

Routledge is an imprint of the Taylor and Francis Group, an informa business

© 2008 Shaheen Shariff

Typeset in Garamond Three and Gill Sans by
Florence Production Ltd, Stoodleigh, Devon
Printed and bound in Great Britain by
TJ International Ltd, Padstow, Cornwall

British Library Cataloguing in Publication Data
A catalogue record for this book is available from the British Library

Library of Congress Cataloging in Publication Data
Shariff, Shaheen.
    Cyber-bullying: issues and solutions for the school, the classroom and
    the home/Shaheen Shariff.
        p. cm.
    Includes bibliographical references and index.
    1. Cyberbullying.   2. Bullying in schools.   3. Computer crimes.
    4. Internet and teenagers.   5. Internet and children.   I. Title.
    LB3013.3.S467 2008
    371.5'8 – dc22   2007039912

ISBN10: 0–415–42490–9 (hbk)
ISBN10: 0–415–42491–7 (pbk)
ISBN10: 0–203–92883–0 (ebk)

ISBN13: 978–0–415–42490–5 (hbk)
ISBN13: 978–0–415–42491–2 (pbk)
ISBN13: 978–0–203–92883–7 (ebk)

Cyber-Bullying

'Th   d
to (I
cou   d
use

Shaheen   e
rise of c   :s
to contr   n
because   is
ground   /e
provide

As t   e,
schools   )n
the oth   to
free exp

The   al
book,

- is
- addi
- provic
- develops
- obligation   eir
- highlights ways   m, technology providers and community organizations to provide support systems for victims (and perpetrators) of cyber-bullying.

Written by one of the few experts on the topic, *Cyber-Bullying* challenges reactionary school responses and encourages you to reconsider whether the culprits defined in this battle as kids and technologies are instead victims of a society in which the adults model intolerance and discrimination. The author peels away the layers chapter by chapter, to help you reconceptualize cyber-bullying to discover the educational potential of children and digital literacies.

Now teaching at McGill University, Montreal, **Shaheen Shariff** comes from a background in educational law and policy studies. Increasingly she is seen as the global expert on the topic of cyber-bullying.

This book is for my family

Hanif, my pillar of strength

Farhana, you will heal and be healed . . .
always be happy

Zahir, my ever-present soul-mate

In memory of Hamed Nastoh and his plea to educate

Dear Mom and Dad:

The first thing is, I love you Mom and Dad, but you didn't understand why I had to commit suicide. There was so much going on, and I tried to cope with it, but I couldn't take it anymore . . .

It was horrible. Every day, I was teased and teased, everyone calling me gay, fag, queer, and I would always act like it didn't bug me . . .

But I was crying inside me. It hurt me so bad, because I wasn't gay. And when people said it, my own friends never backed me up. They just laughed. I would pray to God every night for every one to stop saying that.

I know that you are going to miss me and that you will never forgive me, but you will never understand. You weren't living my life. I hate myself for doing this to you. I really, really hate myself, but there is no other way out for me.

Sure, I could have taken a gun and shot everyone in the head . . . but what would the point be?

I know I left my room messy. You can clean it if you want, but please don't sell or throw anything away. Even though I won't be there, I still want that room. It has to be my room . . .

I love you Dad and Mom. Please, please tell the people at the school why I did this. I don't want somebody else to do what I have done.

Mom, after my death please, please go to schools and talk to kids that bullying and teasing has big consequences. And tell them to please stop crying. That's just my only wish and I hope people will miss me. Please visit my grave often, so I'm not lonely.

(Used with the permission of Nasimah Nastoh, Hamed's mother)

Contents

Illustrations

Figures

Tables

Box

Preface

When I first developed the prospectus for this book, I had not envisioned that by the time I finished writing it, the issue of cyber-bullying would expand to such an extent. It is now at the forefront of educational policy agendas throughout the world. Moreover, the study of cyber-bullying is now, more than ever, a moving target. This made it difficult to stop adding new information to this book as it emerged on a daily basis. If I had continued to do that, I would never have finished writing.

Twelve months ago, even I could not have imagined that, in such a short time, cyber-bullying would evolve to become the polemic issue it is today, resulting in angry protests and petitions that demand forceful action by national teachers' unions and legislators. On one side of the controversy, teachers are petitioning school boards and unions to enforce student expulsions; and ban social networking web sites with a view to regain control of student respect for school authorities. The perception at national and international levels is that the Internet gives students too much power, allowing them to run rampant circles around their supervisors. To control this, some governments are investing millions of dollars into filtering technologies that restrict access to chat rooms and social networking sites that have, in some cases, been 'hacked' through by sixteen-year-olds within minutes! At the other extreme, some students, parents, librarians and civil libertarians insist that expulsions, suspensions, attempts to ban web sites, filters and blocking systems are futile. They argue that schools have no right to intervene in online expression because this infringes student rights to freedom of expression that takes place off school campuses and outside of school hours. They argue that zero-tolerance policies do not foster positive or respectful learning environments, but instead create poisoned and chilled environments that perpetuate cyber-bullying.

The media has characterized the issues as a 'battle', with cyberspace as its battleground. What is at the heart of this hotly debated controversy? What changed over the last year to reach such intensity? While academics and policy-makers were attempting to understand the phenomenon of cyber-bullying among school children (where pre-adolescents and teenagers harassed, threatened, demeaned and bullied each other online), many teachers and school principals shrugged their shoulders and suggested this had little to do with them. The consensus was that because most cyber-bullying took place from home, on personal computers and cellphones, outside of school time. It was therefore a parental responsibility. As such, they argued it should be addressed in the home. Many teachers, as evidenced by studies presented in upcoming pages, knew little about the extent of cyber-bullying that took place among their students, or their own legal responsibilities to protect students from abuse by classmates.

What changed was the advent and sudden popularity of a range of online social networking sites among teenagers. These sites unwittingly opened the doors to student online discussions in which teachers and school officials became the (intended or unintended) focus of student conversations. While most students use such networks responsibly, young people in many countries began to demean and sometimes express deeply offensive comments about certain teachers, school officials, university and college professors. For example, Facebook.com, a web site initially launched by a Harvard student to encourage online social relationships among Ivy league university students, suddenly became popular among high school students because of its capacity to upload hundreds of photographs and textual postings and connect large groups of friends. At the same time, YouTube.com also garnered the attention of teenagers, who discovered they could post amateur videos online without objection.

In the UK, one form of peer cyber-bullying known as 'Happy Slapping' was already popular. This form of bullying involved groups of teens slapping and beating selected victims, filming these actions, and posting them online. Other forms of peer cyber-bullying included setting up web sites and bulletin boards containing photographs of a classmate, and inviting insults, demeaning sexual comments and ratings to be posted and viewed by an infinite cyber-audience. A third form of peer cyber-bullying involved filming or taking pictures of victims, modifying the photographs to depict sexually graphic images, uploading them online and inviting comments from global audiences. All these forms of cyber-bullying among young people were paid negligible attention by school authorities in general. Now that teachers and school officials have become the subjects or focus of discussion on some social networking sites and bulletin boards, the matter has come to a head. Comments about teachers are posted on the public 'walls' of Facebook participants in the same way that grafitti about teachers was written on school washroom walls by previous generations of students. The Internet however, has far greater public reach than washroom walls. Insinuations that some teachers are paedophiles combined with other sexual insults; criticism of their manner of dress, appearance, accent, hygiene, and teaching styles, can have detrimental psychological impact, ruin teacher reputations and cause significant embarrassment.

In the past week, as I typed and edited the closing chapters of this book, I was contacted by several local school administrators from public and private schools. Most seemed quite anxious for advice before the school year started up again. I also received calls from several upset parents. All of them complained that their schools and school boards did nothing last year to protect their children from bullying or cyber-bullying despite numerous pleas for help. They were afraid to send their children back to school.

A number of organizations are beginning to take steps to gain an improved understanding of the issues. The Canadian Teachers Federation has invited me to join a task force its officers have created in response to teachers' demands for action; the Ontario College of Teachers conducted an interview and released it at the same time as a new survey on teachers' experiences with cyber-bullying in that Canadian province; and the Quebec School Boards Association has invited my participation in a task force on cyber-bullying. The Lester B. Pearson School Board in Quebec, thanks to the efforts of Mrs Nancy Hain, has already implemented a task force and workshops for teachers.

Most requests for guidance were received just prior to the new Fall term before pupils return to school. They indicate that there is a policy and practice vacuum that creates anxiety, tension and deep dilemmas for parents, educational policy-makers, administrators and teachers. The issues that have emerged with increased use of technologies have turned the notion of education and its administration, as we traditionally knew it, on its ear. Although the organizations that contacted me are all Canadian, the preliminary findings from an international research project I launched last year, with colleagues in Japan, China, India, Australia, New Zealand, United States and the United Kingdom (www.cyberbullying.co.nr), disclose that each of these countries are experiencing similar issues relating to cyber-bullying. Therefore, in this book, I have attempted to highlight some of the emerging issues internationally; analyse cultural and contextual differences in the way that young people in different parts of the world are engaging online; and consider legal and policy responses that have emerged at the global levels to address cyber-bullying. Unfortunately, we are still in the very early stages of researching the phenomenon of cyber-bullying. Research in many parts of the world is just beginning to get underway. Consequently, there is not a significant amount of scholarly research available in many Asian countries, other than examples of cyber-bullying cases that have caused concern. There has been significantly more activity relating to the study of traditional bullying in the UK and North America. This has naturally led to research initiatives that also take into consideration cyber-bullying in Western schools, resulting in more scholarly examination of the subject. However, even this was largely limited to behavioural perspectives over the last decade. It is only recently that the issues are being studied from interdisciplinary and critical perspectives that take into account contextual and systemic influences on children when they engage in online activity.

Given this context, I believe that my book will be timely and valuable as a guide for educators, policy-makers, parents, the media, technology providers and indeed anyone with a stake in understanding the complexities of cyber-bullying. My goal is to help readers to reconceptualize the way they think about education, student citizenship, socially responsible discourse and discipline in a digitized world. I put particular emphasis on the need to *value* our children and look more carefully for their participation and potential as leaders to resolving the issues we confront today. I believe that given sufficient responsibility and respect, youngsters can work collaboratively with adults towards new and digitized forms of learning that will detract from a focus on negative use of online tools.

My methodology is to provide readers with a foundation that informs them about the profile of traditional and cyber-bullying; the biological and sociological influences on children's behaviour; the power hierarchies among stakeholders within school systems that ultimately control what children learn and express on and off-line, to help them appreciate why typical approaches to address traditional and cyber-bullying are seemingly sensible, but do not work.

I bring together in laymen's terms, notions of substantive law and critical educational pedagogies that show greater promise of grounding educational responses to cyber-bullying. I present simple stakeholder models and guide-lines that can inform teacher education and professional development towards the development of non-arbitrary, ethical, educational and legally defensible policies.

We must remember that our generation developed and continues to introduce the online communications tools that create children's digital realities. They are growing up in a world that is simultaneously physical and virtual. Cyberspace is very much an integral aspect of their world. Moreover, my book explains why I believe that the discriminatory attitudes young people express through cyber-bullying are merely reflections of attitudes and hegemonies that permeate our societies, embedded within the very structures of our institutions. We often fail to recognize or acknowledge their existence. While the stated intent of our school mission statements talk about fostering 'inclusive and respectful school environments' there seems to be a disconnect in the actual implementation of those mission statements in many schools. The Internet has simply provided the wide open spaces that allow for society's attitudes of prejudice and disrespect to surface, opening up a Pandora's box of challenges.

Many young people cannot imagine a world without computers, cellular phones or text-messaging. These tools, despite their growing pains, present infinite opportunities for improved learning, and the development of global networks, friendships and connections that we could never have envisioned as children, let alone partake. It is these exciting and innovative opportunities that we must integrate into a reconceptualized approach to education, rather than dwelling too heavily on the dark side of technologies. While it is of course important to address the forms of cyber-bullying that have emerged, I hope to show in this book, that if we contextualize what is taking place and revisit the way we control and administer children's learning and expression we will make greater strides in navigating the dilemmas of cyber-communication. We ought to learn and grow *with* our children in an age of digital literacies, and empower the future generation to become responsible and contributing citizens, both of the physical and virtual worlds of cyberspace. Ultimately, we need to trust them to become better global citizens than we have been. To do this, they must have our committed support.

Shaheen Shariff, Ph.D.
Faculty of Education,
McGill University

Acknowledgements

I would like to begin by thanking Ms Frances Helyar, Ph.D. candidate, without whose commitment, persistence, efficiency, thoroughness and patience this book would not have come together. Frances worked with me to bring together years of work from scattered sources, including journal articles, book chapters, case studies and media reports, but insisted on taking no shortcuts that might compromise the quality of the book, despite tight deadlines. Frances, thank you for your high standards, which reflect the incredible individual that you are.

I would also like to thank the Social Sciences and Humanities Research Council of Canada (SSHRC) for making the research that went into this book and related projects possible. It is encouraging to have a federal granting agency that recognizes the need for cutting-edge research on a moving target, bringing together interdisciplinary research paradigms such as law, technology and education in an international forum. Connected with my SSHRC projects, I would like to thank my colleagues: Professor Colin Lankshear who was instrumental in helping me bring together my understanding of the mind-sets people adopt with respect to digital literacies; Dr Dawn Zinga, Dr Dianne Hoff, Mr Roderick Flynn, Dr Roland Case, Dr Edward Brown, Professor Hasegawa, Mr Zhang, Dr Jaishankar, Dr Patricia Ehrensal, Mr Kusminder Chahal and Mr John Fenaughty, all of whom are collaborators, co-investigators or consultants involved in the international project in its educational or legal aspects. All of your unconditional collaboration and input have helped me to gain an informed perspective on navigating the emerging complexities of cyber-bullying worldwide. Thank you to PREVNet for partnering our project.

I am also indebted to Ms Cathy Wing and Mrs Catherine Pearce of Media Awareness Network, for their invaluable support, research contributions and joint conference presentations. I look forward to working with them to develop much needed online professional development and teacher education programmes. Thank you to Mrs Nancy Hain, Assistant Director of Secondary Schools at the Lester B. Pearson school board, for her support as we conducted research in the schools, and her initiative in setting up a local task force; Mr Myles Ellis of the Canadian Teachers' Federation for authorizing use of the

CTF's recent resolution in this book; Ms Joyce Mason and Ms Beatrice Schriever of the Ontario College of Teachers (OCT) for getting my message out and approving use of the OCT's most recent survey on cyber-bullying of teachers; Mr David Birnbaum, Executive Director of the Quebec School Boards Association, for taking the initiative to collaborate; Dr Jamshid Beheshti and Dr Alan Large for authorizing the reference to their valuable bonding model; and to all school administrators, teachers and parents, too many to be named, who have contributed in some way to my research.

To the research assistants who have worked on both my cyber-bullying SSHRC research projects, I want to thank you for your conscientious commitment and dedication. In particular, I would like to thank Andrew Churchill for his leadership, enthusiasm and intelligent insight; Tomoya Tsutsumi for his precision in encoding the data in Quebec; Julie d'Eon, Yasuko Senoo and Lanxu Zhang for helping me develop collaborative networks in Japan and China and for translating the work; and my legal research assistants, Pavel Matrosov, Sujith Xavier, Amar Khoday, Katy Frattina and Sarah O'Mahoney for their valuable contributions.

Thank you to the following publishers for permissions granted for use of sources from my current and earlier work, as follows: Sense Publishing; *Education and Law Journal*; *Atlantis – A Women's Issues Journal*; *International Journal of Cyber-Criminology*; *International Journal of Learning*; *McGill Journal of Education*; *The Educational Forum* ; University of Toronto Press; Trentham Books; Peter Lang and Cambridge University Press.

To the Nastoh family, thank you for allowing me to publish your son's very personal letter. Nasimah, you have had enormous impact in educating people about the devastating consequences of bullying in any form.

Last, but by no means least, a very special thank you to my son, Hanif Shariff, for lending me the cartoon he developed on the 'horns of the dilemma' aged 10, and for his patient help (as a university student) with the tables and figures in this book. To my husband, Zahir, for his never-ending patience and support during my writing of this book, for his belief in my ability to produce good writing at all hours of the night, for the cups of tea in bed to wake me up the next morning to start yet another chapter, and to both Hanif and Farhana for lighting up my days.

Chapter 1

Cyberspace

Battleground or opportunity?

Teachers declare war on cyber-bullying!

(Brown, 2007)

School war against the bullies brings academic success!

(Asthana, 2007)

Prof raises alarm about cyber-bullying!

(Lampert, 2006)

Curb 'cyber-bullies' prof urges!

(Bohn, 2006)

Internet gives teenage bullies weapons to wound from afar!

(Harmon, 2004)

Introduction

Until very recently, the mention of the word 'cyber-bullying' conjured images in people's minds of a computer game with 'Star Wars-type' characters engaging in battle. It was difficult to convince people that this topic would attract much global attention and soon arrive at the forefront of public policy debates in education and parenting. That time has come. The issue of cyber-bullying often tops the agendas of government officials, educators, parents, civil libertarians and legal practitioners. The rapid advancement of cellular phones and Internet technologies has opened up new and infinite spaces that young people can explore with fewer restrictions. If we are to believe the above media headlines, ironically, the issue of cyber-bullying *has* become a battle of sorts in cyberspace. It appears that students, civil liberties advocates and some parents defend student rights to free expression in cyberspace, whereas educators, teachers' unions, other parents and government officials want to restrict them.

The purpose of this book is to introduce readers to the key issues that inform the heart of this debate or 'battle' and provide guidelines for schools, parents and other influential stakeholders, to address the emerging policy vacuum. My book presents international profiles of traditional and cyber-bullying and draws attention to the tensions that arise as a result of intersecting power relationships among stakeholders, all of whom are significantly impacted by emerging forms of student online expression. My goal is to raise awareness of the key dilemmas that confront schools, students and their parents, with a view to encourage reconceptualization of cyber-bullying, towards the development of proactive, educational and legally defensible responses. In much the same way as a painter might take time out from painting to have his eyes checked and his lenses readjusted so that the images he paints on his canvas become less blurred, so, too, I invite readers to take time out to readjust their assumptions and perceptions relating to the issues and reconsider them from the unique perspectives ventured here. The Internet and digital literacies have become part of young people's lives, their social relationships and their learning. I hope that the approaches I present in this book will facilitate this learning in school and home environments, both physical and virtual, that are conducive to children's well-being, learning and development as civil minded and socially responsible, contributing citizens of a global society. Young people cannot contribute in positive ways if there is a battle raging all around them.

Battles in cyberspace

This battle is consistently reflected in the media headlines that now appear regularly, giving the impression that one is reading about a *Star Wars* episode in cyberspace, with the Internet as the starship and kids as alien enemies. Consider the following headlines: 'A gift from the devil: Worry about online activities' (Soloyon, 2005); 'Cyber-bullying: The Internet is the latest weapon in a bully's arsenal' (Leishman, 2002); 'Internet gives teenage bullies weapons to wound from afar' (Harmon, 2004); and 'Cyber-bullying blighting our lives' (*Reading Evening Post*, 2006). These examples are a drop in the ocean of headlines that proliferate in news reports, which have global reach through the Internet. Most reports are framed to highlight the dangers and not the potential of online communication, often describing online tools as 'weapons'.

The news reports, as their headlines suggest, focus less on *why* kids might be using online communications networks as weapons to wound than on the dangers of using them. If we look at the headlines more closely, we discover that there is also a separate 'battle' taking place. This other war uses a different genre of 'weapons', commonly known to adults as 'policies' and 'legislation'. Consider the following headlines: 'Teachers *declare war* on cyber-bullying' (Brown, 2007); 'School *war against the bullies* brings academic success' (Asthana, 2007); 'Regina bylaw to *target* cyber-bullies' (CBC News, 2006); 'Web giants like You Tube are being *urged to get tough* with the *cyber-bullies* that use their sites to make pupils' and teachers' lives a misery' (Goff, 2007). A school

Dean's article is entitled '*Foiling* Cyberbullies in the *New Wild West*' (Franek, 2006). (Emphasis has been added in all examples.)

It seems ironical that these sensational headlines create a fear of online technologies, but focus on 'fighting', 'curbing', 'controlling' and 'clamping-down' on the '*cyber-bullies*'. The headlines refer to children, teenagers and young adults who appear to be ensnared by evil technologies. It is even stranger that so many media reports sensationalize and indicate support for an adversarial approach by educators to control and manage young people's online expression.

Worthy weapons?

The 'weapons' being used in attempts to control cyber-bullying, consist of lobbying by teachers' unions, parents and school administrators who want their governments to implement laws and policies that censor social communication tools such as Facebook and YouTube from being accessed at schools. Some call for bans on cellular and mobile phones that have photographic and text-messaging capabilities. Others want to restrict computer use while children are at school; impose school board monitored firewalls; and enforce zero-tolerance policies that include suspensions and, in some cases expulsion, as deterrents to bullying (Education Act, R.S.O., 1990). In the southern United States, some governments have also declared cyber-bullying serious enough to come under the umbrella of 'homeland security' legislation (Shariff and Johnny, 2007b).

Two of the headlines at the start of this chapter, namely, 'Prof raises alarm about cyber-bullying' (Lampert, 2006) and 'Curb 'cyber-bullies' prof urges' (Bohn, 2006) refer to a public presentation that I gave at McGill University in February 2006. These national headlines took me by surprise the following day. My talk for educators had called for responses to cyber-bullying that are grounded in educational and non-arbitrary, proactive responses. I do not want to raise alarm bells but I certainly want to raise awareness. The last thing I wish to do is make people fearful. As I have discovered, the media does an adequate job of that.

What drives this 'battle'?

The media headlines discussed above do not clarify *what* we are fighting. If the *technology* is dangerous, then why are we clamping down on the 'cyber-*bullies*' instead? In this book, I want to examine carefully the notion that violence can be controlled, banned, censored, fire-walled, managed or snuffed out in a contemporary and globalized world using violent or intolerant responses (zero-tolerance and suspensions). What do we seek to achieve as a society in our current responses to technology use among young people? Is there really an 'enemy'? Do there have to be scapegoats, and does society attach unrealistic notions of danger to the Internet or to youngsters who engage in online teasing and torment of peers and authority figures? Can cyberspace be 'controlled', and, indeed, can the communications that take place using electronic tools and media be 'managed' or 'supervised'?

There are two aspects to the issue of cyber-bullying that I plan to address in this book.

Peer-to-peer cyber-bullying

The first, which is less controversial, involves cyber-bullying among peers. Although this aspect of the issue has, in and of itself drawn a significant amount of media attention, there have been fewer vocal calls by educators for strong action. Cyber-bullying among students has been assumed to be an extension of traditional bullying that has nothing to do with school responsibilities because it generally takes place from home computers and personal cellphones. There is disagreement among parents and schools as to who is responsible for monitoring and preventing children and young people from bullying their peers online. As I will explain when I present the profiles of traditional and cyber-bullying, there is always a power differential when bullying takes place. In peer-to-peer bullying (physical or virtual), the power differential is at the level of young people, where a certain number of peers have a power advantage over their target(s).

Anti-authority cyber-expression

The second form of student expression, also commonly referred to as 'cyber-bullying', has recently attracted substantially more attention. There have been stronger calls for action from school and government officials, teachers and teachers' unions, because this form of cyber-bullying involves postings by students on social networking sites. Although most young people use social networking sites responsibly, a number of students have used them to demean and put down their teachers or school administrators, joke about them, modify photographs and invite insults and comments by students. There is disagreement among students (supported by civil libertarians and some parents) and school authorities as to whether this form of online expression by students constitutes 'cyber-bullying'. While the upcoming chapters engage in analysis of this debate, I have included it in this book as a form of cyber-bullying because it has attracted so much attention and concern from educators and policymakers. The power differential involved in this form of student online communication is reversed. The 'victims' of such expression are teachers, school principles and college and university professors (authority figures), who are disempowered because they have little control over who sees the online comments about them. Because the jury is still out as to whether this form of student expression constitutes cyber-'bullying', I also refer to it as 'anti-authority cyber-expression' or 'anti-authority online expression'.

'Raveger, Raveger'

My first experience with cyber-bullying began with an email from 'Raveger, Raveger [sic]'. The email was sent to our daughter Selina (pseudonym), when she was about 15, in Grade 11 at a high school in British Columbia, Canada. We came home one afternoon and found her pale and frightened, which was unusual for this normally feisty teenager. She handed us a printout of the email which read:

> You don't know me . . .
> But I know you . . .
> I've been watching you at school . . .
> And if you don't want to die . . . I'd sleep with one eye open
> Down on your knees, bitch!
> Raveger, Raveger
> (Shariff, 2001)

As a parent, I was concerned about Selina's safety. Was this a paedophile? Was it an adult at school? If a student was involved, did he know her walking route home from school? The reference to watching her at school brought the threat into the realm of the physical school environment, despite the fact that it was sent over the weekend from a home computer. School police liaison officers were unsuccessful in tracing the email, and our efforts to trace the source of the email through the ISP provider met a brick wall. At first there was no response to our calls and emails. When eventually contacted, an ISP manager explained that he could not shut down the email source to protect the client's free expression rights.

A male classmate eventually confessed that he and three others had sent the email from his home computer. Once the boy learned police were involved, he owned up to being coerced by the primary instigator, Mike (pseudonym). Apparently Mike had wanted to date Selina, who had refused his advances, and he sought revenge through email. Though school administrators were provided with the perpetrators' names, the boys were not disciplined because the email was not sent from school. Consequently, the harassment continued at school, where Selina was stalked and verbally bullied by the boys, who continued to go by the name of 'Raveger'. During one classroom project, the boys insisted on having Selina join their group. The teacher saw no problem with that, becoming impatient at Selina's reluctance to join them. Selina burst into tears. Once the problem was explained, the teacher confessed to having no prior knowledge of the incident, despite the Principal's commitment to us that he would inform all Selina's teachers about the threats the four boys had perpetrated.

Little did the 'Raveger' boys know how often the words contained in their email would be repeated in educational contexts – at conference presentations, in published journal articles and book chapters, in media reports (Shariff and Strong-Wilson, 2005) and, now, in the first chapter of a book on cyber-bullying. 'Raveger' helped me launch a career dedicated in large part to researching and addressing the complex issues of student communication in cyberspace, the spill-over effect in physical space, and the blurred boundaries of student safety, privacy and free expression. More importantly, it helped me launch research into the extent of school responsibilities and those of parents, policymakers and law enforcement agents to intervene when school-mates engage in bullying outside school hours, on home computers or personal cellphones. Although this email was sent eight years ago, the issues it raised continue to challenge parents, school administrators and teachers worldwide, as technology use among pre-teens and adolescents flourishes. Ravager sets the stage for discussion of some key dilemmas that have surfaced with increased proliferation of new technologies among young people, and that continue to become significantly more complex as innovative social communication tools such as Facebook, MySpace, YouTube, Bebo, LinkdIn, Orkut and rapidly advancing cellphone technologies become established as contemporary modes of communication among the younger generation.

I believe it is important to provide readers with a sense of the broader societal context, which highlights the range of stakeholder influences such as the power of the media, government officials, school boards, school administrators, technology corporations, teachers and parents in shaping how we conceptualize, perceive and respond to technology and digital literacies. We ought to critically question whether we should be controlling to such a great extent what children learn in the home, at school and online. Alternatively, we need to consider how we can empower them, through engaging educational endeavours that develop respect and trust and enable informed and thoughtful decisions when they use technologies. I believe that adult mindsets that emphasize control of behaviour over mentorship and guidance result in ineffective policies and practices. These, in turn, bring out the forms of expression young people adopt to assert their developing identities, sense of space, privacy and security. It becomes a vicious cycle because our responses to children's actions and expressions online determine the extent to which they are empowered to take responsibility and leadership in their own growth, learning and social interactions, or whether they decide to break rules, hack through firewalls and search for independent spaces where adults cannot intervene. I suggest that the way in which online conversations and dialogues are defined, understood and responded to may also shape children's actions and reactions in a particular space and time, depending on environmental influences, past experiences and biological triggers. Electronic space can be perceived as complicating the issues. Alternatively, it can be viewed as providing opportunities that open up young people's worlds. The mindset with which we approach technologies makes all the difference (boyd and Jenkins, 2006; Lankshear and Knobel, 2005). Although rules have their place in schools, officials who enforce those rules might want to apply some flexibility in certain contexts. For people who do not have a lot of experience with technologies, inflexible rules can cause considerable problems. Consider the following situation that almost cost an inexperienced substitute teacher her freedom.

In a controversial case involving Julie Amero, an American substitute teacher in Connecticut, Ms Amero was charged and convicted of accessing pornography on a classroom computer and allowing students to view it. Students had previously accessed a pornographic site and triggered a virus that kept bringing up pornographic pop-up screens, much to their amusement.

Amero maintained, with the support of academics and technology experts (Willard, 2007), that she was innocent and did not purposely access the porn site. She tried to explain that she simply switched on the classroom computer, and a pop-up screen for a pornography web site repeatedly surfaced through a 'mousetrap' trigger. According to Willard, this trigger is caused by 'malware' – a virus that lurks in the background and is designed to kick in when certain pornography sites are accessed either purposely or by mistake. Julie argued that the children could have accessed the web site that set off the trigger. In some schools, teachers are not allowed to turn off computers. Therefore Julie, trying to obey school rules, turned the screen away from their view and went to seek help. Regardless of the rules, perhaps a more experienced teacher would have turned off the computer to get rid of the trigger and then sought help. As a result of leaving the classroom with the pornographic site on the computer screen, some of the students viewed the web site, and she was subsequently charged. After six appeals and enormous public outcry, Ms Amero was acquitted and released from a sentence that would have committed her to forty years in jail – the penalty under Connecticut's S. 53–21 of the General Penal Code on Risk of Injury to a Minor.

In this situation, the school rules disallowing teachers from turning off the computer exacerbated the problem. This is why my objectives in this book include a review of the emerging complexities of cyber-bullying for teachers, schools, parents and policymakers generally. I want to bring a more human element into examination of some of the policy, rule-making and definitional challenges related to cyber-bullying and use of technologies. To that end, I will highlight the range of influences and stakeholders that can impact our understanding and *response* to the kinds of activity that students are beginning to engage in online. With each chapter, I peel away the layers of complexity to develop legal and educational guidelines that culminate in pragmatic but practical solutions in Chapter 8. Although these solutions do not, by design, include any check-lists or rubrics, I believe they show greater promise of helping stakeholders navigate the challenges of student expression in cyberspace.

My analysis in this book brings a particular focus on the fostering of school environments (physical and virtual) that should be inclusive and empowering and support the education of children growing up in an increasingly wired world. I hope that the concerns I raise throughout this book, and the critically informed pedagogical approaches that I advocate at the end of the book, will raise awareness that bullying has always been complex. Technologies have simply brought these complexities into new spaces. I argue that the root causes or motivators for this type of online communication have not changed, and that technologies have provided new spaces in which information can be exchanged at far greater speeds for infinite audiences.

Hence, it is now more important than ever to adopt well-informed, educational, non-arbitrary, ethical and legally defensible policies and responses, no matter how upset we become with the content and challenges to authority contained in young people's online expressions. This book explains some of the tensions between balancing free expression, privacy, safety and supervision as student expression moves with fluidity between the boundaries of physical school settings and virtual spaces. I reiterate that, although I do not bring a 'to-do list', 'blue-print' or 'rubric' that parents and educators can follow to reduce cyber-bullying, I can certainly facilitate an appreciation of the nature of traditional bullying and cyber-bullying and draw attention to the gaps and root systemic considerations that are often overlooked when adults respond in anger and frustration.

As my experience with 'Raveger' discloses, I am a parent and educator who has experienced cyber-bullying and found the legal tensions fascinating to study. In the process I have dug deeper into the root causes of bullying and cyber-bullying and have discovered the need for a shift in the way we frame cyber-bullying, and conceptualize the policy development and practise dilemmas to address it. Even though rapidly emerging technologies make the study of cyber-bullying difficult because it is a moving target, I maintain that we are dealing with issues that have plagued social interaction among humankind for hundreds of years. Power hierarchies still exist that sustain and perpetuate discrimination and systemic oppression, grounded in racism, sexism, homophobia and ableism, which marginalize some people more than others. We cannot address a complex issue such as cyber-bullying without taking into account stakeholders' political agendas and parental prerogatives that influence what schools teach and what students learn. It is these issues that are rearing their heads through cyber-bullying at an increasingly rapid and infinite pace given the capabilities of new technologies. The underlying attitudes and motivations are not new. They are the same as they have always been. It is those aspects of bullying and cyber-bullying that we need to address through improved *education* – not control and censorship.

Before we turn to these issues, I would like to introduce readers to a general understanding of the nature of traditional bullying, its forms and profile and the conditions under which it occurs, as it has been studied within the paradigms of developmental psychology and sociology. The profiles of traditional and cyber-bullying that I present in Chapter 2 will establish that I appreciate the devastating impact of bullying and cyber-bullying that has tragically taken the lives of many young people through suicide or even murder. I have researched the subject sufficiently to understand the deep and lasting psychological consequences of bullying and cyber-bullying on children and adults who are victimized, especially at the hands of large groups of peers or unknown individuals on the Internet. And although I fully support a need for some form of consequences for those who engage in cyber-bullying, I contend that we place too much emphasis on discipline and punishment after the fact. I would like us to think about long-term proactive responses that might not have immediate impact, but over time should make their mark more permanently.

Background on traditional bullying is important because it lays the foundation for an improved understanding of emerging profiles of cyber-bullying. Chapter 3 presents a transnational snapshot of how cyber-bullying is emerging and being perceived in various countries with emerging technology use. In Chapter 4 I discuss the biological and socializing influences that greatly influence young people's propensity to engage in bullying, particularly from the perspective of gender differences. Chapter 5 then looks at how adults supervise and control kids' spaces, from home and playground spaces, to policy and legislation. Chapter 6 looks at the power hierarchies among the various stakeholders that influence what children learn and how they in turn express themselves on- and off-line. Chapter 7 addresses the debate on student free expression and supervision by looking at a range of judicial decisions under tort law, human rights and constitutional laws to culminate in a set of reasonable standards that can guide educators on their responsibilities. Finally, Chapter 8 considers pragmatic and practical solutions on how we might meet those legal responsibilities but, more importantly, engage children through educational endeavours that incorporate digital literacies and a critical pedagogical perspective that guides us to empower students and teachers through a collaborative and cohesive dialogue. These guidelines show greater promise of addressing the 'horns of the dilemma' of cyber-bullying than do the 'weapons' and 'battles' that are so enthusiastically endorsed in current conceptions and approaches to cyber-bullying.

Chapter 2

Profile of traditional and cyber-bullying

> Mom, after my death, please, please go to schools and talk to kids that bullying and teasing has big consequences . . . That's just my only wish and I hope people will miss me. Please visit my grave often, so I'm not lonely.
>
> (Hamed Nastoh, bullying victim)[1]

What is bullying?

(Bullying among school children is certainly a very old phenomenon, though it was not until the early 1970s that it was made the object of systematic research. In schools, bullying usually occurs in areas with minimal or no adult supervision. It can occur within or around school buildings, though it more often occurs in physical education classes, hallways, bathrooms or classes that require group work and/or after school activities. Bullying in school sometimes consists of a group of students taking advantage of, or isolating, one student in particular and outnumbering him/her. Targets of bullying in school are often pupils who are considered strange or different by their peers, making the situation harder for them to deal with. Bullying can also be perpetrated by teachers, or instigated against them.

Historically bullying was not seen as a problem that needed attention, but has rather has been accepted as a fundamental and normal part of childhood (Campbell, 2005; Limber and Small, 2003). In the last two decades, however, this view has changed, and schoolyard bullying and cyber-bullying are seen as serious problems that warrant attention.

In the 1990s, the United States saw an epidemic of school shootings (of which the most notorious was the Columbine High School massacre). This continued into 2006, in Virginia and in Montreal, Canada, where in separate incidents two young men went on shooting sprees at two post-secondary institutions, taking in their wake their own lives and those of peers and teachers. Although most of the young people who carry out these shootings take their own lives, there is a pattern that disclosed that all of them were, at some point in their lives, victims of bullying by peers (Dedman, 2000).

In most cases, it was discovered that they resorted to violence only after the school administration repeatedly failed to intervene, as in the case of the shootings in Virginia and Columbine. As a result of these trends, numerous anti-bullying programmes and zero-tolerance policies have proliferated as schools attempt to reduce and control bullying. According to Hoover and Olsen (2001), up to 15 per cent of students in American schools are frequently or severely harassed by their peers. Only a slim majority of fourth to twelfth graders (55.2 per cent) reported neither having been picked on nor picking on others (ibid.). Furthermore, bully-victim cycles are found where individuals are both bullies and victims (Ma, 2001; Pellegrini and Bartini, 2000; Schwartz et al., 1993; 1997).

Numerous surveys of students have found that face-to-face bullying by peers in school is a frequent experience for many children (Genta et al., 1996; Kumpulainen et al., 1998; Whitney and Smith, 1993). One in six children report being bullied at least once a week (Rigby, 1997; Zubrick et al., 1997) although that figure is as high as 50 per cent if the duration of the bullying is taken as lasting only one week (Smith and Shu, 2000). In another study, 40 per cent of adolescents reported having been bullied at some time during their schooling (Mynard et al., 2000). However, the percentage of students who report longer term bullying of six months or more decreases to between 15 per cent and 17 per cent (Slee, 1995; Slee and Rigby, 1993).

Bullying has been understood and defined as an age-old societal problem, beginning in the schoolyard and often progressing to the boardroom (Campbell, 2005; McCarthy, et al., 2001). 'Bullying' is often defined by developmental psychologists as an aggressive, intentional act or behaviour that is carried out by a group or an individual repeatedly and over time against a victim who cannot easily defend him or herself (Campbell, 2005; Olweus, 2001; Whitney and Smith, 1993). Bullying is a form of abuse that is based on an imbalance of power; it can be defined as a systematic abuse of power (Rigby, 2002; Smith and Sharp, 1994). Bullying may be physical, including behaviours such as hitting, punching and spitting, or it may involve language that is browbeating using verbal assault, teasing, ridicule, sarcasm and scapegoating (Campbell, 2005; DiGiulio, 2001; Slee and Rigby, 1993). It involves a minimum of two people, one the perpetrator and the other the victim. However, a large number of people may be involved in an indirect manner as an audience. These bystanders may be other students who witness the bullying event but remain uninvolved. They are frequently afraid of becoming the next victim if they do interfere. They often feel powerless and show a loss of self-respect and self-confidence (Campbell, 2005; Harris and Petrie, 2002).

Canadian studies tell us that approximately 10 per cent to 15 per cent of children are bullied or engage in bullying at least once a week.[2] Bullying begins in kindergarten, involves various degrees of violence and comprises various forms of harassment. Bullying can be physical or psychological, overt or covert, random (indiscriminate) or discriminatory. For a variety of reasons, educators may not recognize bullying for what it is, and victims sometimes find it difficult to substantiate covert or psychological forms of bullying. This is because such behaviour is easily confused with teasing and generally occurs on playgrounds, in hallways and now most frequently in cyberspace (email, text messaging, web sites), away from the watchful eyes of teachers or other supervisors.

Emerging litigation against schools indicates that victims and their parents are prepared to sue schools for failing to protect them from bullying and cyber-bullying. If schools are to keep students safe and avoid litigation, the first step is to learn how to recognize the various forms of bullying in the physical school environment and, in particular, the conditions under which it occurs.

The etymology of bullying

Ironically, bullying began as a term of endearment. The *Oxford English Dictionary* notes that it originated in the 1600s as 'boel', meaning 'lover of either sex' (Simpson and Weiner, 1989, p. 645). The dictionary also references a 1721 edition of *Bailey* that contains the word 'boolie', meaning 'beloved'. The word was also used to describe one's 'brother' (ibid., p. 645). From lover to brother, the word eventually took on the meaning of close friendship as between good buddies, companions and mates. Implicit in this relationship was amiable teasing, cajoling and joking among friends. For example, Shakespeare prefixed 'bully' as a title, for example, 'Blesse thee, bully doctor' (ibid., p. 645).

British coalminers described co-workers as bullies and thus began an association with bullies as 'rowdies' or 'ruffians'. By the late 1800s bullying began to refer to cowardice, weakness, tyranny and violence.[3] It also began to be associated with gangs: 'A gang of bullies was secretly sent to slit the nose of the offender' (ibid., p. 646). By 1883, to act as a bully was 'to treat in an overbearing manner; to intimidate, overawe' (ibid.), or to 'drive or force by bullying; to frighten into a certain course' (ibid.).

The etymology tells much about the problem of recognizing bullying. Its transition from general rough-housing to hostile treatment highlights interesting parallels between the historical evolution of the word and bullying in contemporary schools. First, many researchers (Glover, *et al.*, 1998; Roher, 1997; Smith and Sharp, 1994; Tattum, 1997) acknowledge that, until the last twenty years or so, bullying in schools was widely accepted as an unavoidable part of growing up. Smith and Sharp (1994) point out that, although the topic was addressed in novels such as *Tom Brown's Schooldays*, almost no research on it was published outside Norway and Sweden until the late 1970s, when the Norwegian bullying expert Olweus (1978) published an English version of his book *Aggression in the schools: Bullies and whipping boys*. As the etymology discloses, this is around the time that notions of bullying shifted to incorporate negative characteristics.

Bullying was not recognized as problematic in the UK and North America, however, until the 1980s. In the army and university fraternities, bullying took the form of 'hazing' of new recruits. In British boarding schools that I attended, new students were often put through a form of bullying known as 'squashing' by their prefects. Authorities were well aware that this took place but tolerated it as a toughening up that rookies needed to build character. Similarly, with playground bullying, there was an underlying assumption by teachers that such behaviour was acceptable because it forced quieter children to learn to assert themselves.

Bullying or teasing?

In the context of the etymology, it is important to explain why teachers may not recognize teasing as bullying. Bullying has two forms: physical and psychological (which includes verbal teasing). Curiously, verbal bullying in contemporary schools fluctuates between terms of endearment and hostile treatment. For example, a significant amount of adolescent discourse occurs in the electronic medium and is often influenced by lyrics in rap and grunge music (Ashford, 1996). Drawing from such lyrics, teens might greet each other by saying, 'What's up dawg?'(derived from African American rap lyrics). They may chide a friend, 'I'm going to kick your ass'. They may tell a friend he's 'bad' (meaning he's 'cool'). They may challenge a friend to roughhouse by saying, 'Bring it on f— face' ('let's fight').

Much of this language, when directed at friends, is meant without harmful intentions. Take for example a recent human rights bullying case (*Jubran vs North Vancouver School Distr. No. 44* [2002] B.C.H.R.T.D. No. 10 (Q.L.) 221) in which Azmi Jubran, a high school student of Iranian descent, suffered four years of incessant bullying at his North Vancouver high school in British Columbia. After graduating, Jubran brought a human rights claim against the school for failing to protect him from the homophobic discrimination that comprised a large part of the bullying. He insisted he was not homosexual but was harassed based on his appearance. One of Jubran's persecutors, referred to as 'Mr Richardson', testified that, in high school, taunts that might be interpreted by adults as homophobic are not always meant that way when directed towards friends:

> Mr Richardson testified that the words used by the students were 'part of the high school vocabulary', and words like 'gay' were used to describe someone, something, or a situation that a student didn't like. Mr Richardson testified that he himself used those words 'all the time'. He testified it would be common for a student to say: 'that shirt is so gay' or the 'long jump is so gay' if the student didn't like it. He also said that the words 'queer', 'faggot' and 'homo' were commonly used as part of normal conversation, even among friends, *as terms of endearment*. He further

testified that he still has a friend who says to him 'what's up homo?' and that those words are used without reference to sexual orientation [emphasis added.]

(Tribunal Judge Robertson, *Jubran vs North Vancouver School Distr. No. 44* [2002] B.C.H.R.T.D. No. 10 (Q.L.) 221, p. 7)

This discourse emulates the amicable teasing among buddies in the early 1800s, such as 'My over jolly bully-boy, let be' (Simpson and Weiner, 1989, p. 645). Bullying begins to reflect the shift in its etymology from a 'buddy' relationship to its more hostile and overbearing character when identical words and actions are directed towards someone who is not a friend. For example, the words 'homo' and 'gay' make the transition from being terms of endearment between friends to hostile words intended to harm. The testimony from *Jubran* is again useful to illustrate how this happens. A number of his perpetrators, referred to by their last names in the tribunal transcripts gave the following testimony:

Mr Howard, Mr Higgins, Mr Kai and Mr White all testified that when the words were spoken by someone who was not a friend, the terms 'dork', 'geek' 'gay' and 'faggot', were used interchangeably as words of insult or as a put-down. Their evidence was that the words were not intended to imply that Mr Jubran was homosexual, and that neither they nor others who called Mr Jubran those names were of the view that Mr Jubran was homosexual. Mr Howard and Mr Kai denied that any of the 'sting' of the words resulted from the fact that they related to homosexuality; they testified that the word were simply used as another form of insult.

(Tribunal Judge Robertson, *Jubran vs North Vancouver School Distr. No. 44* [2002] B.C.H.R.T.D. No. 10 (Q.L.) 221, p. 7)

This language, used in two entirely different ways, might explain why teachers continue to tolerate verbal bullying. Although teachers try to stop students using swear words and sexist language, they cannot monitor every word or conversation.

Glover *et al.* (1998) report Boulton and Hawker's (1997) British study that found teachers commonly look for physical injury and generally ignore verbal bullying. In keeping with the popular adage, 'sticks and stones will break my bones but words will never hurt me', they found many teachers turn a blind eye to verbal bullying. Middle-school students reported that teasing was the most common aspect of the bullying they experienced (90 per cent of the time), and their responses suggest various reasons as to why teachers might tolerate bullying. One student noted that, 'Teachers turn a blind eye to name calling because they believe it doesn't hurt you' (Boulton and Hawker, 1997, p. 32). Another observed, 'It seems that action is only taken if someone is really hurt [physically]', and a third complained, 'Teachers want a school with no bullying and so they pretend it doesn't exist' (ibid.).

Other studies support these findings,[4] and although most researchers have moved away from stereotypical views about bullying as simply a physical assault,[5] many teachers and students apparently still perceive bullying as physical and not verbal. For example, Glover *et al.* (1998) studied the responses of British teachers and students in junior and secondary schools who were provided with a list of behaviours (including a range of physical activities such as kicking, hitting and shoving, and verbal behaviours such as teasing, name-calling and threatening). In their study, a significantly higher proportion of responses by teachers (90 per cent) described physical behaviours as bullying, compared with verbal behaviours. Students also identified physical bullying as being more serious than verbal bullying, but to a lesser extent than teachers.

Moreover, most of the teachers who were interviewed believed children should cope with teasing on their own. One teacher responded, 'It happens so much that I just tell them [the children] to get on with it. It's no good encouraging them to be too sensitive, they should learn to ignore it' (ibid., p. 55). These results are significant, as teachers' perceptions of bullying affect how they respond to complaints, and students' perceptions of verbal bullying as harmless may encourage them to participate in it.

These findings illustrate how important it is to ensure that educators and the courts understand the complexities of bullying well enough to recognize and appreciate the range of bullying behaviours and their effects. This is also important to bear in mind when we turn to the profile of cyber-bullying – because a significant amount is verbal, with greater psychological ramifications than physical bullying.

General characteristics

Bullying entails overt or covert behaviour and takes verbal or physical forms. Good-natured horseplay and teasing escalate into bullying when victim(s) and perpetrator(s) cease to agree when the behaviour should stop and when a power imbalance is created between them. Askew (1989), for example, suggests bullying comprises a continuum of behaviours that involve the perpetrator(s)' attempt to gain power and dominance over others.

Girls and boys display similar levels of bullying. However, boys report bullying more often and generally engage in overt, physical forms of bullying, whereas girls tend to engage in covert, psychological bullying (Crick *et al.*, 2002; Hall, 1999; Pepler and Craig, 1997; Rauste-Von Wright, 1992). Nonetheless, there is now evidence of a trend in increased physical bullying and violence by females.[6] Tremblay (1991) suggests that the disparity between genders is due to extensive focus on male aggression and lack of focus on female aggression.[7] The disparity in rates could also be explained by changes in the way girls are socialized and how females are depicted in the media and in society – another point to remember when we go to a discussion of gender differences and cyber-bullying.

Research suggests that male students are more likely to carry a weapon onto school property and they constitute 83 per cent of all victims of school-related homicides or suicides. In addition, boys are more likely to fight among themselves, whereas girls fight with either sex. After extended periods of relentless bullying, victims of both sexes are more likely than students who are not bullied to bring weapons to school for protection (DiGiulio, 2001; Olweus, 1993).

Current research identifies a broad consensus that the following general factors contribute to bullying in schools. Make a note of these conditions because they also exist in cyberspace and inform the profile of cyber-bullying:

- There is always a power imbalance that favours the perpetrator(s) over the victim.
- The perpetrators are often supported by a group of peers, some of whom actively encourage the bully and others who watch, but do nothing to help peers who are targeted.
- Targeted students draw the negative attention of their peers and are actively pushed out of the group and isolated (Bukowksi and Sippola, 2001; Crick et al., 2002; Schuster, 2001).
- Exclusion and isolation from the larger peer group fortify the power of the perpetrator(s).
- The perpetrators' behaviour is uninvited and unwanted by the victim.
- The perpetrators' actions are deliberate, repeated and often relentless.

Why is the combination of power and exclusion so characteristic of school bullying? Other types of violence may involve power but not necessarily exclusion. In bullying, the perpetrator's primary objective is the isolation and exclusion of certain peers, and, as we will see in the profile of cyber-bullying, in cyberspace, teachers and other authority figures are also isolated and demeaned. The perpetrator's actions draw the support of the larger peer group, increasing the victim's vulnerability. In addition, although not all members of the group will support bullying, the frightening reality is that a larger number of peers (an average of 30 per cent) (Henderson and Hymel, 2002; Olweus, 2001; Salmivalli et al., 1996) will support individual bullies rather than help the victim. This is a key consideration to bear in mind when we move to the profile of cyber-bullying.

Other researchers agree that the most lethal aspect of bullying is the group effect, which perpetuates and sustains abuse of individual victims (Bukowksi and Sippola, 2001; Crick et al., 2002; Henderson and Hymel, 2002; Juvonen and Graham, 2001; Perry *et al.*, and Perry, 1990; Salmivalli, 2001; Schuster, 2001). Perpetrators are generally driven by the need for power and recognition, in order to make up for a lack of confidence and self-assurance. They crave acceptance. Recruiting the support of the peer group by isolating and demeaning someone satisfies that need. Note at this stage that I prefer to use the word 'perpetrator' rather than the label of 'bully', because a perpetrator initiates a certain action or actions in a specific context, whereas labelling an individual as a 'bully' gives the perception that such an individual is a bad or 'evil' person at all times – it connotes a negative flaw in the person's character, whereas a perpetrator may only engage in bullying once – he or she may, as research has found, also be a victim of bullying by others. Hence, for me, it is important that we move away from labels. Although I have used 'victim' and 'target' interchangeably throughout this book, their use depends upon the context of the discussion. Suffice it to say that labels such as 'disruptive', 'aggressive', 'evil' and 'terrorist' essentialize and justify blame-laying and scapegoating.

Perpetrators and targets

People often ask about the characteristics of kids who engage in bullying. Are they the popular kids or the so-called 'losers'? There is a discrepancy in the research on this question. The NCPC (1997) reported that perpetrators are generally unpopular, whereas a number of more recent studies have confirmed that perpetrators exhibit high levels of leadership and confidence and are often popular with peers and teachers (DiGiulio, 2001; Katch, 2001; Olweus, 2001). DiGiulio (2001), for example, contends that the instigators are popular with teachers because of their leadership skills and academic abilities. Unlike the stereotypical 'bully' who is perceived to be dejected and unpopular, perpetrators are often classroom leaders and peer tutors (Salmivalli *et al.*, 1996) – those whom teachers might assume would defend victims, rather than instigate or reinforce bullying. It is plausible, however, that peer leaders who engage in bullying may not be as self-assured as they seem. They may crave attention and take on peer leadership roles as a way to gain prestige and power.

Targets may thus be chosen based on whether they are perceived to advance or hinder the effective functioning of the peer group. Individuals who are perceived as 'different' are singled out for exclusion, which then triggers the bullying (Artz and Riecken, 1997; Katch, 2001; Olweus, 2001; Salmivalli, 2001).

To obtain more specific information on children's motivation to single out and bully certain victims, Glover *et al.* (1998) interviewed 3,417 elementary and high school students in Britain. The students were asked if and why they had engaged in specific anti-social behaviours, without having to admit they had 'bullied'. The researchers were also assessing the reasons children gave for discrimination. Interestingly, the greatest justification to bully someone (14 per cent for boys and 12 per cent for girls) was based on whether the victim was perceived as 'too clever' (ibid., p. 27). A victim's looks were another motivator (14 per cent for boys and 13 per cent for girls). Other responses included the following: 'I hadn't got on with her ever since primary school . . . I don't know why . . . it's the way he looks at me and makes me feel I don't like him' (ibid.). Parental or peer pressure provided another motivation for victim exclusion: 'we weren't allowed to mix with them . . .' (ibid.). The author summarized his findings as follows:

- Ethnic background and religion are more frequently mentioned among older males as reasons for bullying, whereas gender is more frequently the reason for discrimination by adolescent males as a male taunt (sexual harassment).
- Perceptions of being rich or poor and family background are of limited concern, but the way people look and dress is a significant motivation to bully, especially for girls.
- Boys attack hard workers more than girls in adolescence, but victim 'cleverness' motivates students of both genders to bully until grade 11. Learning problems and lack of sporting aptitude are also motivations for boys to bully until grade 11.
- Being different causes 10 per cent to discriminate, with little reduction until grade 11. This is especially true for students who are new to a school and speak with different accents.

Once a target is identified, he or she is presumed to deserve the punishment and 'get what is coming to them'. This justifies the exclusion that is a ubiquitous aspect of bullying. Katch (2001) inadvertently discovered that children's motivation to blame, exclude and victimize begins as early as kindergarten.

> When I first started audio-taping the children's play and talk, I cut out every discussion about exclusion. I thought it did not relate to my subject of violence. But when exclusion kept coming up, I decided to listen to those discussions, and I found that exclusion and violence seemed to be inextricably intertwined. Excluding someone from the group seemed to justify violence, both by the excluded child and by those who exclude him, just as when Seth and Patrick called Joel a baby before knocking him down and when Caleb called Nate a girl before punching him. On the other hand, . . . as we learned from the killers at Columbine, the excluded child can feel justified in using violence to hurt those who exclude him. I wish I could just tell the children to be more inclusive, but it's never that easy.
>
> (Ibid., pp. 129–30)

Wason-Ellam (1996) believes that race, combined with class, is often a reason for exclusion, although girls tend to exclude on race more than boys do. She also notes that toys, such as Barbie, can reinforce negative stereotypes that contribute to bullying. Barbie is still popular with young girls, and Wason-Ellam observes how it became a tool of privilege and race that girls used to exclude a Punjabi student who did not own the doll. The girls dressed their Barbies and shared lip-gloss, make-up and hair clips in 'gestures of intimacy' (ibid., p. 97), but when the student, Surinder, would try to join in, she was dismissed with, 'Go away, we don't want you in the group' (ibid., p. 96) and 'I'm going to Renee's house after school to play with make-up because we are best friends. I am not going to invite you, 'cos your clothes are funny and you're a paki dot' (ibid.). Wason-Ellam recalls Surinder's response when she called her a 'princess': 'I inadvertently address Surinder as a "princess" as she arrives in school in a fancy dress. Soulfully, she looks up at me and says, "I can't be a princess because I don't look like a princess, Linda"' (ibid., p. 97).

Surinder's response illustrates how this type of exclusion negatively affects students' self-image. These findings also suggest that perpetrators bully to fill an emotional void resulting from a lack of confidence or self-worth. Victimizing others based on their differences allows the bully to gain status and recognition (whether positive or negative) within the peer group. The finding that gender is an important motivator, especially for boys, is not surprising. What is surprising is that gifted students, or those with a strong work ethic, appear to invite bullying – perhaps because young people subconsciously want to achieve academic success when they realize the career success and social status it brings. Chapter 4 expands on some of these socializing and attitudinal influences in greater detail.

Types of bullying

As I have noted, there are two principal types of bullying: physical and psychological. Both can be carried out in overt and/or covert ways and may involve indiscriminate or discriminatory forms of behaviour.

Physical bullying

Physical bullying is generally described as 'overt' because it usually involves open attacks on a victim (Olweus, 1993) that often grow worse if others are watching. Studies have, in fact, found that the longer the perpetrators are encouraged, the more serious the physical abuse (Salmivalli et al., 1996).

Extreme physical bullying can take many forms, including beating, locking peers in school lockers, strangling, shooting or using other weapons or objects to cause harm. Other methods of harassment include flicking rubber bands at the victim's face, throwing nails and wood-chips in the eyes, spraying victims with harmful substances, pouring acid or gasoline on the person's body, tying him or her up or blindfolding (NCPC, 1997; Olweus, 1993). These are only a few of the many examples of the kinds of activity students engage in to enforce a power relationship in which victims are overwhelmed and helpless.

(Physical bullying can also, however, be 'covert'. This kind of bullying takes place in the absence of supervisors or adults and might involve actions such as locking a victim in a school locker – or rape. A well-known example of covert bullying resulted in the murder of a South Indian teenager. Reena Virk (Jiwani, 1997) was tricked into meeting peers by a grocery store and later beaten to death and drowned. She was accused of stealing a friend's diary and calling all the boys who were listed in it. Indiscriminate forms of physical bullying do not identify the victim on the basis of an enduring prejudice such as race, sex, gender or ability, but might be triggered on a whim or spontaneous sense of annoyance or discomfort. A victim's look or body language, if misinterpreted as hostile, can trigger bullying, or a perpetrator may identify a suitable victim as someone who seems vulnerable (Artz, 1998a).

More often than not, physical bullying takes on discriminatory forms, such as sexual or racial harassment of a physical nature, or physical attacks on children with special needs. The pervasiveness of sexual bullying and harassment in schools is well documented, and updated studies on sexual cyber-bullying in Chapter 4 confirm that it continues to persist. For example, Stein (1991, 1995, 1999) disclosed that approximately 80 per cent of girls and 60 per cent of boys report they have been victims of sexual harassment. Sexual harassment incorporates at least four of the characteristics of bullying described above:

1   there is usually a power imbalance between the perpetrator(s) and victim;
2   the harassment is unwanted;
3   it is deliberate and relentless; and
4   it is based on the victim's gender.

Sexual harassment is included in the Canadian NCPC's (1997) description of types of bullying. Although kissing and hugging are gestures of care, they become bullying when they are unwanted and imposed on victims against their will. This kind of bullying could include pulling down someone's trousers; flipping up girls' skirts or snapping or unhooking bras; crude gestures; exposing genitals, or forcing someone to commit a sexual act against their will (all of which can also be defined as sexual assault) (Stein, 1995, 1999; Welsh, 1998). This type of sexual harassment is discriminatory because the victim is selected because of gender (with girls generally victimized more than boys).

Homophobic physical bullying incorporates random forms of physical bullying described above, combined with verbal insults about the individual's sexual orientation. Tolman et al. (2001) found that adolescent boys in grade 9 are most susceptible to homophobic bullying, based on their appearance. If they are not strong athletes, or are physically smaller than others, boys may become targets. However, it is important not to oversimplify the reasons for this kind of bullying, as research suggests that victim identification depends as well upon the self-assurance, relational attitudes and emotional well-being of victims

(Racial attacks include the forms of physical bullying described above or they can be combined with sexual harassment or other forms of discrimination.) The difference is that they are directed either by mainstream students towards victims from visible ethnic groups based on colour, appearance, manner of dress, manner of speech and cultural background (Dei, 1997; Janoviček, 2001; Jiwani, 2001; Razack, 1998), or by students from visible ethnic groups against each other. For example, in her study of immigrant and refugee girls, Janoviček (2001) reports that students of Iranian lineage bullied Iraqi students, Koreans bullied Philippinos, Hispanic and African American students conflicted, and so on. This illustrates how complex racial attacks can be, and reminds us that it is not always mainstream students who instigate racial bullying.

(It has been suggested that race was most certainly a factor in the case of Reena Virk, whose brutal murder was noted earlier (Jiwani, 2001). The initial assault was overt: she was attacked on an open bridge and later under a tree by a group of adolescents. However, after most of the adolescents left, Kelly Ellard and Warren Glowatski followed her to the water and continued the 'covert' beating and drowning. Ellard, smoking a cigarette, held Reena's head under the water with her foot until she no longer surfaced. Significantly, even though word spread that Reena had been killed, none of the many students who knew about the murder reported it for at least a week. Another alert for the reader, as it relates to cyber-bullying)–(the code of silence and the sense of entitlement to privacy among perpetrators, bystanders and reinforcers. These examples illustrate how covert physical bullying can be harder to substantiate than overt bullying, particularly if perpetrators and witnesses have a code of silence. Researchers (Glover et al., 1998; Smith and Sharp, 1994) report that observers are afraid to 'rat' or 'grass' on the offenders in case they become the next victim.)

This network of covert support for perpetrators was also evident in the Jubran case. Covert bullying was part of the homophobic bullying Jubran endured for four years at Handsworth Secondary school in North Vancouver, British Columbia. Friends shielded a classmate who set fire to Azmi Jubran's shirt, and, although each boy owned up to the abuse, each also later denied it. School administrators had difficulty identifying the individual who carried out the assault, making it difficult to discipline him.

(Children with special needs are also highly susceptible to physical bullying because they may have difficulty with speech or mobility and as such are already in a position of vulnerability.) Smith and Sharp (1994) (report that physically disabled children, for example, may not be strong or fast enough to protect themselves or retaliate. They found that approximately two-thirds of the special needs children interviewed reported being bullied, compared with one-quarter of mainstream students. One special needs student complained, 'They kick me and punch me and they are horrible to me. They smack me and spit on my back' (ibid., p. 222). Another stated that, because he had difficulty carrying his lunch tray, his friend always carried it for him, but then he was challenged to a fight because other students accused him of being lazy.'

Finally, as DiGiulio (2001) observes, students in contemporary schools are raised in a commercial and media driven society that tells them how they should look and dress to be 'cool' or acceptable. Children who cannot afford the latest fashions or may simply refuse to conform to the popular dress code may be physically attacked. At the other end of the spectrum, affluent children who wear desirable clothes are also vulnerable to physical attacks in which their clothes and watches are stolen from them. This form of bullying is also known as 'taxing'. A government survey in Quebec, Canada (Séguin, 2002), found that 11 per cent of 16,600 young people in the province reported being victimized this way.

Psychological bullying

Psychological bullying generally involves either inflicting mental anguish to cause their targets to fear for their physical safety, or breaking down self-esteem and confidence. This is obviously an integral aspect of cyber-bullying, as discussed in Chapter 3. Again, at least three or more of the characteristics of bullying are always present:

1   the harassment is unwanted and uninvited;
2   it is relentless; and
3   the victim is singled out for the abuse.

Verbal psychological bullying is 'overt' in the sense that joking and insults can be heard or read by witnesses and substantiated by victims.

Covert (non-verbal) psychological bullying is intended to exclude and isolate by stalking and/or ostracizing the victim. It is the most difficult form of bullying for victims to substantiate, because teachers cannot see it, or prove it occurred. Perpetrators might suddenly ignore victims or refuse to work with them on class projects or other activities. They may spread unsubstantiated rumours that embarrass the victim or make him or her appear dishonest or untrustworthy to peers.

Psychological bullying, like physical bullying, can also be indiscriminate or discriminatory. Indiscriminate psychological bullying might involve teasing, making repeated derogatory statements about the victim or other kinds of verbal harassment. For example, a boy might be called a 'loser' because he does not have a girlfriend or cannot afford clothes that help him fit in with the 'cool' crowd. He may be called 'cry baby' if the pressure fro[...] gets to him and 'four eyes' or 'geek' or 'dork' if he wears glasses[...] Olweus, 1991).

Bullying often stems from the social inequities that adult[...] fosters, sustains and continues to grapple with. Research confirms that a significant amount of psychological bullying is discriminatory (Dei, 1997; Glover *et al.*, 1998; Janoviček, 2001; Wason-Ellam, 1996). Students are excluded and purposely isolated through covert psychological bullying because of race, gender, sexual orientation, disability, accent, or because they are good students and do well in class. Children from these categories are already marginalized because of their differences, which are then exacerbated through bullying. Peers may not pick them for sports teams or class projects and they may be ignored, stalked or stared at. Scholars observe that, not only are such children marginalized by one form of discrimination, they often face a combination of discriminatory factors (for example, they might experience covert bullying through exclusion because of their race as well as their gender or sexual orientation, and possibly a learning disability or giftedness) (Jiwani, 2001). This results in intersecting and interlocking barriers of discrimination that victims find difficult to overcome, understand or explain. They know they are isolated but may not understand why.

Covert psychological bullying makes it difficult for teachers to support the victim. For example, teachers cannot punish someone simply for staring and may not be able to establish for certain that it was done with malicious intent. Alleged stalkers, for example, could defend their actions by saying they simply happened to be walking the same way as the victim. Similarly, children cannot be disciplined for laughing unless the teacher overhears inappropriate language or unfair innuendoes. And students will undoubtedly be embarrassed to have a teacher insist that they be accepted into a group or sports team when they are clearly unwanted.

Psychological sexual harassment can also be overt or covert, comprising sexual proposals and threats, name calling or repeated demands for sexual acts, among other demands. Girls may be called 'bitch', 'hoe' (whore), 'dyke', 'butch', or 'lesbian', whereas boys will be called 'gay', 'homo', 'sissy' or 'girl'. As with physical bullying, children from visible ethnic groups are especially vulnerable to psychological bullying. Studies on refugee and immigrant students from these groups disclose that these students are subjected to significantly more bullying than mainstream students. Racial slurs include comments such as 'go home to India . . . or China . . . or Iran' and taunts about appearance and manner of dress. Refugee and immigrant students are often referred to as 'FOBs' (fresh off the boat) and are sometimes also harassed by peers from their own communities who were born here and see them as an embarrassment (Handa, 1997).

Finally, children with special needs are particularly vulnerable to verbal bullying because of their disabilities. Smith (1995) explores how devastating this bullying is for these children. Children reported being called 'cabbage', 'maggot' and 'whale' (ibid., pp. 223–4) and having their peers jeer at their low marks in class. At the other end of the spectrum, gifted children are also subjected to harassment as 'teacher's pet', 'dork', 'geek' or 'walking encyclopaedia'.

Boulton and Hawker (1997) explain that, because teasing is characterized by a combination of irritating and light-hearted qualities and often contains hidden messages, it can be difficult for teachers and students to recognize it as bullying. Indeed, what one child finds upsetting, another may find playful, and what one child finds funny on one occasion may not be appreciated when it becomes persistent. It can therefore be difficult for the victim as well as adult observers to determine the teaser's intention and for the perpetrators to appreciate fully the effect of their words and actions.

Changing roles

Adding to the difficulty in identifying and addressing bullying is the fact that the roles of perpetrator and victim can be interchangeable. The National Crime Prevention Council (1997) reports that children who find themselves victimized can also perpetrate violence and are often perceived as 'bullies'. Studies conducted in Scandinavia by Salmivalli (Salmivalli, 1999, 2001; Salmivalli *et al.*, 1996) identified six distinct participant roles that children take in bully/victim situations: bully; victim; assistant (joins the bully); reinforcer (encourages the bully by observing and laughing); defender (assists the victim by siding with him or her or trying to stop others); and outsiders (students unaware of the bullying or who avoid such situations by staying away). The researchers studied 573 sixth-grade students and found they represented six participant roles in the following proportions:

	Per cent
Bullies	8.2
Victims	11.7
Assistants	19.5
Reinforcers	17.3
Defenders of victims	23.7
Outsiders	12.7

Although they found that 23.7 per cent of students said they would defend the victim, a larger percentage (an aggregate of 33 per cent of the children in this sample) exhibited some level of support for the behaviour.

Pepler and Craig (1997) found that, although 83 per cent of students report discomfort in watching someone being bullied, their actual observations showed that 25 per cent of bystanders supported the perpetrators. Henderson and Hymel (2002) note that peer bystanders who watch but do nothing contribute significantly to the problem. Equally disturbing is the fact that bystanders are often friendlier towards the instigators after such episodes, which increases the latter's excitement and aggression.

O'Connell *et al.* (1999)[10] identified three major reasons for peer inaction:

1   the personal responsibility is diffused because of the presence of others;
2   children are intimidated by the power differential between themselves and the perpetrator and are afraid of becoming victims themselves; and
3   children may not have strategies for dealing with bullying and opt not to intervene.

Notably, another group of studies confirms that peer witnesses lack the courage to report bullying because they are not confident of receiving assistance and protection from teachers or administrators (Besag, 1989; Henderson and Hymel, 2002; O'Moore and Hillery, 1991; Tattum and Herbert, 1993). In sum, peer inaction contributes to a negative school environment where victims cannot rely on their peers for support, and, as we shall see in the next chapter, in cyberspace, peer support for perpetrators can multiply to millions of onlookers and bystanders. Their inaction adds significantly to the victim's humiliation and creates a negative online and in-school environment for them.

Henderson and Hymel (2002) also report that the greater the number of children present, the longer the behaviour continued, and, concomitantly, the abuse intensified. Again, this should be noted because it is especially true of cyber-bullying, when large numbers of kids can get involved at any time of the day or night. These studies support Boulton and Hawker's (1997) findings that a greater proportion of students, like their teachers, did not perceive verbal harassment as bullying. It is possible that the bystanders do not see themselves as actual participants, even though they watch and may verbally contribute to the harassment.

Effects of bullying

As Hamed Nastoh's dedication at the beginning of this book illustrates, the tragic consequences of extreme bullying, as witnessed in cases involving suicide and murder,[11] are well known. The impact of bullying on children in the normal course of school life is not as well recognized but can also be devastating. Mental anguish from the social exclusion caused by physical and psychological bullying is sufficient to destroy the confidence of any adult, let alone a child, on whom it can have lifelong effects. As the evidence illustrates, the impact of bullying (on victims *and* perpetrators) should not be taken lightly.

Researchers (Haynie *et al.*, 2001; Hodges and Perry, 1996; Juvonen and Graham, 2001; Kochenderfer-Ladd and Wardrop, 2001; Rigby, 2001) find that victims and bullies experience greater psychosomatic problems, including depression, anxiety, low self-esteem and poorer overall mental and physical health than those not involved in bullying. Interestingly, children who are both victims and perpetrators are at even greater psychological risk than those who are one or the other (Haynie et al., 2001; Kumpulainen et al., 1999; Nansel et al., 2001). They demonstrate greater psychological problems, tend to seek out deviant peers and perform more poorly in their schoolwork. They also report poorer self-concept and greater social dissatisfaction. Boulton and Hawker (1997) point to a growing body of research that shows that teasing and exclusion in particular can have devastating consequences, including school avoidance and poor school functioning. These findings are corroborated by victims' own descriptions in their legal claims against schools and by parents of students who committed suicide (Dufour vs Howe Sound Board of Education (2000) (Case abandoned); Jubran vs North Vancouver School Distr. No. 44 [2002] B.C.H.R.T.D. No. 10 (Q.L.) 221).[12]

Bullying and bystander support for perpetrators have serious consequences for students from marginalized groups such as immigrants or refugees. These students are less likely to complain to authorities because they are new to the school system, do not speak English well and may be too shy to build a rapport with their teachers. They may not understand the role of school counsellors, or their own cultural protocols may require them to maintain deference to authority (Handa, 1997). Similarly, disabled students, gays and lesbians and heterosexual children of same-sex parents may exhibit poor school performance and related depression (Sears, 1993).

It is important to point out that the effects of bullying can be profound and lifelong. Devlin's (1997) study of British prison inmates is instructive here. Devlin found that most of the inmates had experienced severe bullying during their lives, and although much of the bullying was probably physical, the psychological impact clearly affected them long after the physical scars had healed. Many became hardened criminals, owing to pent up anger and frustration, and lack of trust in peers, teachers and other adults in their lives.

The consequences of most physical bullying are easily recognizable. Teachers can easily see when a student has bruises, a black eye or broken bones. Internal injuries such as bleeding or broken ribs, however, are more difficult to detect and may be dismissed as whining until external signs make it clear that the student is in pain. For example, Hamed Nastoh was sent home with a stomachache two days before he killed himself, and his mother noted that he did not tell either her or school officials that he had been kicked in the stomach. The stress and anxiety of bullying can also cause physical conditions such as headaches, stomach upset and lethargy, but teachers and parents might reasonably assume that the child has a physical illness. Not surprisingly, perpetrators also sustain serious physical injuries and tend to become involved in substance abuse and criminality (NCPC, 1997; Olweus, 1991). Those who fluctuate between bullying and being victimized show the greatest tendency for serious aggression and criminality in adulthood (physical fighting, weapons use and theft) (DiGiulio, 2001; Hall, 1999).

It is clear that bullying is a serious problem in schools that needs to be addressed by schools and parents. The day-to-day victimization of students is as important to ameliorate as the extreme cases. Not only are the safety, health and well being of victims affected, but those of all students at a school where bullying occurs – and that is virtually all schools, because it creates a chill and poisons the entire school environment. I come back to the issue of school environment in later chapters, because this is one of the primary areas where schools and parents can work together. It is also an aspect of school responsibility that the courts have highlighted as of paramount importance to learning.

Bullying today

In the wake of the Columbine and Montreal (Dawson College) shootings and, more recently, the mass random shootings at Virginia Polytechnic University (Agence France Presse, 2007) and Dawson College in Montreal in 2006, and the media attention to those and other serious bullying cases, many parents and stakeholders are concerned that school violence is on the rise[13] and possibly even out of control. Easy access to guns and the high population in the United States might contribute to the current rates of violence there. Students in Canada, Australia, China, Japan or the UK, for example, may not experience cases of extreme violence as often because there is less ready access to guns. This does not mean, however, that bullying is not prevalent in schools in those countries, nor that it is not a serious concern. It is an issue in many countries, but it usually does not involve extreme violence nor result in death. Given the media attention to bullying, however, it is important to consider it in context.

Canadian and US researchers (Dolmage, 2000; Roher, 1997; Tanner, 1996) concur that a very small number of young people (4 to 6 per cent) actually engage in serious acts of violence.[14] DiGiulio, in fact, contends that schools are the 'safest places in the world' (2001, p. 23). He notes that violent deaths from murder and suicide in American schools declined by 40 per cent between 1995 and 2001, whereas the risk of violent death for students who dropped out of school, were expelled or suspended increased 'several hundredfold' (ibid.).[15] These statistics, although less recent than those I provide on cyber-bullying in the next chapter, are crucial. Let me repeat the fact that the risk of violent death for students who were expelled or suspended increased 'several hundredfold' (ibid., p. 23). When we consider school and government responses to bullying and cyber-bullying in later chapters, these statistics will play an important role. DiGiulio also provides data that disclose a 14 per cent reduction in physical fights in US schools between 1991 and 1997 – another positive finding; however, as we will see in Chapter 3, it may be simply that the physical bullying has moved into the covert realm of cyberspace with far wider reach.

In the meantime, it is notable that typically only extreme bullying cases are reported by the media, thus giving an inaccurate picture of its frequency and seriousness. According to Dolmage (2000), media-reported statistics that reflect a rise in youth violence are rarely presented in context. The numbers may instead reflect higher rates of overall violence because of a growing population[16] or because schools now report incidents of a less serious nature to police more frequently.[17] Put another way, it is important to question critically the statistics presented by the media that are often geared to sensationalize and draw attention to aspects of a story without attention to the context. This in turn has significant impact on the policy and practice response by schools and education ministries.

I spend quite a bit of time addressing the influence of the media in creating fear and shaping the public's perceptions about bullying, cyber-bullying and the dangers of communication technologies in later chapters. For now, it is notable that a lot of bullying is psychological – both in terms of how it is carried out and its effects. In contemporary society, much of it flows between physical and cyberspace as 'cyber-bullying', and it is to this form of bullying that I now turn.

Definitions of cyber-bullying

One of the problems I have always had with definitions of 'bullying' is that they were too simplistic and therefore invited reactions, policy and program-matic responses that failed to recognize its nuances and complexities. In the case of cyberspace, because of the range of possibilities, the fluidity with which it is possible to move from one form of technology such as email, MSN, Facebook, MySpace, web-blogs, chat rooms and so on, and the capacity for millions of people to read and participate in various forms of communication, any definition of cyber-bullying must be applied with a caveat. Cyber-bullying must be understood in the specific paradigmatic context in which it is presented.

More importantly, when we define a behaviour, it is important to remember it as an action that takes place in a particular context, at a particular time, with various influences operating on the individual(s) who take the action. Moreover, it is the particular lens or conceptual approach that we bring to our understanding of bullying or cyber-bullying that will determine our response. I began to hint, in my introduction to Chapter 1, that descriptions and definitions of reality can be deliberately framed to develop people's under-standing of an issue by the words that are used to define it. So, for example, if the Internet is described as a 'gift from the devil' (Soloyon, 2005), or 'Web ensnares teens up to eight hours a day' (Soloyon, 2005) and if use of communi-cations technology by young people is consistently described in this way, then it follows that no matter how they use it, there will be a negative connota-tion attached to it. For example, I gave the example of the teenage boys who testified at the Azmi Jubran human rights tribunal and explained that when they call someone 'gay' or a 'homo' and if the expression is directed towards someone they like, then they mean it as a term of endearment. When it is against someone they dislike, then it is meant to hurt.

With so much of popular teenage discourse infiltrated with words such as 'ho' (prostitute) and 'bitch' and quick communication codes such as 'omg' which means 'Oh my God', which have developed through MSN and text messaging, teenagers are increasingly blocking out the adults in their lives. Moreover, as Lankshear and Knobel (2006) point out, kids approach cyberspace with a very different understanding of its fluidity or capacity, whereas adults tend to see cyberspace as something that can be controlled in the same way as physical space.

For example, adults might perceive that online firewalls are like brick walls that cannot be hacked through. As adults have always had some kind of 'control' over the spaces that kids occupy, and over forms of knowledge young people access at home and school, they might define cyber-bullying as 'anti-authority', 'rampant' and 'out of control'. Although, in the last five years, numerous studies have reported on the forms, extent and impact of cyber-bullying, it is important to bear in mind that that these findings may help us understand only one part of the puzzle, and that we ought to look at the range of influences that might tacitly condone cyber-bullying through the behaviour and responses we ourselves model.

We should also be cognizant of the very fine line between youth expression that we generally accept when they interact among themselves and that which is truly harmful and offensive. Here are some definitions of cyber-bullying that illustrate the forms it takes, the tools that are used to engage in it, and ways in which it is understood to differ from traditional bullying.

It is not clear whether the term 'cyber-bullying' was first coined by Canadian Bill Belsey (2005) or American lawyer, Nancy Willard (2003). Belsey defined cyber-bullying as follows:

> Cyber-bullying involves the use of information and communication technologies such as email, cellphone and pager text messages, instant messaging, defamatory personal Web sites, and defamatory online personal polling Web sites, to support deliberate, repeated, and hostile behavior by an individual or group that is intended to harm others.
>
> (Belsey, 2005)

A more comprehensive, though shorter, definition is presented by Nancy Willard, Director for the Center for Safe and Responsible Internet Use, who describes cyber-bullying as speech that is 'defamatory, constitutes bullying, harassment, or discrimination, discloses personal information, or contains offensive, vulgar or derogatory comments' (Willard, 2003, p. 66). Remember that, if we adopt this definition, the defamatory nature of the expression would have to be first established in a court of law. According to Willard, other forms of cyber-bullying can include flaming (sending derogatory messages to a person(s), harassing and denigrating (put-downs), masquerading, outing and excluding (Willard, 2005).

The term 'cyber-bullying' describes forms of bullying that use technology. According to some reports, it is a phenomenon that children and adolescents seem to increasingly be using to harm others (Campbell, 2005), although there is also significant evidence (Media Awareness Network, 2005) that many adults are equally guilty of engaging in cyber-bullying. I will give examples of adult cyber-bullying as we go along.

There is no dearth of definitions of cyber-bullying. Elsewhere, and within the context of certain articles, I have defined peer-to-peer cyber-bullying (Shariff and Strong-Wilson, 2005) as comprising covert, psychological bullying, conveyed through the electronic media such as cellphones, weblogs and web sites, online chat rooms, 'MUD' rooms (multi-user domains where individuals take on different characters) and Xangas (online personal profiles where some adolescents create lists of people they do not like).

In 2007 I would add to that definition to include social communications networks such as Facebook, YouTube, Orkut, LinkdIn, MySpace and count-less others that are surfacing on the Internet. Some researchers have defined cyber-bullying as 'willful and repeated harm inflicted through the medium of electronic text' (Patchin and Hinduja, 2006). Other researchers define it as an 'an aggressive, intentional act carried out by a group or individual, using electronic forms of contact, repeatedly and over time against a victim who can not easily defend him or herself' (Smith, 2004).

It might be a good idea to check the description of cyber-bullying on Wikipedia. The definitions and explanation of cyber-bullying are compre-hensive and helpful because they cover a range, although not all, of cyber-actions that could be included as cyber-bullying:

> Cyberbullying (also spelled Cyber-bullying, Cyber-bullying, or online bullying) is the term used to refer to bullying and harassment by use of electronic devises through means of email, instant messaging, text messages, blogs, mobile phones, pagers, and web sites. Other terms for cyberbullying are 'electronic bullying', 'e-bullying', 'SMS bullying', mobile bullying', 'online bullying', digital bullying', or 'Internet bullying' . . .
> (Wikipedia, 2007)

Wikipedia goes on to explain that, in some countries, provinces and states, cyber-bullying is defined as a crime. As with the profile of traditional bullying presented earlier, cyber-bullying is described as:

> [W]illful and involves recurring or repeated harm inflicted through the medium of electronic text. According to R.B. Standler, bullying intends to cause emotional distress and has no legitimate purpose to the choice of communications. Cyberbullying can be as simple as continuing to send

e-mail to someone who has said they want no further contact with the sender. Cyberbullying may also include threats, sexual remarks, pejorative labels (i.e. hate speech). Cyber-bullies may publish personal contact information for their victims at web sites. They may attempt to assume the identity of a victim for the purpose of publishing material in their name that defames or ridicules them.

(Wikipedia, 2007a)

These definitions all state in common the fact that communications technology tools and media are being used to engage in online bullying, that the communication is, as with general bullying, deliberate and wilful, repeated and exclusionary. So the question that arises is: Do we blame the medium or the message? (McLuhan, 1964). I would argue that the medium of cyberspace simply provides an avenue for expression of the message. As Campbell (2005) asks, 'is cyber-bullying, an old problem in a new guise?' (p. 68). The message is no different from that which is often expressed when bullying occurs in physical space (overtly or covertly). If we are to carry out Hamed Nastoh's goal of education effectively, then it is critical to focus on the message, but also important to understand the medium so that it too can be used to empower learning and convey an altogether different message.

Methods used in cyber-bullying include text messaging of derogatory insults on mobile phones, with students showing the message to others before sending it to the target; sending threatening emails, and forwarding a confidential email to all address-book contacts, thus publicly humiliating the first sender. Others gang up on one student and bombard him/her with 'flame' emails or set up a derogatory web site dedicated to a targeted student and emailing others the address, inviting their comments.

In the United States, high school student David Knight lived this nightmare. David had been teased, taunted, kicked, threatened and punched for most of his years in high school. In an interview with CBC National News (Leishman, 2002), David explained that the most devastating aspect of the bullying was the humiliation he suffered every time he logged onto the Internet. Students from his school had set up a web site about him where they continued the threats, insults and gossip. The derision against David spread quickly and globally. He was told by peers to check out a certain web site originating in Thailand. To his horror, the web site was titled, 'Welcome to the page that makes fun of Dave Knight' – an extension of the web site that was set up by his Canadian peers. In an interview with CBC National News, David explained:

Rather than just some people, say 30 in a cafeteria, hearing them all yell insults at you, it's up there for 6 billion people to see. Anyone with a computer can see it . . . and you can't get away from it. It doesn't go away when you come home from school. It made me feel even more trapped.

(Ibid.)

It took the threat of litigation against the Internet provider and David's school before the web site was finally taken down – approximately six months after his family's initial request for removal (ibid.).

In addition, web sites can be set up for others to vote on the biggest geek, or sluttiest girl in the school (Campbell, 2005; Snider, 2004). In one instance, a video of a teenager masturbating for her boyfriend was uploaded and emailed to her entire class when the relationship soured (Harmon, 2004). Other examples of this kind of bullying include the following.

The previous section presented a profile of traditional bullying as either physical or psychological, and overt or covert. Although I have described it as primarily 'covert', cyber-bullying can be as open, aggressive and 'overt' as other forms of psychological bullying – especially now that comments derogating teachers and persons in authority can be loaded on the Internet for everyone to see. Cyber-bullying generally takes the form of verbal and written bullying. Written forms of communication, especially online, can often be saved, reproduced and have an element of permanence, whereas the spoken word, if not recorded, is difficult to reproduce.

As I have mentioned several times and will continue to emphasize and expand upon throughout this book, cyber-bullying is not restricted to children and youths. The Internet and email, for example, have provided a medium for many adults to vent their anger and frustration, harass, threaten and exploit the reputations of other adults. Some take on virtual personalities in MUD rooms and sexually harass other players. In Chapter 7, I will also highlight cases involving online harassment and cyber-libel against teachers by parents, and introduce examples of Internet web sites created by adults that perpetuate hate and violence.

Before presenting statistics drawing from a range of international studies to gauge the extent of technology use and cyber-bullying in various parts of the world, it is important to highlight some of the key characteristics of cyber-bullying that are not aspects of traditional bullying.

Characteristics of cyber-bullying

Electronic media by their nature allow for traditional forms of bullying to take on characteristics that are specific to cyberspace.

Anonymity

The anonymous nature of cyberspace first made it attractive to young people, especially when there is a nexus to the school, because it allows for the targeting of classmates and/or teachers without being easily detected (unless they are using social networking sites on which is it easier to identify those who post comments). Most cyber-bullying is anonymous because perpetrators are shielded by screen names that protect their identity. Anonymity in cyberspace adds to the challenges for schools (Harmon, 2004). Furthermore, although cyber-bullying begins anonymously in the virtual environment, it impacts learning in the physical school environment. The consequences can be psychologically devastating for victims and socially detrimental for all students (Gáti *et al.*, 2002). Fear of unknown cyber-perpetrators among classmates and bullying that continues at school distracts all students (victims, bystanders and perpetrators) from schoolwork. It creates a hostile physical school environment where students feel unwelcome and unsafe. In such an atmosphere, equal opportunities to learn are greatly reduced (Devlin, 1997; Shariff and Strong-Wilson, 2005).

An infinite audience

Second, and as I mentioned earlier in this chapter, research on general bullying finds that 30 per cent of onlookers and bystanders support perpetrators instead of victims (Boulton, 1993; Salmivalli, 2001). The longer it persists, the more bystanders join in the abuse (Henderson *et al.*, 2002), creating a power imbalance between victim and perpetrators. Isolation renders victims vulnerable to continued abuse, and the cycle repeats itself. What might begin in the physical school environment as friendly banter can quickly turn into verbal bullying that continues in cyberspace as covert psychological bullying. The difference in cyberspace is that hundreds of perpetrators can get involved in the abuse, and classmates who may not engage in the bullying at school can hide behind technology to inflict the most serious abuse.

I have already used the well-known example of an abusive web site designed to insult David Knight, which found its way into Thailand. A similar situation occurred with a Trois Rivières, Québec teenager, Ghislain Reza, who became known worldwide as the 'Star Wars kid'. Ghislain had taped himself playing a Star Wars character and doing a dance with a light sabre. He mistakenly left the tape in the media room at his school. The tape was stolen by two classmates who uploaded the video onto a web site. The web site received approximately 15 million hits and over 106 clones of the video were made. This resulted in Ghislain becoming known as the 'Star Wars kid'. He was teased everywhere he went at school. The Hollywood director of the Star Wars movies, George Lucas heard about Ghislain. The American corporate mentality kicked in, and some entrepreneurs began to produce 'Star Wars kid' memorabilia and souvenirs. At his school, students would jump up on tables and dance chanting 'Star Wars kid!' everywhere he went. His parents eventually sued the two classmates who uploaded the tape and settled out of court for approximately C$360,000 in April, 2006. Ghislain had to move to another school to avoid the teasing. Although the settlement was good for Ghislain because it took him out of the public eye, if the case had proceeded to trial it would have been the first of its kind on cyber-bullying. Most of the court cases that are instigated for bullying and cyber-bullying seem to get settled out of court because legal costs are generally too high for parents, and school insurance companies use all kinds of delay tactics to avoid trial. Moreover, courts are reluctant to hear cases of cyber-bullying because of the definitional challenges and their concern of opening up the floodgates to litigation. David Knight's situation is a case in point. His claim was delayed for at least three years by the school's insurers and is now under settlement negotiations.

Prevalent sexual and homophobic harassment

A third concern is that sexual and homophobic harassment is emerging as a prevalent aspect of cyber-bullying, and this may be related to the gender differences in the way that males and females use the Internet and cellphone technologies. Certainly, the international findings that I discuss later on are very interesting in this regard.

Permanence of expression

Fourth, online communications have a permanence and inseparability that are very difficult to erase. Cellular phones are generally carried all the time, making them difficult for victims to ignore, and computers are generally used everyday. Although, of course, a cellphone can be ignored, text messages and emails can be sent so that every time the phone or computer is turned on, the nasty messages are waiting. Most people have a cellphone and need their computer for learning and work activities. Moreover, emails and defamatory material or modified photographs about a person on the Internet are extremely difficult to remove once posted, as millions of people can download and save it immediately. These forms of expression can then be forwarded on to hundreds of other people and saved in their desk or laptop computers.

MySpace, Facebook and YouTube

Online social communications tools such as MySpace for pre-teens and teenagers began to surface approximately five years ago and caught on like wild-fire. Especially for girls, who engage in more social and verbal forms of communication, MySpace was the perfect way to connect with friends, but also exclude peers, harass, and demean them. Disney has recently created a MySpace of its own to capitalize on its popularity. Until this year, incidents of cyber-bullying involving MySpace were generally restricted to peer-to-peer cases. However, with the advent of Facebook and YouTube, the world of social networking entered entirely new realms.

Facebook was launched on 4 February 2004, at Harvard University, by twenty-two-year-old Mark Zuckerberg. It was developed to be a social networking tool for Ivy League university students, and, within two weeks, one-half of Harvard students were members. By 30 May 2004, students at Stanford and Yale had joined, and, by September 2005, Facebook was opened to high school students. By June 2006, the site was opened to business networks with more than 20,000 networks of employees. Within a span of three years, Facebook gained over 19 million registered users. It is the sixth most trafficked site in the United States, and 1 per cent of all Internet time is spent on facebook.com (Roher, 2007). One of its attractions is that it is a photo-sharing site on the web. Six million photographs are uploaded daily and are expected to bring Zuckerman, US$100m in revenue in 2007. Yahoo offered to purchase Facebook for US$1bn and was turned down.

According to a California ethnographer, danah boyd (her legal name is in lower case), the competition between Facebook and MySpace is based on class. In an article entitled 'Facebook is for "good" kids – MySpace is for freaks' (Harris, 2007), *The Gazette* reports boyd's research that Facebook teens tend to be from families who are wealthier and emphasize a college education, are predominantly white, take honours classes and 'live in a world dictated by after school activities'. The young people who communicate on MySpace, however, are described as 'geeks, freaks or queers' from lower-income families and are expected to get jobs after graduating from grade 12. The reason for this divide according to boyd is that people tend to gravitate to social groups where they feel most comfortable. This was verified in a survey by Comscore (an Internet data collection company) that found almost 50 per cent of Facebook users – compared with the overall web average of 40 per cent – live in households in which the annual income is higher than US$75,000. The media article notes that, although boyd's findings were presented as a 'blog essay' rather than an academic article, her reputation as a leading analyst of online behaviour makes her study convincing.

I agree with other academics who found boyd's study interesting because it identifies the online subtleties of discrimination, which are difficult to recognize. In light of this study, it is not surprising that the US military prevented their soldiers from accessing MySpace but allowed access to Facebook, which is preferred by officers.

Online social communications tools

In a recent interview, boyd described MySpace and Facebook as follows:

> MySpace and Facebook are social network sites where individuals create profiles and link to others ('friends') within the system. The profile serves as an individual's digital representation (similar to homepages) of their tastes, fashion, and identity. In crafting this profile, individuals upload photos, indicate interests, list favorite musicians and describe themselves

textually and through associated media. The social network feature allows participants to link themselves to others within the system, revealing their affiliations and peer group. These sites also allow friends to comment on each other's profiles. Structurally, social network sites are a cross between a year book and a community web site.

These sites also provide numerous communication tools. Both have a messaging system similar to email; MySpace also has a bulletin board where people can post messages that all friends can read and a blogging service where people can post entries for either friends or the public at large. When youth login, their first task is typically to check messages in order to see who has written to them. While email is still used to communicate with adults and authorities, MySpace is the primary asynchronous communication tool for teens. After checking personal messages, youth check friend additions, bulletins board posts, event announcements and new blog posts by friends. They visit their friends' pages to see new photos or check out each other's comments. The vast majority of social network site use amongst youth does not involve surfing to strangers' profiles, but engaging more locally with known friends and acquaintances.

(boyd and Jenkins, 2006 (May 26))

According to boyd, MySpace has over 78 million registered accounts, and Facebook has approximately 8 million. Although over 85 per cent of college students participate on Facebook if it exists on their campus, she explains that MySpace is a cultural requirement for American high school students. She quotes one teenager as saying: 'If you're not on MySpace, you don't exist' (ibid.). Not all MySpace users are teenagers but most American teenagers have MySpace accounts.

boyd explains that these sites play a key role in contemporary youth culture:

These sites play a key role in youth culture because they give youth a space to hang out amongst friends and peers, share cultural artifacts (like links to funny web sites, comments about TV shows) and work out an image of how they see themselves. They also serve as digital publics, substituting for the types of publics that most adults took for granted growing up, but are now inaccessible for many people – neighborhood basketball courts, malls, parks, etc. and allow them spaces *where they can escape adult culture* [emphasis added].

(Ibid.)

I ask readers to make note of boyd's remarks because they are important to my discussion of how we supervise student spaces in Chapter 5.

Because of its more elitist status and the fact that its enrolment is popular with so called brighter and more educated youngsters, prospective employers have begun to check applicant's profiles on Facebook to see what kinds of friend they have; how much they drink (as evidenced by photographs of themselves either posted or tagged by friends); what kinds of personal conversation they have with friends on their walls; how they generally dress, behave and so on (Sankey, 2007).

As more teens join Facebook, this social networking web site has run into problems relating to high school and middle school students posting anti-authority cyber-expression about teachers and school officials. What is surprising is that many of the kids who post the online comments argue that their conversations should not be accessed by adults (even if those adults are on Facebook and can see their postings through other people's profiles). This fuels the debate about private and public spaces, and the argument by students that they are not 'wilfully bullying' their teachers but simply having conversations among themselves that are not meant for their teachers' or school officials' eyes. They argue that they do not intend to harass, threaten and generally bully their teachers and that they have every right to a free conversation. I return to an analysis of these issues later in the book. In the meantime, other networks, such as YouTube, are also drawing their share of problems

YouTube allows for the downloading of videos for all to see. Internationally, YouTube has caught on as a site where all kinds of video-tapes can be posted. In some cases videotapes are modified and placed on YouTube. Examples include videotaping student fights, filming peers undressing in gym changing rooms and washrooms; filming angry teachers in classrooms; and students dancing at a school dance (Roher, 1997).

Other social networking tools include Orkut, the equivalent of MySpace in India, and Freevote.com. Using Freevote.com, students can set up a web page for an individual school that permits students to vote on issues at their school. Although the philosophy is positive, this site also allows students to make personal, degrading and offensive anonymous comments about others. Similarly, RateMyTeacher.com and RateMyProfessor.com sometimes invite vitriolic comments when students are angry with teachers or professors for a variety of reasons. Bebo.com is popular in New Zealand, Australia, the UK and Ireland and contains categories such as 'people search', 'background check', 'find friends', 'find people', 'chat room', 'black dating', 'photo album', 'online photo albums'. Although it is important that the web site has background checks, Bebo has also had its share of young people engaging in cyber-bullying on its site.

These online social networking tools are both public and private to a limited extent, opening up important debates about which stakeholders have the authority (and responsibility) to intervene in cyberspace to monitor young people's social communications. The jury is still out on this issue as the courts have yet to provide clear direction on these issues. The social communications networks present an exception to the anonymity of cyber-bullying, because the names of those who post comments can be made visible and accessed by others who join the same network. Because of the overwhelming global reaction to these social communication networks, I deal with them in upcoming chapters through detailed analysis, because it is through these issues that we can sift through and tease out some of the boundaries of responsibility that at present remain unclear.

Online sexual discrimination

In 2005, I wrote several articles and book chapters with a graduate student, Rachel Gouin, on the prevalence of sexual and homophobic harassment in cyberspace. I reiterate here some of the findings we reported. This form of cyber-bullying is largely influenced by both biology (hormonal and pre-pubescent influences) and environment (gender socialization).

The research suggests that, although both genders engage in cyber-bullying, there are differences (Chu, 2005; Li, 2005). It has been argued that children who engage in any form of bullying are victims. They are influenced by biological and environmental forces, including intersecting and interlocking systemic barriers of oppression based on race, gender, sexual orientation, (dis)-abilities, cultural hegemony, androcentrism and Eurocentrism, that continue to pervade many institutions, including schools and courts (Razack, 1998; Shariff, 2003). I expand on these influences in Chapter 4.

Numerous scholars have written about online gender harassment (Brail, 1996; Finn, 2004; Gáti et al., 2002; Herring, 2002; McCormick and Leonard, 1996). Some have outlined categories such as gender harassment, unwanted sexual attention and sexual coercion (Barak, 2005). Others have written about virtual rape (Dibbell, 1993; MacKinnon, 2001), cyberstalking (Adam, 2001; 2002; Spitzberg and Hoobler, 2002; Tavani and Grodzinsky, 2002), identity theft (Finn and Banach, 2000), cyber-bullying (Shariff, 2004; Ybarra and Mitchell, 2004a,b) and cyber-violence more generally (Herring, 2002). The studies highlighted below illuminate ways in which gender-based cyber-bullying or violence differs from, and is linked to, what occurs in physical (non-virtual) space.

Female victims

Barak (2005) defines three categories of sexual harassment:

1   gender harassment;
2   unwanted sexual attention; and
3   sexual coercion.

She divides the first category into four subcategories:

1   active verbal sexual harassment, which includes offensive sexual messages from harasser to victim, gender humiliating comments and sexual remarks;
2   passive verbal sexual harassment, which includes offensive nicknames and online identities (such as wetpussy, xlargetool);
3   active graphic gender harassment, which includes unwanted erotic and pornographic content through mail or posting in online environments; and
4   passive graphic gender harassment, including pictures and movies published on pornographic sites (such as forced pop-up windows).

The second category, unwanted sexual attention, 'refers to uninvited behaviours that explicitly communicate sexual desires or intensions toward another individual' (ibid., p. 78). Finally, sexual coercion entails the use of various online means to pressure the victim into sexual co-operation. Even though the use of force is not possible online, the threats can be perceived by the victim as being as realistic as a face-to-face situation. This is illustrated by the telephone threat that caused Canadian teenager Dawn Marie Wesley to commit suicide. The words 'You're f——g dead!' from a classmate caused her to believe real harm would come to her. Her perpetrator was convicted of criminal harassment because the court observed that perceived harm by the victim amounts to the same thing as actual harm (Shariff, 2004).

   This perspective that electronic threats are as real as, or even more frightening than, those made face-to-face, is supported by Herring (2002), who explains that online behaviour that leads to assault against the physical, psychological or emotional well-being of an individual or group in effect constitutes a form of violence. She distinguishes four types of cyber-violence:

1   online contact leading to offline abuse (misrepresentation leading to fraud, theft, unwanted sexual contact);
2   cyber stalking, which comprises online monitoring or tracking of users' actions with criminal intent;
3   online harassment, which consists of unwanted, repeated and deliberate threats, abuses and alarms; and
4   degrading online representations of women through words or images that invite disrespect or put-downs.

Adam (2001) observes that cyber-violence studies disclose that the majority of perpetrators are men and the majority of victims are women. He reports that as many as one in of three female children reported having been harassed online in 2001 alone. Among children, girls appear to be targeted twice as much as boys (Finkelhor et al., 2000).

According to Herring (2002), 25 per cent of Internet users aged ten to seventeen were exposed to unwanted pornographic images in the past year. Eight per cent of the images involved violence, in addition to sex and nudity. The Alberta study of middle school children referred to earlier (Li, 2005) disclosed that boys owned up to cyber-bullying more frequently and girls were more frequently victimized. Furthermore, Mitchell *et al.* (2001, as cited in Barak, 2005), in a survey of American teenagers, found that 19 per cent of these youths (mostly older girls) had experienced at least one sexual solicitation online in the preceding year.

Female perpetrators

Although girls may be more likely targets of cyber-violence because of their location along a hierarchy of power, adolescent girls are increasingly surfacing as active instigators of cyber-bullying. Although Ybarra and Mitchell (2004a) found that males and females were equally likely to report having harassed someone online, a recent study of 3,700 adolescents (Kowalski, as cited in Chu (2005) found that, in a two-month period, 17 per cent of the girls surveyed confessed to online bullying compared with 10 per cent of the boys. Given that girls aged twelve to eighteen have been found to spend at least 74 per cent of their time on chat rooms or instant messaging (Berson *et al.*, 2002, this is not surprising. It is even less surprising when considered in the context of the biological and environmental (socializing) influences that are address in Chapter 4.

Given that preliminary research on cyber-bullying discloses a significant amount of sexual harassment and gender differences in the way Internet harassment is carried out, we cannot ignore role of gender and its manifestations of online violence. Later, I will present examples and statistics that impact and motivate young men and women and show how this in turn affects learning environments (both physical and virtual). These examples will set the stage for introductions of judicial and legislative responses to legal claims of sexual harassment in cyberspace in later chapters. For now, it is important to note that, although girls and women appear to be the primary targets in cyberspace, sufficient research suggests that girls, internationally, are increasingly found to perpetrate cyber-bullying in groups and are more frequent users of social networking tools

Male targets and perpetrators

Sexual orientation also features heavily in general and cyber-bullying. Cases of general bullying include the devastating suicide of Hamed Nastoh, the pouring of acid and four-year-long homophobic bullying of Azmi Jubran by his classmates at Handsworth High school. In Azmi's case, his perpetrators testified at the human rights tribunal that, when friends are teased about being gay, it is a term of endearment; however, when the insult is directed at someone who is disliked, the words are meant to hurt. Based on the persistent, long drawn out and deliberate nature of homophobic bullying endured by Azmi Jubran and David Knight, the words were meant to hurt. In David Knight's case, he was described as a homosexual paedophile, with invitations to an infinite audience to write insults and comments below his photograph.

A study conducted by Tolman *et al.* (2001) at the middle school level in the United States made important observations relating to sexual harassment and homophobic bullying at the adolescent level. What they found was that sexual harassment significantly increased at pre-adolescence and adolescence. It was largely perpetrated by male students, who also engaged in homophobic bullying of their less aggressive male peers. Tolman *et al.* suggest two reasons – first, the raging hormones and interest in females and second, the need by adolescent males to prove their manhood. In doing so they engage in sexual harassment of females and put down males who are either perceived to be competitors or perceived to have more 'feminine' characteristics, resulting in the homophobic bullying. These issues are addressed in greater detail in Chapter 4.

Intersecting forms of discrimination

To complicate matters, in each of the cases discussed here, it is not simply the sexual orientation that invites the derision. Each of the victims I have mentioned were teased for something else as well – in Hamed and Azmi's case, it was the fact that they were also of Iranian heritage, although both were born in Canada. In David Knight's case, his intelligence and good looks might have played a role. In Ghislain Reza's case, his weight certainly played a role.

The international context

Although there have been limited studies over the last few years, and many new studies have either yet to be completed or are emerging as this book goes to print, it is nonetheless important to summarize them here, and underscore the fact that cyber-bullying is emerging as a global concern. Although significant media and research attention has been paid to addressing it in countries such as Britain, New Zealand, the Netherlands, Australia, the United States and Canada, research in South Asia is just getting underway, as the use of technologies begins to proliferate among young people in those countries. My own research project, which includes collaborators in Japan, India, China, New Zealand, Australia and the United Kingdom (www.cyberbullying.co.nr/) is a two-year project that will culminate in a conference in New Zealand in

July 2008 to disseminate findings. For the purposes of this book I present preliminary data as they trickle in from my international colleagues and research assistants in Japan, India and China, and also briefly discuss what is taking place in the West. The South Asian countries are interesting from the perspective of understanding the impact that technologies are having on their respective cultures and the way in which their young people are beginning to break traditional roles through online communication. It is to this snapshot I now turn in Chapter 3.

A transnational snapshot

SNERT . . . That's what some call the trouble-makers of cyberspace. Attributed to Kurt Vonnegut, the term stands out for 'Snot-Nosed Eros-Ridden Teenager'. It concisely captures much of what many cyberspace deviants are all about. They thumb their noses at authority figures and smear their discontent all over themselves and others.

(Suler and Philips 1998)

Introduction

SNERTS live all over the globe. They are not restricted to Britain, Canada and the United States. Accordingly, in this chapter, I would like to provide a transnational snapshot of Internet use, prevalence of cyber-bullying and brief case examples, to give readers a general appreciation of what is taking place in various parts of the world under the definition of 'cyber-bullying'.

Cyber-bullying has only recently emerged in many countries and is only now becoming recognized as a serious issue that needs to be addressed. The research emerging from my academic colleagues in various countries is varied and sporadic. Moreover, I have just embarked on the first year of my international research project. To begin presenting the transnational snapshot, therefore, I have prepared two tables. Table 3.1 provides a general snapshot of what is taking place internationally, in terms of increased use of communications technologies, and emerging data on experiences with cyber-bullying. Table 3.2 provides available country-specific data. The sources for the statistics in both tables are given in footnotes, and can be accessed by readers for more information on preliminary findings from each country. The tables should not be read as an effort to engage in comprehensive quantitative comparisons by country at this stage. My intention in presenting the data this way is to ensure that the available statistics are highlighted and organized in a somewhat coherent form for this chapter, and to provide readers with a 'glance' at the kinds of information that are beginning to emerge internationally. Table 3.1 does not contain *all* the available data either. It simply contains sufficient examples to provide an idea of what is taking place.

Table 3.1 A transnational snapshot of technology use and reported cyber-bullying

	Access to computers/ Internet	Cellphones (own cellular phones)	Cyber-bullying
Australia[a]	• 61% of homes have computers • 46% have Internet access • Global leader SMS • 500 SMS messages per month in 2005	• 46% of 14-year-olds • 55% of 15-year-olds • 73% of 16-year-olds • 12% of kids aged 6–9 use SMS every day • 80% 15–17-year-olds SMS daily	• 13% of students experience cyber-bullying by age 8 • 25% know somebody who had experienced cyber-bullying • 42% of girls aged 12–15 experienced cyber-bullying
Canada[b]	• 95% of 11–15-year-olds have Internet access at home	• 37% of 11–15-year-olds • 80% 16–17-year-olds • 32% 8–10-year-olds	• 84% of teachers cyber-bullied • 23% bullied by email • 35% bullied in chat rooms • 41% bullied by text messages • 50% knew someone being cyber-bullied • 40% did not know perpetrators
China[c]	• 137 million people use Internet • 17.2% of web users under 18 • 32.3 % of Internet users are in high school	• 487,343 cellphone users • 304.65 billion instant messages sent per month	• Case studies are available; few statistics available • Mainly dealt with by legal system under criminal or defamatory laws • Research just beginning
India[d]	• Internet connections and users grown from 10,000 (1995) to 30 million (2003). Modest for country with billion+ population • 15% of homes have computers, of which 61% subscribe to Internet • Teen users represent 8%	• Fewer formal statistics available on cellphone use although similar to Japan; landline phones are more expensive so mobiles are more readily available. Research is underway to determine mobile phone use. However cyber-bullying seems done via mobiles	• Mobile bullying more common in students • 65% of students were victims of cyber-bullying using phones • 60% bullied others using mobile phones
Japan[e]	• 20% use computers by the age 11 • 70,072,000 Internet users • 99% have Internet access at school	• 24.1% of elementary students have cellphones • 66.7% of junior high • 96% of senior high	• Although few formal studies • Numerous cases of *netto-ijime* (cyber-bullying) as set out in this chapter

Table 3.1 (continued)

	Access to computers/ Internet	Cellphones (own cellular phones)	Cyber-bullying
Singapore[f]	• 69% of students have Internet access at home	• 75% carry cellular phones	• 14% of 1,100 students were bullied via text messaging • 13% were bullied on instant chat
United Kingdom[g]	• 69% students have access to Internet at home	• 75% carry cellular phones	• 20% out of 770 young people cyber-bullied • 73% knew perpetrators • 26% by strangers • 1 in 20 admit involvement in cyber-bullying • 1 in 8 send threats to others • 1 in 12 admit posting false info about others on a blog
United States[h]	• 70% of children aged 4–6 years used computers • 68% under age 2 used screen media • 91% of 12–15-year-olds access Internet • 99% of 16–18-year-olds use it • 74% of girls 12–18 years old chat online	• 84% of children 10–14 carry cellular phones • 45% between 8 and 10 years carry cellular phones and engage in text messaging	• 75–80% of 12–14-year-olds have been cyber-bullied • 43% children bullied while online • 35% threatened online • 53% admitted being mean/hurtful online • 1 in 17 children threatened online • 1 in 4 aged 11–19 threatened

Notes:

a Lee (2005); Davidson (2004); Australian Bureau of Statistics (2005); Campbell (2005); MacLean (2006).

b Shariff (2007b); Churchill (2007); Li (2005); Ontario College of Teachers (2007).

c Zhang and Wei (2007a,b).

d Jaishankar and Shariff (in press); McMillin (2005).

e Morita et al. (1999) as cited in Yoneyama and Naito (2003); Senoo (2007); Hasegawa et al. (2006, 2007); Research committee for protection of children (2006); Mainchi Daily News (2007); Itoh (1999).

f Forss (2006; 2007).

g NCH (2005); Rivers (2003); Land (2006); Livingstone and Bober (2005).

h Chu (2005); Finkelhor et al. (2000); Ybarra and Mitchell (2004b); Portsmouth Herald Editorial Board (2005); Swartz (2005); Hinduja and Patchin (in press); Lenhart (2007); Ybarra and Mitchell (2004a); Ybarra et al. (2007).

Table 3.2 Country-specific considerations

	Country-specific considerations
Australia[a]	• Global leader in mobile and text message use • Autocratic-positivist legal and policy approach • Banned access to YouTube in 1,600 schools in Victoria State • Spent $84m on Internet filters, hacked by 16-year-old in 30 minutes
Canada[b]	• Ontario Teachers Association Survey found 84% teachers defamed on social networking sites • Canadian Teachers' Federation passed a resolution to address cyber-bullying • Ontario amended legislation to include suspensions for bullying • Gender differences apparent in the way males and females engage in cyber-bullying. Females more likely to inform adults than males • 46% of students do not believe cyber-bullying is school responsibility • 26% of students strongly disagree that schools must intervene • 63% said it starts at school • 72% would report cyber-bullying anonymously • 71% more likely NOT to bully if they were happy at school • 83% would like to create a more kind and respectful world
India[c]	• Cultural considerations are important in India • Bullying socially accepted part of the culture between people of different castes • Applicable laws include Information Technology Act (2000), but this pertains more to pornography, less effective in addressing cyber-bullying • Girls can gain independence through Internet from safety of their homes – retain domestic role but build identities and career possibilities • Girls engage more in chat groups and social networks and attend cyber-cafés in groups
Japan[d]	• Cultural considerations important in Japan • 80% of bullying is carried out by a peer group rather than individuals • Collective power vs individual power • Teachers/parents push victims of bullying to integrate into the group • 40 cases of student suicides occurred between 1999 and 2005 as a result of parental pressure • 30% of the suicides occurred because suicide is culturally considered a respectful way out of a problem • Japanese girls use *shuojo anime* – form of online fan club • Cellphone and text bullying more common and transfers to online defamation and threats
South Korea[e]	• Recent law implemented for Internet use but deals largely with extortion • Koreans reveal name and ID number before sharing opinions • Described as the most wired country in the world
United Kingdom[f]	• Livinstone and Bober (2005) study well worth reading – see references • British government web site gives comprehensive advice – worth a visit • 18% of girls vs 7% of boys reported being cyber-bullied • 35% of girls vs 17% of boys knew someone who had experienced cyber-bullying • 31% of youths received sexual comments on the Internet • 33% of youths received nasty comments on the Internet • 46% admit divulging personal info over the Internet • 40% engaged in identity play on the Internet • 18% of parents did not know how to help their child use the Internet safely

Table 3.2 (continued)

	Country-specific considerations
	• 35% of children said they had filtering software • 69% of children did not like the restrictions by parents • 63% of children have tried to hide their online activity
United States[g]	• 32% of white students encountered online bullying • 18% of black students encountered online bullying • Females preferred text messaging vs face-to-face • Girls more likely to be victims • 58% of students grades 4–8 said nothing to parents if threatened • Over 2 million kids never tell anyone • 67% students believe bullying happens more offline than online • 28% students believe of bullying happens more online than offline

Notes:
a Lee (2005).
b Li (2005); Shariff (2007b).
c Jaishankar and Shariff (in press); McMillin (2005).
d Gibson (2006); Akiba (2004); Morita and Kiyonga (1994); Senoo (2007); Tanaka (2001); Song (2006); Itoh (1999).
e Forss (2006, 2007).
f Livingstone and Bober (2005); British Educational Communications and Technology Agency (2007).
g Lenhart (2007).

The tables are followed by a discussion of known incidents of cyber-bullying in the tabled countries. Where available, I provide a contextual analysis of deeper cultural nuances of identity formation, privacy considerations in physical and cyberspace, and the legal and policy responses of various countries to these forms of cyber-bullying. Over the next couple of years, my international research project (www.cyberbullying.co.nr) will begin to compile and engage in comprehensive quantitative and qualitative comparisons by country. This will culminate in a conference in New Zealand in July 2008 with NetSafe to present an update on progress, with an edited book by all the international researchers involved. That publication will provide more detailed perspectives on transnational cyber-bullying and discuss the responses to it in the respective countries. I am very excited about the collaborative way in which our researchers from India, China, Japan, the United States, the United Kingdom, Australia and New Zealand have come together to engage in this long-term but very important project. Here is some preliminary information.

Context and analysis

My contextual discussion of the preliminary findings tabled above will be more interesting to readers if I begin with the findings in the Asian countries such as Japan, China, Singapore, India and Thailand and follow up with some of the findings in Western countries, namely, Australia, the United Kingdom, United States and Canada. I have decided to present them this way, because a significantly larger amount of news media and academic research has focused on cyber-bullying as a Western phenomenon. Preliminary findings in Asia suggest that this is not the case. Globalization and new technologies are proliferating at a rapid pace in Asia. The following findings and case examples illustrate that they are having a similar impact on adolescents and teachers, and creating identical challenges for schools and parents.

Japan

On 6 November 2006, the Minister of Education, Culture, Sports, Science, and Technology (MEXT) in Japan received an anonymous letter that warned him of a potential suicide due to *ijime* (bullying). This incident made an enormous impact on the Japanese administration. It had already been more than two decades since *ijime* became understood as a serious educational issue in Japan. *Ijime* was first identified as a social problem in Japan in 1984–5 when sixteen pupils committed suicide under suspected bullying circumstances (Morita, *et al.*, 1999, cited in Yoneyama and Naito, 2003). Senoo (2007) explains that, since 1985, the number and variety of *ijime* cases have rapidly increased. Among scholars it is widely believed that the nature of *ijime* is related to Japanese cultural and social characteristics such as collectivism and homogeneity (Akiba, 2004; Rios-Ellis *et al.*, 2000). However, as Hasegawa (2007) explains, although several severe cases have been reported, there have been no scholarly reports yet on the topic of cyber-bullying.

In Japan, a country considered to be digitally ahead of the rest of the world by at least two generations (Mitchell, 2004), children are exposed to digital gadgets at a very early age. The research on technology use in Japan is therefore quite surprising, given the number of serious cases of cyber-bullying that I highlight in this chapter.

Technology use: computers

Approximately half of Japanese children aged eleven use the Internet; however, only about 20 per cent were regular users in 2004 (Dickie *et al.*, 2004). Hasegawa *et al.* (2006) asked students to answer the question: 'I have a computer at home, but I don't use/am not allowed to use the computer.' They report that even though many high school students own computers, a large percentage of them do *not* use a computer, even if they have one at home. Computer use among elementary schools is even lower.

As a result, the researchers found that both junior high and high school students lack knowledge in maintaining computer security and pay little attention to the security status of computers when they use them. The researchers say that part of the reason for parents' restricting computer use at home might stem from the popularity of '*shoujo anime*' (animated characters). *Shoujo anime* appears to be a popular form of Internet sharing and fan clubs for young Japanese. It is especially popular with girls, who participate in *shuojo* fan clubs where they talk about their favourite male character whom they idolize (Gregson, 2005). Parents are concerned about some of the animated characters that are passed from computer to computer because they carry viruses. One of these popular characters is known as 'Winny'. Senoo (2007) observes that computers can become infected very easily as Winny gets passed among school-children.

As Table 3.1 shows, the percentage of households that use high-speed Internet reached 36.2 per cent, Internet users numbering 70,072 as of February 2005 (Hasegawa *et al.*, 2006). Advancement and innovation of information technology can be seen in the field of education as well. Research done by the Ministry of Education and Science (as of 30 September 2005) (ibid.) shows that 99.9 per cent of schools have Internet access. 84.0 per cent of these schools have high-speed Internet access. 48.8 per cent of the regular classrooms have a LAN installed and 89.6 per cent of the computer rooms. The subject of information technology became compulsory at primary school and junior high school in the academic year 2002 and at high school in the academic year 2003.

Technology use: mobile cellular phones

The findings relating to cellular phones are quite different from home computer use in Japan. This form of technology is far more popular among Japanese students, as Table 3.1 shows. These findings are corroborated in Professor Hasegawa's study (ibid.), where he and his colleagues reported a high rate in students' cellphone use (junior high school students, 80.8 per cent and senior high school students, 92.9 per cent). Hasegawa *et al.* (2007) also report that 85.7 per cent of the junior high school students they surveyed and 96.6 per cent of the high school students had their own cellphones.

Interestingly, 80.8 per cent of the junior high school students and 92.9 per cent of the high school students did not have any restriction on their cellphone use. It appears that Japanese parents are less worried about cellphone use because mobiles cannot attract viruses. Apparently, parents do not make the link that cellphone technology and Internet communication are integrally connected, and that text messaging and photographs taken on cellphones can be easily posted and dispersed online. Moreover, as Hasegawa *et al.* observe, parents are more worried about students engaging in blogging and chatting, which could detract from their school-work:

> Parents can monitor what web sites their children access to some degree for the PC use because they share the family PC; however, for the cellphone use, children use their own cellphone without any restrictions. *Parents do not interfere with their children's Internet use by their cellphone.* We can assume that the use of tools which enable to send information easily such as blogs

will spread rapidly. Therefore, we need to educate students to be able to judge what kind of information they can send and what kind of information they should not send to the general public.

(Hasegawa *et al.*, 2006)

Although the Hasegawa study suggests that the most trouble students admitted to experiencing online was virus infection of their computers, a number of worrisome cases involving cyber-bullying have drawn attention to cyber-bullying in Japan, which is only recently being taken seriously subsequent to the anonymous suicide note received by the Ministry.

Cyber-bullying among Japanese peers

Two of my graduate research assistants, both of whom have lived and taught in Japan, Julie d'Eon and Yasuko Senoo (2007) began to investigate the prevalence of cyber-bullying in Japan. Initially, their research disclosed very little, with the exception of Professor Hasegawa's study. They stumbled on a police web site in Japan and found numerous Japanese cases of cyber-bullying – or *netto-ijime* (bullying on the Net). Readers will see many similarities in the cases presented below to those that have been reported by Western media on what has been taking place among American and British students.

Case 1: d'Eon and Senoo (2007) found that girls, who are generally perceived to be less assertive, undertook what is believed to be first case of cyber-bullying in Japan. A few grade 9 girls (around thirteen years) bullied a grade 7 student (around eleven years old), using a cellphone camera. They took her to a washroom in a shopping mall, removed her clothing and took pictures of her naked, using two of the group members' cellphones. They then showed the picture to friends and threatened the victim that it would be shown to more people if she reported the incident to teachers. One of them sent the picture to another friend by cellphone. In this case the school interfered, deleted the picture and stopped further spreading of the picture (Hasegawa *et al.*, 2007; Senoo, 2007).

Case 2: In February 2007, six middle-school girls in Kobe used their cellphones' digital cameras to photograph another naked (female) victim. They posted the photographs on a bulletin board, inviting online visitors to rank their favourite parts of her body. The Kobe Prefectural Police filed charges for engaging in obscene acts (Senoo, 2007).

Case 3: In a tragic Japanese case involving a female perpetrator, a young girl was murdered after receiving a threat on a contentious web site (Associated Press, 2004). Satomi Mitarai, aged twelve, bled to death in a study room after her neck was cut open with a knife. Her closest, eleven-year-old friend was taken into custody by police who stated that the dispute arose on instant messaging. The accused admitted to summoning Satomi out of their homeroom classroom with the intention of killing her. The *Japan Times* reported that the girls each had a web site and often used their personal computers to communicate via text messaging.

Case 4: In November, 2006, a grade 9 male student in Akita saw his name used on a pornographic novel web site. The student was mentally shocked and could not attend the school for a few days. His name was used with the names and depictions of female students in indecent scenes of a novel. The novel was written by anonymous readers using computer and cellphone relay formats. The victim talked to the police, and the matter was under investigation for libel. The web site administration deleted the novel in December at the request of the police (Senoo, 2007).

Case 5: Two grade 9 male students sent around 800 anonymous emails to a female student's cellphone via their home computer in mid December 2006. These messages said 'Die! Feel sick to be with you! Ugly! . . . Do not come to school!' and so on. The victim's parents found her depressed and asked the police for advice. The boys were arrested for unreasonable nuisance under prefectured measures. The prefectural measures set down a maximum of six months imprisonment and a the maximum of Yen500,000 (around $5,000) fines for unreasonable nuisance (ibid.).

Case 6: In November 2006, a first-year high school student in Sapporo posted moving images of himself undergoing physical bullying by several classmates. Two of the offenders, one boy and one girl, were subsequently suspended from the school.

Case 7: In December 2006, eight members of a high school baseball team in Nagano Prefecture were found to have slandered a teammate on a bulletin board. Six offenders were ordered to be restricted to their homes, and the team was banned from competition for three months.

Cultural considerations

Researchers have found that, in Japan, 80 per cent of the bullying is carried out by a peer group rather than individuals. It happens in close friendships, where the victim is not excluded from the group but harassed for a period before it is someone else's turn. Not unlike patterns found in Western countries, it is students who are perceived to be 'good students' that perpetrate and are involved in bullying, rather than those who are generally perceived as 'problem kids' (Gibson, 2006).

Ijime *and* netto-ijime

Ijime has changed its character as traditional Japanese communities collapse and give way to economic and technological development. According to

Akiba (2004): 'privatization (individualism), along with economic changes in [Japanese] society, have collapsed traditional Japanese communities' (ibid., p. 220). She observes the importance of examining the impact of the gap between societal change and the traditional role of schools to foster Japanese cultural values. Senoo (2007) explains that with technological advances, *netto-ijime* (cyber-bullying) is becoming more prevalent. McVeigh (2003) suggests that the technology necessitates individual practices that isolate the individual from the social masses. In Japanese culture, this is a new phenomenon.

When Japanese parents use the term *ijime*, it usually describes extreme psychological and verbal aggression rather than physical aggression (Smorti *et al.*, 2003). In that connection, it fits well within verbal and psychological forms of cyber-bullying. Another main characteristic is its collective nature. Because Japanese students spend so much time together in groups, individual leaders single out one member of the group for bullying. The rest of the group follows the leader in isolating the victim (Akiba, 2004; Morita and Kiyonaga, 1994).

Because of Japanese homogeneity, victims are generally targeted for personal characteristics, or through sexual forms of harassment. Non-Japanese students are rarely mistreated. Rather, they are more likely to be treated as idols because of their racial difference. Certain invisible characteristics of Japanese victims have been suggested by Akiba (2004). From her interviews with middle school students, she found common characteristics of victims that trigger the feeling of irritation in the *ijime* perpetrators such as 'selfish', 'persistent' and 'noisy'. These types of behaviour cannot be easily accepted in Japanese society. Historically, for complex reasons of traditional social organizations, collective power rather than individuality was required for survival. This collectivism exists deep inside Japanese society and is tacitly understood. In this context, being selfish, persistent or noisy is not an understandable behaviour. The person who behaves in these ways is reactively perceived as different from other people. Senoo refers to a well-known Japanese proverb that says: 'the nail that sticks out gets hammered down'. The victims are chosen 'because they are somewhat different from others' (Tanaka, 2001, p. 463) in their behaviour. Accordingly, difference can be a point of contention even in homogenous societies, and perhaps more so in order to encourage conformity to the normative culture.

Regarding limited use of computers, despite global perceptions that the Japanese would be avid users of the Internet, Senoo (2007) explains that the Japanese have some strong and unique traditional beliefs in their everyday life that are quite different from those of religious communities. Many of them do not believe in a specific religion or believe only in Japanese Shintoism (Japanese myth). These traditional beliefs have a great influence on their behaviour and thinking. One of these traditional beliefs is that *hard* work is more valuable than *smart* work. The person who uses a computer or the Internet for his or her homework would be considered as being lazy. Many teachers and schools prefer their students to take their time doing homework using hard copies (i.e. books, newspapers and dictionaries); hence, they do not strongly recommend that students use computers and the Internet unless there is a special need to do so. This cultural preference might be a main cause that formed the resistance to the implementation of computer education in schools.

Gakko ura saito: *mobile-bullying*

As the statistics in Table 3.1 show, the use of mobile phones is very popular. This is partly owing to the expense of landlines in Japan. This has resulted in considerable 'Mobile bullying' among students. Pupils have created clandestine school sites (known as '*gakko ura saito*') that can only be accessed via mobile phone. These sites have created a new form of group bullying that encourages an entire generation of what Professor Hasegawa calls 'anonymous slanderers' (Hasegawa *et al.*, 2007). As Senoo comments, in the old-style *ijime*, at least the tormentors were known. The electronic version is as vicious, if not more so, because electronic communications afford complete anonymity. As I have noted in the profile of cyber-bullying, a key aspect of cyber-bullying is its anonymity, which makes it far more difficult for school authorities to intervene, let alone identify the instigators or implement disciplinary and educationally preventative measures. This dichotomy in the cultural orientation towards reduced use of computers to do 'work', and the increased incidence of cyber-bullying using both cellphone and Internet technology is quite specific to Japanese culture for the reasons explained above.

Ijime-jisatsu *(suicide linked to* ijime*)*

Another cultural aspect of *netto-ijime* is the increased rate of suicide among young people. *Ijime-jisatsu* is one of the disastrous and culturally incidental consequences of the *ijime* phenomenon in Japan. The number of reported cases of *ijime-jisatsu* had been decreasing for the last two decades before the Minister of Education received the anonymous suicide note on 6 November 2006. Senoo (2007) cites a BBC newscast that reported five students killing themselves in four days in November 2006. Following these cases, the police force determined that *ijime* was involved in fourteen of the forty cases of student suicides in 1999–2005, after previously reporting that there was no such case in January 2007 (ibid.). As of 2 February 2007, two suicide cases in 2006 had been officially determined to be *ijime*-related cases by the police. The number increased dramatically by November because of the lack of appropriate intervention.

As Hamed Nastoh's dedication at the opening of this book shows, suicide from bullying or cyber-bullying is not limited to Japanese society. However, as Senoo observes, there are some traditional Japanese beliefs and values that make this act an incidental solution of the *ijime* problem in Japan. Unlike other societies, this solution is not strongly tabooed in Japanese society because of their historical warrior culture (*bushido*), which traditionally regarded suicide 'as a responsible way to deal with a problem when faced with no other option' (Hogg, 2006). This view has not yet completely changed, even though Japanese life style became modernized a while ago.

Another traditional belief underlying Japanese suicide is its high value on patience related to group harmony. Chinese business management advisor Song Wenzhou comments that Japanese society demands of its people extreme efforts and patience to ensure harmony. Consequently, teachers and parents push victims of bullying to struggle with the problem or make better efforts to integrate into the group, leaving some of them few options other than suicide (Song, 2006). This statement is supported by one actual *ijime-jisatsu* case in Iwaki, Fukushima. The Fukushima district court allocated 30 per cent of the responsibility for one suicide victim's demise to the victim's parents, because they forced him to continue attending school despite the bullying (Ito, 2002, as cited in Senoo, 2007). His forced return to face the perpetrators was built on the notion of *Iwaki-shi ijime-jisatsu jiken hanketsuni tsuite*. This means 'Japanese form their identities based on their role and responsibility in a group' (Shiizu and Levine, 2001, as cited in Akiba, 2004, p. 231). This treatment, although seen as very reasonable and natural in Japanese society, has negative implications for children in the formative years of identity development. If they are excluded or not given any roles or responsibilities within the classroom group, the psychological damage is enormous.

South Korea

Cyber-bullying has also emerged as a concern in South Korea, where the government has implemented a law to prevent Internet misuse. South Korea's Ministry of Information has developed a law that will no longer enable cyber-perpetrators to hide behind false identities. The new law took effect in July 2007 and will compel ISP providers to track the originators under the 'Internet real-name system' by recording the identification records of users when they post entries. Portal operators will be obliged to disclose personal information such as names and addresses of cyber-attackers when their victims want to sue them for libel or infringement upon privacy. Ministry director Lee Ta-Hee observed that, 'South Korea is an Internet powerhouse and it is probably the most wired country in the world. But sadly, the dark side is too dark' (Bartlett, 2007).

In South Korea, online mobs distribute victims' home addresses, credit card details and even their employer's phone numbers. All of Korea's police stations now have a cyber-terror unit to help deal with the problem. The number of cases referred to Korea's Internet commission tripled last year. The cyber-terror unit recognizes the impact on victims' social status as well as the fear that this generates. According to Chun Seong Lee, liaison officer at the Cyber-Terror Response Centre, cyber-bullying and cyber-crime occur so often in South Korea that they are impacting people's social lives, causing people to drop out of work and school and causing mental illness. In 2008, a new law is expected to come into force that will demand that online users reveal their names and ID number before joining chat rooms and social networking sites (Simmons, 2006). Although no formal studies are yet available from South Korea, follow-up studies will be pertinent in a year or two to determine whether the new laws have been effective in tracking down perpetrators.

Singapore

In Singapore, psychologist Ng Koon Hock is reported to have found that 69 per cent of students have access to the Internet at home, and 75 per cent carry cellular phones. Of these, at least 14 per cent of 1,100 students surveyed were bullied via text messages, and 13 per cent were bullied on instant chat networks such as MSN (Forss, 2007).

China

Table 3.1 discloses some interesting facts on Internet use in China (Zhang and Wei, 2007a,b). The population of cyber citizens has reached 137 million, with an average online time of 16.9 hours per week, according to statistics from the China Internet Network Information Center (CNNIC) as of 23 January 2007; 17.2 per cent of China's cyber citizens are under eighteen; 32.3 per cent of them are high school students, which is the highest percentage according to their career (ibid.). The number of mobile phone users reached 487,434 by the end of April 2007 according to statistics from the Chinese informational industrial department. The instant messaging service is frequently used, reaching a height of 304.65 billion across the country, representing an increase of 39.9 per cent compared with last year.

The influence of the Internet on teenagers has raised concerns in China. People pay more attention to its influence and characteristics. For example, a recent 'survey in media demand by teenagers under 18' (cited in Zhang and Wei, 2007) conducted by the Shanghai communist youth league, Shanghai China young pioneers committee and Shanghai social science young pioneers research bureau indicates that the Internet has played an important role in teenagers' lives. Although they consider newspapers and magazines as primary 'information broadcasting tools', the preference is clearly moving to use of the Internet because it provides a freer platform for the sharing of opinions anonymously without worrying about political consequences. This is an especially important consideration given China's human rights record.

Concerns about cyber-bullying

Although the concept of 'cyber-bullying' have not yet been officially accepted by Chinese government officials, the Chinese media has begun reporting cases and data concerning cyber-bullying that have occurred in foreign countries. Chinese newspapers are following US and UK's cyber-bullying research reports. 'The Star Wars kid' case was broadly reported in China. Moreover, Chinese educationists, lawyers, media and Internet experts have paid more attention to teenagers who were cyber-bullied all over the world. According to Zhang Yang (2006, as cited in Zhang and Wei, 2007b), the 'Internet can easily raise a teenager's anxiety, as indicated through loss of privacy, Internet violence, Internet threat, Internet fraud, Internet sex and Internet viruses, which all represent factors for nervousness and anxiety'.

Chinese cases related to cyber-bullying

'Internet violence' is the term in China that refers to use of the Internet, and cyber-bullying is described as an 'attack force' (Zhang and Wei, 2007b). Although some of the meaning may get lost in translation, here are some of the considerations expressed in a recent report. I have left the translation as it is without making grammatical corrections on purpose:

> Some people post critics to express their dissatisfaction with someone in their real life by employing irresponsible words under the cover of anonymous characteristics of Internet. Others follow without consideration which might twist the truth. Most people receive information by word of mouth, but they can not tell the truth. In turn, truth is distorted eventually. Furthermore, cyber stalking happens and privacy is opened to public. To some extent, abuses will replace the rational. It is an intrusion of privacy, reputation and a large amount of people participate, and therefore, it causes enormous damage. So we call it 'Violence'.
>
> (Zhang and Wei, 2007b)

Professor Zhang's report provides the following examples of cyber-violence or abuse:

Case 1: Cat abuse

One case included the serious abuse of a cat, which was filmed and posted on the Internet. The post was titled: 'Cat abused by Student of Peking University' and reads like this:

> A little white cat sneaks into Medical Library of Peking University, and is caught by a student. Most of people think that he just intend to take

the cat out, however, something terrible happens – the student throw cat towards wall, and the cat's brain breaks and blood flow around in front of hundred students. This student becomes a target on Internet because of the cat. Over 500 pages critics posted on most of comprehensive web site and news web site in China. Someone intends to post the student's name in public, someone criticizes his behavior, and someone is against his action. 10 thousand people post their critics.

Eventually someone tells the truth, cats often get in the library since the library is warm. On that day, the little cat scratches the book of the student. The student tries to take the cat out of the library but is bitten by the cat. The student is so nervous that he can not control himself and throws the cat out un-deliberately. After that, that is the end of the story.

The student is the forth year student in medical department, behave normally and was selected as student representative of Medical department. During the case, he was taking an internship in a hospital, and bear pressures from society. After that, he stays in the dorm alone and refuses any interviews.

(Zhang and Wei, 2007, p. 2)

Although clearly the violent action against the cat was abhorrent, the case illustrates how situations can be taken out of context. The student had a cat phobia and was afraid of the cat. The ensuing rage against his actions had an enormous psychological impact.

Another Chinese example involves a telephone group fight.

Case 2: Telephone group fight

This case involved a strong and angry response to the telephone harassment of a woman. A posting was made 'To attack all disordered/deranged people' at 9.45 a.m. in June 2006. The person who posted the online thread reported that one of his female co-workers received phone harassment. He demanded suggestions that would solve the problem. People started to post their comments such as 'Call him during the middle of the night; send a virus to his cellphone; post his cellphone number everywhere'. All kinds of suggestions were posted in the span of 10 minutes. A number of people called the harasser's cellphone number and reported it on the blog: 'I have already called the number' at 10.06 a.m. Another responded: 'Maybe he is outside, too much noise, and he hangs up the phone.'

This suggests a form of cyber-vigilantism that is emerging as cyber-'bullying' in response to reports of harassment. This form of vigilantism, if it gets out of control, can become equally dangerous, especially if the violence spills into the physical context, and the harasser is located, stalked and beaten up.

Case 3: Internet prank (kuso)

Another form of cyber-bullying involves 'pranks' or what are called '*kuso*'. These online pranks have become very popular in China, but they are quite complex and warrant a dictionary explanation. Wikipedia (2007b) explains that online pranks in China have become a product of entertainment in China, similar to plays or movies. This is the official explanation of Chinese '*kuso*':

> 'Kuso' is the term used in the Chinese world for the Internet culture that generally includes all types of camp and parody. Generally speaking, an Internet meme is any faddish popular phenomenon on the Internet. The term may refer to the content itself, the subject of the content, or the phenomenon of its spread. It is discrete, identifiable content as opposed to more general things like a philosophy or a trend. It is spread voluntarily, rather than by trickery, compulsion, predetermined path, or completely automated means. Some people liken Internet memes to a form of art, and digital art on the net to a form of meme. An Internet meme may stay the same over time or it may mutate over time, by chance or by the aggregation of commentary, alternate and parody versions, and news about the meme.
>
> A typical Internet meme is simply a digital file that gets passed from one user to others using whatever formats and transmission means are readily available on the Internet (for example, email, blogs, social networks, instant messaging, and the like). Usually, what is passed is either the content itself or a link (such as a hyperlink) to where the content may be found. The content might be in text, video, image, or other format, and might consist of a joke, a rumor, an amusing picture, a video clip, animation, or graphic, or an offbeat news story.
>
> In general, content that is actually notable or useful is not considered a meme, it is simply content. Thus, though it has meme-like qualities a newsworthy story, videogame, web service, song by an established musical group, or the like, is not a meme. Some web sites collect and popularize memes, or are devoted to the spread of specific memes.
>
> One common form of meme is created when a person, company, product, musical group, or the like, is promoted on the Internet for its pop culture value. Vanity sites, for example, are among the first recognized Internet memes. People use photo sharing sites like Flickr or video sharing sites like YouTube to promote themselves or their musical groups. In extraordinary cases where an otherwise non-noteworthy person or incident gains great popularity this way it is often considered a meme.
>
> Often, a person or company becomes infamous by virtue of an embarrassing video, email, or other act. These arise, for example, in the context of dating and relationships, job applications, security cameras and other hidden videos, or collections of bizarre news stories.

Many memes are urban rumors, fraud schemes, slander, or false news stories that are either planted deliberately to become a meme, evolve by mistake or rumor, or that jump from an offline source to the Internet. . . . Some web services like snopes.com and the urban dictionary collect lists of such hoaxes, or offer services by which users can fact-check popular claims they find on the Internet in order to determine their source and whether or not they are true. This definition of Kuso was brought into Taiwan in around 2000 by young people who frequent Japanese web sites and quickly became an Internet phenomenon, spreading to Hong Kong and subsequently the rest of China.

(Wikipedia, 2007b)

There is a popular sentence online that seems quite contradictory: 'If I like you, I would like to prank you, even though I do not like you but I would still prank you' (Zhang and Wei, 2007b, p. 3). According to Zhang and Wei, the behaviour of 'prank (*kuso*)' is a form of bullying. Here are some typical case examples of *kuso*.

Example 1: Kuso *against a teacher*

Four photographs of a middle-school teacher in Foshan Guangdong, including photographs of his face with a naked human body, the body of a monkey and the body of a chicken, respectively, had been posted online, it was reported in the *Foshan Daily Forum*. It took the police 48 hours to find the perpetrator, a second-year high school student, whose name is Xiaorong. The student admitted that he downloaded the teacher's pictures from the school's web site, searched pornography and animal pictures online and used Photoshop software to combine those pictures into seven photos. He claimed that he did not know he had broken the law and, like some of the North American and British cases that I will discuss later on, thought what he had done was simply a joke. It was not meant to harm the teacher at all. He reported doing it to draw attention to himself. Make a mental note about this student's perspective because, when it comes to posting defamatory and libellous anti-authority materials online, there is a definite pattern that emerges globally, one aspect of which is the students' desire to draw attention to themselves. When we get to the chapters that consider solutions to dealing with these kinds of prank, we will need to think about how we help students draw positive attention to themselves, and, second, how we can help them come to an understanding of the definite line at which pranks can become abuse.

In Xiaorong's case, although the police felt that he should be punished, they took into consideration that he had no motivation to insult others subjectively and, because he is still a high-school student, they gave him a caution and fines of 500 Yuan. According to Chinese criminal law, those behaviours that harm society but do not belong to criminal activities are penalized by the public security organ based on Regulations of the People's Republic of China on administrative penalties for public security.[1] This case was judged according to Article 42.[2] There was no report as to how the school responded to these actions – whether educationally or in any disciplinary forms (Zhang and Wei, 2007b).

As with emerging North American and British cases, Xiaorong's case is not exceptional in China. Belew (2007) reports that a video posted on YouTube filmed students swearing at their teacher's photograph, knocking his hat off and taking other belittling actions. This in turn drew many protests until YouTube took it down.

Students in China have also experienced altered photographs with postings online. Consider the case of Piggy (ironically, the same name that was given to Golding's 1954 bullying victim in Lord of the Flies).

Example 2: Piggy

Piggy's real name is Qian Zhijun. Piggy participated in a transportation security fair when he was a second-year high school student three years ago. One of his poses as a pig was captured by someone on camera. The pictures were posted on the marketing for the fair. Photoshop was used to combine Piggy's face with Dingdang Cat, Ali Baba, Shrek, Mona Lisa and the Statue of Liberty and Jia Baoyu. According to Zhang and Wei's (2007b) report, Qian soon became the first person abused by the Internet. Someone even called him 'changeable Piggy'. Since then, Piggy has become a popular part of movie posters in China. According to the report, Piggy initially said 'he felt bad and terrible at the very beginning. After that, he thought most people were not deliberately trying to hurt him because most of them described Piggy as cute and funny' (Zhang and Wei, 2007b).

Example 3: Little fat boy

Another case that became famous in China involved the face of a young, overweight student described as 'common and normal picture of him' on the Internet (Jaishankar and Shariff, in press). Nobody could have anticipated how many hackers the picture would attract. Thousands of people signed onto the site to alter and make fun of the 'little fat boy'.

Example 4: Ning

Ning is a second-year student in the high school of Dian Jiang District, Chongqing province. During the summer of 2004, Ning used his father's cellular phone to send several instant messages containing sexual insults to his Chinese teacher Xiao's phone. Xiao reported this to the school principle and warned Ning to stop his improper behaviour. Ning admitted he was at fault and wrote a report. Xiao also demanded a personal apology, which Ning refused. Xiao took legal action in December 2004. The court considered that Ning used sexual messages to insult Xiao deliberately and that his behaviour intruded on Xiao's personal rights; however, because Ning is a teenager under eighteen, his guardians were deemed responsible. Finally, Ning's guardians wrote an apology letter and paid 500 Yuan for mental damages.

This case again is very interesting from a range of perspectives. Although the teacher was initially agreeable to an apology and compensation for mental damages, the student maintained that he was simply joking and that he only sent her one message for fun. In China, it appears that the courts consider parents to be responsible for the student's behaviour, with no reference to whether the school has an obligation to educate against these forms of online expression. The report from my Chinese colleagues (directly from the translation) suggests that the school ought to have an educational responsibility:

> What Ning did was just broken the school's rules. The teacher should educate the student but not sue the student. However, after the judgment, both parties did not look for appeals. Concerning about the case and the popularized instant message harassment phenomena, Dian Jiang District Court's judge Huang thought that sending instant messages deliberately could easily cause the violation of rights. However, if those activities want to be defined as violation of rights activities, there must be validated evidences. In this case, Ning admitted the written material about the instant message harassment. The material became the key evidence for the case and determined the judgment.
>
> (Zhang and Wei, 2007b, pp. 5–6)

Another emerging area of cyber-bullying in China is referred to there as Internet slander. This involves openly insulting others using force or other methods or fabricating stories to slander others. Under Chinese law, they are considered guilty according to Article 246.[3] Zhang and Wei (ibid., pp. 6–7) report that there is a lot of slanderous behaviour on the Internet. Here are some examples.

Example 5: Slander through identity theft

Wang Shunhe stole a password from a web site and used it to send an insulting instant message to another student, Zhou, and to Zhou's family. They claimed that this caused psychological damage to the entire family from 24 September 2003 to 2 October 2004. Wang Shunhe also used the Internet to post a thread containing insulting words. He also published the names and phone numbers of members of the family. Family members were inundated with phone calls from across the country and even as far as Singapore. Strangers from Singapore called Mr Zhou to arrange a one night stand with his daughter. This action destroyed Ms Zhou's health and destroyed her reputation. The family filed criminal action, and Wang was eventually sentenced to two years in prison. This pattern, again, is not significantly different from in North America, although in China there appear to be extremes – either imprisonment or simply a fine.

These examples suggest that the Chinese are not immune from cyber-bullying and that additional studies are needed in China to understand the real extent of cyber-bullying in a country with such a large population. I am especially interested in the kinds of responses that will emerge to reduce it.

Most reports in China relate to adult on adult cyber-bullying. In a well-known case of cyber-vigilantism that again turned into cyber-*bullying*, a man posted information about another individual who allegedly had an affair with his wife. He identified his wife's suspected lover by his web name. This led to a series of postings that revealed the man's name, phone number and address. Thousands of web postings denounced the lover, and Internet users telephoned or showed up at his home to shout abuse at him and his family. Lawyers are now calling on the government to protect people from having their personal information made public on the Internet (Bartlett, 2007). Administered in anonymous cyberspace, cyber-vigilantism can impinge on many personal and privacy rights.

Thailand

Sending cruel and sometimes threatening messages and racial or ethnic slurs is frequent in Thailand as well. Because computer proficiency is second nature to many youngsters today, it is not surprising that web sites that contain audio-based stories, cartoons and pictures that ridicule others spread to an international audience. For example, David Knight, a Canadian, was told to check a certain web site in Thailand. To his horror, the web site was titled, 'Welcome to the page that makes fun of Dave Knight . . .'. This was a clone of a web site created by his peers in Canada.

Moreover, pictures of classmates are often posted online, along with questions asking students to give negative ratings of the individual targeted. For example, 'Who is the biggest . . . (choose your own derogatory term)?'. Hacking into an email account and sending vicious or embarrassing material to others is also becoming a common practice in Bangkok. Somsak (not his real name), a local fourteen-year-old, entered his class one day to find everyone glaring at him. A boy he barely knew approached him and shouted, 'Why did you call me a [disparaging term]?'. Somsak was as shocked as the boy making the complaint. Eventually, the problem was resolved, but Somsak still had no idea who accessed his account to send the offensive email. Another technique is to engage someone in instant messaging, trick that person into revealing sensitive personal information, and forward that information to others. The practice of taking a picture of a person in the locker room or toilet using a camera phone and sending that picture to others is another method that's gaining momentum here (Payne, 2007).

India

Although there are many Western studies related to cyber-bullying, there is no empirical research in India to unearth this modern phenomenon. Jaishankar and Shariff (in press) cite an unpublished Indian study that found that mobile bullying is common among school students. This study investigated the nature and the extent of school students' experience of cyber-bullying using mobile phones. The results showed that 65 per cent of the students were victims of cyber-bullying using mobile phones, and 60 per cent of the respondents had also been involved in bullying others using mobile phones.

Although bullying is predominantly considered to be a serious issue in Western countries, the Indian criminologist Jaishankar (ibid.) writes that bullying in India is an acceptable part of the culture within, and between, people from different castes. He notes that bullying in schools or colleges is prevalent. It is sometimes called 'ragging', or, when directed at young women, it is known as 'Eve teasing' (teasing a virgin). Consequently, few laws or policies to address bullying have been put in place. Given the enormous surge in technology and the involvement of Indian computer programmers and IT people in outsourced American technology firms, the use of modern technologies such as Internet and mobile phones has proliferated, increasing the prevalence of bullying by school and college students. Today, Internet and mobile phones have become part and parcel of everybody's lives, and most students carry mobile phones. Here is an example of an email sent out by tenth grade students of a respected Mumbai school, about the students of a rival school:

> If u think they r hot . . . Well, let me tell u they're not They're ugly, they're fat, they look like ratz!!!! Even alienz look better dan dat!!!!!
>
> (Ibid.)

Although this may seem to be more of a playful prank than a serious offence, it is only the beginning of a trend that can escalate into a serious problem. In this case, the teachers intervened, and the problem was eventually resolved. According to one Indian news report, 'In India, where younger and younger kids are discovering the power of the Internet cyber-bullying has already started trapping Indian teenagers in its insidious Web' (Kapoor, 2003).

Although few formal studies have been undertaken, a cursory look at www.orkut.com (a social networking site) shows many similar postings to those on Facebook and MySpace. There is more information available on adult cyber-abuse and cyber-crime and very little so far on cyber-bullying among students. Orkut came to India in February 2006 with a mission statement claiming to help people to create a closer, more intimate network of friends and hoping to put them on the path to social bliss, similar to Facebook. It is apparent from the mission statement that the network was established to enable people to interact with each other across the globe by bridging geographical distances. However, according to Rahul (2007), it has since been used for superfluous activities leading to moral degradation and upheaval. A management student from Mumbai was arrested by the police following a girl's complaint about tarnishing her image in the public forum, namely Orkut. The boy was trying to entice the girl for some time. He threatened her with dire consequences when she resisted his advances. Later, he posted an obscene profile of her on the Orkut portal along with her mobile number. The profile has been sketched in such a way that it draws lewd comments from many who visit her profile. Later, the boy was arrested under section 67 of the Information Technology Act, 2000 (India has no separate law for cyber-bullying).

According to Kapoor (2003), legal experts in India do not believe this legislation has the teeth to reduce cyber-crime because it was initially designed to promote e-commerce. It is not very effective in dealing with cyber-stalking, cyber-bullying and other forms of online harassment. Kapoor explains that the law does not even define 'cyber-crime'. A brief search in the Orkut profile will reveal 'many modified profiles of beautiful girls' (Sengupta, 2006).

More recently, India has brought in an Internet censorship policy (Fratina, 2007) allowing it to close down offensive web sites and blogs. A number of actions have also been brought under cyber-defamation laws.

In another case involving Orkut, a malicious profile of a Delhi schoolgirl was uploaded on the site. The perpetrators posted obscene photographs and contact details such as her home address and telephone numbers on the profile, using suggestive names such as 'sex teacher' to describe her. The matter came to light after the girl's family started receiving vulgar calls; thereafter her father contacted the cyber cell of Delhi police's economic offences wing. According to the Delhi police sources, the girl is a student in a South Delhi school. The obscene pictures and personal information brought two strangers to the girl's door suggesting that the girl had invited them for sex through the Internet.

This is the second incident demonstrating Orkut's misuse in New Delhi. Earlier, an air hostess alleged that someone had opened an account in her name on the web site, in which she was described as a 'sex struck woman'.

The majority of cases reported by Jaishankar and Shariff (in press) relating to Orkut involve sexual harassment of women. The unpublished research report by my law student, Sakina Fratina (2007), includes information on India's first case of cyber-stalking. Mrs Ritu Kholi complained to the police that a person had been using her identity to chat over the Internet at the web site www.mirc.com, for four consecutive days. The individual was using obscene language and giving out her telephone number, encouraging people to call her at odd hours. Consequently she received over forty calls from Kuwait, Mumbai and Ahmedabad. Finally, the IP address was traced, and her perpetrator was arrested under the Indian penal code, which among other crimes prohibits the interference with a woman's modesty. However, there have also been cases where school principals have been insulted on Orkut.

The foregoing cases of cyber-bullying, and cultural considerations that are specific to the countries involved, provide a general idea of the forms of cyber-bullying that have begun to emerge on the Asian continent and surrounding areas. The need for increased and more focused research relating to Internet use, digital literacies, the use of mobile cellular phone systems and, more particularly, school responses to those forms of cyber-communication in Asia is urgent. Technological advancement is moving so quickly that it is difficult for researchers, academics and policymakers to keep up. The enormous challenge is that 'solutions' are needed urgently to contain the rapid prolifieration of this kind of globally popular expression among young people. At the same time, there has not been sufficient time to collect and analyse the data on such use; nor to place it in its appropriate cultural contexts. Hence, the primary emerging responses tend to be positivist and legal, with particular attention to the criminal aspect of such expression. The educational component is largely missing; as we saw in Japan, it is largely the police and not the school that becomes engaged. Similar responses are implemented in China, India and South Korea. Let me turn now to the Western hemisphere and highlight some of the emerging research in the United Kingdom, United States, Canada and Australia.

United Kingdom

Table 3.1 summarizes the significant amount of research that has emerged with respect to bullying and the use of technologies. There are fewer studies that specifically focus on cyber-bullying; however, it is important not to discount what we can learn from those who have studied online use among young people. As the data show (Dickie et al., 2004), over 80 per cent of children and teens in the United Kingdom access home computers, and 75 per cent of eleven-year-olds own a cellphone. A survey by MSN disclosed that over half of the young people surveyed had instant messenger (IM) conversations at least once daily, and 33 per cent chatted on IM several times a day. One in ten respondents reported visiting online blogs (diaries) daily, and 48 per cent of those surveyed said that they checked their email at least once daily (ibid.).

According to a 2005 survey by the National Children's Home charity and Tesco Mobile (NCH, 2005), of 770 youths between the ages of eleven and nineteen, 20 per cent of respondents revealed that they had been bullied via electronic means. Almost three-quarters (73 per cent) stated that they knew their perpetrators, whereas 26 per cent stated that the offender was a stranger.

Another interesting finding was that 10 per cent indicated peers had photographed them on cellular phone cameras and that this made them feel uncomfortable, embarrassed or threatened. Many youths are not comfortable telling an authority figure about their cyber-bullying victimization. Although 24 per cent reported the abuse to a parent, and 14 per cent told a teacher, 28 per cent did not tell anyone, and 41 per cent told a friend (ibid., p. 6). A survey of over 500 British twelve to fifteen-year-olds found that one in ten experienced cyber-bullying, most commonly through threatening emails, exclusion from online conversations or through the spread of rumours about them on the Internet. The survey, entitled 'MSN cyber-bullying report: Blogging, instant messaging and email bullying amongst today's teens' was published by MSN using data from British market research company YouGov's study of 518 young people and their parents in January 2006. Other findings from the report disclosed the following information:

- More than twice as many girls (18 per cent) as boys (7 per cent) reported that they had been 'cyber-bullied', and twice as many girls (34 per cent) as boys (17 per cent) knew someone who had experienced cyber-bullying.
- One in twenty respondents admitted involvement in bullying someone online.
- One in eight reported sending threats to others, and one in twelve admitted to posting fabricated information about someone on a blog (online diary).
- Thirteen per cent of respondents judged cyber-bullying to be 'worse than physical bullying'.
- Seventy-four per cent of respondents did not approach anyone for help after experiencing cyber-bullying.
- Forty-eight per cent of parents were 'unaware of the phenomenon of cyber-bullying'.

A news media article entitled 'Bullies inflicting "extreme misery" on UK school pupils' (Land, 2006) reports the findings of the largest ever investigation into school bullying by Bullying Online, which surveyed 8,574 children, parents, teachers and adults in the first six months of 2006. The researchers found that 69 per cent of pupils who participated in the survey said they had been bullied within the last twelve months, and 50 per cent of those said they had been physically hurt. Eighty-seven per cent of the parents who took the survey said their child had been bullied, and 77 per cent reported that their child was bullied more than five times. It is not clear from this news report whether cyber-bullying was included in the survey. The report quotes one of the Bullying Online researchers as saying:

> There have never been so many trendy methods of dealing with school bullying but the results of our survey are shocking and it's time to find

out which methods work and ditch the rest . . . Parents will be shocked to learn that bullying is big business but that none of the anti-bullying methods being used in schools have been evaluated in independent long-term trials.

(Liz Carnell, quoted in Land, 2006)

Although I agree that it is time do to something, I am not convinced that evaluating the thousands of anti-bullying programmes will do anything to reduce traditional or cyber-bullying. I hope to convince readers as we move through this book that we need to reconceptualize the way we approach and address these issues. As the United Kingdom has taken bullying and cyber-bullying very seriously, there are, no doubt, many more surveys to assess its prevalence. Suffice it to say that these findings suggest there a definite need to consider alternative responses. Parental awareness and confidence in reporting the issues to parents and school authorities are important aspects of addressing cyber-bullying.

A comprehensive study reported by Livingstone and Bober (2005a) for the Economic and Social Research Council in Britain, entitled 'UK children go online' is highly instructive in this regard. This study, the first of its kind, focused largely on the thoughts and feelings of the children themselves, and also surveyed their parents. Here is a brief summary of their findings.

The study involved direct interviews with 1,511 children and young people between the ages of nine and nineteen, with an anonymous survey of 906 of their parents, followed by a series of focus group interviews and observations focusing on children's use of the Internet.

Access to the Internet

Consistent with the other studies reported in this chapter, the researchers found an increase in home access (75 per cent) and universal school access (92 per cent). They note that access platforms are diversifying, with 71 per cent of homes with computers, 38 per cent of these young people have a mobile phone, 17 per cent have a digital television, and 8 per cent have a games console with Internet access. They found socio-economic factors were sizable. Eighty-eight per cent of middle-class but only 61 per cent of working-class children have access to the Internet. Nineteen per cent have access in their bedrooms.

Nature of Internet use

Most are daily or weekly users: 41 per cent use it daily, and 43 per cent weekly. Most are online for less than an hour a day, 90 per cent using it for homework, and 94 per cent use it for other things. Twenty-one per cent admitted to using it for less appropriate activities, such as plagiarism by downloading papers from the Internet and submitting them as their own work.

Inequalities and the digital divide

Context is important, and this study took the time to look at socio-economic class and related factors. For example, middle-class teens and those who have spent more time online obviously have better online skills. Only 25 per cent say they are not interested in the Internet, but 47 per cent of occasional and non-users say that they do not have access. Fourteen per cent said they lacked the time to use it. Children of parents who use the Internet more frequently use it more often and have more expertise. The study found that most of those who use the Internet are not taking full advantage of it and are restricted to a narrow range of sites. This is important for my discussion of solutions later on. The researchers observe that 'a new divide is opening up between those for whom the Internet is an increasingly rich, diverse, engaging and stimulating resource and those for whom it remains a narrow, un-engaging, if occasionally useful resource of rather less significance' (Livingstone and Bober, 2005b, p. 2).

Education, learning and literacy

The authors report that many nine- to nineteen-year-olds have not received lessons (30 per cent), and only 16 per cent of the parents consider themselves advanced, in comparison with 32 per cent of the children. Children lack key skills in evaluating online content, and this could be problematic when dealing with individuals or blogs that might draw them into cyber-bullying behaviour or victimization. For example, 38 per cent said they trusted most of the information online, and only 33 per cent had been taught how to judge the reliability of online information.

Communication

The mobile phone is the preferred mode of communication for flirting and gossiping with friends or getting advice, and text messaging is preferred to email. Online communication with friends to stay in touch with them at all times is highly valued, and, unlike the media warnings of strangers waiting to pounce on naive users, few expressed an interest in contacting strangers, although 21 per cent had been contacted by people they did not know in chat rooms. Another encouraging finding was that 53 per cent stated that talking face to face was better than communicating online. Twenty-five per cent seek advice online.

Participation

Another aspect of this study that will be useful when I discuss solutions are the findings that 44 per cent of these students participate or make a useful contribution through their participation. For example, 54 per cent are interested in political and civic issues; 44 per cent have completed online quizzes; 25 per cent have sent an email or text message to a web site (protesting about something wrong with the web site), and 22 per cent have voted for something online. Seventeen per cent have sent pictures or stories to a web site. This is good news, and it goes to show that online use among young people is not as all bad as the media would have us believe.

Risks of online communication

That said, the study did find some negative risks. Researchers note that parents underestimate their children's negative experiences, and that one-third of those interviewed reported receiving sexual (31 per cent) or nasty comments (33 per cent), although only 7 per cent of the parents were aware their child had received such comments or been bullied online. Forty-six per cent owned up to divulging personal information online, and 40 per cent engaged in identity play – pretended they were someone else. These findings are corroborated in my own study in Quebec described below, with similar percentages. Thirty per cent have made an online acquaintance, and 8 per cent of those actually met with someone they met online.

Regulating the Internet at home

Parents interviewed made it clear that they seek to manage their children's Internet use. Most of the parents whose children had Internet access at home said they directly share in and/or support their child on the Internet, although their children were less likely to admit this. And as with many other studies on parental confidence and competence, parents in this study also admitted they face some difficult challenges. Eighteen per cent said they do not know how to help their child use the Internet safely, and, whereas 35 per cent of the children said they had filtering software, 45 per cent of their parents thought they had such software. Not surprisingly, 69 per cent of the children did not like their parents placing restrictions on their computer use, and 63 per cent said that they have taken some action to hide their online activities from parents.

As regards gender differences in Internet use, this study has found that, although girls are more likely to visit civic sites and less likely to encounter pornography online, they are more likely to experience contact risks (such as bullying) than boys.

Although this report was very general, much of the information could be highly useful in developing policies to combat cyber-bullying, because the study takes an in-depth look at how children use and relate to the Internet, and provides the views of their parents. I was quite surprised though, that cyber-bullying was not investigated more extensively in the report. As the statistics suggest, parents may not be as clued in to their children's use of technology as they think. Parents often seem to focus all of their attention on children accessing unsuitable material, or being targeted by paedophiles, and don't take cyber-bullying as seriously.

The recommendations of this report are discussed in Chapter 8, to complement some of the solutions I suggest in the final chapters.

There is also a new information web site on cyber-bullying for parents, educators and other stakeholders set up by the Department for Children, Schools and Families (2007) that is quite good. I review this web site as part of my analysis on official responses covered in Chapter 7. At the same time, teachers' unions in the United Kingdom are reported to be demanding a 'shut-down' of web sites such as YouTube, citing a recent Scottish case where students filmed a teacher in the classroom and posted it on YouTube with the caption 'You are dead' (Riga, 2007).

Happy slapping

It is worth mentioning one form of bullying that originated in the United Kingdom and has been copied worldwide. The practice of 'happy slapping' is believed to have originated in London, in the garage music scene, in 2005, and has been widely reported in the British media. Assault charges have been brought against youths in various happy slapping incidents in the United Kingdom, but as yet there has been no move to legislate specifically on the issue.

In one case, in 2005, a sixteen-year-old girl was seriously assaulted on her way home from school. A video of the incident, filmed on a mobile phone, was then circulated throughout her school. Despite the fact that a huge amount of the distress the victim suffered was due to the video being shown to her peers at school, a school spokesman was quoted as saying simply 'this is a police matter which happened outside school' (BBC, 2005). When dealing with the Internet and third generation mobile phone technology, which is accessible by students both during and outside school time, such an approach does not begin to deal with the problem.

United States

Table 3.1 again confirms the extensive use of technologies by young people in the United States. Approximately 70 per cent of children aged four to six have used computers, and 68 per cent under the age two have used screen media.

An American survey of 3,700 middle school students found that 18 per cent were cyber-bullied (Chu, 2005). In the year 2000, a University of New Hampshire study found that one out of every seventeen kids in the United States, or 6 per cent, had been threatened or harassed online (Finkelhor *et al.*, 2000).

By March 2006, statistics showed that 75 to 80 per cent of twelve- to fourteen-year-olds had been cyber-bullied. Furthermore, 20 per cent of kids under eighteen have received a sexual solicitation. So cyber-bullying is clearly on the rise, and it affects both genders in the United States. A study presented at the American Educational Research Association, in 2006, shows that female perpetrators preferred to use text messaging harassment versus face-to-face bullying by two to one (Toppo, 2006). Ybarra and Mitchell (2004b) in the United States reported that 15 per cent of their sample identified themselves as Internet bullies, and 7 per cent said they had been targeted online. The growth of cyber-harassment was recognized as far back as 1999 with a report from the United States Attorney General to the vice president Al Gore, suggesting that incidents were an increasing problem for law enforcement officials (Beckerman and Nocero, 2002).

The *Portsmouth Herald* reports that pre-adolescents and teens averaging nine to fourteen years of age use anonymity to engage in cyber-bullying (Portsmouth Herald Editorial Board, 2005). In Westchester County in the State of New York, school officials invited 600 students, parents, educators and law-enforcement officials to a one-half day conference on cyber-bullying. When officials asked approximately 200 students how many had personally been a cyber-victim or perpetrator, or knew a friend who was either, 194 students raised their hands (Swartz, 2005, March 7). A poll commissioned by Fight Crime: Invest in Kids found that more than 13 million children in the United States, aged six to seventeen, are victims of cyber-bullying (Kharfen, 2006). One-third of all teens and one-sixth of all pre-teens have had mean, threatening or embarrassing things written about them online. Over two million kids never tell anyone – a teacher, a parent, a sibling, a friend.

I would like to focus on a recent study conducted by PEW/Internet and American Life Project that disclosed some interesting findings (Lenhart, 2007). The study involved a nationally representative phone survey of 935 teenagers and found that one in three teens using the Internet experienced online harassment (see Table 3.3). Not surprisingly, as with other studies, girls are more likely to be the victims. What is different in this study is that most of the teens surveyed said they are more likely to be bullied *offline* than online. Lenhart reports that about one-third (32 per cent) of all American teenagers who use the Internet say they have been targets of a range of annoying and potentially menacing online activities – such as receiving threatening messages; having their private emails or text messages forwarded without consent; having an embarrassing picture posted without permission; or having rumours about them spread online. Older teens (ages fifteen to seventeen) said

Table 3.3 Making private information public is the most common form of cyber-bullying (%)

Have you, personally, ever experienced any of the following things online?	Yes	No
Someone taking a private email, IM or text message you sent them and forwarding it to someone else or posting it where others could see it	15	85
Someone spreading a rumour about you online	13	87
Someone sending you a threatening or aggressive email, IM or text message	13	87
Someone posting an embarrassing picture of you online without your permission	6	94
Answered 'yes' to any of the four previous questions	32	68

Source: Pew Internet and American Life Project Parents and Teens Survey, October–November 2006. Based on online teens [*n* = 886]. Margin of error for the overall sample is ±4%.

they were more likely to have had someone forward or publicly post private messages – 18 per cent of older teens have experienced this, compared with 11 per cent of younger teens.

Depending on circumstances, these behaviours may be really threatening, simply annoying or benign; however, teens who share their identities and thoughts online are more likely to be targets than those who do not communicate as much online. In other words, the PEW/Internet report notes that, when teens have trusting relationships with peers and share information in confidence, they stand a greater chance of having that trust broken and the content being publicly posted without their permission (15 per cent). Approximately 13 per cent admitted to spreading a rumour online and another 13 per cent had received aggressive emails, instant messaging or text messages. Like David Knight in Canada, 6 per cent reported having an embarrassing picture of themselves posted online without permission.

Bullying happens more often offline

Two-thirds of all teens (67 per cent) said that bullying and harassment happened more *offline* than online. Fewer than one-in-three teens (29 per cent) said that they thought that bullying was more likely to happen online, and 3 per cent said they thought it happened both online and offline equally. Girls were a bit more likely than boys to say that bullying happens more online (33 per cent of girls versus 25 per cent of boys), though, overall, both boys and girls say that kids their age are more likely to be harassed offline. In focus groups conducted by the Project, one sixteen-year-old girl casually described how she and her classmates bullied a fellow student:

There's this boy in my anatomy class who everybody hates. He's like the smart kid in class. Everybody's jealous. They all want to be smart. He always wants to work in our group and I hate it. And we started this thing, some girl in my class started this I Hate [Name] MySpace thing. So everybody in school goes on it to comment bad things about this boy.

(Lenhart, 2007, p. 2)

This corroborates the earlier UK studies I have reported in Chapter 2, where students are often bullied because they are 'smart' or perceived as too intelligent (Boulton and Hawker, 1997).

Gender differences

As with many studies of cyber-bullying, the PEW/Internet Project also found that girls are more likely than boys to say that they have ever experienced cyber-bullying. Thirty-eight per cent of online girls reported being bullied, compared with 26 per cent of online boys. The study found that older girls are more likely to report being bullied than any other age and gender group, with 41 per cent of online girls aged fifteen to seventeen reporting these experiences. Teens who use social network sites such as MySpace and Facebook and teens who use the Internet daily are also more likely to say that they have been cyber-bullied. Nearly four in ten social network users (39 per cent) have been cyber-bullied in some way, compared with 22 per cent of online teens who do not use social networks.

The online rumour mill

The studies on gender differences mentioned earlier are corroborated by the PEW findings with respect to the online spreading of rumours. This study found that at least 13 per cent reported that someone had spread rumours about them online. Girls are more likely to report someone spreading rumours about them than boys, with 16 per cent of girls reporting rumour-spreading compared with 9 per cent of boys (see Table 3.4). Social network users are more likely than those who do not use social networks to report that someone had spread a rumour about them (16 per cent versus 8 per cent). The report quotes one middle school girl as saying:

I know a lot of times online someone will say something about one person and it'll spread and then the next day in school, I know there's like one of my friends, something happened online and people started saying she said something that she never said, and the next day we came into school and no one would talk to her and everyone's ignoring her. And she had no idea what was going on. Then someone sent her the whole conversation between these two people.

(Lenhart, 2007, p. 3)

Table 3.4 Online rumours tend to target girls (%)

Have you, personally, ever experienced any of the following things online?	Boys	Girls
Someone taking a private email, IM or text message you sent them and forwarding it to someone else or posting it where others could see it	13	17
Someone sending you a threatening or aggressive email, IM or text message	10	15
Someone spreading a rumour about you online	9	16*
Someone posting an embarrassing picture of you online without your permission	5	7
At least one of the forms of cyber-bullying listed above	23	36*

Source: Pew Internet and American Life Project Parents and Teens Survey, October–November 2006. Based on online teens [*n* = 886]. Margin of error for the overall sample is ±4%. * Indicates statistically significant difference.

Threats against older girls

As with the studies reported by Ybarra *et al.* (2004a, 2007), the Pew/International survey also found that at least thirteen per cent of the older girls had received threatening emails. The comments by one fifteen-year-old boy are also pertinent to my later discussion of adolescents who are unaware of the line beyond which their pranks and jokes can be perceived as real threats, causing their targets to become extremely frightened.

> I played a prank on someone but it wasn't serious . . . I told them I was going to come take them from their house and kill them and throw them in the woods. It's the best prank because it's like 'oh my god, I'm calling the police' and I was like 'I'm just kidding, I was just messing with you'. She got so scared though'.
>
> (Lenhart, 2007, p. 3)

A study by Ybarra *et al.* (2007) analysed data from a 2005 telephone survey on 1,497 youths in the United States aged ten to seventeen and found that the frequency of use tended to increase the odds of being sexually harassed. Ybarra considers this an important health issue that needs to be addressed by pediatricians who ought to help parents assess their online behaviour globally ('Survey identifies teen online behaviors associated with online interpersonal victimization', *Medical News Today*, 2007).

Modified photographs

Not as many teens (6 per cent), but enough to cause concern, reported having embarrassing pictures of themselves posted online without permission. I agree with Lenhart when she notes that this is not surprising, given the number of photographs that are posted on social networking sites such as MySpace and Facebook. She reports that 9 per cent of those who used social networking sites reported this, compared with 2 per cent of those who did not use such communication tools. Moreover, the PEW/Internet study found that students who post photos themselves are more likely to report that someone has posted an embarrassing photo of them without their permission. One seventeen-year-old boy explained:

> I'm not a big fan of MySpace. Well, I got in trouble from one of them at my school . . . I had one and they [other friends] put a bad picture up there [on her page] and I got in a little trouble at school . . . Some girl just put up like pictures of us on New Year's Eve and the Dean saw it.
>
> (Lenhart, 2007, p. 4)

Again, this example is pertinent to the discussions of students who get themselves into trouble when school officials access social networking sites.

Finally, the study also found that young people who engage in intense Internet use are cyber-bullied to a greater extent. As the report states, online teens who have created content for the Internet – for instance, by authoring blogs, uploading photos, sharing artwork or helping others build web sites – are more likely to report cyber-bullying and harassment than their peers. Content creators are also more likely to use social networks – places to create and display and receive feedback on content creations, and social network users are also more likely to be cyber-bullied (see Table 3.5).

Table 3.5 Do social networks facilitate cyber-bullying? (%)

Have you, personally, ever experienced any of the following things online?	Social network user	Non-social network user
Someone taking a private email, IM or text message you sent them and forwarding it to someone else or posting it where others could see it	17	12
Someone spreading a rumour about you online	16*	8
Someone sending you a threatening or aggressive email, IM or text message	16*	8
Someone posting an embarrassing picture of you online without your permission	9*	2
At least one of the forms of cyber-bullying listed above	39*	23

Source: Pew Internet and American Life Project Parents and Teens Survey, October–November 2006. Based on social network users [n = 493] and non-social network users [n = 393]. Margin of error is between ±3% and ±5%. * Indicates statistically significant difference.

Racial differences

According to the study, white teens are a bit more likely than African-American teens to think that bullying is more of a problem online – 32 per cent of white teens said bullying happens more often online, whereas 18 per cent of African-American teens said the same.

Why teens engage in cyber-bullying

As part of their focus groups, the PEW researchers asked teens about online experiences they had with bullying and harassment. *The students informed them that adolescent cruelty had simply moved from the school yard, the locker room, the bathroom wall and the phone onto the Internet.* This is really important to remember for the discussion on space that comes in later chapters. I have reminded readers throughout this book that cyber-bullying is not much different from the adolescent cruelty that has always taken place – including the graffiti on bathroom walls about disliked peers and teachers. What has changed is not the *kids*, but the *medium*. Therefore, we must be careful where we place the blame. As Lenhart observes, the simplicity of being able to replicate and quickly transmit digital content makes bullying quite easy. As one of the research subjects commented: 'Just copy and paste whatever somebody says'. Her middle school peer warns:

> You have to watch what you say . . . If that person's at their house and if you say something about them and you don't know they're there or if you think that person's your friend and you trust them and you're like, 'Oh, well, she's really being annoying', she could copy and paste and send it to [anyone] . . .
>
> (Ibid., p.5)

Another middle school girl describes how the manipulation of digital materials can be used to hurt someone. 'Like I was in a fight with a girl and she printed out our conversation, changed some things that I said, and brought it into school, so I looked like a terrible person' (ibid.).

Interestingly, some of the teenagers felt that the mediated nature of the communication insulated teens from the consequences of their actions. One high school boy responded to the question whether he had heard of cyber-bullying:

> 'I've heard of it and experienced it. People think they are a million times stronger because they can hide behind their computer monitor. Also known as "e-thugs." Basically I just ignored the person and went along with my own civilized business.' A middle school girl described 'stuff starting online for no reason'.
>
> (Ibid.)

Homophobia

Some of the students in the focus group spoke about homophobia and intoler-ance as fuelling cyber-bullying. One middle school girl related witnessing the following harassment:

> 'I have this one friend and he's gay and his account got hacked and someone put all these really homophobic stuff on there and posted like a mass bulletin of like some guy with his head smashed open like run over by a car. It was really gruesome and disgusting'.

> (Ibid.)

As Lenhart observes, bullying has entered the digital age; however, the 'impulses' behind it are the same. It is those impulses that we need to address so that teens become more thoughtful about their actions.

Canada

My own recent research in elementary and high schools in Montreal, Canada, where we surveyed students in grades 6–9 (eleven to fifteen years of age), corroborates many of the Lenhart findings, although the sample of students was smaller. We surveyed to over 500 students at four high schools and two elementary schools in the English Montreal School Board. Of these, 54 per cent were male and 46 per cent were female. We are yet to begin our work in the French-speaking schools, and, once those data are gathered, it will be interesting to see the differences between anglophone and francophone students. Of the students surveyed, 95 per cent have Internet in their homes, and 5 per cent do not. Surprisingly, only 37 per cent own a cellular phone, and 63 per cent do not. Table 3.6 shows the response of students to questions regarding their experience of being cyber-bullied or engaging with others in cyber-bullying. Although at first glance, these statistics do not seem too disturbing based on individual questions, for example, the highest response was for 'have you ever been called a negative name or been harassed because of your physical appearance?', whereas 28 per cent answered 'occasionally', we noticed that 70 per cent said 'often' or 'occasionally' to at least one question; 35 per cent said 'often' or 'occasionally' to at least four questions; 16 per cent said 'often' to at least one question; and 16 per cent said 'often' to at least three questions. As all the questions relate to some form of racial, sexual, homophobic or other threat, harassment, insult and so on, it can be concluded that the percentages of students in this sampling experienced fairly high rates of cyber-bullying.

We also asked about their 'alternative' online behaviours, such as taking on different ages or personalities. We found that 43 per cent admitted to having pretended to be a different age online, and 22 per cent have tried a

Table 3.6 Experience of being cyber-bullied (%)

	Often	*Occasionally*	*Never*
Called negative name or harassed because of physical appearance	6	28	66
Called a negative name or harrassed because of ability	5	27	68
Called negative name or harassed because of clothing or dress	4	16	81
Been labelled as gay/lesbian even if not	4	23	73
Been cyber-bullied by a student who attends your school	3	12	80
Called a negative name or harrassed because of disability	3	9	87
Continued to receive even when asked person to stop	3	9	89
Called a negative name or harassed because of ethnicity	3	9	89
Received a threatening message that made you afraid	3	8	89
Received angry/rude/vulgar email via Internet	3	26	72
Discovered someone else pretended to be you online	2	21	77
Received a threatening message from someone you do not know	2	12	86
Been deliberately excluded by others online	2	10	89
Been put down, harassed or targeted on a web site	2	7	91
Called negative name or harassed because of religion	2	5	93
Had someone send/post personal information about you	2	11	88
Received a threatening message from someone at school	2	11	87
Been subjected to unwanted sexual suggestions	2	5	94
Had any sexually explicit pictures sent to you	1	8	90
Called negative name or harassed because of gender	1	6	93
Called negative name or harassed because of sexual orientation	1	2	87
Were afraid to open email or real cellphone messages for fear of cyber-bullying	1	5	95
Received angry/rude/vulgar messaging via cellphone	1	3	96

Source: Shariff (2007b)

different personality. Again, what was most telling was that 58 per cent of the students said 'yes' to at least one question, and 14 per cent said 'yes' to at least four questions. Other questions included:

- Have you tried to be older so that you can get into adult web sites? (15 per cent said yes)
- Have you done wild and crazy things you could never do in real life? (14 per cent said yes)
- Have you taken a different physical appearance? (13 per cent said yes)
- Have you acted meanly as if you never would face to face? (12 per cent said yes)
- Have you said hurtful things you would never say face to face? (10 per cent said yes)
- Have you taken someone's name and pretended to be them? (9 per cent said yes)

(Shariff, 2007b)

The lower percentage rates for 'act meanly as you never would face to face' or 'say hurtful things you would never say face to face' might be due to the fact that popular discourse among adolescents in physical settings already contains expletives and words such as 'you're a ho (whore)' and 'I'll bust a cap in your ass (I'll shoot you)' as part of the regular conversation when they are speaking among themselves. As observed in Chapter 2, at the Jubran human rights tribunal, students testified that they often speak to friends this way. Therefore, when asked a question about whether they might say mean things online, the responses are lower because kids have a higher threshold for what they define as 'mean' things – i.e. it would have to be really nasty to be meant hurtfully, hence, the lower numbers. This corroborates with some of the case examples I presented earlier from India, China and Japan, and, later in this book, where young people do not quite realize when they are being 'mean' and find it hard to recognize the line beyond which their expression can be hurtful.

I was particularly interested in analysing the results of our survey because the Lester B. Pearson school board, where we conducted our research, has been doing a considerable amount of awareness work relating to cyber-bullying. I wanted to see whether the board's initiatives had made a difference. Accordingly, we simultaneously conducted twenty-seven adult interviews with their teachers and school administrators (nine school administrators and eighteen teachers) and juxtaposed some of their answers with the results from the student surveys. Some of the students had given examples of the kinds of cyber-bullying that were taking place:

- An eighth grade boy randomly sent emails from the school computer lab quoting a threatening line from a movie.

- An elementary teacher was told by students that a student was writing bad things about her online.
- A mother responded to inappropriate comments coming to her son online by telling them they were behaving inappropriately. The students responded rudely and inappropriately to her.
- A student sent harassing audio messages repeatedly to another student's email account.
- Two girls had a falling out, and one of them threatened to post some compromising pictures on a web site.
- A girl or a group of girls were insulting another girl on her own web site.

Adult perceptions

When asked whether they were aware of any children in the school receiving threats or being harassed through electronic media all nine school administrators said yes, but when the teachers were asked how informed they were about the issue of cyber-bullying, here are some of their responses (Shariff, 2007a):

- I can realize and conceptualize how easily it's done but no, I don't have a lot of experience with it . . .
- It's hard for me to say if it goes on often, if they don't tell me . . .
- I don't think that they communicate that well to adults. Maybe out of fear . . .

When asked where it starts, 63 per cent of the students said it starts at school. This is what the educators said:

- The monitoring of our computer labs is very strict no one is allowed to use the labs without supervision.
- A lot of those sites are blocked, so a lot of that stuff doesn't happen in the school.

Opinions about cyber-bullying

When respondents were asked their opinions about cyber-bullying, the surveys revealed some very important information. For example, 32 per cent agreed/strongly agreed with the statement that online bullying can't hurt you, 'it is just words in cyberspace'. Moreover, 34 per cent agreed/strongly agreed that it is a normal part of the online world, and no one can do anything to stop it. Paradoxically, 88 per cent agreed/strongly agreed with the statement that 'People can be really hurt and I know some of them'. These are high statistics that suggest students do realize people can be hurt. When we see the examples of cyber-bullying and the typical forms of denial by students that they did not mean to hurt others and were just 'joking', there appears to be a dichotomy. This dichotomy is complex, and I will explain it in later chapters. It is noteworthy at this stage, however, that students are often confused as to whether they are being hurtful or not.

Moreover, 48 per cent agreed/strongly agreed with the statement that it is the school's responsibility to stop online bullying, but, in response to the statement 'If students bully each other at home, it is only the parents' responsibility', 24 per cent strongly agreed, and 36 per cent agreed (60 per cent).

Again, these statistics are important when we come to analysing them in subsequent chapters, within the larger context of the influences that play on young people, the contexts in which they exert their agency to act a certain way (given that many of these responses were quite mature and aware about the seriousness of cyber-bullying).

Consider Figure 3.1. There is a clear difference of opinion between what the students consider to be a matter of privacy to be dealt with by parents, and what the school sees as its responsibility. Notably, 46 per cent

Student perspectives:

	Strongly agree	Agree	Disagree	Strongly disagree
If students bully each other at home, the school has a responsibility to stop it	7%	21%	46%	26%
It is the school's responsibility to stop online bullying	15%	33%	40%	11%
If students bully each other at home, it is only the parents responsibility	24%	36%	34%	7%
If someone is being hurt online using line school network, the school should be told	53%	35%	9%	3%

Adult perspectives:

- It's our responsibility 100%.
- We do get involved. Even though parents say that's none of your business, that didn't start here. As soon as the school environment changes, as soon as the child does not feel safe in the environment and their ability to learn is impeded. Our mandate is 100% for the safety and security of the people in this building.
- This is such as new area and it's so fast and convenient and so blurry that I don't know that there's only one right answer (. . .)

Teachers
- Yes
- No
- I don't know

Administrators
- Yes
- No
- I don't know

'blurry'   'complicated'   'grey area'   'boundaries'

Figure 3.1 What is the school's role?

Source: Andrew Churchill, research assistant, Shariff, cyber-bullying SSHRC project (2007c)

disagree and 26 per cent *strongly disagree* (70 per cent) with the statement that, if students bully each other at home, the school has a responsibility to stop it. Put simply, students do not believe schools have a right to intervene when the expression takes place on home computers. Paradoxically, 100 per cent of the educators interviewed stated they had a responsibility to intervene, even if it takes place at home. As we will see later, these are the differences of opinion that have fuelled the controversies between students, schools and parents on the privacy issues – and boundaries of responsibility. The schools see it as a 100 per cent mandate to keep students safe.

These questions were designed to obtain some idea of the students' and educators' understanding of civil rights on and off campus, in school, outside school and in cyberspace. Whereas the students we interviewed did not seem to think their rights were being infringed by school interference (which appears to contradict the case examples involving student protests), the educators were clearly upset with the general parental stance that schools have no right to interfere when the expression occurs at home (see Figure 3.2).

Significantly, in response to the statement 'The solution to cyber-bullying lies with students because they know the online web', 42 per cent agreed, and 23 per cent strongly agreed (65 per cent).

Another very important finding in my opinion was the response by students to the following statements: 'If adults treated young people more kindly

Student perspectives:

	Strongly agree	Agree	Disagree	Strongly disagree
I have the right to say anything I want online because of freedom of expression	10%	16%	37%	38%
Adults created the Internet, now they should live with the consequences	15%	19%	49%	18%
Adult's should stay out of young people's communication	15%	20%	45%	19%

Adult perspectives: relevancy of the charters

☐ Yes
■ No
☐ I don't know

Teachers and Administrators

- *They thought that **I was invading their children's privacy** and actually rather than appreciating my efforts **I got an earful** of you know, 'what's it your business, or what are you doing?'*

Administrator

Figure 3.2 What about rights?

Source: Andrew Churchill, research assistant, Shariff, cyber-bullying SSHRC project (2007c)

students would treat each other the same way' (62 per cent agreed/strongly agreed). Seventy-one per cent said they were less likely to bully if they were happy at school; 83 per cent said 'I would like to create a more kind and respectful world'. Moreover, 81 per cent agreed/strongly agreed with the statement that cyber-bullying is a worse problem than last year; 72 per cent would report it if they could do it anonymously.

What did the school think about all this? One administrator simply chalked it down, acknowledging that there is a 'problem':

> Well we tell, we educate them, we tell them what it is, but after that we have tell them (. . .) you can come and speak to us, we do have a program if you do, we do have a plan, if we do. But it's a matter of getting, first of all acknowledging there is a problem, educating the kids as to what it is, and then making sure those kids feel comfortable telling staff and admin about what is going on. But it's so new to them and so new to us . . .
>
> (Shariff, 2007c)

This response demonstrates the lack of confidence in many school administrators – the uncertainty with which they approach the issues, which might sensitize the students to the fact that their administrators and teachers simply don't know what to do. However, the students have made it clear that, if they were in a school environment where the adults were kinder to them, where they could be kinder to others and where they were happy, there might be less bullying. There is certainly a will on the part of young people not to engage in bullying and, as we will see in the next chapter, this largely depends on the environment that the school creates – whether welcoming or autocratic.

I would also like to highlight one more finding of the research in Quebec. An important part of a welcoming school environment is the confidence with which students feel they can report bullying or cyber-bullying. Table 3.7 shows what we found when asking these questions.

Even though 66 per cent would report it to their parents, and 58 per cent would report it to their teacher, principal or school counsellor if someone was being hurt, it is disturbing to see that 30 per cent said they would not report it to school officials, even if someone was being hurt. Moreover, 40 per cent would only report it if they could do it anonymously.

An Alberta middle school study (Li, 2005) disclosed similar findings to the Quebec research in terms of the relative percentages of students being bullied and engaging in bullying. Li found that 23 per cent of the 177 respondents were bullied by email, 35 per cent in chat rooms, 41 per cent by cellphone text messaging, 32 per cent by known schoolmates, 11 per cent by people outside school, and 16 per cent by multiple sources, including schoolmates.

Table 3.7 Would I report it? (%)

If you were a victim would you:	Yes	No	Blank
Tell your parents or guardian about it	66	25	8
Tell your friends about it	65	26	9
Report it to your teacher/principal/school counsellor	51	41	9
Report it to the police	23	62	9
Keep it to myself and not tell anyone	12	76	12

If you witnessee cyber-bullying taking place and a student was being hurt would you?	Yes	No	Blank
Report it to your teacher/principal/school counsellor	58	30	13
Tell your parents or guardian about it	44	41	14
Tell your friends about it	58	27	15
Report it to the police	21	79	20
Keep it to myself and not tell anyone	11	71	18

	Strongly agree	Agree	Disagree	Strongly disagree
I would report cyber-bullying if I could do it anonymously	32	40	21	7

Source: Shariff (2007c)

Over half of the students reported that they knew someone being cyber-bullied. Almost half of the cyber-bullies used electronic means to harass others more than three times. The majority of the cyber-bully victims and bystanders did not report the incidents to adults. When gender was considered, significant differences were identified in terms of bullying and cyber-bullying. Males were more likely to be bullies and cyber-bullies than their female counterparts. In addition, female cyber-bully victims were more likely to inform adults than their male counterparts.

As I will be detailing some Canadian and American case studies later in the book, I present only brief examples of the kinds of cyber-bullying or anti-authority cyber-expression that are taking place in Canada, as reported in *The Gazette* recently (Riga, 2007).

Case 1: St Thomas High School, Quebec

In April 2007, six students were suspended and more than twenty students attended a school session on cyber-misconduct after insulting material about staff was posted on Facebook. Students referred to one teacher as a paedophile, suggested two others were having a lesbian affair and suggested one teacher took heroine. The school has actively sought to learn more about the issues of cyber-bullying since this incident and are looking into hiring consultants, carrying out workshops for teachers and students and participating in research surveys. This is an important step in the process of addressing anti-authority online expressions. I expand of the advantages of adopting these forms of response in later chapters.

Case 2: Rosemont High School, Quebec

Eight grade 11 students were suspended in May 2007 for their involvement in a Facebook page devoted to a teacher's backside. It included salacious remarks and a picture of the woman's behind.

Case 3: Gatineau, Quebec

Two high school students were suspended in November 2006 after they secretly recorded their teacher's angry outburst and then posted three clips of the incident on YouTube.

Case 4: Birchmount High, Ontario

Four high school students were arrested in March after a protest over the suspension of a fellow student turned violent. The student had been asked to leave the school over derogatory Facebook postings about school staff. In later chapters I discuss some of the media reports regarding this controversy, in which students and administrators were pitted against each other. The way in which the media framed the story, some of the inaccuracies, and school and governmental responses are discussed and analysed in significant detail; therefore I do not expand on them now.

Moreover, I have not indulged in a discussion of the policy responses, or legal considerations for the North American data from the United States and Canada or those from the United Kingdom at this point in the book. Courts in these countries have heard a number of cases on issues that can be applied to cyber-bullying (although few cases specifically addressing cyber-bullying have been adjudicated). In later chapters I present court decisions and emerging standards based on established and emerging jurisprudence that will inform the development of international policy guidelines. As we have seen in this chapter, there are many common elements in how cyber-bullying plays itself out across the world. These legal aspects are discussed in Chapter 7. At this point I ask readers to make note of the disconnect between the way that students and some parents perceive school responsibility and privacy rights, and the way in which schools approach their obligations to address it.

Finally, there are two more countries, from 'down under' (Australia and New Zealand) that deserve mention in this chapter in connection with the extent of, and responses to, cyber-bullying.

Australia

The data emerging from Australia, as presented in Table 3.1, suggest that it is certainly a global leader in mobile phone and text messaging use and in that regard has had its share of challenges with regard to cyber-bullying. Campbell (2005) conducted a study of 120 Australian students in grade 8. Her results indicate over one-quarter reveal they know someone who had been bullied using technology. Further, 11 per cent of the students admit they have cyber-bullied, and 14 per cent reveal they were targets. Campbell's study also disclosed that most of the targets were bullied through text messaging, followed closely by chat rooms and then by electronic mailing.

This was supported in a 2006 joint survey by The National Coalition Against Bullying and a teen magazine *Girlfriend* (MacLean, 2006). The project surveyed over 13,000 girls between the ages of twelve and fifteen, disclosing that 42 per cent of the girls surveyed had either been harassed, intimidated or denigrated through mobile phone text messaging.

Rape online

The most difficult thing about reporting case examples is the frustration that young people have the capacity to engage in such severe acts of abuse. In March 2007, a group of schoolboys filmed themselves sexually abusing and degrading a female classmate. Their film was then uploaded onto YouTube. The film showed twelve youths surrounding a seventeen-year-old girl, who has a mild mental disability, bullying her to perform sex acts, urinating on her and setting her hair alight. The education minister in southern Victoria State, where the attack took place, decided that the state's 1,600 schools would block access to YouTube. She is reported to say: 'The government has never tolerated bullying in schools and this zero tolerance approach extends to the online world' (Bartlett, 2007).

The director of the Australian police's high tech crime centre, Kevin Zuccato, is quoted as saying at the time of the attack that this was a disturbing example of cyber-bullying. 'Cyber-bullying between children online is on the rise', he said. 'Social networking sites are also putting children at risk.' 'The dark side is too dark' (ibid.). Although indeed this was one of the more disturbing acts of cyber-bullying that even I have read about (and I have read thousands of case studies), I believe that the provincial government's focus on the *technology*, namely the banning of YouTube, detracted the focus away from the terrible abuse that the girl suffered at the hands of her perpetrators. As I will argue in later chapters, it is impossible to ban social networking sites such as YouTube, for several reasons. These sites have become immensely popular and they have become a source of enormous revenue for the web providers. Moreover, if one social networking site is closed down on a certain day, a hundred others could be created the next day, or within minutes of the ban. Blocking such sites does not work either, as the Australian government recently found out. Consider another Australian case.

Case 5: The hacker

The *Herald Sun* in Melbourne (Higginbottom and Packham, 2007), reports that sixteen-year-old Tom Wood, a Melbourne schoolboy, broke through the Federal Government's new $84 million Internet porn filter within 30 minutes. Apparently, it took him just over half an hour to bypass the Government's filter. Tom also showed reporters from the *Herald Sun* how to deactivate the filter with a few clicks of his mouse. The report says that the teenager ensured the software's toolbar icon was not deleted. This left his parents under the impression the filter was still working. Tom is a former victim of cyber-bullying and feared that other computer proficient children would bypass the government filter and put it on the Internet for their friends to use. According to the report, the boy had already spoken to Australian communications Minister Helen Coonan about cyber safety during a forum in May 2007, saying it was a 'horrible waste of money'. He had suggested the Federal Government could have developed a better Australian-made filter that would be cheaper than the overseas blocking devise that cost so much.

In response to the *Herald Sun*'s enquiries, the Australian government added an Australian-designed filter, Integard, to the web site on Friday. Tom promptly proceeded to break through the new Australian filter within 40 minutes. The government's response to that feat was that they had anticipated children would find ways to get around the NetAlert filters. To prevent that from happening too often, they had contracted suppliers to provide continuing updates. After spending so much tax-payer's money on these filters, the minister noted: 'Unfortunately, no single measure can protect children from online harm and . . . traditional parenting skills have never been more important.' The filters are designed to stop access to sites on a national blacklist and bar use of chat rooms, and can be tailored by parents to stop access to sites.

Tom stressed that the filters were missing the mark by a long way, regardless of how easy they were to break. His words illustrate how little credit we give to youngsters who can see beyond the immediate need to control online expression to the larger and deeper issues that ought to be addressed. Tom's words are wise beyond his years and certainly more thoughtful than the Minister's:

> Filters aren't addressing the bigger issues anyway . . . Cyber-bullying, *educating children on how to protect themselves and their privacy are the first problems I'd fix* . . . They really need to develop *a youth-involved forum* to discuss some of these problems and ideas for fixing them [emphasis added].
> (Higginbottom and Packham, 2007)

No expert on cyber-bullying or technology could have put this more succinctly or so insightfully. It is really essential that we involve and educate the children, but it appears that there is a need for educating ourselves first.

It turns out that the NetAlert scheme cost *$189 million*, which includes $84.4 million for the national filter scheme, plus funding for online policing, a help line and education programmes. The Australian government will also offer the option of filtering by Internet service providers. The report states that, under its filter programme, households can download the filter from www.netalert.gov.au/ or have it sent out to them. Tom's words and activism in showing the lack of thought and futility that go into many government policy responses are crucial to an improved understanding and response to cyber-bullying. As we work through this book, I will present support for Tom's position, to explain why it is essential that we engage young people in developing responses and 'solutions' to cyber-bullying that absolutely cannot be resolved simply through the purchase of expensive blocks and filters. Nor will it be resolved through the censorship of technologies that are too far advanced to be controlled in traditional ways.

New Zealand

Australia's neighbour, on the other hand, has had some success in addressing cyber-bullying through early foresight and networking among stakeholders. Supported by the government of New Zealand, an organization by the name of NetSafe (www.netsafe.org.nz/home/home_default.aspx) has, over the last few years, developed networks between schools, web providers, cellphone corporations, parent groups and community organizations to develop comprehensive policies and supportive links for students, schools, teachers and parents. These links include a kid's online phone system, referrals to counselling, assessment of anonymously reported situations and so on. This organization has adopted a contextual approach that seems to work. Our international research project (www.cyberbullying.co.nr) will be looking further into what aspects of the NetSafe stakeholder networks work best, and why.

Before we move on to discuss suitable approaches, responses and possible solutions to cyber-bullying, I would like to provide readers with some background on the biological and socializing influences that motivate young people to engage in the forms of bullying activities that they undertake. This background is important because it lays the foundation from which to understand why so many of the zero-tolerance programmes and filtering programmes fail to work. Moreover, readers may have noticed from Chapters 2 and 3 that gender plays an important role in how bullying and cyber-bullying are engaged in, the forms such expression takes, and who gets victimized.

Breaking news

US controversy: Mrs Drew and Megan

As noted in my Preface, new developments relating to cyber-bullying emerge everyday. I would be remiss not to mention at the proofing stage of this book, a highly disturbing and controversial case that has drawn significant attention since my manuscript was submitted. The case involves a forty-seven-year-old Missouri woman, Lori Drew, who took on the identity of a sixteen-year-old boy named Josh, to lure her daughter's thirteen-year-old friend Megan into an online relationship. Posing as Josh, Mrs Drew's messages, initially friendly, suddenly turned nasty on 15 October 2006, culminating in a statement that read: 'The world would be a better place without you' (Maag, 2007). Megan Meier had trusted in 'Josh' as her online boyfriend. Devastated, she took this message literally and committed suicide. While the teen was already on anti-depressants, this email is assumed to have pushed her over the edge. Her mother discovered her in a cupboard, hanging from a belt (Ibid.).

Controversy has arisen over the fact that local and federal authorities in Missouri investigated the case but did not press charges against Mrs Drew because her online behaviour 'might've been rude, it might've been immature, but it wasn't illegal' (Ibid). However, the US Attorney's office in Los Angeles is reported to be looking into the case with a view to charge Mrs Drew with federal wire fraud, as well as cyber fraud against MySpace, as its head office, New Corp., is based in Beverly Hills, California. Although the possibility for successful prosecution of MySpace is minimal because of established legal precedents I detail in Chapter 7, this case is worth watching for its own precedent-setting value if Mrs Drew is successfully prosecuted for wire fraud. Regardless of the legal issues it raises, it supports my argument from an ethical perspective, that adults are sometimes the worst abusers of cyberspace.

New law in Pakistan

Finally, adding to the list of international laws that are making their appearance with regard to the Internet, the *Hindustan Times* (2008) reported on 11 January that the Pakistan government has passed a new Cyber Crimes Ordinance, issued on 31 December 2007, that the government will set up special Internet technology tribunals in Islamabad to investigate and counter cyber-crimes that currently go unpunished due to lack of specific legislation. The ordinance covers crimes such as cyber terrorism and stalking, criminal data access, electronic fraud and forgery, misuse of electronic systems or electronic devices, unauthorised access to codes, malicious code, misuse of encryption, spamming and unauthorized interception.

The statistics and forms of cyber-bullying at the international level evidence a significant amount of gendered cyber-bullying – whether it is sexual harassment against females or homophobic harassment against males. There is also a large amount of literature that looks at why this might be the case. Therefore, I have dedicated Chapter 4 to investigating the biological and socializing influences in the home and in greater society, especially as they contribute to the ways that traditional and cyber-bullying play themselves out. It is to these considerations that I now turn.

Chapter 4

The role of gender

Biological and environmental influences

What's bred in the bone will come out in the flesh.
(Boyd, 2000, p. 95)

Introduction

The international statistics highlighted in the previous chapter suggest a number of gender differences in the way males and females engage in cyber-bullying and communicate with friends through online social networks. As we have seen, many of the perpetrators are teenagers. Is aggression really bred in the bones of young men, or is it simply the way in which their biological conditions at pre-puberty and during puberty combine with the social messages they receive from their caregivers and educators?

Although gender is not the only aspect that influences the emergence of cyber-bullying and the range of responses to it, I believe that the way in which gender differences are shaped, how they play themselves out in online use and in cyber-bullying, as well as societal responses to it, are sufficiently prevalent to warrant the attention of an entire chapter.

I have organized this chapter to inform readers about the biological and social influences that contribute to the development of male and female identities within their homes and cultural contexts, followed by socializing influences that shape their sense of location or identity within those contexts and greater society, including cyberspace as a social environment.

The statistics presented in the previous chapter clearly demonstrate that females are more often targets of sexual harassment, cyber-threats, cyber-stalking and unsolicited pornographic materials. More fascinating, however, are the studies that suggest that cyberspace has had, in many countries and cultures, a liberating effect on girls. I will highlight studies in this chapter that report how communication technologies have helped girls and young women become more social and confident and develop a new sense of identity and agency that helps them break free from cultural and social non-feminist expectations and stereotypes.

The role of the home, especially parents and caregivers, in supporting and enhancing these perspectives, and the media's portrayal of such caregivers as incompetent and incapable of protecting children from cyber-ills, are also highlighted here. This chapter illustrates the ways in which gender roles that are allocated from a very young age play themselves out in cyberspace. Those roles also influence the ways in which adults approach technology use by girls and boys. They also play a significant role in informing the perspectives of government and school policymakers, teachers and other members of the community, each of whom have a stake in what children learn and express.

It is not surprising then that the sheer expanse and speed at which expressions can be conveyed and preserved online can be especially disturbing to parents and members of society who have traditionally controlled the flow of information and, ultimately, what information children access when they are away from home, what they express, and to whom. Rapid changes in forms of communication and their use by girls, boys, men, women and transgendered individuals; the spread of information that was for so many generations carefully controlled through 'selection' and censorship of educational resources such as text-books and library books; values and role models that spoke loudly through hidden curricula (Jackson, 1986; Kincheloe, 2004; McLaren, 1998) all can be framed as threats to the status quo of traditional homes, schools and political institutions. This apparent loss of control can play itself out by downplaying the root causes of bullying and cyber-bullying (such as discrimination). It magnifies the dangers of individuals who challenge the hegemonic status quo (Gramsci, 1971; 1975), and creates a sense of public panic, with calls for forceful responses that are perceived necessary to return young men and women to their gendered roles as strong assertive boys and good little vulnerable girls.

I also return to my opening discussion in Chapter 1, on the ways in which the media exert control to influence what is learned by the public about threats to children, to 'home-grown' or traditional values, and to public safety, all of which schools are expected to respond to under pressure from media, parents and governments. Although these issues are discussed at greater length in Chapter 6, I highlight a number of cyber-cases here, to illustrate how the media 'frames' its reports to sustain an image of girls as fragile and incompetent users of technology, making them more vulnerable and in need of protection from cyber-predators. Boys continue to be portrayed as aggressive and more likely to perpetrate cyber-bullying, connect with harmful web sites and become cyber-predators; and law-makers and law-enforcement officers are generally revered as their saviours. A critical reading of these frames of control discussed in the context of the international research on cyber-bullying and Internet use will, I hope, by end of this chapter, begin to provide readers with a clearer appreciation of why the 'battles' about cyber-use rage on.

Socialization in the home

As soon as children come out of the womb, while still at the hospital, they are learning. When they come home with their parents, they begin to incorporate, through sense, smell, sound, movement, language and their parental responses, various cues about communication and the fact that they are social beings in their new world. Before we move on to consideration of the social factors that so often define gender roles in our society, we might ask whether biology has anything to do with whether children will eventually engage in bullying in any of its forms, as they get older. The debate about whether the tendency for violence is rooted in biology or the environment has not been entirely resolved.

The biology of bullying

There are some who suggest that nature and nurture both affect bullying. Biology and the social, family and educational environments students experience are the primary forces involved in bullying. Genes, hormones, personality traits or physiological impairments occurring during pregnancy or early infancy, can significantly affect later development. As Boyd observes, 'What's bred in the bone will come out in the flesh' (2000, p. 95). Seven years later, we can now add: 'What's bred in the bone will come out in physical and virtual flesh', as kids take on new personalities in cyberspace. Environmental influences can be considered the 'nutritional elements' that interplay to result in positive or negative behaviours. It is important to look at the biological and environmental factors in schools, in the home and in cyberspace that affect student identities, attitudes about themselves, and behaviour towards others. Understanding how these factors affect students helps us understand how and why bullying of any kind occurs.

Scholarship on bullying in the last two decades has largely defined it as a 'developmental' problem – focusing on aggressive tendencies or behaviour of individual 'bullies' and suggesting that those individuals need 'intervention' or 'treatment'. In other words the matter has been studied, and still continues to be from a paradigmatic, psychological perspective, as a *health* issue. This is slowly changing as developmental psychologists and other researchers globally have begun to realize the importance of *context*.

It is important, nonetheless, to briefly highlight some of the biological influences that might make a difference in whether or not a student engages in bullying, becomes constantly targeted as a victim, or stands by as an observer.

Biological factors, including genetics, hormones, allergies, overactive thyroids, attention deficit disorders and other physiological influences, can influence young children's propensity to bully. Children who exhibit chronic behaviour problems from biological sources comprise approximately 6 per cent of the school population (NCPC, 1997; Shariff, 2000, May). Two major sources of concern here are nutrition and medication. Research tells us, for example, that substance abuse and lack of nutrition during pregnancy or the pre-school years impair the growth of brain cells and that fetal alcohol syndrome (FAS) affects one-third of young offenders (NCPC, 1997). A number of researchers found that violent offenders have distinct personality traits that originate in early childhood, such as hyperactivity, impulsivity, poor concentration, an inability to defer gratification and low empathy. Others have found these traits remain constant through to adulthood (Reiss, *et al.*, 1993).[1]

The Olweus (2001) international study on bullying corroborates these studies. He found that bullying behaviour starts early and persists into adulthood.[2] However, according to the NCPC (1997), the neurological effects of FAS, including hyperactivity, disruptive behaviour and attention deficit disorder (ADD), can be offset by good nutrition and emotional support from adults. Furthermore, studies reported by the NCPC found that reading to children at an early age stimulates nerve and cell growth. Children who are malnourished at home can be hospitalized and nurtured back to health (although the damage may not be completely reversed). What is not known is whether children with these kinds of physical challenge engage in, or perpetrate, cyber-bullying. This would be an interesting study to undertake, given the numbers of young people in majority countries who experience malnutrition from poverty.

Another significant factor is genetics, with a special focus on gender differences, being the primary reason that I have introduced biological considerations in this chapter on home and gender. Given that, in general, boys tend to engage in more aggressive forms of bullying, and girls in more psychological and covert forms, it is plausible that the differences might be due to genetics. It is noteworthy that psychological forms of bullying can be equally aggressive, as we will see in studies reported later in this book. Some studies show that human aggression is biologically determined but that its influence on human behaviour is minimal.[3] Boyd (2000), however, argues strongly that genetic factors in male aggression cannot be discounted. He points to empirical evidence that the criminality of biological parents is more strongly correlated with crime in children who were put up for adoption than with the criminality of parents who adopted them.[4]

There is considerable research evidence that hormones play a role in influencing behaviour.[5] Boyd (2000) makes a case for testosterone as a critical factor in male aggression. He traces the research on this all the way back to Aristotle, who, 2,500 years ago, noted the physiological effects of castration on men. Although castration can have a social impact on men's behaviour, approximately 100 years ago, scientists determined that the internal secretions of the testes also have a physiological effect on male aggression. D.H. Starling coined the word 'hormone' (to set in motion) for the 'chemical messages' that cause certain behaviours (ibid., p. 119).

Boyd refers to what criminologists call the 'age–crime curve' (ibid., p. 121) to support his claim that hormones are critical contributors to male aggression. He observes that, in the United States, Canada and the United Kingdom, violent crime by young men increases markedly around the age of fifteen, reaches a peak before the age of twenty, and then declines by the age of thirty. By the age of forty it becomes a rarity. Significantly, this pattern of male violence can be found in every nation for which reliable evidence is available. According to Boyd (2000), the age–crime curve for homicide in the United States, for example, is shaped like Mount Everest. And significantly, although the curve in the United Kingdom is about one-tenth the height of the US curve, it is identical in shape. This might confirm the prevalence of cyber-bullying at adolescence and, in particular, sexual and homophobic harassment online, as we shall see later on.

A number of studies (Artz, 1998b; Boyd, 2000; DiGiulio, 2001; Lanctot, 2001) indicate that both genders increase their violent behaviour between grades 5 and 10 or 11 (ages nine to fifteen or sixteen) around the first onset of puberty and through to the mid teens. Tolman *et al.* (2001) report an increase in, for example, homophobic bullying and sexual harassment amongst adolescent boys. They surveyed eighth grade students (148 girls and 133 boys) in a suburban middle school serving working-class and middle-class white and Latino students. Students were asked to report the types and levels of sexual harassment they had experienced at the school. The researchers were struck by how the teenagers' emerging sexuality and exploration of early romantic relationships pervaded the school environment. They heard how people 'hooked up' and 'broke up' and how the boys watched each other 'kicking g's' (kicking gays). They noticed that boys experienced tremendous pressure in publicly demonstrating their heterosexuality to their male peers. This translated into making sexual comments about girls and their bodies, or acting in an overtly sexual way in relation to girls. The researchers observed that:

> Participating in this form of sexual harassment, whether by making the comments or colluding with boys who do, was not only *normalized* by the boys as simply part of being a boy, but an integral aspect of *proving that they are not gay and therefore not subject to harassment themselves.* Further, through listening to boys' and girls' descriptions of their experiences with harassment, alongside their experiences with early romantic relationships, sexual harassment in early adolescence began to sound like a 'dress rehearsal' of sorts for heterosexual relationships [emphasis added].
>
> (Tolman *et al.*, 2001, pp. 1–2)

They explained that sexual harassment is so normalized that both genders often fail to report it. As I mentioned in my discussion of the statistics on cyber-bullying in Chapter 2, this is an important observation that researchers could miss. This is why narrow definitions of bullying' or 'cyber-bullying' might miss important statistics on sexual, homophobic or racial harassment, or combinations of those forms, because the children being surveyed may not consider them to fit within their understanding of bullying. An increase in the prevalence of sexual bullying just prior to and during adolescence is definitely corroborated in the research findings on cyber-bullying presented earlier. The Tolman study has important implications for the safety of both genders. The more intense the pressure is on boys to prove they are not gay, the more girls are subjected to increased sexual harassment. Boys perceived to be gay are also targets for severe and persistent homophobic bullying.

Suicide and homicide rates are other indicators of the influence of testosterone. Before puberty, girls and boys have approximately equal rates of homicide and suicide (Boyd, 2000; DiGiulio, 2001). However, by the age of thirteen, male rates of homicide and suicide are twice as high as female rates, and, by the age of sixteen, male rates are four times as high, supporting Boyd's argument that genetics play an important role:

> Testosterone is inextricably tied to male sexuality, and the intensely sexual period of adolescence is when we all begin developing relationships. We are competing with our peers, advertently or inadvertently, for the attraction of potential sexual partners; we learn of betrayal, of unrequited love, and of love lost . . .
>
> At any age problems with intimate relationships can produce conflict, hostility, and violence. But in adolescence, when testosterone is rushing about the testes, and young men are still on a learning curve, the potential for aggression and violence is at its apex. What happens when, in these circumstances, young men experience confusion, misunderstanding, and disappointment? In the absence of corrective influences, it is not surprising that young men express anger, irritability, aggression and violence.
>
> (Boyd, 2000, p. 137)

Puberty and hormones might also have this effect on girls, although less dramatically than the effects of testosterone on boys.[6] Most serious cases of female bullying[7] involve disputes about relationships with boys that might also be influenced by hormones, as the girls reach puberty and experience sexual arousal. It appears that biological influences might explain at least part of the equation. Consider now the environmental influences on bullying, which I believe have a significantly larger impact on the persistence and extent of bullying and cyber-bullying.

Environmental influences

Society at large, the home and school are the principal environmental influences on bullying. General attitudes towards violence in society may influence children to engage in bullying. For example, when adults model high levels of tolerance for violence, children may decide that it is an acceptable form of behaviour, regardless of whether or not adults tell them it is wrong. Moreover, children and adolescents internalize the violence they see on movies, TV and music videos and may regard it as socially acceptable.

Gender socialization in the home

Gender socialization begins at home. Depending on whether young people are supported through dialogue and communication with parents, invested in trusting relationships, and are happy and comfortable at home, the way in which they are socialized also impacts how young people might participate in cyber-bullying, or adopt leadership roles in trying to prevent their peers from engaging in it.

Environmental influences in the home, especially during early childhood and adolescence, might account significantly for children's motivations to bully (NCPC, 1997). When parents do not bond with their infants in a trusting relationship, children cannot develop confidence to explore their social environment or develop autonomy, and are motivated to seek power and validation through aggression and bullying.[8] A large body of literature establishes a correlation between early negative familial experiences and aggressive behaviour in children.[9] The research confirms that child abuse in the home contributes significantly to a range of negative consequences such as poor self-concept, aggressive tendencies, alcohol and drug abuse, sexual promiscuity and depression. Studies have also found, however, that a strong parent–child bond reduces aggression in later life (Farrington *et al.*, 1992, as cited in Hall, 1999; Nelson and Lewak, 1988). In the context of cyberspace, this could make the difference between engaging in cyber-bullying, and accessing pornographic and hate sites, or making the decision to avoid those sites and stay away from peers who engage in online harassment and insults.

Female gender roles

These findings are consistent with the research on bullying that shows that it begins at an early age, and that perpetrators and victims experience low self-esteem, lack of confidence and suicidal feelings. This does not, however, explain the behaviour of girls who also engage in aggressive physical bullying or persistent and vicious cyber-bullying. Some studies suggest that this tendency might have something to do with the girls' fathers. Artz (1998b) reports interesting findings in a study of physically aggressive girls from middle-class homes. She discovered that girls with aggressive fathers tended to exhibit the level of aggression expected of males. The girls also engaged in more typically female bullying techniques, such as stalking or tricking others into meeting them in isolated places so that they could beat them up.

In her interviews, Artz found that each girl who engaged in aggressive physical and covert psychological bullying had been sexually abused by either her father or a male family member or male family friend. The girls were neglected and received little support from their mothers, who were also dominated by their spouses. To regain their sense of power, the girls blamed victims for breaking unwritten rules – such as calling them a 'bitch' or a 'whore' – or accused them of stealing a boyfriend. In their minds, this justified the violence. Artz believes that the girls engaged in physical bullying to seek attention and admiration from boys and to fill the void from lack of attention by their fathers. They were also more sexually active than most girls their age.

Imagine the power that the anonymity of the Internet might provide to girls who seek power in this way. Rumours and gossip in the physical and/or virtual school environment have been identified as reasons for increased violence in a number of high-profile bullying cases.[10] In each case, the perpetrators spread rumours about the victim's attempts to steal her boyfriend or spread the word that the victim had called a popular girl a 'bitch'. Also in each case, the social group began to gossip and churn up resentment against the victim. This method of bullying is covert, because victims do not have the opportunity to defend themselves but suffer the effects of the lies and whispering about them. This results in isolation and ostracism, increasing the power imbalance that helps the perpetrators convince themselves that their actions are justified.

Moreover, it is plausible that girls, who may be more submissive in face-to-face communications, may not feel so constrained by online communications. Their assertive online communication skills may lead to online harassment. Ybarra and Mitchell (2004a) found that young people who are victims in offline environments are significantly more likely to harass others in online environments (51 per cent). This issue is further complicated by caregiver–child relationships, delinquency, psychosocial challenges and Internet use. Similarly, Wolack et al. (2003) found that children who had high levels of conflict with parents and those who were highly troubled (with higher levels of depression and victimization or troubling life events) were more likely to engage in close online relationships, increasing their vulnerability to online exploitation.

Boyd (2000) has drawn our attention to environmental conditions that influence male biology towards aggression. One could reasonably assume, then, that the way girls are socialized can promote psychological and covert forms of bullying. The social norm regarding girls is that they are more delicate than boys and should express themselves verbally, rather than physically. It is regrettable, but not surprising, then, that girls would use their verbal and social skills to manipulate and isolate those they bully. An incidental finding of the Artz (1998b) study was that when asked what they would most like to do in the future, all subjects answered that they wanted to be married and have children.

It is ironical that so ingrained is the traditional female role of home, marriage and children in the psyches of children, regardless of whether they are from unhappy homes, they have nonetheless been socialized to view marriage and family as desirable goals.

These findings are also interesting when juxtaposed with the online experiences of girls in North America, India and Japan. According to McMillin (2005) and Gregson (2005), online social networking among girls in India and Japan, in particular, has helped them develop identities that are both independent of their traditional domestic roles in the home, but, in many ways, also integral to those roles. The social networking sites have provided these girls and women with the ability to interact with peers with similar lived experiences, and yet not come into conflict with family members who do not like them to socialize outside of the home before they are married (or even after they are married). The Internet has allowed them the freedom to construct online identities that are significantly more confident. In a number of cases, these identities have led to job opportunities outside the home that would not have been available to them without those social networking sites. Consequently, it is important to appreciate the liberating role of social networking sites, which researchers in India and Japan have found are used predominantly by girls and women.

McMillin (2005) reports on a study of computer use by teenage girls in Bangalore, India. Only 30 per cent of those surveyed responded (most likely because many girls in India still do not have access to technology despite the burgeoning IT industry in India). The author notes that email and surfing for the teenage girls in India, although disclosed to be only a small part of their leisure activities, were, 'an integral component of a matrix of rituals of identity expression' (ibid., p. 175). McMillin observes that computer use actually facilitated a continuation of their gender roles:

> As a new media technology, the computer, with television, facilitated a continuation of their gendered roles as residents of the private, domestic sphere. Yet, through their Internet and email connections and their consumption of limited global products despite the dangers associated with them, they could cautiously explore new boundaries in virtual space. While the nation around them lumbered along according to a postcolonial clock that measured only the nation's backwardness and developmental lag as compared to industrialized metropolis, the teen girls in this study were right alongside their Western counterparts, communicating through email, surfing the Internet, and watching current news, fashions, music albums, and comedies in concurrent time . . . With the increase in multi-national corporations in Bangalore and more specifically, call centres, which are hungry for young, English-speaking, urban females fresh out of private, English-language high schools and colleges, the Indian teen may indeed be on the brink of discovering the Internet as a medium that

transports her from private restrictions to public freedom . . . Of course, IT-based call centers are themselves hierarchical and may replicate exploitative colonial regimes, yet it is evident that the Internet, coupled with television, will present a formidable influence in how the Indian teenage girl visualizes her urban, gendered and national identities and articulates her freedom and consuming agency.

(Ibid.)

In terms of online harassment, girls in India use cybercafés in groups because they have gained a reputation for being able to 'safely' (ibid., p. 174) connect the girls to public spaces. Although some of the girls admitted to using chat rooms to keep in touch with friends, one of the girls, Swetha, a seventeen-year-old, said she stayed away from these spaces:

> I am not regular in chat rooms I used to be when I was younger but now I know there's a lot of bullshit, lots of porn and cyber sex. You should be careful – many girls go in (to chat rooms), then cyber sex things happen, then they get really depressed.

(Ibid., p. 170)

In discussing the attachment to *shuojo anime* in Japan and participation in fan clubs in the shuojo series, Gregson (2005) notes that Japanese girl fans of *shuojo* do not necessarily identify with the female lead characters. She notes that they do not engage with the characters because they want to see talented or sweet, kind girls become heroines in the story. These girls use web sites to talk about the boys they like from their favourite *anime* stories and to put up pictures of those boys on their web site. Gregson suggests that the girl fans of *shuojo anime* have 'moved their bedroom discussion to the Web' (ibid., p. 137). As with the teens from India, the Internet has become a safe haven within which Japanese girls can try out their independence online from the safety of their homes, but engage in very public discussions about topics they would never share in public offline. Hence, the anonymity of the Internet in some cultures provides a cocoon that allows young women to engage more actively in a public sphere without giving up their cultural ties and commitments to their families.

Male gender roles

It is also important to consider how men and boys are socially constructed as perpetrators, and women as victims. Although there seem to be hundreds of studies on female behaviour online, there is a dearth of articles relating to males, with one or two exceptions. There is a need to understand the gendered nature of the phenomenon. Adam (2002) contends that the ways in which virtual and non-virtual violations of the body enforce authority and reinforce the submission of the victim cannot be discounted. I agree, especially as there is also sufficient evidence in the research to suggest that homophobia directed at male victims is prevalent on the Internet (Chu, 2005; Harmon, 2004; Leishman, 2002). However, to ignore the larger gender pattern associated with violence is to miss a basic insight into the social reality of violence as a means of control and intimidation. In other words, it tends to be perpetrated downward through a power hierarchy, reinforcing societal gender inequalities (Herring, 2002).

A very interesting article by Suler and Phillips (1998) investigated the ways in which social hierarchies develop online communities such as the 'Palace (created by The Palace Incorporated (TPI) client and server programmes)', 'Mansion' and 'Welcome' (related chat rooms). Suler and Phillips observed that two factors shape the universal and specific forms of what they refer to as 'deviant' behaviour within these communities. One is technical, and one is social. The technical aspects play an important role, because every chat community is built upon a unique software infrastructure that offers specific technical features for how people experience the environment and interact with each other. They suggest that, no matter what technical features are offered, someone will find a way to abuse them. Suler and Phillips explain that 'if you build it, some will exploit it' (ibid., p. 276). For example, 'snerts' can use sounds and visual images to harass others, where these features are technically available in the chat room.

They also note that social factors may be partially or completely independent of the technical aspects of the environment, and this is owing to the fact that every culture or subculture develops standards of acceptable or unacceptable behaviour. They reference theories of 'cultural relativity' to explain that what is normative behaviour in one culture is not necessarily considered 'normal' in others. Thus, that what may be considered normal or deviant within one chat-room culture may not be perceived as deviant in another. Here are excerpts from their description of the ways in which the anonymity of the chat rooms, where 'avatars' or different personas are adopted within the chat rooms, reflect some of the participants' deeper problems that emerge as a result of their earlier socialization (ibid.):

> Much has been said about how anonymity on the Internet disinhibits people. Feeling relatively safe with their real-world identity hidden, people say and do the things they otherwise would not normally say or do in the face-to-face world. Parks and Floyd explained this phenomenon in terms of the social context cues, theory and social presence theory. The absence of relational cues (visual, tactile, auditory) as well as physical proximity to another person may result in behaviour that is nonconforming according to usual social norms. In some cases, that has a positive effect. People may be more honest, open, generous, and helpful. In other cases, however, the nasty side of a person gets unleashed, accompanied by a tendency to de-personalize others. Hence the snert. It is possible that the positive effects

may outweigh the negative. In their research of Usenet newsgroups, Parks and Floyd were rather surprised that the deviant behaviour was not as widespread as believed.

(Ibid., p. 277)

As Suler and Phillips observe, not everyone wants to be totally invisible, with no name, identity, presence or interpersonal impact. They argue that everyone wants and *needs* to express some aspect of who they are and to have those aspects acknowledged and reacted to. They suggest that anonymity on the Internet allows people to set aside some aspects of their identity in order to safely express others:

> Snerts need someone to react to and affirm their offensive behaviour. This need is a bit different than simply catharting their frustrated drives, as the 'Eros-ridden' idea suggests. Snerts are trying to express some unresolved and warded-off feature of their troubled identity in an attempt to have it acknowledged. Unfortunately, they do it in a way that abuses other people. Under ideal conditions, they may be able to accept and work through those inner feelings and self-concepts that torture them. If not, they will continue to venture that ooze through their online snert identities, while safely dissociating it from their 'real world' identity.

(Ibid., p. 277)

They explain that, instead of the anonymity releasing their nasty side, individuals may experience the anonymity of lack of an identity as toxic. Consequently, they may feel frustrated about not being identified nor having a place in the group. This may cause some 'newbies' to act out their frustration in an antisocial manner online. They need to feel that they have some kind of impact on others, regardless of whether it is negative or positive. This is similar to the child who acts out when he or she wants attention and is being ignored, even if they know full well that the attention might be in the form of scolding and punishment. They note that humans predictably prefer to connect with others if the alternative is no connection at all. Some snerts who join chat rooms may unconsciously justify their misbehaviour and blame the online community for taking away their identity. In other words, they reject people because they feel rejected themselves.

If we consider this assessment of the reasons why some teens may act out online in chat rooms and even on social networking sites such as Facebook and MySpace, then it allows us to appreciate a need to address the *reasons underlying* that behaviour and *not* the behaviour itself. This certainly puts into perspective that some of the students who post negative comments about their teachers may realize it will be detected, and may in fact be calling for attention from those particular teachers.

Suler and Phillips also explain that, although some studies suggest that girls engage in more discriminatory, exclusive forms of psychological violence than boys, they seem to be outnumbered by males, who tend to engage in more sexual and violent forms of bullying. They argue that perhaps online males – especially teenage males – 'have a more difficult time restraining or constructively expressing their Eros-ridden nature – i.e. they are not as mature' (ibid., p. 275). However, there are also other early socialization factors that may be significant here. In his book, *Real boys,* Pollack (1998) describes what he has learned after many years of working with boys with severe emotional and behavioural problems. He explains that at birth, and for several months after, male infants are more emotionally expressive than female infants, but, by the time they reach elementary school, they tend to internalize most of their feelings – a pattern that continues throughout their lives.

Pollack cites two reasons for this general trend. The first is the use of shame in the 'toughening-up' process as it applies to boys. Pollack notes:

> Boys are made to feel shame over and over, in the midst of growing up, through what I call society's shame-hardening process. The idea is that a boy needs to be disciplined, toughened up, made to act like a 'real man' be independent, keep the emotions in check. A boy is told that 'big boys don't cry;' that he shouldn't be a 'mama's boy'. If these things aren't said directly, these messages dominate in subtle ways in how boys are treated – and therefore how boys come to think of themselves. Shame is at the heart of how others behave toward boys on our playing fields, in school-rooms, summer camps and in our homes.
>
> (Ibid., pp. 11–12)

The second reason, argues Pollack, is the separation of a boy from his mother at an early age and then again in adolescence (coming out from 'behind his mother's skirt'). Pollack suggests that these separations are responsible for boys' suppressing feelings, which surface as physical aggression when they reach puberty. Pollack found that boys deal with their shame by suffering silently and retreating behind the mask of masculinity – and by failing to report bullying if it happens to them. Consequently, it can be difficult for parents and teachers to gauge what is really going on in young men's heads – and whether or not they might be either the victims of perpetrators or perpetrators themselves.

Another psychologist supports many of Pollack's observations. In a heart-rending book entitled *Lost boys*, Garbarino (1999) reports on the early life experiences of young American men, most of who are on death row for murder. He explains that neglect and abuse of boys, combined with socialization that requires them to hide their emotions and maintain a tough exterior, can have explosive results. He provides four reasons for male aggression: Boys become hypersensitive to negative social cues. They may interpret non-threatening glances or looks as threatening: 'This one looked at me funny yesterday . . .

That one is bothering me . . . See that guy there? I think he's got a blade hidden' (ibid., p. 81). They also become oblivious to positive social cues. This means that even when people are kind to them they cannot remember – they remember only negative social cues. They develop a repertory of aggressive behaviours that are readily available and easily invoked in order to protect themselves and prove that they are strong. Finally, they conclude aggression is a successful way of getting what they want, and, in most likelihood, the Internet could provide the tools through which to obtain the power they need and the validation they crave in their lives.

The socializing influences of the home and family therefore play a significant role and, to a lesser extent, the biological factors discussed earlier. In Chapter 6, I also discuss the roles and influences of other stakeholders in young people's lives – institutional and systemic influences that also largely shape their experiences and social relationships on and offline, especially when it comes to their experiences in school. Included in that chapter, I highlight how the news media shape and inform the opinions of parents and school officials to create a perception about the seriousness or urgency of certain situations. Because the media can create such strong perceptions about the impact of cyber-bullying, I thought it important to introduce, at this point in the book, a short discussion about how the media go about framing reality for stakeholders, especially as they impact a gender-biased reality, that then translates into hierarchical social relationships online.

How media frames reality

As I alluded at the outset of this book, the way in which the news media present information about our world can have significant ramifications that impact the heart of a society's values, beliefs and educational responses. Edwards (2005) explains that news is not reality – it is a *representation* of reality that does not 'tell it like it is' but rather, 'like it means' (Bird and Dardenne, 1998, p. 71, as cited in Edwards, 2005, p. 14). Edwards describes the news as a 'meta-language' that derives its meaning (and therefore creates the meaning of our reality) through specific arrangements of its elements, which give it the power to legitimate the meaning it repeatedly conveys to the public:

> From the traditional inverted pyramid and narrative forms as to the 'facts' of 'who, what, where, when, why and how' as related by 'sources', news is a unique symbolic system that has the power to legitimate for consumers the very symbols it presents . . . It is the ongoing, daily repetition of this meta-language that allows news to sustain its cultural power. As our cultural scribes and repositories of knowledge, journalists and the institution of the news media play a role in defining social and political discourse and, by extension, our social and political reality'.
>
> (Ibid., p. 14)

By telling people what to think about, the media are culturally empowered to take on a surveillance function in our society that allows news producers to select *what* information we receive, from *whom* we receive it, and *how* we receive it. According to Wright (1986), this function results in several important consequences. It reaffirms and maintains our social order by defining our villains (in the case of cyber-bullying, they appear to be technology tools and the kids themselves); it confers status on issues and individuals featured in the news; and it increases anxieties using sensational words about the dangers of certain individuals or an impending situation – particularly when no interpretative or mediating information is provided. Edwards notes that the news therefore provides the impression that we can control our world by reaffirming the values of our social and political order. It also implicitly teaches us which behaviours are rewarded and who is punished. As part of this process, ordinary people are elevated to important status, regardless of whether they are willing to be, and these sources become powerful forces in the construction of news.

This assessment of the power of the media in reaffirming and reinforcing our understanding of social issues of concern comes through loud and clear in the headlines and articles that I mentioned at the beginning of this book. The media have been instrumental in shaping the public understanding of bullying over the last decade. They are clearly having the same impact with respect to cyber-bullying, the dangers of children who engage in use of social communications systems and the dangers of the Internet.

This process is called 'framing', which organizes information in a way that provides particular interpretations or meaning for the audience (Gamson and Modigliani, 1989; Ivengar, 1991; Neuman *et al.*, 1992). Frames develop 'cultural resonances' on larger themes of public interest – such as youth violence and now, of course, what is on everyone's minds, cyber-bullying. Edwards argues that the problem with cultural resonance is that experts with their own agendas, for example police officers, can use the media to direct public conscience of the issue. Media framing involves story selection, sources quoted, editing and information organization. Edwards suggests that this contributes to over-reliance on official sources that, in turn, contributes to the predominance of law-and-order frames in the news. This again explains the focus in the news on banning, suspending, legislating and punitive responses to bullying and cyber-bullying.

The use of words such as 'war 'and 'battle' is common in media framing – such as a 'war on drugs' (Mackey-Kallis and Hahn, 1994). These researchers argue that framing drug issues as a 'war' may actually contribute to our failure to solve the problem by 'misdiagnosing' the issues – misdiagnoses lead to ineffective solutions. And this is my greatest worry as regards the framing of cyber-bullying, its dangers and the need for urgent responses. Framing our responsibility to address cyber-bullying as a 'war' gives it a totally different focus that attracts positivist legal responses that are punitive, controlling and reactive, as opposed to proactive and educational. It magnifies the dangers of the Internet and the kids who use it – rather than looking for ways to guide young people as they grow up in a world confused by hormones, overprotective parents and adults who condone and model violence but expect youngsters to avoid it. It is like putting someone in a pool of water and asking them to stay dry! In my opinion, framing played a significant role in the misdiagnosis of general bullying, which resulted in a plethora of anti-bullying programmes and policies that were found to be minimally effective (Shariff, 2005; Shariff, 2006 a,b,c).

Media framing of gender roles

Mazzarella and Pecora (2002) conducted an empirical analysis of newspaper coverage of adolescent girls' lives. They concluded that 'While not scape-goating girls for broader social problems, it is clear that the press constructs girls *themselves* as social problems' [emphasis in original] (ibid., p. 16). These researchers noticed that, based on the interest of feminist researchers and high-profile studies of girls who are growing up in an era where they were described by Phipher (1994) as 'coming of age in a more dangerous, sexualized and media-saturated culture [where they] . . . face incredible pressures to be beautiful and sophisticated' (ibid., p. 12), the media picked up on many of these studies and began to print headlines such as *'Perils of puberty: girls 'crash and burn' in adolescence'* (Eicher, 1994); *'Crossing "confidence Gap" poses high hurdle for girls'* (Brecher, 1994); *'A perilous age for girls'* (Mann, 1997). Mazzarella and Pecora note that, more recently, the public's concern about girls (and boys) as reflected in the media has centered on the Internet and its dangers, with descriptive headlines ('Girls lured via Internet', *The Advertiser* (2003)).

Cyber-news on girls

Edwards (2005) examined 125 articles about teen girls and cyber-crime (and related topics) between 1 January 1990 and 1 January 2002, in five major daily newspapers. Her analysis included headlines, leads, sources quoted and six frame categories: girls as risk; girls at risk; adults as risk; adults at risk; police as hero; and civil liberties at risk. What she found was a stark contrast in the number of articles that were categorized under the girl-frames versus those in the adults-as-risk frames (32 per cent), compared with 6 per cent for girls as victims and 2 per cent for girls at risk. Attorneys were cited as sources in twenty-five of the forty articles (63 per cent) on adults as risk, and police were cited as sources in twelve (30 per cent). Adults at risk were featured in 6 per cent of the articles. The largest block of articles (forty-eight out of 125 – 38 per cent) were framed as police-as-hero and featured police as sources in

73 per cent of the articles. Finally 10 per cent were framed as civil liberties-at-risk, with police and parents cited as sources in 15 per cent of the articles.

Helpless online girls

Edwards found that the articles on girls as risk situated the girls' crimes in female 'spaces', suggesting that the use of technology was merely an extension of stereotypically female behaviour that continued to occur in female spaces such as the kitchen and bedroom. Moreover, the girls were made to appear technologically inept and lacking the agency to successfully commit the crimes on their own, as police and law enforcement officials are quoted in 100 per cent of the articles. One of the articles read:

> 'Girl, 15, arrested making drugs at home with Internet recipe' the lead describes the crime this way: 'Investigators say a 15-year-old girl they caught cooking up narcotics in her home learned the recipe on the Internet.'
>
> ('Girl, 15, arrested', 1997, cited in Edwards, 2005, p. 17)

Edwards observes that the purposive use of the words 'recipe' and 'cooked up' involves food metaphors that are usually linked to female stereotypes in the home who are relegated to the kitchen. Officers reported the girl had already thrown away 'two failed batches', conjuring up a picture of burnt muffins rather than drugs. The word 'recipe' surfaced in two other articles – another on drug recipes, which were considered dangerous because they came from Internet, that also highlighted the second girl's lack of power or expertise on the Internet by suggesting she 'toyed with danger' and 'tangled with danger'. Edwards notes that words such as 'tap of a key-board' remove the seriousness of the activity that the girl was involved in. A third article referring to recipes did so in connection with a girl's attempts to make a bomb.

The fourth article came closest to cyber-bullying: a teenage girl sent herself a threat through MSN and accused two peers of doing it. The official sources quoted in the article downplayed the criminal activity and placed the blame on the technology. This take on the issue misdiagnosed the fact that she was actually engaged in harassing others: 'Authorities characterized the episode as a high school dispute gone wrong and said it is an example of how the Internet has become a frequent source of crime for youngsters' (Edwards, 2005, p. 13). The article further diminished the girl's actions by stating 'Teenagers may assume they are anonymous on the Internet, but there are ways of finding out who they are. Frankly, it's not that tough to figure it out . . .' (ibid.). Edwards notes that, by citing an official source a saying it was not 'tough to figure it out', the article discounts the intricacy of the crime and the efforts the girl took to implicate others, while at the same time reinforcing the school's and police officer's ability to restore order. Indeed, it is not that difficult to concur with Edwards that this is all about showing the public that everything is under control.

She brought it on herself

Examples of the girls-at-risk type include the story of Christina Long, a thirteen-year-old who was murdered in May 2002, by Saul Dos Rei, a twenty-five-year-old man she met in an Internet chat room. Immediately, the headline assigned blame – not to her murderer, but to Christina – 'Slain girl used Internet to seek sex' (Kilgannon, 2002, as cited in Edwards, 2005). Christina was framed with a Jekyll and Hyde character:

> By day, she was Christina Long, a 13-year-old altar girl and co-captain of the cheerleading team at St. Peter Roman Catholic School in Danbury, Conn., where the principal said she was a 'good student and well-behaved' . . . But in the evenings, the authorities say, she logged onto the Internet using the screen name 'Long Toohot4u' and the slogan, 'I will do anything at least once'. In her bedroom, the police say, she used her computer to troll chat rooms and meet adult men for sex, her marital status listed as, 'I might be single and I might not be'.
>
> (Edwards, 2005, p. 20)

By framing Christina as a 'good girl' in the day and a 'bad girl at night', the media took the focus off the crime committed by her murderer and placed it squarely on the shoulders of a thirteen-year-old (who should have known better than to solicit men on the Internet?). By stating that her 'online profile' does not resemble her 'official' tomboy image, the journalist assigned blame to Christina.

Authority figures

The adults-as-risk category contained a higher number of articles (32 per cent) and addressed cyber-crimes committed by adults against girls. According to Edwards, these articles juxtaposed the occupations of the cyber-predators as a threat to the social order, if they were teachers or coaches, but did not mention their occupations if they were not in such positions of authority: 'Teacher in pornography case has county ties' and 'Teacher arrested on sex charge'.

Clueless parents

It is interesting to note that the concept of 'space' resurfaced in discussions of parents at risk if the computer is in the home and supplied by them for their children's use. Make note of this example as it will be relevant to discussions about space in the upcoming chapters. Out of 125 articles, 6 per cent fitted this category, and, interestingly, in 29 per cent of the articles, youths were cited as secondary sources. However, professional experts such as police were again the primary media sources in 71 per cent of the articles. Parents themselves were quoted in three of the seven articles reviewed (43 per cent).

Edwards notes that parents are made to appear ignorant and uninformed about the Internet and its dangers and, in some cases, oblivious to their children's activities. The articles send conflicting messages that trivialize the children's conversations with potential predators online if they are 'safe' in their homes, while in the same story reporting on police investigations that led to questioning of 200 suspects. Here are some examples:

> Genevieve Kazdin, a self-appointed crossing guard on the information highway, remembered the day last September when she found an 8-year-old girl attempting computer conversations with a group of transvestites. Seemingly safe at home, the child was playing with her favourite $2,000 toy; using her computer and modem to make new friends through a service called America Online.
>
> (Schwaratz, *et al.*, 1993)

Although this article warns of the dangers of the Internet, it suggests that friendly intervention when adults are not around can protect children on the Internet. What it does *not* say is how few of these self-appointed information highway patrol people children are likely to meet. Next, Edwards notes that the article suggests that, when they are unsupervised on computers, children are only 'seemingly' safe in their homes. Another article also highlights the ignorance of a parent who comments about her thirteen-year-old son: 'I would be thinking how nice that he's spending so much time developing his writing and typing skills, when suddenly he would ask, "Hey, Mom, what does '69' mean?".' The expert source, cited in the article, a sociology professor at the University of Illinois continued to stress the idea that children are not safe in their own homes by saying: 'We call it the IUD syndrome . . . Parents are ignorant, technology is ubiquitous, and some of the information is deleterious' (Edwards, 2005, p. 23).

A third article again belittles the seriousness of online predators by quoting a girl who says she just tells her parents when she receives pictures every once in a while, or simply deletes them. Instead of picking up on the fact that this child dealt with potentially threatening material very appropriately in the absence of her parents' supervision, the article quotes a source from the National Center of Missing and Exploited Children who said: 'We're pro-cyberspace . . . But for an awful lot of parents, there's a false sense of security . . . Millions of people are coming into their home via cyberspace' (ibid.). Rather than stressing the need for improved communication between parents and kids, these articles position parents as victims of the *technology* – and *reduce the agency* of parents and their children to deal with it appropriately. There is little about communication or the teachable moment between mother and son when the thirteen-year-old boy asked what '69' was.

Heroic policemen

Not surprisingly, Edwards' analysis found that the largest number of articles, forty-eight out of 125 (38 per cent) were framed as police-as-hero and featured police as sources in 73 per cent (thirty-five articles). Lawyers were cited in nineteen, and experts in seven articles. In support of my argument that the social hierarchies of power in society extend from physical to cyberspace, Edwards argues that the predominance of this frame suggests that cyberspace, like the home and school, is gendered and problematic. She suggests that the headlines purposely promote police authority with headlines such as: 'FBI cracks child porn ring based on Internet' (ibid., p. 25). The *New York Times* article 'Setting the traps to snare online predators' provides examples of how police spent 'countless hours in the dim glow of computer screens' to protect 'young victims, blurry-eyed with romantic visions' (Richter, 2001, as cited in Edwards, 2005). Edwards finds the parallels between the police and predators ironic, as both huddle in front of computer screens for hours in attempts to capture the girls.

Civil liberties for perpetrators

Edwards found that the articles that related to civil liberties played down the dangers of the Internet to protect high-profile predators when they were caught accessing child pornography online. This example is also one that will be revisited in the upcoming chapter, to discuss how information is presented in contradictory ways to maintain control of it. Cyberspace again poses a threat to examples such as this one, where reality is manipulated to arrive at a certain 'truth' or evidence. In one case involving a well-known newsman, Larry Matthews (Castenada, 1997, as cited in Edwards, 2005), the judge, in supporting Matthews' First Amendment rights, refused to disclose his name publicly. Edwards observes that, in contrast to the other articles about cyber-predators, this article about a journalist accused of exchanging child pornography over the Internet suggests that his claim that he was simply doing research was perfectly legitimate and that our fears of the Internet are putting people's civil liberties at risk:

> 'I think this is an area of law that has to be watched very carefully. It's always in the name of some horrendous evil, like child pornography, that important rights tend to get stripped away' said Robert Corn-Revere, a Washington lawyer who represents journalistic agencies on First Amendment issues.
>
> (Edwards, 2005, p. 27)

Other articles on civil liberties involving high-profile cases such as 'Jeanine Piroo's sting: visiting chat rooms to chase paedophiles' cited civil liberties lawyers as likening sting operations to 'witch hunts'.

This final example is a good place to move on to the discussion in Chapter 5, where I begin to lay out the tensions between supervised and unsupervised space, towards introduction of the debate about student free expression rights and the rights of stakeholders, including parents, to determine what information children express and are exposed to. In Chapter 6, I then work through a list of relevant stakeholders that include government policymakers and school boards, school administrators, teachers and teachers' unions, and technology corporations, all of whom have an interest in controlling expression and information, so that it can be more easily handled and managed. That chapter shows how institutions in particular can censor their own ability to address issues of cyber-bullying because they often place too much emphasis on school reputation, good housekeeping, management and control of students, rather than on dialogue with students and empowering engagement in their learning.

This backdrop allows me to delve into the deeper considerations about who defines the parameters of learning in cyberspace; who controls expression in a democracy – especially when cyberspace has elasticized and blurred the boundaries of privacy and is presented by the media as a threat to the interests of the greater good (when it suits official agendas). At other times it is presented as no threat when online predators turn out to be important people (Edwards, 2005). And, although the policy debate about boundaries between free expression, privacy, supervision and safety is still being worked out, we need to ask what happens to the children and adults who are facing harassment and cyber-bullying. It is important to remember that children are watching while the policy vacuum is being debated among school and government officials, teachers' unions and law-enforcement officers who want to 'crack down' on cyber-bullies. They observe the on and offline power plays among adults; deference to authority and manipulation of realities; they notice the scapegoating, and the denial of responsibility and accountability. Remember that youngsters look to the adults in their lives as role models, and it is thus important to ask whether we are meeting that mandate adequately, if at all. As teachers and parents get caught up in the fear-mongering and fray relating to cyber-bullying that is 'out of control', educating the next generation about the spirit behind the fundamental principles of justice, equality and free expression in a democracy becomes a low priority, whereas in fact, it ought to be at the top of the agenda. Within the context of cyber-bullying, how many educators are providing students with comprehensive knowledge that draws upon the histories, lived realities and cultural values of many of their peers and teachers who may come from different cultural backgrounds, or who may espouse a different sexual orientation? How many teachers are putting away their 'to do' lists and instead taking the bull by the horns to have a heart-to-heart dialogue with kids who are engaging in cyber-bullying and defaming teachers and peers? How many stakeholders are giving lip-service to getting young people involved in addressing bullying, youth violence and now cyber-bullying, but forget to hear the students' side of things.

Although I do not condone cyber-bullying, and understand the deep hurt and humiliation that result from forms of cyber-bullying that are causing so much concern globally, I believe the only way of reducing its prevalence involves a slow but very worthwhile process. Such a process is needed to adjust systemic power imbalances and get young people involved in defining codes of conduct and consequences. Instead of treating children and young people as behavioural specimens to be studied in our research, and instead of determining their fate through suspensions when they cross certain boundaries, it is incumbent on us that we guide them to take responsibility for their actions. The role of schools, parents and school community stakeholders is crucial to better equip young people to navigate virtual spaces, where they are more comfortable and proficient than most adults. It is to these issues of control, private and public spaces that I now turn.

Chapter 5

Controlling kids' spaces

'Where's the man with the megaphone?' . . . 'Aren't there any grownups at
all?' 'I don't think so'. The fair boy said this solemnly; but then the delight of
a realized ambition overcame him.

(Golding, 1954, p. 7)

Introduction

Elsewhere (Shariff and Hoff, 2007), I have discussed why there are many
parallels between what happens when adolescents are left on a deserted island
without supervision, as in Golding's (1954) fictional study, and what is happening in cyberspace today. Left alone with no supervision, for example,
Golding's boys harass, then terrorize and ultimately kill one another. Peer-
to-peer cyber-bullying similarly puts students on a virtual island with no
supervision and very few rules, which allows bullying to escalate to dangerous,
even life-threatening levels, as illustrated in the examples presented in the
chapters on profile. Furthermore, the boys on the island realize that being
hurtful to peers is easier when they assume a different persona, and so they
paint their faces for anonymity before they attack. Cyber-perpetrators are no
different; they hide behind pseudonyms (recall 'Raveger' (Shariff, 2001)) and
well-disguised IP addresses, making it difficult, if not impossible, for the
victim to determine the source of the threat. This anonymous nature of cyber-
bullying is perhaps the most troubling of all for students because it leaves
them wondering in the classroom or school playground, 'Is it him?'. Is it her?'
Indeed, it might be anyone. Like being on an island, there is no escape.

Moreover, the emergence of anti-authority expression, perceived as cyber-
bullying by teachers, has complicated the issue because of the lack of clear
boundaries between private and public spaces, which makes it difficult to develop
and implement rules and policies that do not infringe free expression rights.
Chapter 7 will clarify some of these issues. However, before proceeding to discuss
the legal considerations, it would be helpful to think about the sharing of space
between adults and young people, because this is ultimately what the debate
is about. In physical space, there are visible boundaries signified by the types

of room in a school, or adult and student spaces where respect for authority is to be maintained to a certain degree. Classrooms and school administrative offices are examples. Although classrooms are primarily student spaces, once the teacher is present there is generally an unspoken rule about acceptable use of language, respect for the teacher and so on. On school property, the grounds and buildings are generally places where children know that a certain standard of behaviour is expected. Generally, administrative offices in a school represent the ultimate positions of adult power, where students are only summoned to the Principal's office if there is an issue or problem. I have been inside some schools, however, where the administrative offices (including those of the head teacher or principal), are spaces where students feel sufficiently comfortable and confident to enter and chat about their work or accomplishments. This is uncommon. In general, most schools have the physical dividers of authority. In cyberspace, these boundaries are not well-defined at all. There are no specific allocations of space that demark the separation between authority figures and students. Cyberspace, like the open sea at the threshold of Golding's island, is a vast and public space, with fluid boundaries that can be extended and in some cases reduced, depending on who is using the space and which participants within that space define the rules of the game.

Human beings, like animals, have always been territorial, and, as Darwin (2003) informed us, it is all about survival of the fittest. What makes us different from other animal species is that most animals nurture, protect and teach their young survival skills for short periods of time and then let them roam independently to learn and fend for themselves. Although clearly, in the animal world many dangers lurk in unknown spaces, there is almost an instinctive element of trust by the adults that they have done their best to prepare their young for these dangers. How their offspring use learned survival skills to navigate the dangers is left up to them – unsupervised.

Supervising kids' spaces

As human beings, we teach children how to eat, clean themselves, and communicate, and we protect and nurture them, until they are old enough to go to school. Once they are at school, we suddenly place more emphasis on supervision, discipline, authority, subordination, punishment and consequences, with less attention to the social survival skills they will need in the contemporary world. High schools rarely teach students how to sustain long-term partnerships with a spouse; learn parenting skills; manage finances, budget and food shop; or run a home, although most home economics classes make a superficial effort to do so. Few social studies classes teach students how to network with people who could mentor them in their careers, or even how to use a credit card, avoid getting in debt and stay healthy (although, admittedly, schools are increasingly focusing on improved wellness). Nonetheless, we have generally shifted the focus away from preparing our young for life, to controlling their behaviour, making them conform to rules and laws designed for the benefit of adults, such as zero-tolerance policies and legislation. If those rules do not work, we bring in the police and criminal justice system to keep them in their proper place (Apple, 1990; DiGiulio, 2001; Giroux, 2003; Kincheloe, 2005; McLaren, 1991).

In his insightful book, *Educate, medicate, or litigate* (2001), Robert DiGiulio provides disconcerting evidence to show how children in the United States, who might be victims of systemic barriers in society – poverty, neglect, ill-health, abuse, racial discrimination, immigration or refugee status and so on – are consistently labelled as 'disruptive' and 'unco-operative' when they cannot adjust to a school system that has little meaning or relevance in their lives. DiGiulio provides statistics to show how many perfectly healthy children are placed on Ritalin and other drugs to control their behaviour at the insistence of school teachers and authorities in the United States.

Moreover, as one of my graduate students, Andrew Churchill, aptly observes, we supervise children's play spaces from a very young age. Andrew cites as examples soccer and baseball leagues that are set up to formalize young people's games from the age of four and five. How often have we heard about overzealous and competitive coaches and parents pressuring children to perform at soccer or hockey games, to the point of abuse and breakdown from stress? Moreover, in the last two decades or so, fear of paedophiles and murderers kidnapping children while they play outside has resulted in around the clock supervision, even though most adult boomers remember roaming free to play for hours without adult supervision.

As the parent of younger children I, too, was guilty of over-supervising my children, often worried to the point of paranoia about someone kidnapping them. I could never relax when they played outside, even under my watchful eye. I do not want to trivialize these concerns. They are legitimate worries for parents. Unfortunately we live in a society where people do kidnap, rape and murder children. But, at the same time, there is also a responsibility to educate children, and make them aware of strangers who might entice them into vehicles, prepare them to know when and where to seek help, or stop at an invisible line at the end of the driveway before running onto the road to chase a runaway ball.

Confusing and disengaging children

Substantial literature exists to illustrate how our schools are doing a less than effective job of providing education that is useful or relevant to all children (ranging from highly gifted to severely disabled). We teach to the perceived 'norm', by preparing pupils to pass standardized tests so that *we* can manage how many students move on to higher education and enhance the reputations of our schools as academically superior, based on student performance on standardized tests (Apple, 1990; DiGiulio, 2001; Dolmage, 2000; Egan, 1997; Giroux, 2003; Kozol, 2005; Robertson, 1998).

As Kieran Egan (1997) explains in his book *The educated mind*, schooling in Western democracies runs into problems because we attempt to implement three conflicting educational philosophies of: rationalism (academics based on Platonic ideals – geared towards elitist standardized tests); individual development philosophies (based on Rousseau's teachings, which, in theory, make sense but are difficult to implement in schools without significant planning, monitoring and evaluation); and socialization philosophies developed from John Locke's influential work towards developing civic-minded citizens. Again, as a number of scholars argue, the desire to run democratic schools and provide inclusive environments looks impressive in the stated intent of policies and mission statements. In reality, however, democratic principles are minimally understood by most teachers and less successfully implemented in classrooms (Shariff and Sarkar, 2004). Throw into the mix John Dewey's 'organic model' of education, and the results are a confusing mix of conflicting ideologies that lack focus and keep students disengaged from learning.

Children are more perceptive than they are given credit for, and most can recognize this lack of direction and focus. Students in many schools are bored and alienated from what they learn in schools, turning to violence for stimulation (Ashford, 1996; Giroux, 2003; Kincheloe, 2005). At the same time, they are consistently supervised, told what *not to* do, and repeatedly informed about the *consequences* of certain 'behaviours'. Less time is spent on dialogue with students about *why* describing peers and teachers as 'sluts', 'hos' and 'homos' is not very helpful to developing positive social relationships or school environments. How often do we tell students to respect *everyone*, including *themselves*, in addition to respecting authority figures? We certainly tell them that to get respect you have to earn it; however, when it comes to asking them to respect authority figures it might be worth considering whether those in authority model or deserve the respect they insist upon receiving from students.

McNeil (1988) found that, in schools where the administration was top-down and bureaucratic, students were less engaged in their learning, whereas, in schools where students were empowered to help direct their own learning in an environment where adults demonstrated respect for the students as people, the results were amazing. A study on student engagement conducted by McGill University researchers in 1998 (see Butler-Kisber and Portelli, 2003) studied ten inner-city Canadian schools and found a significant reduction in violence and improvement in learning. For example, the curriculum in one school studied was revamped to represent a 'curriculum of life'. In another school, the core curriculum was refocused on the arts. One positive outcome of this was that students who would never have seen the inside of an art gallery had opportunities to present their work in a major art gallery in Halifax.

Moreover, Ashford (1996) did considerable research to establish that when students are bored they experience a sense of *anomie* and are more likely to turn to violent or high risk activities that challenge the rules and laws adults put in place to keep them in line.

Enter the digital divide

Jenkins (Jenkins and boyd, 2006) suggests that most parents understand their children's experiences in the context of their memories of their own early years. For the baby boom generation, those defining experiences involved playing in backyards and vacant lots within suburban neighbourhoods, socializing with their friends at the local teen hangout, and participating within a social realm which was constrained by the people who went to your local school. All of that, he says, is changing.

His colleague, danah boyd (ibid., 2006), agrees. She notes that social networking tools such as MySpace and Facebook play a key role in young people's lives because they service as 'digital publics'. This is best explained in her own words:

> These sites play a key role in youth culture because they give youth a space to hang out amongst friends and peers, share cultural artifacts (like links to funny web sites, comments about TV shows) and work out an image of how they see themselves. They also serve as digital publics, substituting for the types of publics that most adults took for granted growing up, but are now inaccessible for many young people – neighbourhood basketball courts, malls, parks, etc. Youth are trying to map out a public youth territory for themselves, removed from adult culture. They are doing so online because their mobility and control over physical space is heavily curtailed and monitored.
>
> (Ibid.)

In support of these comments, Jenkins explains that much of the activity that our generation enjoyed as kids is being brought online:

> What teens are doing online is no better and no worse than what pervious generations of teens did when their parents weren't looking. The difference is that as these activities are being digitized, they are also being brought into public view. Video games bring the fantasy lives of young boys into the family room and parents are shocked by what they are seeing. Social networks give adults a way to access their teens' social and romantic lives and they are startled by their desire to break free from restraints or act older than their age. Parents are experiencing this as a loss of control but in fact, adults have greater control over these aspects of their children's lives than ever before.
>
> (Ibid.)

Jenkins goes on to observe that digital technologies simply bring to the surface teenage behaviours that have always been present. These are recorded more permanently online:

> Indeed, one of the biggest risks of these digital technologies is not the ways that they allow teens to escape adult control, but rather the permanent traces left behind of their transgressive conduct. Teens used to worry about what teachers or administrators might put in their permanent records since this would impact how they were treated in the future. Yet, we are increasingly discovering that everything we do online becomes part of our public and permanent record, easily recoverable by anyone who knows how to Google, and that there is no longer any statute of limitations on our youthful indiscretions.
>
> (Ibid.)

Cyberspace to kids is like a forest that awaits discovery for a formerly caged animal. There is much to explore, learn, navigate – an infinite world of wonders but also many dangers. I use this exaggerated metaphor on purpose, to argue that technologies have provided youngsters with the spaces they need to explore and learn about issues that are relevant and have meaning to them. Cyberspace provides an arena that gives the impression it is largely unsupervised by adults. In cyberspace, they can roam free and socialize with peers in a world where parents and teachers are not welcome. So valued has this space become for young people, that even those who are victims of cyber-bullying, are reluctant to report it for fear that the technology (cellphones or computers) will be withdrawn, or that the adults will not understand what is taking place because some of them 'do not even own a cellphone' (Campbell, 2005).[1]

And yet, as danah boyd (Jenkins and boyd, 2006) reminds us, because of mobile phones, college students report greater ongoing communication with their parents than in previous generations. She cites Misa Matsuda as arguing that networked technologies allow young people to maintain 'full-time intimate communities'. Hence, new media are allowing young people to become more deeply connected to their peers, and also to their family members. This provides powerful open channels for communication. These are positive factors that are rarely communicated in news headlines or referred to when we hear how the 'web ensnares' teens (Schmidt, 2006).

Kids' perspectives – their own private space

As the cleverly selected name for the popular networking tool 'MySpace.com' suggests – young people perceive the online communication spaces as their own – this is 'my space' or 'our space', and adults should not be privy to what we say. Consider the following case examples of cyber-bullying as reported by news media.[2] The first case is that of Brad Parsons.[3]

Case 1: Brad's bungle?

Post meant for friends only, teen says:

Brad Parsons says he never imagined he'd be bounced from his school and see friends arrested when he created a Facebook group for his friends to use to vent about a vice-principal. 'We made the group as an inside joke', the 16-year-old student at Birchmount Park Collegiate said in a phone interview.

But the teen who 'likes hanging out and chilling' with his friends and says he's never caused any trouble, stepped into a grey area when he created the space on Facebook.com, a popular social web site, that slagged his school's vice-principal, Mary Burtch and other staff.

Internet experts say Parson's case once more raises interesting questions that don't have clear answers.

'These issues are arising with increasing frequency and I think it's tough to identify how much of this is a legal issue, how much of this is a conduct issue within a school', said Michael Geis, Canada Research Chair of Internet and E-commerce Law at the University of Ottawa. 'I think it is hard to identify a right or wrong.'

For instance, does a conversation intended to be privately shared among friends, as Parsons says, constitute cyber-bullying, as the school says, if it becomes publicly available?

Parsons argues that while the comments made were mean-spirited and made fun of Burtch, they shouldn't be considered bullying because they were not intended to be seen by her. 'It was not online harassment', Parsons said. 'We were not in any way trying to get the message to her. We were just talking amongst each other.'

Parsons, who plays house-league hockey and is studying to take his G1 driving test, led a protest Friday to decry the school for 'suspending people and suspending freedom of speech and opinions on a private chat line'.

Four other Birchmount Park students were suspended earlier this week after school administrators discovered the derogatory comments on the web site.

What started as a protest with fewer than 100 students tripled in size after someone pulled a fire alarm. Four students were arrested when police were pelted with objects as they tried to direct traffic.

Parsons was told Monday he would be expelled from school but has since heard his punishment might be lighter. He has a meeting tomorrow with the school board that he hopes will clear things up.

His mom, Sylvie, 52, said that as punishment she is taking away Internet access from her son. But she noted that when she went to school, she and her other friends would stand around and say mean things about teachers.

'The technology has changed so it's become a much different thing now', she said.

Parsons said he and his friends have long had problems with Burtch, who Parsons says has singled them out because they hang around in the back of the school where there have been problems caused by students not in his group.

Parsons, whose favorite classes are English and drama, says he was getting good grades and was finishing an essay on *MacBeth* when he was expelled. 'I'm losing out on my education because of this and it's going to set me back', he said.

(Chung, 2007)

In Brad's case, it is clear from the support he received that he and his fellow students believed strongly that the comments they made were 'private' and not for the eyes of school authorities, least of all Ms Burtch and her staff. The student protest comprised resistance to the idea that any rules were breached. The students argued that, although the comments were mean spirited, they were not by any means meant personally to harass Ms Burtch or her staff and, hence, should not be defined as cyber-bullying.

Brad's case is no exception. There are hundreds of such incidents being reported in the news globally, involving statements by students about school authorities. Consider Bram's situation for example. Bram took a similar position regarding his freedom of expression rights, and focused less on the libellous connotations of his online 'joke' that he saw his teacher masturbating in the back of the class.

Case 2: Bram's botch-up?

Bram Koch, a student at Willowbrook Public school in Ontario, appeared in a radio interview with his father, David Koch, on a Canadian Broadcasting Corporation Radio One talk show, *The Current* (Findlay, 2007). Bram explained to a national radio audience that he did not realize his joke about his teacher would cause so many problems. Bram wrote a joke about his teacher on a friend's Facebook saying that he had seen her masturbating at the back of the classroom. This was brought to the school administration's attention. Bram was subsequently suspended from participating in a field trip to Montreal with his friends, which he had been excited about attending.

Neither Bram nor Brad thought twice about the possibility that adults might see what they wrote online, both believing it to be a private space for kids. Moreover, both explained that their expressions were just jokes to be shared with friends. Neither boy realized the ramifications or impact of their very public words. Bram admitted that he never thought of this as cyber-bullying.

Moreover, neither boy gave any thought to the possibility that millions of people access Facebook (Jenkins and boyd, 2006; Roher, 2007). Even with the privacy settings on, the comments on their wall are accessible to friends. What their friends make accessible to others who are not part of the original group is where Facebook conversations can move easily from a private domain into a far more public one. Similarly, when photographs are tagged by friends, even if they are within a person's privacy settings, those friends may provide access to many other registered communicators. The posting can spread very quickly to the computer screens of thousands. Moreover, when comments like this are made about authority figures, rumours among school kids circulate faster, motivating hundreds of kids to log-in within minutes, with the specific purpose of reading the comments. It takes only one whistle-blower to report the posting. Alternatively, as more adults, including prospective employers, join Facebook to verify the profiles of applicants, what might have started as a private conversation among friends can become highly public. As both these boys found out, this can lead to a lot of trouble.

Although both boys admitted their jokes were mean-spirited, neither one conceded that the school should have the right to intervene. Both insisted that they really believed they were having private conversations. Bram stated that, although he no longer uses Facebook, he will continue to look for other spaces (presumably online), where he can communicate privately with his friends.

In both cases, the boys were angrier about the school response than ashamed of their comments. They did not seem to care that, when placed in a 'public' forum such as the Internet, their words might be interpreted as undermining school authority, which in turn could impact the school environment and the learning of all students in the classroom.

When asked whether he still attends the teacher's class, Bram said he sits in the back of the classroom and does not look at her. They do not speak at all. I would ask readers to make note of this, because I return to a discussion of how teachers ought to handle such situations, in Chapter 8. In Chapter 6, I also address some of the serious political and systemic influences that in some cases might indirectly fuel negative comments by students. The most difficult aspect for schools, as explained in personal accounts by school administrators, is the deep anger of the teachers. Surprisingly, it is the colleagues of teachers who are not defamed online who express the strongest protests against such speech. Those teachers seem to take up the torch to call for harsher consequences in defence of their demeaned colleagues. There is often a deep sense of injustice, and, as one school administrator who called for advice worried, when the teachers return to school in the fall, they will be 'seeking blood'. This is a major point of concern that I will also deal with in the context of stakeholder relationships and power hierarchies in the upcoming chapter.

Going back to the two boys for a minute, it appears that they were not alone in taking the position that their expression was legitimate. Brad's supporters who carried signs supporting free expression did not believe he did anything wrong. Research suggests that most pre-teens and adolescents would agree. An Ipsos-Reid poll conducted for Microsoft Canada in 2007 found that 70 per cent of respondents aged ten to fourteen said they believe the information they put online is private (Thomas and Canadian Press, 2007). In the United States, there have been similar student protests.

Case 3: Indiana outrage

Similarly, students in Indianapolis publicly protested over suspensions for on-line postings on MySpace. A Fox news report, in usual sensational fashion, reported the following:

> *Indiana Students Outraged Over Schools' Blog Crackdown*
> Increasing crackdowns on what educators deem inappropriate online behaviour have outraged students and free-speech advocates who see them as pursuing school rules too far beyond the classroom.
>
> The battleground is online journals, or blogs, and popular Web sites such as MySpace.com where teens post comments about their daily lives – including school.
>
> School officials say such postings can be disruptive to education; critics say schools should not have the power to punish students for comments posted from a home computer.
>
> 'The school system has no right to sit there and tell us what we can and cannot do at home. They can control what we do at school, but when it gets home, the only people who can tell us what to do is our parents, not the school', said Kayla Wiggington, a 17-year-old junior at Whiteland High School in suburban Indianapolis who uses MySpace to keep in touch with friends.
>
> The school board in the Whiteland-based Clark-Pleasant school district will vote October 17 on a proposed policy that would put students and teachers on notice that they are legally responsible for anything they post online, including material deemed defamatory, obscene, proprietary, or libelous [emphasis added].
>
> (Associated Press, 2006)

The American students, like their Canadian counterparts, also perceived their social networking spaces as their own territory. Cyberspace has become their play space away from adults. They see it as empowering and liberating, and it comes as a shock when they are discovered and punished. They almost feel betrayed and, in many cases, are pushing back with lawsuits, stating their schools have infringed their freedom-of-expression rights by clamping down. Some of these law-suits and court decisions are presented in Chapter 7 as they relate to the debate between free expression and supervision in cyberspace. For now, it is important to recognize young people's mindsets towards cyberspace as their own territory. Ironically, Brad and Bram are not much different from the boys on Golding's island in *Lord of the flies*, who created their own ethical rules in the absence of adult supervision. In addition, as Suler and Phillips (1998) suggest, cyberspace provides a venue for people to express aspects of their personalities that they cannot express in physical spaces. They do this to seek recognition and validation of those spaces. Moreover, these researchers suggest that such expressions are a cathartic form of venting for students whose frustrations are not addressed in physical spaces. The same Fox news story also quoted a school official from a separate school that had also expelled students for writing racial comments about their teachers on MySpace. The school official is quoted as saying 'Kids look at the Internet as today's restroom wall . . . They need to learn that some things are not acceptable anywhere' (Associated Press, 2006).

There is food for thought here. Even as Brad Parson's mother observed, we all said mean things about teachers when we were young. Are the youngsters correct to a certain extent in saying that schools are overreacting? Does it make such a difference that the online expression is open for all to see? If we consider this in the context of smaller communities in the past, before the Internet existed, the writing on the walls of a public washroom might have been perceived to be as humiliating as those in a globally wired community that has grown to infinite proportions.

We need to pay attention to the fact that, although the entire focus of the anti-authority expression has been about how badly behaved the students are, and how this affects their teachers, few accounts or reports have paid attention to the possibility that where there is smoke, there is fire. In some cases, I have been approached by school administrators who have informed me that some of the comments made about the teachers online were fairly accurate and therefore less libellous and defamatory than the teachers made them out to be. This could include comments about a teacher's hygiene; their didactic and disrespectful manner towards students; their inflexible and unreasonable application of rules; their tendency to ignore and marginalize certain students more than others in the classroom; and, in one case, their open admission of being gay or lesbian. Although there is no question that students' statements that accuse teachers of being paedophiles or nymphomaniacs can significantly affect a teacher's reputation, statements about the possibility of teachers' disrespectful attitudes towards students should make teachers reflect on their own behaviour and consider ways in which they might adjust their teaching approaches. I suggest that teachers who are in the profession as committed educators (and there are many), those who are passionate about teaching children, would seize these comments as teachable opportunities instead of taking up a defensive approach. In other words there are degrees of harm that can result from online postings by teens. It is important for teachers to recognize those degrees and act on them accordingly. Truthful (albeit hurtful) student comments might still be turned into opportunities for discussion and dialogue. Discussion of the issues might make a strong contribution to fixing a poisoned environment. As I have asked in the title to Chapter 1, is this a battle or an opportunity? I would argue that these situations provide many opportunities for teachable moments that will help schools move forward to foster school inclusive environments that value mutual respect and trust among students and their faculty.

I proffer that, in some cases where teachers have been cyber-libelled on Facebook or MySpace, there may be underlying frustrations on the part of student that have not been addressed by the teacher. These might then play themselves out through attention-seeking, online comments that help the student feel somewhat vindicated. These situations provided opportunities for teachers and the school administration to consider how they themselves might be contributing to the demeaning behaviour. It does not take a lot of effort to ask students: Are you happy with your learning experience at this school? Are you happy in the classroom? Do you believe the teacher you have defamed has paid sufficient attention to you? Are you unhappy with the way that the teacher communicates with you? Do you feel included or excluded in class discussions? Did something happen between you and the teacher that caused you to react so negatively? Recall the comments of the students I surveyed in the Quebec study reported in Chapter 3. Sixty-two per cent of the students agreed strongly with the statement: 'If adults treated young people more kindly, students would treat each other the same way.' Seventy-one per cent of the students said they were less likely to engage in bullying or cyber-bullying if they were happy at school. Eighty-three per cent said 'I would like to create a more kind and respectful world'. And what were some administrator responses to this?

> Well we tell, we educate them, we tell them what it is, but after that we have to tell them . . . you can come and speak to us, we do have a program if you do, we do have a plan, if we do. But it's a matter of getting, first of all acknowledging there is a problem, educating the kids as to what it is, and then making sure those kids feel comfortable telling staff and admin about what is going on. But it's so new to them and so new to us . . .
>
> (Shariff, 2007)

Administrators always talk about a dependence on a plan or programme. What they lose sight of is that, sometimes, it is not necessary to have a plan. It is simply important, as this administrator said, to acknowledge that there might be a problem. But in doing so, it is critical also to realize that communication with students is a two-way endeavour. Teachers and school officials must begin to recognize that they might be contributing to the problem. If that is the case, no amount of programmes will fix it.

Leaving things suspended in an uncomfortable climate after the incident has been reported and publicized, without talking about it at all in class, as was the case in Bram's situation, does not get to the root of the attention-seeking behaviour. Even though students claim that they consider Facebook to be private, the demeaning comments are in and of themselves attention seeking comments. Pupils might be interested in having only their peers read their concerns (as expressed jokingly), but in other cases, where they are angry enough at their teachers, they might subconsciously want that message to reach the teachers in an indirect way, just as the unruly child behaves badly to get any kind of attention, even if it involves punishment (Suler and Philips, 1998). This cathartic expression empowers students, making up for inadequate feelings they might experience in their relationships with certain teachers. One extreme example is that of Kimver Gill. Kimver Gill had been posting photographs of himself with enormous firearms on a grunge web site, only days before he walked into Dawson College in the heart of Montreal in broad daylight and started shooting at students randomly. It was later determined that Gill had been bullied as a student. Regrettably, those who saw the photographs did not take them seriously or realize that this was a desperate call for help. Gill killed one girl and seriously injured several students before shooting himself and being shot to death by police in the school cafeteria.

In order to be more open to the ways in which students are using the Internet and engaging in digital literacies, it is also important to be aware of the mindsets through which adults tend to approach those tools, compared with the mindsets that young people adopt. Consider what some of the other experts who study technologies and digital literacies have to say on the issue.

Adult mindsets and the digital disconnect

Although most adults use email, Internet and cellphones, they do not rely on them as tools of social communication to the extent that young people do. Such tools are an integral aspect of virtual (and physical) social networks that have emerged among adolescents and youths with the advent of new technologies. Media such as Facebook, MySpace, MSN, SMS, web-blogs, text messaging and bulletin boards have become essentials within the lived realities of young people – much more so than those of adults. Many adults continue to perceive technology as a *means to an end* – a *medium*, whereas, for young people, the *medium is an integral aspect of the message* – a phenomenon that Marshall McLuhan (1964) introduced some years ago. This is why, as *Time* magazine (Chu, 2005) reported recently, teenagers use computers, blackberries and cellphones to communicate, even when their peers or siblings are in the same or neighbouring rooms

Technology has become another normative framework and tool upon which young people rely to communicate with one another. However, virtual spaces are extremely different from physical ones, and as such they generate a new set of social conventions among youths. And yet, from pre-adolescents to university students, young people seem to master the technological tools at their disposal with little or no trouble, whereas adults are generally more technologically challenged, and frequently turn to young people for guidance. Moreover, cyberspace allows for participation by an infinite audience (on public web sites for instance). The world has opened up to children and young people in vastly different ways from what it did for their parents and teachers.

Although more adults are venturing to join social networking groups, I believe their motivations are to understand better the tools, rather than to really enjoy their benefits. Parents and teachers in general rarely use MSN, MySpace or Facebook. This increases the disconnectedness of adults and allows them a superficial understanding of the realm of possibilities. It also limits their appreciation of the potential for knowledge transfer in cyberspace.

Lankshear and Knobel have developed a 'mindset' paradigm that clearly illustrates the differences in the mindsets of most adults and children as they *conceptualize*, use and approach technology. Table 5.1 gives some examples from their comparison of the two paradigms (Lankshear and Knobel, 2006, p. 38).

The mindset paradigm describes the differences in the way that adults (with some exceptions) and most young people have adapted to new technologies depending upon their worldview and mindset. Most adults have mastered email, and computer technologies, but only superficially. They tend to

Table 5.1 Some dimensions of variation between the mindsets

Mindset 1	Mindset 2
The world is much the same as before, only now it is more technologized, or technologized in more sophisticated ways:	The world is very different from before and largely as a result of the emergence and uptake of digital electronic inter-networked technologies:
• The world is appropriately interpreted, understood and responded to in broadly physical-industrial terms	• The world cannot adequately be interpreted, understood and responded to in physical-industrial terms
• Value is a function of scarcity	• Value is a function of dispersion
• Tools are for producing	• Tools are for mediating and relating
• Focus is on individual intelligence	• Focus is on collective intelligence
• Expertise and authority are 'located' in individuals and institutions	• Expertise and authority are distributed and collective; hybrid experts
• Space is enclosed and purpose-specific	• Space is open, continuous and fluid
• Social relations of 'bookspace'; a stable 'textual order'	• Social relations of emerging 'digital media space'; texts in change

Source: Lankshear and Knobel (2006)

conceptualize them from mindset 1 and attempt to accommodate 'it' – what they perceive as 'the' new technology and 'digital literacy' – to their physical world.

Alternatively, as Lankshear and Knobel (ibid.) argue, it is important to understand and approach new technologies and digital literacies as emerging digital media spaces, texts in change (as opposed to the textual order of book space), and a world that focuses on collective intelligences rather than individual intelligence. It opens up a world that provides the tools and media for mediating and relating knowledge rather than simply tools for producing knowledge that can be submerged in orthodoxy and conformity.

Young people have adapted quickly to the cyber-world – a world that cannot be interpreted or responded to in 'physical-industrial' (ibid.) terms but one that enables and accepts collaborative and interactive participation. We have always talked in education about giving students a voice, engaging them in their learning. And yet, now that we have the capabilities (that indeed *they* are opting to use) – the adults in their lives, parents, teachers, school administrators and researchers, feel excluded. We are often held back because of the mindset we adopt. This in turn contributes to a sense of disempowerment, and, for teachers who value their status and authority over that of students, it becomes a crisis.

Richard Lanham (1995) suggests that, under contemporary conditions, the notion of 'literacy' has extended its semantic meaning from that of being able to read and write, to the ability to understand information however presented' (cited in Lankshear and Knobel, 2006, p. 2). This means that digitally literate people must be capable of moving from one kind of medium to another – from text to image to sound and back with fluidity. Lankshear and Knobel explain that the value of digital literacies lies in their ability to help us adapt the message to a range of media that can be used for different audiences.

In the context of schools, it becomes clear that the tendency of school boards is to adopt mindset 1. The immediate reaction is to keep children safe by installing firewalls and block filters as though they were in the physical world (similar to the road blocks, fences and restraints that would work in real space), or ban the use of cellphones, Ipods and social communications networks in the school and sometimes in the home as punishment. The following comments by the school superintendent in the Birchmount School case evidences the mindset towards 'technology' as something that can be controlled as one entity: '[B]ullying using *a new information technology* . . . gives kids way more power than they've had' (School superintendent Anne Kerr, as quoted in Girard and Nguyen 2007).

Levelling the plane of authority and power

Young people adopt mindset 2 and understand the value of digital literacies as *enabling tools – for mediating and relating*. Ultimately, students can easily hack through firewalls – and may seek out the content that schools and parents attempt to censor because of efforts to prevent access. When mindset 2 informs the use of digital literacies, as Lankshear and Knobel observe, expertise and authority are no longer top down, but involve 'collective, hybrid experts' (2006, p. 38). Thus, as they explain, literacy (the ability to read and write) has taken on completely new meanings, such as 'the ability to understand information however presented' (ibid., p. 2). These authors are concerned, however, that once people in positions of authority think they understand digital literacy and apply the 'it' perspective to institutional contexts of learning, they attempt to control, standardize and manipulate the tools, technology and content, as they have done with conventional literacy and the promotion of conformity and orthodoxy:

> Like conventional literacy, digital literacy is being 'schooled' to conform to the logic of manipulative institutions (compulsory consumption of services), and to be made into something manageable at the level of totalizing systems Given space we would run a full argument for cultural practices of computing that parallels [Ivan] Illich's [(1971)] argument for how learning as a cultural practice has been schooled under the logic of manipulative institutions. Indeed, with official constructions of 'digital literacy' cultural practices of computing are actually turned into compulsory, consumption of curricularized and certificated learning.
>
> (Ibid., p. 7)

These experts on new techologies argue in favour of adopting a sociocultural approach to digital literacies instead of an autonomous model. They explain that, according to an autonomous model, literacy consists of skills, tools and techniques, with more of a focus on cognitive competencies and user abilities. The mindset adopted remains the same as that adopted for Western alphabetical literacy – which consists of mastery of letters and phenomena that are coded and printed. They explain further that, unfortunately, when this model is applied to digital literacies, it is too simplistic:

> 'Digital literacy' consists in so many lists of what the abstracted skills and techniques are that a proficient person can 'do.' Once they 'have' them they can then put them to useful purposes in work, at home, at school, etc., and function 'competently.' Courses that set about 'teaching' learners these tools and techniques, and certify them when they are finished (the process is almost precisely the opposite from what, for example, young people do when they set about learning how to play online games and to become part of an online gaming community) . . .
>
> Critique of the autonomous model of literacy from the standpoint of sociocultural theory does not deny that elements of skill and technique are involved in practices of reading and writing. Obviously, they

are necessarily present. The point is, however, that these 'skills' and 'techniques' actually differ in important ways when they are embedded in different practices which involve different purposes and where there are different kinds of meaning at stake (compare, for example, 'searching'). Moreover, the skills and techniques of decoding and encoding do not actually take us very far at all on their own. This is because reading and writing is always 'reading and writing with meaning' and this meaning is not primarily, or even substantially, a function of some 'skill' or 'technique' that might be called 'comprehension.' It is predominantly a function of social practice, social context, and of Discourse (Gee, 1996) in a sense that is very close to Wittenstein's (1953) concept of 'forms of life'.

(Ibid., p. 8)

I find it ironical that, once again, it is the *sociocultural context, value of discourse* and *meaning making* that are overlooked as institutions grapple with adapting to new technologies. This is no different from what we have seen in the physical text book banning controversies (Shariff and Johnny, 2007a). It is no wonder then that when students engage in forms of online discourse defined as 'cyber-bullying', school officials and teachers tend to place the full responsibility on the shoulders of parents, or on behaviour 'problems' with the students.

In adopting the autonomous approach, schools have tended to overlook their obligation, as *educators*, to encourage socially responsible and critically informed dialogue and discourse among students. As we have seen, adults feel lost in cyberspace because their mindset still overwhelmingly resides in the physical world. Hence, when addressing some of the serious emerging issues that concern online harassment, homophobia, death threats, and racial, sexist and homophobic slurs perpetrated by some students against others (which fall under the umbrella of bullying and cyber-bullying), some educators and researchers look for oversimplified and manageable responses. They search for standardized assessment and intervention tools, and evaluation models grounded in their physical world, which they organize into manageable 'buckets', as they search for strategies and national 'blueprints' to control the emerging problems related to cyber-bullying.

For example, at recent advisory meetings on cyber-bullying (PREVNet, 2006), one group of Canadian experts comprised of academics, researchers, school administrators and officials, students and non-governmental organizations (NGOs), were brought together to discuss cyber-bullying. The objective was to understand the problem better, develop policy and plan interventions and programmes to address it in schools. Participants were presented with statements such as 'bullying hurts' and 'bullying is a relationship problem', and asked to consider the cyber-bullying and technology issues within the message of these statements. These 'buckets', or statements, not only ignored the *sociocultural context* and *diversity* in which bullying occurs, but also overlooked the *complexities and range of digital literacies in cyberspace* and their *enabling abilities for mediating and relating*. This approach also ignored the political and systemic hierarchies of power that can develop over time in many schools and greatly impact administrative efforts to foster inclusive, cohesive and collaborative school environments. Ironically, it was primarily the young people seated around the table at the PREVNet meeting who reminded adult experts – the researchers, psychologists, educators and sociologists – that it was important to *reconceptualize* their notions of relationships in cyberspace. The young participants spoke about the possibilities of mediation in cyberspace and most insisted that digital literacies have opened up a world with the potential for positive and interesting social relations. The meeting culminated with the decision to create an online advisory committee, where the young people helped adult scholars and educators navigate through cyberspace. The success of such a committee will largely depend upon the commitment and recognition of a sociocultural dimension by the network leaders.

As Lankshear and Knobel (2006) explain above, the 'it' approach seeks to normalize, manipulate and fit the use of new technologies into a nicely packaged and manageable product that can then be marketed, across the country and internationally, as a 'blueprint' that will help to manage the problem. This is the same conceptual approach that underpinned the overwhelming failure of anti-bullying programmes in the physical school context. Over the last decade, schools were inundated with anti-bullying programmes that were marketed as the 'solution' to all bullying problems. Few were successful because they oversimplified the environmental and biological influences, including systemic forms of racism, sexism, homophobia and ableism (see Anand, 1999; Shariff, 2004; Shariff and LaRocque, 2001). I argue that such an approach yet again represents a form of 'selection' as censorship – where the underlying sociocultural influences and institutional barriers that we have addressed earlier in this book are overlooked as legitimate concerns – whether they occur in the physical school setting or in virtual space.

For the reasons stated above, few adults know how to access or 'supervise' what their students and children are doing on home computers, blackberries and personal cellphones that have text-messaging and photographic capability. Therefore, while young people venture easily into the vast and borderless realm of cyberspace, there are few adult guidelines that help users develop ethical responsibilities, once there.

This loss of 'control' and media framing of the Internet as fraught with dangers invite the desire to regain control through the only means familiar to adults – through punishment and discipline, legalized and 'forceful' means if necessary.

I will address some of the legal considerations in Chapter 7; however, what is preoccupying school authorities to a large degree is the perceived 'war' that young people have apparently waged against authority through online social networking groups. By all appearances, it seems that school authorities perceive this form of 'cyber-bullying', as they have defined it, as disintegrating into a *Lord of the flies* syndrome. I believe Golding was successful in illustrating that humans are territorial, and that there is always an element of society that will take over control to subordinate those who are more vulnerable. In this regard, his message was one about survival of the fittest, and about the way in which power manifests itself under certain conditions. The anti-authority forms of online expression pose a threat to the control that teachers had heretofore exercised over students.

Because 'technology' is understood within an adult mindset to put too much power into the hands of young people, there has been a movement among educators internationally for governments, school boards and teachers' unions to bring in stronger laws and codes of conduct to clamp down on the 'bullies' and avoid the type of anarchy that took hold on Golding's island. Moreover, because 'technology' provides the tools for these forms of bullying, the thrust is to ban and/or manage 'it' to the greatest extent possible by disallowing cellphone, Ipod and laptop use in classrooms and 'banning' access to Facebook and similar networks by withdrawing computer privileges as punishment. It might be instructive to take a look at some of the emerging policies internationally, to assess whether they really do have the 'teeth' to exercise control, and whether they fit the 'clamping down' approach, or whether, in some cases, they might have been developed with a less reactive and more thoughtful and informed approach.

Legal and policy responses: a few examples

As noted earlier, one of the United Kingdom's largest teachers' unions, the Professional Association of Teachers, called for the government to legislate the closing of YouTube because it has attracted many negative postings by students against their teachers (Asthana and Smith, 2007). While the teachers' union works out that censorship 'battle' with UK politicians, it is noteworthy that the United Kingdom already has a very comprehensive and informative web site that specifically informs parents, teachers and other public stakeholders about cyber-bullying, which I detail shortly.

Readers will recall that the response to cyber-bullying in most of the international countries highlighted in Chapter 3 was generally of a positivistic nature. This means that the tendency in many parts of the world is to respond to cyber-bullying or anti-authority online expression through punitive and legalistic means. These can include implementing laws and policies that seek criminal recourse including imprisonment or fines; or civil recourse with compensation under the common law of torts, such as cyber-libel and defamation. I have briefly mentioned legislation and policies implemented or proposed by various countries such as Japan, Singapore, Thailand, India and Australia in Chapter 3. For the remainder of this chapter, I would like to highlight some of the law and policy responses that are emerging in Western democracies.

European Union

At the European level, although cyber safety of children appears to be an important topic, action seems to be currently confined to research. Interestingly enough, the EU encourages legal action by nation states. This is most likely owing to issues of sovereignty and respecting cultural differences as Europe deals with an increasing influx of immigrants and refugees from its previous colonies. Although England has not legislated specifically on the issue of cyber-bullying, there is existing legislation under which it is believed charges could be brought. In France, an existing bill on juvenile delinquency has been amended specifically to deal with the problem of 'happy slapping'.[4]

Council of Europe

The Council of Europe media division (human rights: protecting media freedoms) has sponsored the production of an Internet literacy handbook. This handbook contains a fact sheet on bullying and harassment, that addresses how cyber-bullying and harassment are to be dealt with at school and at home. Under the heading 'Safety and ethical issues', the fact sheet proposes an approach that includes: conflict resolution as part of school curriculum, training staff and students to deal with instances of bullying, provision of positive support to both the students who are targeted and the students who are exhibiting such abusive behaviour, and the implementation of acceptable use policies (AUPs) to monitor how the Internet is used in schools. It also suggests classroom activities such as role-playing activities and discussion groups to deal with cyber-bullying issues, and provides best practice instructions for students. The fact sheet on mobile technology also mentions the growing concern about mobile bullying, specifically, 'happy slapping'.

Council of Europe draft convention on cyber crime

There is a lot of commentary on the flaws of this document (European Committee on Crime Problems, 2001), which could be used to predict the difficulties that would be encountered trying to deal with cyber-bullying at an international level. Criticisms largely centre on the fact that it focuses solely on law enforcement and is seen as detrimental to civil liberties and industry interests. Also, the goal to attain consistency in legislation on cyber-crime among signatory states has led to vague and ambiguous wording in the convention. It is also notable that, although 'cyber-crime' is not explicitly defined in the convention, it does not seem, in this context, to include cyber-harassment, cyber-stalking or cyber-bullying, addressing only computer-related forgery and fraud. The only article that addresses the well-being of children is article 9, 'Offences related to child pornography'.

European Commission (EU): Europe's information society: public consultation on safer Internet and online technologies for children

The European Commission is investigating the harm mobile phones do to young children, including: exposure to inappropriate content, expense, bullying and sexual predators. The Commission mentions bullying 'through the distribution of abusive or compromising messages and photos amongst children as a particular concern'. It was found in May 2006 that 70 per cent of European children aged twelve to thirteen had mobile phones, as did 23 per cent of eight-to nine-year-olds (Out-Law News 2006). The Commission has launched a public consultation with the aim of identifying the most effective way of making the Internet and other communication technologies safer for children. The return date for questionnaires was 7 June 2007, and these are most likely being analysed at present. In the introductory information to the questionnaire, it is mentioned that children may be exposed to harmful content and conduct, such as bullying and harassment, on the Internet. Interestingly, it also mentions that, as the Internet is the primary channel for the distribution of evidence of sexual abuse of children, children themselves may face serious legal consequences for the distribution of such material. It is acknowledged that means of addressing the risks involved with online technology use can involve many actors, at many different levels, including public administration in member states, childcare organizations, the technology industry, financial institutions, schools, parents and the European Commission. The European Commission has already implemented a succession of safer Internet programmes, the most recent of which, 'Safer Internet plus', will end in 2008.

Safer Internet plus programme

The current programme (2005–8) (European Commission, 2007b) established by decision no. 854/2005/EC of the European Parliament, has four main aims: fighting against illegal content; tackling unwanted and harmful content; promoting a safer environment; and awareness-raising. The fact-sheet (European Commission, 2007c) defines harmful content as 'any content that teachers, parents, or other adults responsible for children, think is harmful to them . . .'. The report notes that definitions vary from one culture – and one person – to the next. This highlights one of the major difficulties attached to international action against cyber-bullying, respecting cultural differences, and yet this, I would argue, is the most important aspect of the response. It is encouraging that the EU is taking into account the contextual (personal and cultural) differences in conceptualizing its policy approaches.

The fact-sheet also states that, although the EU has set standards and clarified many legal issues, Internet issues cannot be tackled by law alone and are generally far greater than parents realize. Concerted action is needed as greater access to broadband Internet and third generation (3G) (Internet) mobile phones is becoming common. *Emphasis is placed on education of parents and children, with action at member state level essential, but stimulated and encouraged by the EU.* This approach is commonly taken by the EU towards controversial topics (subsidiarity). In order to respect sovereignty and cultural differences, the Union puts vague guidelines in place and allows the individual member states to implement the suggestions as they see fit. Ironically, in the case of the Internet and cyber-bullying, this approach runs into immediate problems, as the Internet does not respect sovereign borders. An important aspect of this programme is that it has a wide scope covering diverse technologies such as 3G phones, online games, chat rooms, instant messaging, peer-to-peer file transfer and also diverse content, including racism and violence. The drafters of the programme name networks of civilian hotlines as essential to combating cyber-bullying, as many people are wary of contacting the police. The safer Internet plus programme currently funds a project called EU Kids Online (European Commission). The project, which will run from 2006 to 2009, will examine research carried out in eighteen member states into how children use the Internet and new media. It aims to evaluate the social, cultural and regulatory influences affecting both risks and parents' and children's responses to them. One of its main aims is to examine methodological issues relating to cross-cultural analysis in order to establish best practice guidelines for research on children's Internet use. The web site has a data repository of empirical research projects concerning children and the Internet in Europe and encourages contact from other researchers working in the same area, as well as publishing a biannual newsletter.[5]

Legislation in France

In March, the French government signed into law a bill amending previous delinquency laws, with the purpose of criminalizing 'happy slapping' (Wikipedia, 2007c). As I described in Chapter 3, happy slapping involves a physical attack on an unsuspecting victim, which an accomplice tapes, usually with a videophone, and then disseminates by mobile phone or on the Internet. Article 44 of the bill,[6] equates the filming or photographing of certain violent crimes with being an accomplice to that crime, and creates a new felony for the broadcasting of such crimes. This law has been criticized by civil rights groups as inhibiting people from recording incidents of police brutality or engaging in civilian journalism. This approach, unlike that mentioned below in the United Kingdom, addresses the harm caused by the *filming* and dissemination of such videos and not simply the harm *caused by the assault* in question. This approach is not significantly different from the Canadian school approach that took issue with the filming of a beating and punished the camera person, instead of focusing on the beating itself (see Chapter 2).

British responses[7]

As noted in Chaper 3, happy slapping is believed to have originated in London, England, as part of the garage music scene. Although there is no legislation specifically dealing with it as in France, assault charges have been laid in certain cases. In the case of the sixteen-year-old girl who was seriously assaulted on her way home from school and the incident filmed and posted online, it is worth again pointing out that, despite the fact that a huge amount of the distress the victim suffered was due to the video being shown to her peers at school, a school spokesman was quoted as saying simply 'This is a police matter which happened outside school' (BBC News Online, 2005). When dealing with the Internet and 3G mobile phone technology, which is accessible by students both during and outside school time, such an approach does not begin to deal with the problem.

Don't suffer in silence web site

There has been considerable work done in the United Kingdom however, to address bullying and cyber-bullying. The government has published very comprehensive guidelines for schools dealing with cyber-bullying accessible at this web site, called 'Don't suffer in silence' (Department for Children, Schools and Families, 2007), which offers extensive information for children, parents and school staff about cyber-bullying, including links to many other web sites on the topic. Under the heading 'what can you do about it?', it states, 'The law is on your side', and that the Protection from Harassment Act, the Malicious Communications Act 1988 and section 43 of the Telecommunications Act may be used to combat cyber-bullying. A link is provided to a web site called 'Wired safety', one page of which provides information on British law relating to cyber-stalking and harassment (WiredSafety, no date).

Under section 1 of the Malicious Communications Act 1998, it is an offence to send an indecent, offensive or threatening letter, electronic communication or other article to another person, and, under section 43 of the Telecommunications Act 1984, it is a similar offence to send a telephone message that is indecent, offensive or threatening. In both cases, the offence is punishable with up to six months imprisonment and/or a fine of up to £5,000. Because the malicious communications offence is wider ranging than the telecommunications offence, it is more likely to be used by the police than the Telecommunications Act offence.

In most cases involving malicious communications or cyber-stalking, however, there will be more than one offensive or threatening letter or telephone call, and therefore the police will often choose to charge the offender with an offence contrary to section 2 of the Protection from Harassment Act 1997, also punishable with up to six months imprisonment. Part of the reason for using this charge is that, when someone is convicted of an offence under the Protection from Harassment Act 1997, the court can make a restraining order preventing him or her from contacting their victim again. Breach of a restraining order is punishable with up to five years' imprisonment. A restraining order cannot be imposed for a conviction under the Malicious Communications or Telecommunications Acts.

If the emails, cyber-stalking and other forms of harassment that come under cyber-bullying cause victims to fear that violence will be used against them, then the police can choose to charge the offender with an offence contrary to section 4 of the Protection from Harassment Act 1997, which is punishable with up to five years' imprisonment and also allows the court to make a restraining order.

If the emails, cyber-stalking and other forms of cyber-bullying are racist in nature or motivated by religious hostility, then charges of 'racially or religiously aggravated harassment' contrary to sections 32(1)(a) or 32(1)(b) of the Crime and Disorder Act 1998 can be brought against the perpetrators. If convicted, offenders could face up to seven years' imprisonment.

In many situations, the recipient of malicious messages knows who the sender is. It may be a former partner or a relative, which may mean that the victim is reluctant to involve the police. In those circumstances, the victim could consider taking out an injunction under section 3 of the Protection from Harassment Act 1997. However, the web site advises readers always to inform the police, especially if the messages are in any way threatening. Even if the police decide not to prosecute, they may give the offender a formal warning, which could be used in evidence if perpetrators repeated their behaviour in the future.

In addition to criminal prosecutions, victims of harassment can sue the offender under section 3 of the Protection from Harassment Act 1997 for damages arising out of the anxiety caused by the harassment and any financial loss it caused.

The UK web site does not make mention of any cases that have been filed under these forms of legislation in the context of cyber-bullying. The focus of the various applicable legislative frames referred to on the UK web site is largely punitive. Nonetheless, the web site contains some important educational information for parents, teachers, students and other stakeholders. For example, it urges parents and young people to work together to prevent and 'tackle' it whenever it occurs. Some of the advice for various stakeholders contained on the site provides that school governors and head teachers have a duty to ensure that they include bullying via mobile phone and Internet in their mandatory anti-bullying policies, that these policies are regularly updated and that teachers have sufficient knowledge to deal with cyber-bullying in schools. Significantly, the policy guidelines recommend that:

- all e-communications used on the school site or as part of school activities off-site are monitored;

- clear policies are set about the use of mobile phones at school and at other times when young people are under the school's authority;
- Internet blocking technologies are continually updated and harmful sites blocked;
- the school works with pupils and parents to make sure new communications technologies are used safely, taking account of local and national guidance and good practice;
- security systems are in place to prevent images and information about pupils and staff being accessed improperly from outside school;
- the school works with police and other partners on managing cyber-bullying;
- the school provides accessible information, advice and support for students who need it.

The site also recommends the Becta schools e-safety site (Becta, 2007), which has some excellent suggestions for the development of AUPs in schools.

What I like best about Becta's suggestions is that creating a safe ICT learning environment must include 'an infrastructure of whole-school awareness, designated responsibilities, policies and procedures; an effective range of technological tools; and a comprehensive Internet safety education programme for the whole school community' (ibid.). The Becta policy guideline suggests three basic components:

1 Raising awareness of the issues and how they impact the particular school environment and the pupils within particular schools. They suggest awareness can be raised, in part, by a comprehensive Internet safety programme for the entire school community. Importantly, the guidelines suggest that the programme should be continuous. Although it should respond to specific incidents and issues, it should also provide information about emerging technologies, as well as those already embedded within the culture of the school.

2 The second priority is to establish a clear understanding of the responsibilities of all stakeholders involved in the education of children and young people with regard to Internet safety. This includes head teachers and school principals, governing bodies such as school boards, administrators, classroom teachers, school counsellors, librarians and parents, and of course the pupils themselves.

3 The third priority involves an 'infrastructure of effective policies and procedures' described as the 'backbone to effective practice'. AUPs should detail the ways in which the ICT facilities can and cannot be used in school by both pupils and staff. These documents should contain a list of consistent sanctions, procedures and support strategies for dealing with misuse. Although these strategies would include management documents, staff

use agreements, student and parent use agreements, policies for educating staff and students on Internet safety issues, and specific procedures for misuse, an important consideration is that the policies 'need to balance the desirability of fully exploiting the vast educational potential of new technologies with providing safeguards against risks and unacceptable material and activities'.

Although the policy guidelines recommend wide-ranging coverage of fixed and mobile Internet technologies, those provided by the school (such as PCs, laptops, webcams and digital video equipment) and technologies owned by students and staff that are brought onto school property, such as mobile phones, camera phones, personal digital assistants (PDAs) and media players, *they should also recognize the important educational benefits of such tools.* Most importantly, the Becta guidelines recommend attention to the following:

> Remember, also, that an effective Internet safety policy needs to be tailored to the individual needs of your school . . . Your policy must consider the particular circumstances of your school, such as race, gender, ethnicity and religious beliefs of pupils and staff, and factors such as the digital divide and access to ICT outside school, which may all have an impact upon the ways in which children and young people use the Internet, and the types of potentially risky behaviours they engage in. It is not sufficient to merely take a template and insert your school name – the policy will lack ownership and authority, and may leave your school open to risk . . . To be truly effective, all school Internet safety policies need to be regularly reviewed with all stakeholders and updated to take account of new and emerging technologies and changes in local circumstances.
> Ideally, school Internet safety policies should be embedded within a cycle of establishment, maintenance, ongoing review, modification, report-ing and annual review, supported by technological solutions wherever possible. By following this process, schools can ensure that they have a rigorous and effective Internet safety program in place.
>
> (Becta, 2007)

These are important recommendations, because research found that the poor success of traditional anti-bullying programmes and policies was due to the lack of attention to individual differences within schools. Blanket anti-bullying programmes and policies were implemented without attention to cultural contexts, demographics, economic influences and so on, with the result that they did little to address the concerns or motivations of the students who perpetrated bullying (Anand, 1999; DiGiulio, 2001).

Although it is not within the scope of this book to go through everything in the British government web site for parents, teachers and other stakeholders, the site is well worth a visit and, I would argue, well advanced compared with the EU and North American responses as far as comprehensive information and policy guidelines are concerned, as I will demonstrate shortly. And yet, the United Kingdom's teachers' unions are loudly calling for the banning of YouTube. Although I have not attempted to determine whether the government web site is accessed by many teachers in the United Kingdom, it would be worth exploring the extent to which this site has been marketed to educators and parents – how many know about it and use its resources, and the extent to which schools are actually using it to develop their policies to address cyber-bullying in the United Kingdom. It is important to find out whether the tax-payers' money spent by the government on this web site is successful in creating awareness and providing comprehensive education to UK schools and parents. How many parents and students are accessing this web site, and how often?

Among many valuable contributions that the policy guidelines make is a repeated emphasis that addressing cyber-bullying must be *contextual*, taking into account a range of complex factors and the roles and responsibilities of all stakeholders in the school community. In other words, dealing with issues of cyber-bullying in the school context involves much more than getting rid of one social networking tool, such as YouTube or Facebook because ten or twenty more will surface within a week of the closure. Finding a balance through education and learning how to take advantage of the enormous learning potential that comes with ever evolving new technologies must be incorporated into proactive policy and practice responses in schools. Others are urging YouTube and similar sites to monitor and immediately take down the demeaning videos of teachers and student victims as soon as they are posted online (Goff, 2007). This is easier said than done, because of the lack of clout of content monitoring laws and policies discussed in Chapter 7. Although ISP providers, YouTube, MySpace and Facebook are beginning to remove some forms of expression upon request, how quickly they are removed depends upon the nature and degree of the postings. Pornographic, racist, and homophobic postings and films of rape and murder or altered photographs of people in sexual positions that are clearly criminal in nature are generally taken down quickly. Others remain online for long periods of time until the harmful nature is assessed (Roher, 1997).

As far as cellular mobile phone companies are concerned, they too are not generally obliged by law to implement their policies immediately. The appendices to this book contain sample cellular phone company policies. NetSafe, a New Zealand organization that has successfully engaged govern-ment, parents, community based organizations, law enforcement officers and students to come up with a range of policy and practice responses, has also been successful in convincing mobile cellular phone companies to get in touch with parents after about four complaints have been received regarding negative forms of expression that emanate from young people's mobile phones.

Criminology perspectives

Although numerous criminologists and social scientists have documented the threat of online victimization for young people[8] and, internationally, governments and private organizations have attempted to reduce the problem with various programmes and legislation,[9] very few empirical examinations of these programmes demonstrate conclusive evidence of what is effective.

Given that the content of the more recent postings on social networking tools have bordered on pornography and criminal threats, it is worth looking at what criminologists are saying about policy responses to these behaviours. According to Eck (2002), situational or 'place-based' cyber-crime (or bullying for our purposes) prevention strategies are successful, if they are applied in the same way as placing police patrols in certain traffic areas or neighbourhoods. She argues that, rather than attempting to alter the *behaviour* of perpetrators, the purpose of situational crime prevention strategies is to *block the opportunity of committing a crime*, by focusing on actions in context that occur under certain situations. Place-based tactics can be more influential in reducing victimization than 'offender-based' plans, because they pay more attention to immediate situations. Referred to as place improvement processes these types of plan are known for reducing potentially criminal actions because they reduce the attractiveness of committing a crime in certain areas, it is suggested (Brantingham and Brantingham, 1995). Put simply, these criminologists argue for a preventative approach. Criminologists also talk about 'target hardening', which involves a range of security measures to keep away predators or cyber-perpetrators, such as digital locks, passwords and controls set by parents or guardians. They suggest that target hardening not only keeps motivated offenders out of certain areas used by young people, but also provides a 'guardianship' component to restrict young people from accessing areas deemed inappropriate for their viewing.

Based on the large amount of support found for routine activities theory when exploring crime and preventative measures[10] new strategic measures that are developed under the same theoretical basis should work. Programmes that increase guardianship while decreasing target suitability (i.e. digital locks and protections), as well as detering the motivated offender from approaching young people online, would be expected to decrease the likelihood of victimization. Hence, the emerging perspective from these criminologists is that, much like initiatives to make parks and playgrounds safe for our children, we need to make our children's cyber-playground a safer place to play. The key point here is that children should still be allowed to play without being overly supervised. Online blocking should not be so restrictive as to reduce the benefits of online learning.

One example of this type of legislation is a proposed American bill entitled the Deleting Online Predators Act 2006 (Wikipedia, 2007d). This proposed bill has invited a significant amount of controversy because of what some academics argue are extreme forms of censorship of educational content that could be accessed by students online in libraries and schools and from home computers. The arguments around the bill are worth considering for the purposes of looking at what types of 'target hardening' measure are reasonable and which simply amount to censorship.

Deleting Online Predators Act (2006 – H.R.5319 – 'DOPA')

In May 2006, a Republican Pennsylvania representative, Mike Fitzpatrick, introduced the above bill to the United States House of Representatives, with a view to protecting children who use the Internet from online predators. However, there are serious concerns that, if enacted, the bill would censor the autonomy of school teachers and librarians to determine which web sites are safe, and place it in the hands of a government-appointed commission. The bill's broad definition of 'social networking web sites' can include Facebook (www.facebook.com/), MySpace (www.myspace.com/) and YouTube (www.you tube.com/), as well as Wikipedia (http://en.wikipedia.org/wiki/Main_Page), Yahoo (www.yahoo.com/), Amazon (www.amazon.com/) and other informative web sites as well as offending ones. The proposed bill amends the Communications Act of 1934 (Wikipedia, 2007e). Wikipedia reports that similar bills to ban or restrict access to social networking sites have been introduced in Georgia, North Carolina. These bills would impose criminal penalties on any social communications network that allowed children to join the chat room or communications network without parental consent. When consent is granted, the web site would also be required to give parents full access to it. Oklahoma's House Bill 1715 (State of Oklahoma, 2007)[11] would require schools and libraries to block access to the Internet in its entirety for minors who do not have consent. Similarly, the Illinois Social Networking Prohibition Act (State of Illinois, 2007)[12] would require all public libraries and schools to block access to any social networking site for users of all ages. These proposed state bills are consistent with the recent demands made by teachers' unions in the United Kingdom and, to a lesser extent, in Canada. According to Wikipedia, the original legislation on 'commercial social networking web sites' was much less restrictive and defined these sites as follows:

Sec. 2(c) (J) A commercially operated Internet web site that:

(i)   that allows users to create web pages or profiles that provide information about themselves and are available to other users; and

(ii) offers a mechanism for communication with other users, such as a forum, chat room, email, or instant messenger.

(Wikipedia, 2007d)

'Chat rooms' were defined as:

> Sec. 2(c) (K) Internet web sites through which a number of users can communicate in real time via text and that allow messages to be almost immediately visible to all other users or to a designated segment of all other users.
>
> (Ibid.)

Popular web sites that fit this definition include MySpace and Facebook. According to Wikipedia, however, this definition could also include a range of other informative and commercial web sites such as Amazon.com and Yahoo.[13] The proposed DOPA bill has been amended to read:

> (J) COMMERCIAL SOCIAL NETWORKING WEB SITES; CHAT ROOMS Within 120 days after the date of enactment of the Deleting Online Predators Act of 2006, the Commission shall by rule define the terms 'social networking web site' and 'chat room' for purposes of this subsection. In determining the definition of a social networking web site, the Commission shall take into consideration the extent to which a web site:
>
> (i) is offered by a commercial entity;
> (ii) permits registered users to create an online profile that includes detailed personal information;
> (iii) permits registered users to create an online journal and share such a journal with other users;
> (iv) elicits highly-personalized information from user; and
> (v) enables communication among users.
>
> (Wikipedia, 2007d)

This new language allows a federal communications commission to define the terms, and this might mean that it could even restrict web sites such as Wikipedia. Wikipedia reports that, although people on both sides of the debate are in favour of blocking online predators, the larger controversy relates to the effectiveness and drawbacks of the measures being taken by the legislation. The greatest concern involves censorship of professional autonomy.

Wikipedia lists the arguments presented by both sides of the debate. The republican senator, Michael Fitzpatrick, and his supporters argue that the Internet is taking over at a 'dizzying pace' and that he as a parent has serious concerns about dangerous predators. The bill's proponents argue that the Internet makes children comfortable talking to strangers, which is dangerous, hence the need to restrict chat rooms and online social networks.

Opponents of the bill have focused on efforts to revise it to address directly the problem of online predators and prevent blocking of harmless and/or educational web sites. As representative Bart Stupak summarized: 'Unfortunately, child predators are not the target of today's bill. This will not delete online predators. Rather, it will delete legitimate web content from schools and libraries' (Wikipedia, 2007d).

Henry Jenkins (co-director of the comparative media studies program at MIT) and danah boyd, an academic who has done doctoral work to examine how young people use the Internet (both referenced in Chapter 4), were interviewed in May 2006 and asked to provide their opinions on DOPA (Wright, 2006).

According to boyd, the proposed law would extend current regulations that require all federally funded schools and libraries to deploy Internet filters. She noted that the law is so broadly defined that it would limit access to any commercial site that allows users to create a profile and communicate with strangers. Although the partial intent of the legislation is to target MySpace, it would also block numerous other sites, including blogging tools, mailing lists, video and podcast sites, photo sharing sites and educational sites such as NeoPets.

Professor Jenkins agreed with boyd and explained that, in theory, the bill would allow schools to disable these filters for use in educationally specified contexts, yet, in practice, most schools would simply lock down their computers and walk away because of the fear of being charged or fined under this legislation. Jenkins believes that teachers who want to exploit the educational benefits of these tools would face increased scrutiny and pressure to discontinue these practices, and students would lack the ability to explore these resources through independent research or social activities. Moreover, as some of the surveys presented earlier have found, economic status reduces access to technologies because of a lack of affordability in the home. These students are generally left far behind in their learning and ability to function in a world that thrives on technology use. Because of its restrictions on library and school use, this legislation would cut off any possibility for teens who do not have access to computers at home, and would reduce their extended sphere of social contacts outside the school and home.

Moreover, as boyd observed, most major technology companies are moving in the direction of social software, using social features to help users find information, get recommendations and share ideas. All of this would be restricted. Importantly, she argued that the assumptions that underlie the proposed legislation are flawed, because proponents assume that nothing good can be achieved through participation in social networking sites. It would not be surprising to find that none of the proponents has ever signed up to the sites and really examined the potential that can be achieved. The underpinnings of the legislation therefore are clearly rooted in the adult mindsets, as presented in the paradigmatic approaches to technologies presented by Lankshear and Knobel (2006). As an example of the restrictions that would occur even if the legislation was limited to MySpace, boyd noted that many high school students currently contact college students through MySpace to learn about their colleges and universities and decide whether or not to apply. They develop mentorship relationships that would be prohibited by DOPA. Professor Jenkins put this into further perspective:

> Suppose, for the sake of argument, that MySpace critics are correct and that MySpace is, in fact, exposing large numbers of teens to high-risk situations, then shouldn't the role of educational institutions be to help those teens understand those risks and develop strategies for dealing with them? Wouldn't we be better off having teens engage with MySpace in the context of supervision from knowledgeable and informed adults? Historically, we taught children what to do when a stranger telephoned them when their parents were away; surely, we should be able to teach them how to manage the presentation of their selves in digital spaces. The proposed federal legislation does nothing to help kids confront the challenges of interacting with online social communities; rather, *it allows teachers and librarians to abdicate their responsibility to educate young people about what is becoming a significant aspect of their everyday lives. Our responsibilities as educators should be to bring reason to bear on situations which are wrought with ignorance and fear, not to hide our eyes from troubling aspects of teen culture* [emphasis added].
>
> (Wright, 2006)

When compared with the policy guidelines that are instead recommended on the British web site on cyber-bullying, one can see clearly the difference between policy-making mindsets that are rooted in ignorance and fear, and those that can be comprehensively and thoughtfully applied so that the educational benefits of technology use are not compromised.

Going back to DOPA, in its descriptions of various web sites, Wikipedia explains that many allow public user profiles and provide forums. Examples include Yahoo, Amazon.com, Slashdot, RedState, CNET Networks and thousands of others. This potentially qualifies them as social networking web sites, regardless of the content within the web sites. Consider further some of the educational uses for such sites.

Educational use

According to Wikipedia, most American school libraries already have filters on incoming Internet access owing to the Children's Internet Protection Act (CIPA) (Wikipedia, 2007f). Opponents of the bill argue that the language of the bill would simply extend such filtering to include web sites based on specific technologies rather than specific content, including web sites based on those technologies that are used for educational purposes. Some educators have incorporated blogs and Wikis into classroom lessons for students owing to their usefulness as a critiquing and editing tool for students' work and as a forum for comments and suggestions by teachers and other students. These educators also favour such technologies because they enable discussion outside the classroom that can involve students and teachers as well as parents. Here are some examples provided on Wikipedia relating to the educational benefits of such technologies:

> Will Richardson, a teacher in New Jersey, set up a blog for student discussion of The Secret Life of Bees and invited author Sue Monk Kidd to join the chat. She was able to answer the students' questions about the book and give more insight than the teacher alone would have been capable. A separate blog was set up to allow parents to discuss the book in parallel with the students.
>
> Some school administrators are using blogs to communicate news and information about events to parents and students. The homepage for the Meriweather Lewis Elementary School in Oregon is updated with notes from the PTA. The principal and teachers are using blogging software and RSS to allow parents and students to view up-to-date information from the school.
>
> The Pawtucket Public Library in Pawtucket, Rhode Island is one of a number of public libraries that have created their own MySpace profile webpage. These libraries are attempting to communicate with young adult patrons more effectively through the use of online methods to which young adults are becoming accustomed.
>
> The Bering Strait School District relies heavily on a MediaWiki-driven curriculum content system. The district's Open Source student information system, DART, links its teachers and students directly to wiki content, as well as many RSS fed district resources, podcasts and vod-casts. Students have contributed many of the wiki's 4800 or so pages for academic credit during school hours. DART tells them what their key weaknesses are, and links to the resources they need to help master those curriculum standards.
>
> The bill would allow minors strictly limited access to those sites. For schools, access would be allowed only with adult supervision *and* if the site is being used for an educational purpose. For libraries, access would be allowed only if parental authorization is given and the parents are informed that 'sexual predators can use these web sites and chat rooms to prey on children'.
>
> (Wikipedia, 2007d)

So once again, rather than educating parents about the educational potential of such tools, the legislation would further enhance their fear of online predators just waiting to ensnare their kids online.

Library support for online education

The American Library Association (ALA), generally a strong opponent of censorship involving books and literature, is also against introduction of the DOPA legislation, asking its members to oppose the bill. According to the association's former president, Michael Gorman: 'We know that the best way to protect children is to teach them to guard their privacy and make wise choices. To this end, libraries across the country offer instruction on safe Internet use' (Wikipedia, 2007d). On 11 July 2006, the executive director of the Young Adult Library Services Association (YALSA), Beth Yoke, testified before the subcommittee on telecommunications and the Internet under the committee on energy and commerce. She defined the ALA and YALSA combined stance on the issue by saying:

> Youth librarians believe, and more importantly know from experience, that education about safe Internet practices – for both youth *and* parents – is the best way to protect young people. We believe that the overly broad technological controls that would be required under DOPA are often ineffective given the fast-moving nature of modern technology. Further, such technological controls often inadvertently obstruct access to beneficial sites. In essence, we believe that this legislation will lead to the blocking of essential and beneficial Interactive Web applications and will further widen the digital divide.
>
> (Wikipedia, 2007d)

As with the teachers, DOPA would censor librarians' professional autonomy and local support from library trustees, elected school boards and community members, and place it in the hands of federal commissioners who would haven no background or knowledge about the communities in which the libraries were situated.

It is important to emphasize again the lack of attention to *context* by this American bill, and to note how this is a completely different approach from that adopted by the policy guidelines in the UK Becta web site. The UK web site focuses on the local context and environment in addressing cyber-bullying and crime, which makes much more sense. Opponents of DOPA argue that this federal action could degrade the authority of those responsible for safe use of the libraries, whereas up to 80 per cent of the funding for the library or school is locally derived (Wikipedia, 2007d).

Opponents of the bill have argued that the research presented by Rep. Michael Fitzpatrick in support of the bill had found only two cases of rape/sexual assault through Internet solicitations in two surveys covering 3,001 children between the ages of ten to seventeen. Wikipedia reports that, overall, a youth Internet safety survey suggested that the number of children being sexually solicited online in 2005 compared with 1999 is reduced. This suggests that Internet users are becoming more savvy in avoiding such solicitations. Children between the ages of ten to seventeen however, are being harassed and bullied more by their peers and not by strangers.

Canadian responses

In the next chapter I discuss at some length a resolution that has been drafted by the Canadian Teachers' Federation to develop policy responses to cyber-bullying (especially the anti-authority forms emerging on social networking sites). As far as existing legislation is concerned, education in Canada comes under provincial jurisdiction. Ontario has been the most active province in bringing in legislation to address bullying, when it created the controversial Safe Schools Act in 2000. The act gave teachers discretionary power to suspend students indefinitely until a board of trustees could meet and decide on whether they should be expelled. This raised serious concerns among parents as to how this would affect students' education in the meantime. The Act was then embedded into the Ontario Education Act which has recently been amended yet again, to address the outcry by teachers and school administrators about the anti-authority forms of cyber-bullying on social networking sites. Bill 212 of the Education Amendment Act dated 16 April 2007 at a first reading, stated:

> A principal shall consider whether to suspend if he or she believes that the pupil has engaged in any of the following activities while at school, at a school-related activity *or in other circumstances where engaging in the activity will have an impact on the school climate* [emphasis added].
>
> (Roher, 2007)

This section is sufficiently broad as to cover the expressions about teachers on Facebook and similar networking tools. Interestingly, although the amended Act also adds 'bullying' as allowing for suspension (and not expulsion), there is no specific reference to 'cyber-bullying'. Legal experts (Flynn, 2007) suggest this might be owing to the controversial issues raised by the student protests against infringement of their freedom of expression when schools suspend them for what they perceive as 'private' conversations among friends.

Conclusion

In Chapter 7 I will discuss some of the court decisions at established and emerging common law that clarifies the boundaries in this regard to some extent. The irony of the amendment to the Ontario Education Act is that, although the minister of education, Kathleen Wynne, made public announcements stating that the government wants to move away from a zero-tolerance approach, the same government has instituted legislation that supports suspensions for bullying. School suspensions are generally informed by zero-tolerance perspectives. The legislation is not grounded in educational pedagogy. Wynn is reported as saying: 'I want to bring some students together and I want to start talking to kids about what's going on in their lives and their perceptions to cyber-bullying and technology' (Canadian Press, 2007). Her comments beg the question that, if the Ministry was so keen on hearing the youth perspective, would it not have been better to hear what they had to say first, before implementing the amendments to the legislation?

Moreover, as I have noted, the legislation is broad enough to allow sufficient discretion on the part of educators who see value in suspending students for activities that will impact the school climate. As with the proposed DOPA legislation in the United States and the EU legislation that has come under criticism for infringing civil liberties, the assumptions that underpin the Ontario legislation are grounded in the belief that there is no educational value to be gained from discussing online anti-authority forms of expression with students. Similar assumptions underlie a municipal by-law in another Canadian province, Saskatchewan, where the Regina City Council decided to 'take aim at bullying' as the media put it, by allowing fines of up to $2,000 for bullying in public or cyberspaces. The by-law also makes it a criminal offence to take pictures or video-tapes of a fight and post it online (CBC News, 2006). Students under the age of twelve are not subject to the by-law, and, in cases involving youths between twelve and sixteen, parents are required to pay the fine.

In this chapter I have presented two very different responses (UK policies and DOPA legislation), to illustrate the ways in which stakeholders within school communities can either be empowered to work collaboratively to find solutions together (the United Kingdom), or how the local stakeholder autonomy of educational professionals, librarians, school boards and those who understand their communities can be withdrawn. These local forms of autonomy can be replaced by broad powers that are placed in the hands of government officials who censor from a distance (DOPA).

I have also explained that adults compare their children's lives with their own experiences of growing up – which were very different from children's life experiences today. The mindset that adults bring to technologies, online learning and online-social networking among young people is very much akin to Plato's metaphor of the cave. Those who have read Plato's *Republic* (1987) will recall the story of a group of men who were chained in a cave. They faced only one wall of the cave for most of their lives, where the only changes they saw were the shapes of their own shadows shifting with the light of a fire behind them. Release from the cave into daylight, with all its light, colour and visions, would be overwhelming for those cavemen. The conflict would be greater if only a few of the men escape and learn how to function in the outside world. When they return to the cave, they can never adjust to the former rules and power relationships, and those who were formerly in control would naturally have difficulty understanding how and why the power shifts occurred.

Likewise, the Internet, with its rapid growth and infinite capabilities, can be overwhelming for those who are not proficient in its use. This is a stage in modernity, as Jenkins (Jenkins and boyd, 2006) observes, that will pass, as the next generation growing up with technologies become adults. Our young are the cavemen who got away – and learned how to live in the 'real' world (which now requires an adjustment to cyberspace). By the time they grow up, the Internet and related technologies will be an integral part of their lives, social communication and learning. But, in the meantime, we need to address the bungles of the men in the cave who are just released. We watch as they hopelessly try to regain control of life as they once knew it. Once we set one foot out of the cave, it is impossible to go back to one's former reality. In that sense, knowledge as we knew it has been transformed by technologies forever. It is imperative, therefore, that we get used to it and work with it, rather than attempt to control a world that is far broader than our imagination will allow us to go.

In order to identify legal boundaries in cyberspace, we need a frame of reference that informs us about how the rules of the game are, and ought to be, defined in real space. It is in our physical space that power relations among stakeholders have been established. Once we understand the levels of power wielded by stakeholders in physical settings that shape the rules of conduct, discourse and learning, it will be easier to appreciate why certain stakeholders, such as teachers and their unions, are most vocally opposed to the emerging rules of knowledge in cyberspace. The power struggles are not limited to federal and local imbalances – they are further complicated by the power agendas and *desire for agency* in shaping learning. This is because learning ultimately impacts the normative societal hegemonies that have in the past successfully sustained curricula of orthodoxy in schools. As the DOPA example shows, new technologies bring enormous challenges to those who are comfortable with limiting children's ideas, spaces and learning opportunities. Ultimately, banning resources of any kind that limit what students hear, learn, explore and absorb plays out through negative, anti-authority and discriminatory forms of expression that are the objects of control in the first place.

In other words, if we understand how the rules of conduct worked within the cave and determine which stakeholders had the most power and the greatest control, it will help us to appreciate *why* those stakeholders are most afraid of the power that cyberspace provides our young people. It is to these forms of stakeholder power and the conceptual approach certain players bring to supervision in schools that I address in Chapter 6, before moving into a discussion of legal responsibilities in Chapter 7.

Stakeholder power

'Bullying using a new information technology . . . gives kids way more power than they've had'.

(School superintendent Anne Kerr, quoted in Girard and Nguyen, 2007)

Introduction

Battles are all about power. I started off this book with questions about why the issue of cyber-bullying is always presented as a battle. In Chapter 5, I set up the context by suggesting readers think about how we constantly supervise children, and the mindsets that adults continue to adopt to conceptualize communications technologies, even though they have been around for at least two decades.

In this chapter, I want to examine further the mindset that informs the responses of various stakeholders to recent forms of 'cyber-bullying' that have caused such a public outcry globally. This continues the theme of 'constant adult supervision' introduced in the last chapter. I want to examine stakeholder roles in shaping the forms of knowledge and expression accessible to young people. The highly public debate relating to cyber-bullying is largely about expression, privacy and censorship, or control of such expression.

I believe it is relevant to draw upon my knowledge of censorship in schools, to highlight ways in which various stakeholders from school communities have always engaged in it, to shape and sustain a curriculum of orthodoxy that conforms to normative standards and expectations (Shariff and Johnny, 2007a; Shariff and Manley-Casimir, 1999). Any changes to the status quo that threaten to shake the foundations of power in schools and place it in the hands of less powerful stakeholders are generally seen as a threat that must be quelled, using whatever means are necessary, to put the upstarts back in their place. The opening quote at the beginning of this chapter, by a school superintendent (Girard and Nguyen, 2007) confirms the kind of adult mindset that, Lankshear and Knobel (2006) explain, limits adult understandings of digital literacies and their enormous potential for *education*.

When senior administrators complain about too much power in the hands of students, it raises a number of questions: What's wrong with power in the hands of future generations? Can we not work with young people and help them to use the incredible technological tools available to them, in responsible and civil-minded ways? What is the point of suspending them from school instead? Does it take away their online power? Arguably, it does not. There is no educational gain whatsoever. What we ought to focus on is educating them on how not to abuse that power. Work with them to demonstrate transformative leadership approaches, so that they can utilize their technological proficiencies to create a better world. Put another way, it would not be all that unreasonable to 'empower' kids to use their newly acquired 'power' in thoughtful and respectful ways!

Unfortunately, we have rarely empowered children in educational contexts. Many countries have treaty agreements under the United Nations International Convention of the Rights of the Child (United Nations, 1989), where commitments have been made to ensure the three 'Ps' – protection, provision and participation of children. Under the treaty, a report must be filed with the United Nations every four years. The last report filed by Canada received good grades for protection and provision, but did not do as well in the 'participation' category, especially as reported by schools (Howe and Covell, 2000). Allowing students to participate or engage in their learning requires a conscious effort on the part of teachers and school administration to give them responsibility and make them accountable for their actions and learning in contributing ways. I present evidence in this chapter to support my contention that the response to demeaning online postings by students about school authorities and teachers has drawn such a strong and urgent response from teachers, school and government officials globally that it suggests that these school authorities find *their* existing power base under threat:

1   they are worried about 'technology' because 'it' is so difficult to control; and
2   they are worried about too much power in the hands of students because then the stakeholder power bases which have always controlled what children access and learn, will be reduced. This will allow youngsters to access unprecedented forms of knowledge and push the boundaries of free expression, making it difficult to supervise and control them.

If students, through their online proficiency, can access new forms of knowledge and expression that are *not* under the control of authorities, then this poses a threat to the forms of knowledge that have always been produced, reproduced, perpetuated and sustained in schools (Apple, 2000; Kincheloe, 2005; McLaren, 1991).

Knowledge control

Although I do not condone the anti-authority jokes and demeaning forms of expression that are taking place online among youngsters, I wonder what drives students to put down their teachers and school principals? In many of the media reports I have read and referenced in this book, there appears to be an already existing tension between the teachers and school officials, and students who expressed negative or insulting opinions about those teachers and school officials online. Moreover, in personal communications from school administrators and some teachers, I have seen a pattern that suggests that teachers are most upset by the student postings when there is some truth to the comments. That is, when a teacher has difficulty managing a class and students comment on that; when a teacher is didactic and has too many rules and students comment on that; when particular teachers ignore and marginalize some student or always pick on the same students, they could be seriously upset by student comments that reflect those realities. Comments about hygiene and appearance and sexual orientation can also have significant impact on teachers' self-confidence and trust in how they are perceived by the public.

In some cases, it is noteworthy that teachers who were not the subject of online student postings took leadership in having petitions signed by the school or their teachers' union to do something to counter anti-authority online expression. I am informed through a number of personal communications, whose sources I cannot disclose, that often this activism on the part of teachers may have *less* to do with what the students are doing online than it sometimes has to do with *political action*. Teacher activism represents a form of resistance to the policies and practices of their school boards and school administration. In other words, in schools where there is a rift between teachers and school administrators, and indeed among teachers within the same departments, then a relatively innocuous incident can get out of control because of teachers who might overreact, not necessarily to the content of the postings, but as a result of the already poisoned school environment.

School and governmental responses rarely address authority relationships at all – other than reinforcing 'authority' by showing their 'power' through the use of punishment. Accordingly, I invite readers to bear with me while I set the context that explains why responses to student online expressions may be missing the mark, just as they have in traditional bullying. Cyber-bullying as it is perceived to undermine authority has invited strongly adversarial reactions and responses from teachers. These responses, fuelled by the media, pit 'technology' and students in one camp against school and governmental authorities in the other. Teachers bring to their feeling of victimization more than the pain of the demeaning comments against them. These comments are built upon other forms of frustration, such as large class sizes, no time, administrative demands, extra time for children with special needs and so on. The tensions build up against school administrators and school boards. These 'battles' are not simply about cyber-bullying or media framing.

These battles are about control of information, and the shaping of knowledge. They are about maintaining powerful hegemonies that sustain the very systems of oppression grounded in racism, sexism, homophobia and ableism that emerge as bullying. Regrettably, they are modelled, and tacitly condoned by adults in our society. Put another way, students who are punished for their expression against teacher authority often *mirror* attitudes and perspectives that are deeply ingrained within the political and system structures of their school culture and greater society. This is the result of normative forms of knowledge (histories, comprehensive and well-researched textbooks) and forms of expression that governments, schools, parents and special interest groups preclude in schools, and those that they promote towards the sustenance of normative hegemonies. These in turn result in a curriculum of orthodoxy (Shariff and Johnny, 2007a).

Leanne Johnny and I have written (2007) that, through the controlled 'selection' of textbooks, library books, educational resources and classroom discussions, authorities engage in 'censorship' to provide students with an official curriculum informed by hidden agendas of power. Stakeholder agendas influence and shape student values towards normative and easily manageable forms of knowledge. It is when the *management* of knowledge and expression *is at risk* that stakeholder controversies erupt. As in the case of perceived cyber-bullying of school officials and teachers, school controversies are often about free expression, privacy, safety and protection of civil liberties. Students and some parents believe schools have no right to intervene in what they say on home computers. School officials argue that, where there is a nexus to the school, they have every right to intervene.

Parents are among school stakeholders who are also influenced by the way in which the media frames certain situations (as explained in Chapter 3). Parents elect school board trustees, who in turn bow to pressure from government officials to restrict and control what sources of knowledge are presented to children in schools. School principals and teachers, in turn, bow under pressure from parents, schools boards, politicians and the media, concerned about their public image and reputation in educating 'moral' citizens. In turn, they self-censor or restrict access to, or expression of, certain forms of communication by students. What they all fail to realize is that, instead of creating a positive, empowering and engaging learning environment, these intersecting and interlocking systems of oppression (Razack, 1998) stifle creativity and growth, intellectual enquiry and innovation. They instead provide a breeding ground for prejudice and bigotry, autocratic hierarchies of power, and marginalization of students from under-represented or underprivileged groups who do not meet the norm.

Put succinctly, *schools can become breeding grounds for discrimination and intolerance* in society. Not only do some schools foster a culture of orthodoxy, they sustain a culture of fear and overprotectiveness, which validates the need to supervise students all the time. I recently met with school administrators from several schools, all of whom have had to deal with cases where teachers have been defamed or cyber-libelled by students. Some administrators were terrified of the collective power of their faculty and its supporting teachers' union. A common frustration in all of their experiences was time, especially lack of it. There were situations where promises were made that something would be done. In the meantime, a story would be leaked to the media. In at least four cases, early leakage of partial information to the media created mass panic among parents and teachers and misunderstanding in cyber-bullying cases. The following descriptions of two particular cases were conveyed to me by personal communication, the sources are confidential and cannot be divulged.

In the first case, a girl posted a wish list of people at her school whom she wanted to kill. The list included teachers and students. The list was not posted under her name but another, the name of a student she wished to frame. The following day, rumours began among students that there was a killer with a gun in the building. Mass panic broke out. The principal was at a morning meeting outside the school. By the time he arrived, police had surrounded the building. Children had called parents on cellphones, and parents had rushed to pick their children up. Ultimately, the wrong girl was arrested, questioned and suspended. It took a few days to find the real culprit.

At another school, angry teachers petitioned the principal to remove several students from the school. These students had participated in an online forum discussion of teachers that involved over 100 students. Those caught making the most serious comments relating to paedophilia and sexual orientation were suspended. An agreement had been reached between the parents of one student and the principal that the news media would not report her leaving the school. The day that the release documents were to be signed, media headlines talked about a 'student ousted' from the school. The information had been leaked by someone at the school to the media. This perceived breach of trust on the part of the principal caused that pupil's parents to change their mind and insist their child remain at the school. In the politics of it all – between the teachers, school administration and parents – the educational future of the student in question was forgotten. How would he/she be received by the teachers at school? If he/she had left, he/she would have to say goodbye to many friends. At high school, friends and peer relationships mean everything. Teenagers make mistakes. Forcing the teen to leave the school might have been too harsh a punishment. The student was in a Catch-22 situation. Teachers did not want him/her at the school.

As I have shown in Chapters 2 and 4, peer pressure, socialization, family influences and raging hormones can all play a part in how students express themselves. Some of the political wrangling that emerged among adults involved in these incidents ignores the fact that people learn from experience and ought to receive a second chance. Even adults make mistakes and are given reprieve, as I will show in Chapter 7, when I discuss the court cases. When adults take entrenched positions and dig in their heels regarding what is best for students, they quickly forget the legal notion of the 'best interests of the child'. The highest court in Canada has clearly expressed that schools and parents ought to consider what is best for children – rather than placing their own desires at the forefront of decisions involving children's education (*Eaton vs Brant County Board of Education* [1997] 1 S.C.R. 241).

Hence, when we take a closer look at cyber-bullying 'battles', we find that it is adult stakeholders in society, and not the children, who in effect model and fuel 'antisocial' and 'anti-authority' behaviours. When society's young engage in discriminatory, sexual and hostile expression, *they* are the ones who take the rap, *they* are the ones who are suspended and expelled from schools (resulting in academic records that preclude them from entering universities, which would give them a chance to succeed in life). Children and teens pay the highest price for our narrow-minded responses at every step – from suicide victims such as Hamed Nastoh and Dawn Marie Wesley to murdered victims such as Reena Virk, but, ultimately, all of society suffers. Bram, Brad and most young people in their adolescence are simply caught in a battle for power between adult stakeholders who want control over young people's lives – and their spaces. It is no wonder then that cyberspace, with its vast potential for all kinds of expression, information, communication and knowledge, has released the skeleton from the closet that used to preserve school reputations.

This is why it is so unbearable for school personnel to be at the receiving end of cyber-bullying – where the balance of power has shifted to students as they gain proficiency in cyberspace that clearly outdoes that of many teachers and school officials. I believe that when the selection process (in this case, the form of punishment) is motivated for reasons other than the educational value of a learning resource, the fine line at which selection becomes censorship is often crossed.

Influential stakeholders

Before entering a discussion of the legal considerations that these debates raise, it is important to look at how censorship controversies among stakeholders have been played out historically, and examine the power hierarchies that intersect and interlock to result in school policies and practices that may not always be in the best interests of students, the learning environment or the advancement of knowledge and democratic relationships in society.

By way of caveat, I do not suggest that all school initiatives (many of which are thoughtfully implemented to address the problem) are doomed to failure. Moreover, I do not suggest that many sincere efforts by school officials and teachers are *consciously* designed to promote orthodoxy. The message I want to convey is that, so ingrained are certain perspectives within overall hegemonies about authority, discipline, maintaining order, the public good and common values, seemingly sensible and practical responses and resolutions sometimes miss the mark. This is because of the restrictive mindsets relating to student discipline and digital literacies that inform such initiatives. For example, scholars have argued that the reason so many anti-bullying programmes and zero-tolerance policies have failed to reduce traditional bullying is because they provided superficial, band-aid solutions.

According to Skiba and Peterson (1999), the concept of 'zero-tolerance' as a form of discipline emerged from a military model in the army when soldiers were caught drinking. When this model was brought into the school context, it gave educators a sense of being in control. It also fitted in well as an item on their 'to do list' and rubrics on how to 'manage' the 'problem', but did not address the root causes. Root causes are almost always motivated by intersecting and interlocking forms of discrimination (racism, sexism, homophobia, ableism, socio-economic divisions) and power differentials that marginalize some members of society more than others (Dei, 1997; Razack, 1998).

So let me begin with a look at teachers as influential stakeholders, to assess how they position themselves when it comes to addressing forms of expression that directly insult and demean them or peer-to-peer bullying and cyber-bullying.

Teachers and their unions

As I write this chapter, a new study has been released by the Ontario College of Teachers (OCT, 2007). The study reports that 84 per cent of respondent teachers, report having experienced cyber-bullying in the form of students publishing obscene or defamatory pictures or statements online; 41 per cent know about this happening to other teachers; 33 per cent report knowing about it happening to their own students, and 16 per cent know about it happening to students at their school.

> *Question*: As you know, there's been some talk in the media about cyber-bullying, where students publish obscene or defamatory pictures or statements online for the purpose of hurting others. To what extent has each of the following experienced cyberbullying?

Table 6.1 Teachers on experience of cyber-bullying (%)

	Definitely experienced → Definitely not					DNK[a]
	5	4	3	2	1	
Yourself personally	84	3	3	2	5	4
Other teachers or administrators in your school	41	16	11	9	12	11
Your students	33	11	14	12	18	11
Students in your school	16	13	19	17	25	10

(Reproduced with permission of the OCT, August 28, 2007) [a] Do not know.

A. e-mail.
B. Chatroom or bashboard content.
C. Content on personal web sites or blogs.
D. Text messaging.
E. Photographs or video clips.
F. Personal voting-booth web sites.

DNK (do not know/no opinion)

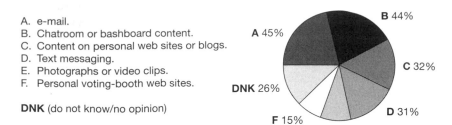

Figure 6.1 Typical forms of cyber-bullying
(Reproduced with permission of the OCT, 28 August 2007)

Forty-five per cent said this happened by email, and 44 per cent said this happens in chat rooms, social networking sites and 'bashboards'. Thirty-two per cent found defamatory content on personal web sites and blogs, 31 per cent via text messaging, 19 per cent through the use of photographs and video clips and 15 per cent on personal voting-booth web sites.

> *Question*: In what form have those incidents of cyber-bullying typically occurred?

The teachers considered criticism of their clothing, appearance and mannerisms and criticism of their grading practices as the most serious forms of anti-authority online expression. When asked whether they believed this contributes to teachers leaving the profession prematurely, 19 per cent of those surveyed believed it did. Twenty-one per cent of the teachers thought this also contributed to students dropping out of school; whereas 24 per cent believed cyber-bullying affected student drop-out rates. Twenty-four per cent felt it decreased classroom quality (thereby the spill-over effect into physical spaces).

Also perturbing are the findings that, whereas 46 per cent of teachers believed that their school or school boards ought to sanction students for these online forms of expression, 41 per cent of English-speaking teachers believed that most or all incidents of cyber-bullying should be reported to the police. French-speaking teachers allocated more responsibility to the schools and school boards (59 per cent) and 30 per cent believed police should be involved.

> *Question*: Which of the answers given in Figure 6.2 best describes your school's position on cyberbullying?

Forty-three per cent of teachers also felt that peer-to-peer cyber-bullying should be reported to the police, although 47 per cent believed their board should sanction students.

A. There are formal, well understood
   rules with potential consequences.
B. There may be formal rules but they
   are not widely understood.
C. There are informal rules.
D. There are no rules.

DNK (do not know/no opinion)

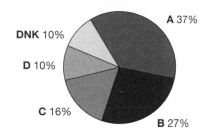

Figure 6.2 School's position on cyber-bullying

(Reproduced with permission of the OCT, 28 August 2007)

A. Schools or boards should sanction
   students involved in harassing other
   students online.
B. Most or all incidents of cyberbullying
   should be reported to the police.
C. There's not much that schools or
   boards can do to protect students
   from other students harassing them
   online.

DNK (do not know/no opinion)

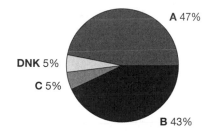

Figure 6.3 Students harassing students

(Reproduced with permission of the OCT, 28 August 2007)

Question: Which of the opinions given in Figure 6.3 on students harassing students with cyberbullying is closest to your own?

This study might provide some indications as to why teachers' unions have come under so much pressure. If 84 per cent of teachers believe they have been cyber-bullied through online postings, it is important to determine what is going on. Are students really running rampant, as media reports suggest? Teachers are increasingly filing grievances with their unions, adding a 'quasi-legal' dimension to already litigious issues. Moreover, many of them (20 per cent) believe that cyber-bullying contributes to teachers leaving the profession. My research on censorship in schools (Shariff and Johnny, 2007a; Shariff and Manley-Casimir, 1999) disclosed that teachers' unions are often pressured by their membership into galvanizing the implementation of laws and policies that help teachers retain positions of power. Anti-authority cyber-expression has the effect of making teachers powerless. Hence, it is not surprising that some of them might want to leave the profession as a result. The OCT, which commissioned the survey, has done a good job of putting a well-rounded perspective on the issue. In the same issue that released the survey results, Shriever (2007) interviewed a number of experts on the subject of cyber-bullying, including myself, and obtained a consensus that banning technologies and suspending students are not the best options. Lawyer Eric Roher and Dr Faye Mishna, an associate professor at the University of Toronto, concurred with my advice that there is an obvious need to engage with students to address why they are demeaning teachers to such an extent (84 per cent). This does not mean, however, that 84 per cent of the children using the Internet and social networking sites are engaging in the behaviours. The OCT reiterates my position that, rather than looking for 'how to' lists, teachers should engage with their students and attempt to learn more about technology use. They also need to find out whether their pupils are engaged in their learning and whether their school experiences are positive or frustrating. To that end, the Canadian Teachers' Federation (CTF) has also taken positive steps.

After several incidents where high school teenagers were caught making derogatory postings about their teachers across CTF, an organization representing approximately 220,000 teachers came under significant pressure to do something about it. Of course the media reported this as a battle, with the headline, 'Teachers declare war on cyber-bullying' (Brown, 2007). They reported the unanimous passing of a resolution to form 'an emergency workgroup to hammer out a national policy this fall on the use of cellphones in class and school penalties for using blogs, email and any form of technology to hurt other people's feelings' (Brown, 2007). In actual fact, the resolution was less designed to 'wage a war', than it was drafted to bring together a task force comprised of experts on the subject, to understand better Internet uses among students, the nature of cyber-bullying and the boundaries of intervention in cyberspace.

As part of this initiative, one objective is to establish ethical standards relating to technology use, identify the legal responsibilities and expectations of Canadian teachers, and develop materials that support these standards towards implementation of consistent national policies and guidelines. I believe the CTF has taken an important step in understanding the issues and that rather than 'hammering' out a national policy, as the media describes it, the federation's policymakers have undertaken in-depth research and are approaching the matter thoughtfully in partnership with national scholars and technology experts. The resolution reads as shown in Box 6.1.[1]

The one concern I have with the wording of this resolution lies in paragraph c), which states 'the need to deal with it forcefully' followed by 'and advice on ways to deal with it'. As a partner in the process I would advise the task force to eliminate the word 'forcefully', especially as they have yet to obtain informed advice from national experts. There are many words that could be substituted for 'forcefully', such as 'collaboratively' or 'the need to deal with it by drawing upon pedagogically sound approaches'. I will talk more about ways that teachers' groups in particular can deal with cyber-bullying when I get to my discussion of recommend approaches in Chapter 8. Suffice it to note at this juncture that, in light of the fact that the primary mandate of teachers is to educate, I believe the word 'educate' could also appear more prominently in the resolution.

Box 6.1: Canadian Teachers' Federation communications technology concern resolution

JULY 12, 2007

BE IT RESOLVED THAT the Canadian Teachers' Federation take urgent action on issues arising from the use of electronic communications in ways that harm students and/or teachers and in ways that are harmful to the education process. Such action should include but not be limited to:

a) Students, teachers, parents and the general public of new communications technologies including, but not limited to, e-mail, Web 2, blogs, social networking Internet sites (e.g. Facebook, YouTube, etc.), text messaging, and cellphones within the context of schools, students, and the professional lives of teachers and administrators. Further, this policy should examine the ethical standards associated with the use of these technologies.

b) Development of partnerships for action to educate students, teachers, parents and the general public of the consequences of inappropriate use of communications technologies in activities that constitute cyber-bullying.

c) Development of materials for distribution by CTF alone or in partnership with Member organizations and others about the seriousness of cyber-bullying, the need to deal with it forcefully, and advice on ways to deal with it.

d) Conduct of research, analysis and dissemination of information gathered by CTF alone or in partnership with Member organizations and others.

e) Formation of a national work group of CTF Member organization staff who will consult with such others as necessary before developing and recommending to the CTF Board of Directors a national action plan on matters arising from communications technology use, including cyber-bullying.

Why the sudden urgency?

What I find most ironic about this 'urgent' need to address cyber-bullying, as expressed by teachers, is that for decades bullying between school children was generally accepted as a part of growing up, especially in schools. Even the OCT Survey (2007) shows that, although 84 per cent reported themselves being cyber-bullied, and 41 per cent knew about their colleagues being cyber-bullied, only 33 per cent definitely knew about their students being cyber-bullied, and 25 per cent of teachers said that they definitely did not know about their students being cyber-bullied. These results suggest that teachers may be less attuned to their students' experiences as victims of cyber-bullying. There is research that supports this proposition.

It was not until Dan Olweus published his work on the serious consequences of bullying in the late 1970s (Olweus, 1978) that interest in the subject really took hold. Before that, children who were victimized and complained were perceived to be 'tattle-tales' and weak of character. It was not until as recently as early 2006, when Facebook, MySpace, LinkdIn, Ratemyteacher.com and other online social networks really began to surface as popular venues to discuss authority figures that a larger number of teachers finally began to pay serious attention to cyber-bullying. It has now become a priority for teachers in many countries. Peer bullying and peer cyber-bullying appear to have been less of a problem. Consider some of my doctoral findings regarding teachers' responses to traditional bullying.

A wall of defence

There is evidence in the research on traditional bullying that suggests that until very recently (within the last five years) teachers and school officials involved in well-publicized cases of bullying and emerging litigation[2] are alleged to display a pattern of denial, culminating in a 'wall of defence'. This wall of defence comes through in complaints filed in court or conveyed in personal communications[3] by at least nineteen Canadian victims of bullying. David Knight, mentioned in earlier chapters, and his mother Nancy Knight supported these claims in a lawsuit they filed against their school in Ontario, Canada, but which is now under settlement negotiations. Several Canadian cases serve as examples where teachers, supported by school officials, refused to take bullying seriously, despite repeated reports by students who were being targeted. From this small number, very few cases went to court as most were settled before trial. However, the parents of these children formed advocacy groups to publicize their experiences and frustration with the way their schools handled their situations.

Teenagers Azmi Jubran, Hamed Nastoh, Jamie Dufour, Andrew Forin and Dawn-Marie Wesley were all victims of bullying. In every case (with the exception of Dawn-Marie Wesley), the parents reported the incidents to the school, and, in each case, the parents publicly claimed that very little action was taken by the school to protect their children. Azmi Jubran eventually brought a human rights challenge against his school and principal; Hamed Nastoh ended his life by jumping off a bridge; Jamie Dufour's parents commenced a civil action for gross negligence but abandoned it prior to the trial; Andrew Forin was suspended from school for filming a school fight that was made public by the media and Dawn-Marie Wesley hanged herself after receiving a threat from one of her perpetrators, despite having visited a school counsellor for help.[4]

Most of the parental accusations have not been adjudicated by a court or tribunal and therefore remain accusations rather than proven facts, because most were settled out of court or abandoned. Nonetheless, the pattern of complaints is so consistent across all the cases that the schools' actions (or lack thereof) cannot be ignored or discounted. All the bullying cases contain the following pattern of complaints against schools:

- Teachers and administrators often assumed the victim invited the bullying and generally denied that bullying was a problem at the school.
- All the schools noted that they had zero-tolerance policies and anti-bullying programmes. They referred to mission statements, school policies and student codes of conduct, apparently assuming that *stated intent* absolved them of responsibility to implement them appropriately.
- Teachers and school officials accused parents of overreacting and apparently viewed them as troublemakers and harassers.
- If the victim retaliated against the perpetrators, the *victim* was more often suspended than the perpetrator.[5]
- The bullying continued well after teachers and school officials were made aware of the situation.
- Victims had to leave the school while the perpetrators remained, without being held accountable for their actions (until, in some cases, public outcry resulted in criminal charges being laid against the perpetrators). Little or no action was taken to suspend or otherwise discipline the perpetrators, despite the existence of zero-tolerance policies.
- Teachers and school officials refused to acknowledge the problem, and therefore did not make a concerted effort to investigate the bullying or provide consistent protection of the victim.

School reputation or support of victims?

Consider Andrew Forin's case. Andrew, a teenager, was an avid videographer who had heard about a prospective fight on the school playground and decided to videotape two boys who were beating up a smaller child, while a large number of supporters looked on, cheering. After taping the fight he went to his weekly job at a television station where he showed his tape to one of his supervisors. She offered him $300 for the tape without explaining the ramifications to him. The tape was immediately distributed to media networks, which aired the tape that evening. School officials were angry that Andrew had sold the tape to the media and suspended him the next day, but did little about disciplining or even interviewing the students who conducted the beating, even though its brutality drew questions from the public about the problem of bullying at the school. Andrew found himself in a Catch-22 situation: the school suspended him, claiming that his video gave the school a 'black mark', and at the same time he became a victim of media sensationalism. The furore over his video diverted attention from the most important issue, namely, the actual bullying and beating of a smaller boy that occurred at the school. The perpetrators were not disciplined until the public called for charges of criminal assault, which were filed twelve months after the beating took place. It appeared that the school seemed less concerned about the bullying than its own reputation and public image.

Larson (1997), who found a similar pattern in her investigation of a racial conflict in an American school, has one explanation for this pattern of denial by teachers and school administrators. She notes that, traditionally, administrators have been more concerned with good housekeeping and school reputation than with examining what drives the conflicts in the first place. When bullying or violence in schools is publicized, it reflects poorly on the school's reputation. Therefore, the initial tendency can be to downplay the situation or deny that a problem exists. Moreover, instead of investigating the root causes of a situation, schools sometimes redefine the problem, blaming the victim, or implying that the victim is a danger to others.

Larson examined a case where black students who were bussed to an all-white school attempted to draw attention to a racial problem by burning a flag at a talent competition. The black students were immediately suspended for being dangerous, even though one of them was an honour role student and had no record of violence. Larson concludes that, by magnifying the perceived danger of the black students' actions, school administrators failed to address the root problem of racism at the school.

Responses by teachers and school officials in these cases have some similarities to a number of the recent cyber-bullying cases involving online postings by students about teachers and school personnel. At a Roman Catholic school in Ontario, nineteen students were suspended for 'bullying' their school principal on a web site. Student postings included calling the school principal 'The grinch of school spirit', directing sexually explicit remarks at him, and displaying pictures of Osama bin Laden and Adolf Hitler. Consider the observations of one school official:

> [W]hile the school board has dealt with students cyber-bullying each
> other, he is not aware of any previous attack on a staff member, which is

a transgression of the board's code of conduct . . . This is very dangerous ground these kids are treading on. It's not conducive to the moral tone of the school, and it undermines authority. It is damaging to the reputation of this school.

(Rusk, 2007)

The reporter interviewed a student who said that suspended students included the student council president and members of the student council who had been added as officers of the chat room without their permission. Although she agreed that the online postings were slanderous, in her opinion the punishment was too harsh because it would go on the students' record and prevent them from being accepted at universities of their choice. Although the undermining of authority is definitely a serious issue, it is not clear why victimization of children who might commit suicide as a result of cyber-bullying is less important. The school official in this case did say that, if it had involved peer-to-peer bullying, the students would have received even longer suspensions. But it still leaves open the question as to what schools believe will be accomplished. Whether students receive a ten or twenty day suspension, to alleviate the issue in schools, it makes little difference, other than get the perpetrators out of school administrators' hair for a few days and calm the teachers down.

Tacit condoning of peer-to-peer bullying

The role of teachers in tacitly condoning peer-to-peer bullying among their students in the long term cannot be ignored. Twenty years ago, a survey of 250 British prison inmates (Devlin, 1997) disclosed that, not only had most inmates either been perpetrators or victims of bullying in school, but that, when those who were bullied complained, teachers paid little attention. According to the inmates, not only was bullying tolerated, some teachers condoned it and participated in it. Devlin reports that teachers often verbally harassed the students, were insensitive to disabilities, and even exhibited overt racial prejudice and outright cruelty.

Smith and Sharpe's (1994) later study involving 7,000 UK students in Sheffield revealed that some teachers showed little concern for bullying victims. In some schools, teachers even instigated bullying through name-calling. Although these teachers represent only a small percentage of teachers in Sheffield schools, it is troubling that such attitudes prevailed. Today, teachers are better educated on how to communicate positively with students, and one would hope that the situation would have improved during this time. Regardless, given the proliferation of information and programmes that have emerged in the last two decades, this sudden concern by teachers to deal urgently with cyber-bullying because they are now its targets suggests that most are for the first time realizing its psychological impact and effect on their *working* environments. Many overlooked the impact of peer-to-peer bullying on students' *learning* environments in the past.

As I noted earlier, perpetrators are often leaders who can be well liked by teachers and peers (DiGiulio, 2001; Juvonen and Graham, 2001; Katch, 2001; Olweus, 1978. This may explain why some teachers do not take victim complaints seriously. If teachers witness only the good behaviour of certain perpetrators, they may not believe victims' claims. Moreover, as the NCPC reports, *victims* are often unpopular with peers or teachers. When victims complain, they might be dismissed as liars, 'tattle-tales' or whiners. As one UK student reports:

> [T]here are some girls who when they are moving about the classroom are butter-wouldn't-melt-in-my-mouth sorts and the teachers think that they are great, but when they are in the girls loo [washroom] with no staff about, they change . . . They are horrible, mean and try to get money from me . . . And I know that I can't get help because the rule is that you don't grass [rat on them].
>
> (Glover *et al.*, 1998, p. 43)

Research by Petersen and Rigby (1999, as cited in Campbell, 2005) also found that many young people do not report bullying or cyber-bullying because they think their report will not be believed or that the incident will be trivialized by adults. They found that fewer than 25 per cent ever report bullying because '[t]hey also do not have much faith that adults can solve the problem and fear that adults might make it worse' (Peterson, 1999, as quoted in Campbell, 2005)

One may well wonder why educators would tolerate bullying among peers and why students have so little faith in their support. One possible reason for it is lack of knowledge or awareness that certain forms of behaviour do, in fact, constitute bullying. Time might also be a factor. Boulton and Hawker (1997) suggest that some teachers might not address psychological bullying (unless it is directed at them) simply because they have little time to deal with the problem. They note that physical injuries take precedence over verbal bullying, as physical injuries can be established with more certainty in court. Teachers they interviewed explained that they cannot respond every time a student reports teasing. For example, one noted:

> It seems to me every break time there is someone saying to me 'Karen is being nasty to me.' . . . I try to take all of them seriously but I just have to let some of them go otherwise I'd have to leave the rest of the class while I sorted them out. I often find myself saying to children who say they have been called names, 'Just ignore them and they will soon find something better to do'. I don't like doing this but I feel I have to.
>
> (Ibid., p. 57)

Thus the various demands on teachers, including classroom instruction, student supervision, and now unlimited possibilities for cyber-bullying of peers, might cause them to become overwhelmed and ignore it unless it involves authority figures. Moreover, MacKay and Flood (2001) observe that budget restrictions and staff shortages may make it difficult for teachers adequately to follow through on policy directives. Teachers today must deal with large class sizes, ethnic diversity and students with a range of abilities and disabilities who come from varying backgrounds and social classes. This level of diversity presents many opportunities for discriminatory forms of bullying and less time for teachers and administrators adequately to address them. Consequently, the school climate can become less tolerant of individual students' differences and more reliant on harsher zero-tolerance policies[6] that are randomly applied to all students, irrespective of each student's situation.

Another reason for the prolonged teacher acceptance of traditional bullying may be a belief that victims should learn to stand up for themselves as part of their maturing process. Teachers might consider the possibility of harm but assess it as minimal when weighed against the harm to the victim of being unable to stand up to the bullies. Accordingly, like the Japanese parents, they send children back out onto the playground to face their tormentors. This was illustrated in British litigation on bullying, where a teacher testified to her belief that bullying victim, Leah Brantford-Smart, should learn to fend for herself:

> [I was] absolutely unwilling to withdraw Leah from where she should have been from the playground and I felt it was the wrong thing to do, that every time she stayed in with me she had a little less practice in going out and looking after herself. I do not want to keep her in very much, and I did not keep her in more than I could possibly help.
>
> (*Brantford-Smart vs West Sussex County Council*
> (2002), para. 11, p. 3)

Leah's teacher adopted the traditional view on bullying, which is that it builds character. She truly believed that Leah should learn to defend herself and therefore she did not tell the perpetrators to stop bullying. The court supported the teacher, ruling that, because the school had anti-bullying policies in place, the teacher was under no obligation to do more.

Some theorists (Jiwani, 2001; Larson, 1997; Perkins, 1997; Razack, 1998; Sefa-Dei, 1997; Wason-Ellam, 1996) suggest that teachers might be particularly insensitive to the needs of children who are already marginalized on the basis of race, sexual orientation, poverty and disability (or ability), unwittingly creating a discriminatory school environment. Glover *et al.* (1998) report that those teachers who had never experienced bullying, racial or other forms of discrimination themselves may not recognize teasing as bullying.

Now that they are at the receiving end of the cyber-bullying, teachers may stand up and take notice. Scholars also make the very important observation that although the student population in Canadian schools (and, increasingly, the United Kingdom, United States and Europe) is very ethnically and culturally diverse, a parallel diversity is not reflected in school staff or administration. Razack (1998), Dei (1997) and others (Epp, 1996; Handa, 1997; Jiwani, 2001; Perkins, 1997) note that the majority of teachers and school administrators in Western schools are predominantly white, whereas the student population includes many students of Asian, African, Hispanic, South Indian and Middle Eastern descent.

They point out that, despite being aware of discrimination, some educators continue to view conflict through Eurocentric, androcentric and middle-class lenses. Teachers apply their own frame of reference to others' reality, and, if the behaviour does not fit their experiences, they may not consider the possibility of harm. This makes it difficult for many bullied students to identify closely with their teachers – and vice versa.

Many schools continue to rely on the traditional authoritarian approaches towards school and student management that have been around for decades, since the times when schools were much more ethnically homogeneous. Unfortunately, those models are less effective in a pluralistic school population, especially when new technologies and cyber-bullying are involved.

As we have seen, the Internet has created new dilemmas for educators that many of them state they are unprepared for and quite uncertain how to handle; yet they are very vocal when the bullying is directed at them. Moreover, reports from the United Kingdom, the United States and many parts of the world suggest that the responses are still *reactive* and heavily focused on *control of behaviour* rather than on *prevention through education options*. Consider these comments in 2006 by a school standards government official, as reported in the *Guardia*n:

> A culture of disrespect and failure to take responsibility will not be tolerated . . . Is easy to lose sight of the fact that pupil behaviour in the majority of schools is good for most of the time . . . But it takes only a handful of poorly behaved pupils to make life difficult for teachers and disrupt the education of other pupils.
>
> (Press Association, 2006)

The Minister's announcement was made prior to the introduction of new legal rights for teachers. The legislation extends the right of teachers to school buses and trains, to get rid of the 'You can't do anything to me miss' attitude, and to preserve school reputations. One school official is quoted as saying: 'A school's reputation can easily be lost through bad behaviour on the buses . . . There is always some uncertainty about the extent of power outside school and this will clarify that right' (Asthana, 2006).

The teachers at one Canadian, formerly Catholic, school were recently up in arms because students discussed some of them in an open, online forum on

Facebook. The anger of the teachers against some of the students was surprising given that even the administration admitted that most student comments were innocuous and very close to the truth. There appeared to be few libellous comments, with one or two exceptions. In attempting to understand the rage of the teachers, who demanded that at least four of the students be removed from the school, I asked the school administrators about the culture at the school.[7] Our conversation disclosed that the school had a history of fractured political relationships. The school was taken over by several different school boards throughout its history and had experienced changes, with many new administrators who came and left while many of the staff remained at the school. Because of its prestigious academic reputation, the school is popular with teachers and parents. The teachers and student body are largely homogeneous (mainly European backgrounds), with few students from other ethnic backgrounds. Many of the teachers are set in their ways, endorsing a disciplinary and didactic approach, rather than the more interactive and open approach advocated by the Quebec ministry's educational reform package. Relationships between the teachers themselves within departments have not been friendly, and relationships between faculty and administration have also been hostile. The teachers' union has not facilitated these relationships.

It became apparent during my conversation with school administrators that the teachers at this school might be using the Facebook incidents as a way to get back at school authorities. Their frustrations, which have festered for many years under the surface, appear to have exploded to the surface. Unfortunately, the students become scapegoats of the power struggles between faculty and school authorities. In this political struggle, the fact that the students are immature, make mistakes and do not realize the impact of their comments is lost. The fact that teachers are responsible for educating students to engage in inclusive and socially responsible discourse is also lost as teachers take entrenched positions. These situations create chilled and poisoned environments in schools. Such environments support violence and discrimination, making it difficult to learn. It is not surprising, then, that the discontent of the school climate was reflected in student online comments about their teachers. While the entire focus has been on the students and their bad behaviour, teachers and schools are missing the crucial signs that indicate that something is very wrong at their schools that needs to be addressed immediately. This could mean an entire restructuring of the school when negative feelings are so embedded and endemic within the school culture. Suspending and removing students who have the courage to comment (albeit in immature ways) on the poisoned culture at the school will by no means fix the problem. The students are not always the problem. The Internet and Facebook and YouTube are not always the problem. The problem resides within the school culture – with the long-time teachers and their negative feelings about the way things are done, and with every new administration who attempts to second guess what exactly the teachers want and who in some ways are afraid of teachers' protests and pressured in to giving into their decisions. These are the hierarchies of stakeholder power that can play themselves out in schools.

Extension of powers to teachers combined with a zero-tolerance environment may also create unequal opportunities for students from traditionally excluded groups or students who are biologically predisposed to behavioural problems. Epp (1996) suggests that, when schools emphasize complicity and competition, they perpetuate systemic violence against marginalized students:

> Systemic violence is found in any institutionalized practice which adversely impacts on students. To be damaging, *practices do not have to have a negative impact on all students. They may be beneficial to some and damaging to others* [emphasis added].

(Ibid., p. 3)

Thus many practices that are assumed to be beneficial may, in fact, be the very processes that marginalize some students.

Selection . . . or censorship?

Although I have already dealt extensively with the role of teachers in addressing bullying and cyber-bullying, it is important to highlight their power in shaping what children learn and access through a censorship perspective. Teachers and principals are the most accessible school personnel, and, therefore, most challenges that relate to what children learn and how they are expected to communicate are first directed to them. Increasingly, we see that what teachers discuss in the classroom is under the lens of public scrutiny, and, therefore, educational specialists often need to engage in a great deal of self-censorship, especially when examining political issues in the classroom. These education officials, in an attempt to avoid conflict or potential legal suits, may acquiesce to the demands of protesters, and, consequently, certain topics or resources may not appear in the classroom. Moreover, educators have been found to engage in self-censorship on a regular basis (Arons, 1986; Dick and Canadian Library Association, 1982; Shariff and Johnny, 2007a; Shariff and Manley-Casimir, 1999). These authors all explain that censorship controversies among parents, students and teachers can cause a chilling effect in the school environment, and thus educational decisions on the types of resource to include and the content of dialogue and classroom discussions may be motivated by a need to protect themselves. The Surrey school board book banning case (discussed later) is a clear example, as parents threatened to sue any teacher on the Surrey School board who ventured into any discussions of homosexuality in the classroom. This resulted in a chilled silence by teachers in the district who did not speak up against the banning of the children's books from kindergarten classrooms, even though many found the books innocuous and helpful in addressing homophobia, bullying and cyber-bullying (Shariff *et al.*, 2000).

Moreover, Noll (1994) confirms that highly publicized educational resource challenges have a ripple effect in the classroom, because they dissuade teachers from discussing certain topics with students. This concludes in a type of self-censorship whereby education officials fail to include materials that are approved by the ministry for fear of invoking anger or dissent in their school communities. As noted before, the tendency by many teachers and school officials is to avoid controversy by banning or attempting to sweep sensitive issues under the rug in the hopes they will go away so that school reputations are preserved. As I have argued elsewhere (Shariff and Johnny, 2007a; Shariff and Manley-Casimir, 1999), this tactic almost always backfires in heated controversy. Whether it is in books or in online communication, the minute there is any disagreement about whether such content should be censored or banned, people run to buy the book before it is taken off the shelves, or immediately log onto the offending web sites to read the offensive content and make a determination of their own. The recent controversies relating to material posted on Facebook, YouTube and so on, have had just that effect. Although technology providers are less reluctant to remove the content, there is often a delay of a day or two before some postings can effectively be taken down. As Roher (2007) explains, the complainant has to establish that the content is sufficiently offensive to be taken down, and, as we will see in the next chapter, the jury is still out on what forms of online content can be considered sufficiently serious to be removed.

In recent years, there have been countless examples of educators who have faced repercussions for expressing political dissent. For example, Giroux (2002) explains that a group of professors at the City University of New York were denounced by the university chancellor for criticizing American foreign policy. Likewise, he observes, Lynne Cheney condemned the deputy chancellor of New York City Schools for suggesting that the terrorist attacks in New York have created an urgent need to teach about Muslim culture in American schools. Such examples raise questions about the extent to which education officials can exercise their right to free speech in the classroom and also demonstrate the challenges that teachers face in trying to broach difficult and sometimes sensitive issues with students.

My observation in all of this is: If teachers are so restricted in what they can say in the classroom, it is no wonder they are concerned over what is said online by students. Whether teachers self-censor or not, the Internet has turned the issue of information control on its head. It is plausible that what is emerging as cyber-bullying is a reflection of what was *not* discussed, what issues were censored but ought to have been part of classroom discussions so that students had access to a broader and deeper understanding of societal issues that can be controversial. It is no wonder that we are facing a *Lord of the flies* syndrome (Golding, 1954), as technologies have provided infinite opportunities for people to express and access so much information. What is tragic and ironical about the entire situation is this. Because our schools have generally catered to mediocrity by restricting access to legitimate and comprehensive forms of knowledge, now that we have the opportunity to take advantage of knowledge that can be available at the click of a mouse, few adults, let alone young people, know where to begin, or how to access it.

Prevailing hegemonies are so deeply ingrained that we struggle to take advantage of what a global world brought together by technologies has to offer. Although I do not suggest that everything on the Internet is well supported, authentic or scholarly, regular and open exposure to a range of perspectives at the school level would certainly facilitate thoughtful and responsible use of technology and digital literacies. As it turns out, it is not surprising that attitudes expressed by students through cyber-bullying were largely developed within school systems that tacitly condone and thereby promote and sustain intolerance and ignorance (Apple, 1990; Kincheloe, 2005; P. McLaren, 1991).

The fact that it took teachers to experience being cyber-bullied themselves before they showed a strong interest in 'forceful' action for dealing with it is disturbing. Most Western democracies, such as the United Kingdom, Canada and the United States, have a legal duty of care to protect children, *in loco parentis*, that was established in 1893 (*Williams vs Eady* [1893] 10 TLR 41) under British common law and still relied upon today in cases involving supervision. As I will explain in Chapter 7, this places a legal obligation on schools to behave like 'careful and prudent parents'.

Lost parenting opportunities

What about parents themselves? How 'careful and prudent' have they been in this controversy and how influential are they in shaping what children learn and express in a school context – whether it is in school or online? Predictably, they are generally their children's strongest supporters, and, in the 'battle' over whether schools have a right to intervene when their children defame teachers, parents have generally come out strongly in support of free expression and civil liberties.

Confused messages: furious father

You will recall Bram, the boy mentioned in Chapter 5, who was interviewed on CBC Radio in the presence of his father (Findlay, 2007). Bram had made up a 'joke' about his teacher masturbating in the back of the class and posted it on Facebook. When interviewed by Gillian Findlay of the Canadian Broadcasting Corporation, Bram's father was furious – but with whom? It might be assumed he was angry with his son for publicly writing sexual and offensive lies about his teacher. Not so. Although he certainly acknowledged the comments were made in poor taste, he was more upset with school officials for suspending his son from a field trip to Montreal.

Although stating that he did not condone what his son did, he strongly asserted that the school had no right to intervene in his son's expression from a home computer. He likened it to being the same as if school officials had walked into his house and told him what to do. Thus the battle over who has the right to intervene in cyberspace once again became territorial – this time between home and school. Parents clearly have authority in the home, but an important point to be aware of is that sometimes parents take up positions to force a certain agenda, much in the same way as the media does. This is achieved by shifting the focus away from the root of the conflict.

For example, by drawing attention away from the content of his son's free expression, Bram's father tacitly reinforced his son's belief that what he did was not that serious. It is important to remember that, although free expression is a constitutional right in Canada, the United States and other Western democracies, it is not an unfettered right. In Bram's case, one would assume that he crossed the line of civil responsibility – whether he was joking on not. The lines of authority between home and school often overlap whenever there is a nexus to the school. By shifting the focus away from the nature of cyber-bullying to place blame on the school for intervening in a so-called private matter from home, I believe a 'teachable parenting moment' was lost, as was an opportunity to work with the school to engage in a dialogue with Bram and his schoolmates to make them aware of the implications.

Confused messages: concerned mother

Similarly, Brad Parson's mother also downplayed the content of her son's expression, implying that the school overreacted because 'we all did it'. Nonetheless, to demonstrate her disapproval, she withdrew Brad's computer privileges. This sent a conflicting message. As she did not believe the expression was that serious, I ask readers to consider whether withdrawing privileges makes any difference in contemporary society, where computers can be accessed in libraries, at friends' homes and in Internet cafes. How much impact does withdrawal of computer access have, especially when the student is not the only one convinced that he did nothing wrong? I believe that here was another lost and 'teachable parenting moment', although it is not clear whether this parent and the school worked together to address some of the issues.

It is important to consider not only the positions that parents are taking with respect to the issue of cyber-bullying under discussion, but also the history of parental prerogative in school censorship controversies. The role of parents in shaping what forms of knowledge and information children are exposed to in schools cannot be discounted. Parents can wield a lot of power when they organize to pressure school boards and school administrators into censoring perspectives they do not want their children to hear.

Parental prerogative in schools

Parents often assert their 'parental prerogative' to intervene in what their children are exposed to, or learn, at school. In the literature on school censorship, there are numerous examples of parents who pressure school boards, administrators and teachers into banning educational resources containing sexual content, witchcraft, references to homosexuality and so on that they do not want their children exposed to (Arons, 1986; Dick and Canadian Library Association, 1982; Shariff and Johnny, 2007a; Shariff and Manley-Casimir, 1999).

My research to date on parental prerogative to challenge schools on educational resources discloses that the majority of protests come from parents who feel that certain topics, books or films are inappropriate for their children. What is very clear is the power parents have over school boards, schools and government to shape what is selected for inclusion or censored from school classrooms (and, now, online learning).

The American Library Association (ALA, 2006) estimates that, in the United States, over 70 per cent of book challenges come from parents alone. Increasingly, parents have also begun to assert their parental prerogative and their rights to have a say in what their children are taught in the curriculum, as well as in the way they are socialized in schools. The following examples of school censorship cases, where parents have challenged what their children are exposed to, may not be directly related to cyber-bullying, but they show the extent of control that parents can exercise on schools to ban certain kinds of information.

Since the introduction of the Johannes Gutenberg printing press in 1455, the issue of banned books has escalated. Foerstel (1994) explains that, once speech could be printed, it became a commodity to be controlled and manipulated on the basis of religion, politics or profit. On the Internet, these opportunities are multiplied infinitely, which in turn limits the amount of control that can be exerted. Until now, books have been challenged and banned worldwide for a variety of reasons. Where young children are involved, over-protective parents have pulled no stops to prevent their children from being exposed to harmful books and resources – from the trivial depiction of a bottle of wine being brought to a sick mother in a picnic basket in the fairytale *Little red riding hood* by the Grimm brothers (ibid., 1994), to witchcraft and wizardry in David Booth's famous fourth grade reader, the *Impressions* series. Booth's reader contains a story entitled 'In my feet', where a pair of giant boots kidnap a child's parents and takes them away. Parents in Alberta, influenced by Jerry Falwell's right wing religious group in the United States, were so upset by the witchcraft in the story, they held the principal of a school in Mayo, Alberta, hostage. These powerful stakeholders threatened not to release him unless he removed the books (Shariff and Manley-Casimir, 1999).

A review by Jalongo and Creany (1991) found that children's books are usually censored for three reasons:

1   mature or realistic content inappropriate for a young and captive audience;
2   profane or obscene language; and
3   inappropriate sexual content.

Herzog's (1995) study on school censorship in the rural hills of Appalachia in the United States supported these findings. Herzog categorized school censorship by looking at the nature of censorship events, the objects of censorship, the initiators of censorship and the motivation of the protestors. Her research confirmed what we have already noted – that the nature of school censorship centres around community values, school location, cultural influences, religious beliefs and public controversies – what Steven Arons (1986, p. 8) refers to as 'corrosive, irreconcilable and proliferating conflict between government and family'.

Herzog also observed that the objects of censorship include curriculum materials, school texts, school library books involving cultural literacy, scary stories, fantasy, folktales, violence, the occult, witchcraft, taboo words, secular humanism, sexuality, creationism versus evolution and political correctness. She observed that the initiators of censorship primarily consist of those who seek to maintain a curriculum of orthodoxy and conformity. This generally involves the far right censorship network. At the other end of the spectrum, censorship is increasingly initiated by liberals and those farther to the left.

Young adult literature has also been targeted by censors. Sacco (1994) notes that literature directed towards young adults emerged in the 1930s, but it was only in 1967 that a new type of adult novel came into play – the 'problem' novel. Problem novels deal with issues that young people encounter in their journey towards adulthood. Topics covered by these books often include taboo topics such as abortion, sex, homosexuality, racism, violence, abuse, and so on. Over the years, the quality of young adult novels has improved significantly, to the point where teachers are increasingly using problem novels as classroom texts, replacing classic novels that students no longer find interesting. However, with the introduction of such novels in classrooms came problematic censorship controversies! Books that contain a lot of swear words and obscenities, for example, are often challenged by parents. Bringelson (2005) explains that, in order for a young adult to be able to imagine a scene, the author must use the slang and vulgar expressions that young people use today. At this point, it is important for the teacher to step in and explain that they do not condone such language. The books are mainly used to help youngsters appreciate that, in some contexts in the real world, offensive language is used.

Sexuality in young adult novels also invites censorship. This can range from a teenager's first sexual experience, to masturbation, sexual desires, abortions, menstruation and homosexuality. It is well known that adolescents are curious about sexuality and thus important that they are exposed to information within a supportive environment. Such books allow students to learn about the realities of life without being embarrassed. Nonetheless, books such as Alice Munro's novel, *Lives of girls and women*, where the main character sees male genitalia for the first time, were petitioned to be banned from a Toronto high school in 1982 (Wallechinsky *et al.*, 2005). Similarly, Mrs Serup, a parent in Prince George, British Columbia, removed the books *Boys and sex* and *Girls and sex* from the Prince George High School library. When asked to return them she filed a lawsuit, claiming her free expression rights under section 2(b) of the Canadian Charter of Rights and Freedoms (the 'Charter') had been infringed by the school administration. The British Columbia court ruled that her behaviour was disruptive to student learning, and that having the books in the school library did not offend her expression rights. She was concerned that she did not want her teenage son to learn about sex at school.

British Columbia in Canada seems to attract censorship controversies. In 1993, in Abbotsford, a right wing Christian community, teenager Katherine Lanteigne wrote a play entitled *If men had periods* and submitted it to a competition for $1,000 scholarship. The play was banned from the competition. This drew so much media attention that the local newspaper, *The Vancouver Sun*, held a debate to assess people's views on whether it ought to have been banned. Katherine was given $1,000 to air the play on the Canadian Broadcasting Corporation airwaves – the country's national broadcasting system. Katherine's teacher commented that the play in and of itself was not good enough to win the competition but should have been allowed by the board to enter. Instead, a mediocre play received more attention than the winning play, which really deserved attention and airing by the CBC. This supports my position that, when educators attempt to sweep sensitive matters under the rug, they in fact emerge with twice the prominence and generally embarrass the censors. Books that are banned often sell more copies than they would have, because people rush out to buy them, to see what the controversy is about. Other young adult books that have sparked controversy include Judy Blume's novel *Are you there God? It's me, Margaret*, which deals with masturbation, menstruation and intercourse.

Violence is also a topic that some parents want their children to avoid. Anthony Burgess' *A clockwork orange*, which depicts rape and violence, has invited many protests as a required high school text. Moreover, the *Captain Underpants* series by Dave Pilkey was reported by the ALA (2006) as the most challenged book of 2005 because its anti-family content was perceived as unsuited to the age group and violence. Steven Arons defines the motivation of the protestors as 'a general struggle for meaning . . . one between the forces of private dissent and the agents of public orthodoxy' (as quoted in Shariff and Manley-Casimir, 1999, p. 161). Those who challenge the school curriculum are often motivated by one or many of the following:

- religious and moral differences;
- fundamentalist parental overprotection or modern liberal values;
- politics, authoritarianism and a desire to protect administrative jobs;
- fear of psychological manipulation;
- different interpretations of the purpose of education;
- fear of change; and
- words and meanings taken out of context.

The popular Harry Potter children's books have appeared on many library and school challenged book lists (Wyman, 2000b). Parents question the appropriateness of Harry Potter books for use in the classroom because they depict wizardry and witchcraft and the books apparently 'carry a serious tone of death, hate, lack of respect and sheer evil' (Shariff *et al.*, 2001). J.K. Rowling's response is generally one of resignation. She states that if we attempt to ban all books that mention witches we would have to remove most classical children's stories. Through her characters, Rowling introduces young readers to the endless conflict between doing good and doing evil. She explains that Harry represents a child with a deep moral conscience who has a 'human underbelly' (as quoted in Wyman, 2000a). Moreover, Rowling stresses the difference between taking the right way as opposed to the easy way out of a difficult moral situation. Child psychologist Bruno Betthelheim (1989) concurred with this perspective many years ago. Bettelheim explained that, when stories force children to confront good and evil through witchcraft, magic and other forms of imagination, it actually helps them develop a moral framework of understanding the differences between right and wrong. The deepest conflicts between stakeholders are related to values – in the following case, the disputes were over religious and secular values.

As noted already, religious parents have had significant impact in having books depicting same-sex families removed from the curriculum in some school districts, while, at the same time, same-sex parents assert their rights to have their children's family backgrounds validated in the curriculum. Parents also assert their rights in the realm of special education, from requesting full integration of children with special needs into regular class-rooms, to streaming of gifted students. With an increasing public distrust of the school system, parents have also expressed their rights to review student records and question teachers' evaluation of their children's progress. At times, parents can get carried away in their zeal to protect their children. This can result in 'parental harassment'. Parental harassment has become an issue of significant concern to educators, as they attempt fulfil their professional responsibilities and cater to the demands imposed on them by parents.

It is no surprise, then, that the complexities of new technologies have parents and schools feeling helpless and out of control. Fear of change and fear of what their children will learn or access in cyberspace are legitimate concerns for parents – especially those who were formerly able to influence the schools to address their parental prerogative. This prerogative is also sometimes shaped by special interest groups that drum up fear in parents' minds.

Special interest groups

Although most censorship challenges in schools come from parents, many such parents do not challenge educational resources on their own. Rather, they are aligned with special interest groups. In the United States, for instance, there have been a number of national and religious organizations, such as the Heritage Foundation, the Eagle Forum and the Pro Family Forum, that have sought to challenge school curriculum and learning materials that address controversial issues such as abortion, teenage pregnancy, drugs and witch-craft (Booth, 1992). Reichman (1993) contends that, over the past decade, several political and religious organizations have advocated the removal of materials. His research shows that members of these organizations are often elected to school and library boards, where they attain positions of power that allow them to engage in censorship.

Ironically, it is groups with similar agendas that have taken advantage of the Internet to promote the highest levels of intolerance and prejudice towards homosexuals and non-European ethnic groups through web sites that appear to be respectable at first glance, but after clicking a few links it becomes obvious that they promote hate. Gerstenfeld *et al.* (2003) found in their study of hate sites is that many give the impression they are neutral by exhibit-ing non-violent statements. This point is exemplified on 'Brotherhood of the Lamb' (www.brotherhoodofthelamb.com), a web site that hosts violent cartoons, photographs and videos of the Middle East. The first page of the web site states: 'BrotherhoodOfTheLamb.com does not condone violence, bigotry or racism against anyone'. Such statements share the same space with phrases such as 'Fascism didn't die with Hitler – Present Day Islamic [are] Fascists' (Brotherhood of the Lamb, no date). Another tactic that these sites use to garner support is the inclusion of educational pages. For example, Gerstenfeld *et al.* (2003) found that, in the hate sites they reviewed 7 per cent included children's pages, some with games, music and alternative history lessons. In the past decade, there has been a growing awareness of the manner in which technology is used to incite hatred. The urgency of addressing this topic was noted at the World Conference Against Racism, where officials met to discuss the regulation of hate speech and racist propaganda on the Internet (United Nations, 2001).

In examining the nature of hate sites, Gerstenfeld *et al.* (2003) note that many groups create sites that have a professional look and feel, in order to lend greater credibility to the sinister messages that they espouse. For example, the 'People's Truth Forum' (www.peoplestruthforum.com) is a web site devoted to news and information on terrorism around the world. It uses a layout similar to that of a professional news web site, thereby intimating that it is produced using journalistic ethics. Although it links to articles on terror from professional news syndicates such as CNN, *Time Magazine* and the *Times of London*, it also has links to e-zines and other less reputable sources, ones that have a clear ideological overlay.

Certainly, online hate and societal influences are not restricted to one group of people – extremists come from all facets of society. As it is difficult to censor such sites, it makes better sense to make young people aware that they exist. As constant monitoring of the sites children visit is also difficult, informed children may be less inclined to get drawn in by their message. Dialogue, open discussion and a range of sources, including books, historical accounts of people from various races and religions and other educational sources, show greater promise of ensuring children know enough to make their own thoughtful judgements about whether to visit such sites, in the same way that we prepare them not to visit pornography web sites or engage in online abuse.

Government influence

Although governments play a vital role in developing responses to cyber-bullying, such as the European Union, UK web sites, proposed American legislation (DOPA) and similar legislation in Singapore, South Korea and India, they also have a large influence on the initial selection of learning resources. Governments have significant influence over shaping the types of student expression that are allowed in schools; informing and moulding young people's attitudes and values within the school itself. Most schools are agents of the state. A primary responsibility of schools is to develop young people's values and dispositions towards civil and social responsibility, so that they can contribute constructively to the democracies in which most of them live. Nonetheless, the political and systemic thrust towards control of information often makes this antithetical to the spirit of education and democracy.

The legislative initiatives that a number of governments have introduced are largely in reaction to demands by the public and educators to do something about cyber-bullying. The proposed DOPA bill referred to in Chapter 5 is one example, as is the amended Ontario Education Act and the legislation introduced by the South Korean government that criminalizes certain forms of online expression (see Chapter 3).

Censorship of expression, whether it is in the form of what students say or what they read and learn, is not a new phenomenon in schools. Governments have always promoted political agendas through the types of learning material they approve. However, until the advent of information technologies, those materials were generally tactile – in the form of text-books, library books, videotapes, photographs, tape-recordings and so on. They were not a moving target as expression and information now are, in cyberspace.

Apple and Christian-Smith (1991) remind us that educational resources are not simply 'delivery systems' that convey a set of objective 'facts'. Instead, they are creations designed and selected by people with a particular set of interests. The recent panic to amend existing legislation and bring in new laws to 'control' bullying and cyber-bullying indicates that many politicians are nervous about online student expression because they cannot control information that is accessed online and, therefore, cannot ban it. In other words, they cannot ban specific online content because it takes different forms, in blogs, chat rooms, email, MSN, cellphone texts, online videos and social networks such as Facebook.

When government officials approve learning materials that favour one worldview over another, it is arguable that they engage in shaping knowledge by failing to represent multiple perspectives. This point is exemplified in a number of conservative states in the United States and some Canadian provinces, where official text-books omit any discussion of homosexuality as a legitimate lifestyle. This in turn might play a significant role in the level of homophobic cyber-bullying that takes place. The United States, of course, is not the only nation where the education system is vulnerable to the interests of politicians. In many countries, the government is one of the primary institutions through which education is offered to the public, and, therefore, the selection of educational materials and policies has close links to the ideological interests of those who govern the nation. Consider China as an example. That country is undergoing enormous changes to the government's ability to control information with the advent of the Internet and the move towards capitalism.

Change often creates a sense of fear and insecurity that elicits the types of 'knee-jerk' reaction that have emerged as a result of teachers experiencing online bullying in countries in the West. As Larson (1997) notes, institutions (and in this case political institutions) maintain authority and regain control of unfamiliar situations by allocating dangerous characteristics to individuals or scapegoats. In this case, cyberspace and its tools of communication have become the designated scapegoats, as have youngsters who choose to test its boundaries. By creating fear in the minds of people that there is an urgent need to control the dangers, the actual issues, such as racism or sexism, which need attention, are ignored, overlooked and swept under the rug by magnifying the dangers and describing the situation as a 'battle'.

When we talk about cyber-bullying as it has emerged in contemporary society, it is not difficult to find that similar attitudes, perspectives and hegemonies originate with adults and significantly impact the forms of cyber-bullying that take place online.

Adult society models intolerance through political and racial conflicts; debates over homosexuality and abortion; and the ultimate forms of violence – terrorism, war, and systemic oppression of some races, religions, peoples and countries, over others. For example, the heinous acts of 11 September 2001 brought to the surface a much-needed political debate and, in particular, a spotlight on all Muslims. Although extremism and terrorist acts in the name of religion cannot be condoned under any circumstances, these acts have brought the world's attention to the plight, hopelessness and desperation that drive generations of young people in the Middle East who have known nothing but war. As the world is beginning to realize, reactionary zero-tolerance responses without addressing the roots of the issue achieve very little and do more to exacerbate the problems. The current war in Iraq is evidence of this. The governments that became involved in instigating that particular battle have demonstrated their power – but infringed some of their own fundamental constitutional provisions, the civil liberties of their own citizens and international human rights treaties in the process. The political unpopularity of leaders such as President Bush and former Prime Minister Tony Blair are clear evidence of the need for diplomatic, ethical and peaceful responses that foster trust and commitment, as opposed to death and destruction where nobody wins. These examples of what I call 'state bullying' greatly shape and influence the opinions, lives and collective education of young people globally.

One California teenager experienced state bullying and discovered very quickly the extent to which governments can become involved when they don't like certain forms of online expression. According to a media report ('California Grade 9 girl questioned about threats to Bush on MySpace' (Yahoo, 2006)), Julia Wilson posted a picture of US President Bush on her MySpace page. In the same vein as the Canadian students who were suspended for posting anti-authority expression on Facebook, Julia scrawled 'Kill Bush' across the top of the picture and drew a dagger stabbing his outstretched hand. She replaced the page last spring after learning in her grade 8 history class that such threats are a federal offence. This however, was too late to prevent a visit from secret service agents. Julia was pulled out of a science class for a fifteen minute interview. The media report noted that her parents were upset she was questioned in their absence as they should have been notified and present during the interview. Here are excerpts from the story:

> On Friday, Wilson said the agents' questioning about her page on the popular teen Internet gathering spot brought her to tears.
> 'I wasn't dangerous. I mean, look at what's (stenciled) on my backpack – it's a heart . . . I'm a very peace-loving person,' said Wilson, an honor student who describes herself as politically passionate. 'I'm against the war in Iraq. I'm not going to kill the president.'
> Her mother, Kristie Wilson, said two agents showed up at the family home in an upscale neighborhood Wednesday afternoon, questioned her and promised to return once her daughter was home from school. After they left, Kristie Wilson sent a text message to her daughter's cellphone, to come straight home:
> 'There are two men from the secret service that want to talk to you. Apparently you made some death threats against President Bush,' the message said.

'Are you serious!?!? Omg. Am I in a lot of trouble?' her daughter wrote back, using code for 'Oh, my God.'

Moments later, the girl's mother received another text message from her daughter that agents had pulled her out of class.

Julia Wilson said the agents threatened her by saying she could be sent to juvenile prison for making the threat.

'They yelled at me a lot,' she said.

'They were unnecessarily mean.'

Julia and her parents said the agents were justified in questioning her about her MySpace.com posting. But they said they believe agents went too far by not waiting until Julia was out of school and questioning her without a parent present.

They also said the agents should have more quickly figured out they were not dealing with real danger. Ultimately, the agents told the teenager they would delete her [posting].

'She obviously is not a threat to society. If you look at her age, her family background, cartoonish nature of the MySpace page' said her father, Jim Moose, an environmental lawyer.

'She is just a typical teenage girl who made a mistake,' said her mother during an interview at their neatly landscaped home.

Assistant principal Paul Belluomini said the agents gave him the impression the parents knew they were planning to question her daughter at school. There is no legal requirement parents be notified.

Spokesmen for the Secret Service in Sacramento and Washington said they could not comment.

The California teen is planning to post a new MySpace.com page, this one devoted to organizing other students to protest against the Iraq war.

'I decided today I think I will because it [the questioning] went too far.'

(Yahoo, 2006)

We ought to be conscious of the fact that this media article may be framed to reinforce the general sense of dissatisfaction in California with President Bush and the Iraq war. Although it played down Julia's innocence (because she was from an upscale neighbourhood where none of its inhabitants could do wrong), the incident in and of itself is important. It illustrates the power of government to get involved in monitoring expression, even among high school students. The pattern in all these cases reflects the fact that many young people do not realize the seriousness with which their online jokes can be taken. Now, substitute a 'homegrown' Muslim teen in Julia's place – let's call him Mohammed Ali. Even if Mohammed Ali's father was an environmental lawyer, and even if he lived in the same upscale neighbourhood with the beautiful landscape, would he have got off as easily as Julia? Based on the fear of terrorism in the United States, the United Kingdom and elsewhere, and given the enormous focus by media especially in the United Kingdom and Canada following the subway bombings in 2005 by 'homegrown' young men, and the arrest of approximately seventeen young men in Canada who were suspected of wanting to blow up the houses of parliament, it is very plausible that the situation might have been much worse for a teen with a Muslim background – regardless of the fact that he might have been as naive and innocent as the story makes Julia out to be. This is why there is such a need to educate young people, not only about the possible ramifications of their online jokes and comments, but also about how their comments may be interpreted out of context because of an 'unconscious fear' (Sadria, 2007) that resides in the minds of people who feel threatened by new technologies as well as people from different cultures. A positive turnout in Julia's case was that, instead of this incident making her fearful, it prompted her to take leadership in doing something about her concerns relating to the Iraq war. She organized a formal protest involving her peers. What came through the article clearly was the supportive relationship Julia had with her parents. Parental support can make an enormous difference in empowering young people to engage in political debates towards *positive* and *educational* changes in society.

Schools in North America, the United Kingdom and Europe no longer cater for homogeneous school populations. Instead, these countries are dealing with the accommodation of students from a range of diverse backgrounds, cultures and religions. The 'curriculum of orthodoxy' I allude to is sustained through the forms of legislation and political guidelines for schools that eliminate perceived undesirable content through resource selection that is limited to a certain genre of curriculum resources. In the West, this in fact sustains a largely Eurocentric and androcentric school environment – where important knowledge that promotes understanding of diversity is omitted or censored. In an era where it is essential for a better appreciation of the diversity, intellectualism and ethic of peace within Islam, for example, my colleague Professor Joe Kincheloe argues for more comprehensive curricula to achieve this. As he observes in his book *Miseducation of the West*:

> Many scholars maintain that the classroom is a central site for the legitimization of myths and silences about non-Western and often non-Christian peoples. If educators who value the power of difference were to teach about the history of Islam, they would have to rethink the canonical history of the West. Indeed, when school texts distort the history of Islam, they concurrently distort all history. Teachers and educational leaders who act on the power of difference forge such recognition into a politically transformative mode of education. Such a pedagogy understands Western societies as collectivities of difference where the potential exists for

everyone to be edified by interaction with the other and the ways of knowing what he or she brings to an encounter.

(Kincheloe, 2004, p.2)

Bakan (1999) argues that how the production of curriculum is organized and whose interests are served in the process inevitably have an impact on its content, which in turn can dispose young people to take on certain perspectives and attitudes that ultimately play out in their social relationships – whether those relationships are at school or in virtual space.

School boards

Along with ministries of education, school boards also have significant discretionary powers. For example, in British Columbia, Canada, section 85 of the School Act states that school boards have the power to both 'determine local policy for the effective and efficient operation of schools' and 'approve educational resource materials and other supplies and services'. Moreover, section 76(3) suggests that 'the highest morality will be inculcated but schools will be run on a strictly secular and non-sectarian basis'. On the one hand, this provides board members with the autonomy needed to select resources and policies suited to the needs of their school community, but, when it advocates the 'inculcation' of the 'highest morality', it raises important questions about whose values can be considered to be of the 'highest morality'.

On the other, it is arguable that even the decisions of board members are susceptible to political pressures and outside influences. For instance, as elected officials, school trustees are accountable to their voters and vulnerable to the demands of special interest groups. One of the ramifications of this structure is that educational decisions are sometimes propelled by a need to appease powerful voices rather than a genuine concern for the diverse perspectives and values of the school community. With the emerging concerns relating to insults that have been posted on social communications tools such as Facebook and YouTube, school boards, like the governments in various parts of Canada, the United States, Ireland and the United Kingdom, have had to bow under considerable pressure from teachers' federations and teachers' unions.

In a landmark lawsuit that reached the Supreme Court of Canada in 1998, one school board, the Surrey school board (SSB) in British Columbia, succumbed to considerable pressure from a vocal group of religious parents arbitrarily to ban three children's books depicting same-sex families, contravening section 76(3) of the British Columbia School Act noted above, that schools would remain strictly secular. A gay kindergarten teacher had submitted the books to his school board for approval to reduce homophobia (and homophobic bullying) at his school. The controversial case proceeded to the Supreme Court of Canada, costing Canadian tax-payers over $4 million dollars in legal fees that might have been avoided. Although these examples do not involve cyber-bullying, they most certainly illustrate the way in which societal stakeholders can influence school policy on what is expressed and learned in the school context.

With the emergence of cyber-technologies, school board officials worldwide are no doubt concerned about how to manage access to information that was previously much easier to control. As the diversity within school populations increases to become multicultural, multi-ethnic, multireligious (and much more interesting!), the challenges for school boards increase as they attempt to navigate competing rights and interests. As the OCT survey shows below, teachers believe that school boards have a significant responsibility (49%) to formulate and explain rules and state the potential for consequences. However, the expectations of school boards by teachers need to be reconceptualized to stress that they concentrate on improving the school culture rather than engaging in punitive codes of conduct.

> *Question*: Which of the following statements given in Figure 6.4 best describes any policy that your school or board may have on how students may communicate on the Internet and web sites or in e-mail and chat rooms?

Other examples of school board interference in student learning (and thereby their attitudes and actions) took place in the Canadian province of Ontario. The Toronto district school board removed the children's book *Three wishes* by Deborah Ellis from its school libraries. PEN Canada (2006) reports that the book had been nominated by the Ontario Library Association (OLA) for the Silver Book Award – a competition in which children in grades 4–6 are invited to vote for the winner. The Canadian Jewish Congress argued that the book's discussion of the conflict between Israelis and Palestinians was inappropriately suited for the age level that the competition was targeting and asked both the OLA and school boards to remove the book from the competition. Although it is clear that school boards have a duty to approve resources that reflect the unique character of their communities and the values

A. There are formal, well understood rules with potential consequences.
B. There may be formal rules but they are not widely understood.
C. There are informal rules.
D. There are no rules.

DNK (do not know/no opinion)

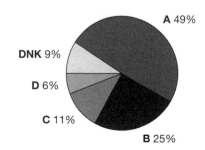

Figure 6.4 School policy

(Reproduced with permission of the OCT, 28 August 2007)

held by its parents, no school is completely homogeneous, especially in plural-istic societies. Therefore, when educational decisions are made, competing agendas and values must be considered. Unfortunately, given the political nature of the education system, this is not always the case, and as such, mater-ials that might contribute positively to public discussion and raise greater awareness of controversial issues are removed from school reading lists. It is plausible that this may no longer be the case as online resources become adopted over time.

Media as censor

Given that issues involving anti-authority cyber-bullying have begun to emerge recently (2006–7), there are few scholarly studies that have yet qualitatively surveyed its incidence and school responses. Therefore, through-out this book, I have had little choice but to rely to some extent on media reports and on personal communications by school administrators and teachers, to discuss case studies. I reiterate that I am all the while conscious that there may be aspects of those cases that are not disclosed in the media reports or personal communications. Nonetheless, I contend that no matter how the media frames the issues, there are definitely clear patterns that emerge in most reports. These reflect the fact that students and technologies have become scapegoats for deeper systemic hierarchies of power within schools and among stakeholders that ought not to be overlooked in our attempts to address the policy vacuum.

I support Edwards (2005) and Mazzarella (2005) when they caution that the news media can control reality to a certain extent, by framing stories to fit certain agendas and control the message to place the spotlight on certain issues over others. When media reporters and editors select information and wording to formulate a new story, they in effect become powerful 'censors' of information that ought to reach the public but is often left out of the picture or given less focus. Engaging in critical media literacy is not a simple task, but it is essential. There is an entire body of scholarship that has emerged in the last decade to convince us about the utility and necessity of engaging in critical media literacy (Chomsky, 2007; Macedo and Steinberg, 2007; Shaheen, 2003; Shaheen, 2000).

Although I did not systematically go through over 100 news report articles on the topic of cyber-bullying to identify specific patterns, as I write this book, I have quickly become aware of very clear patterns. I am at present surrounded by at least forty or fifty print media reports, many of which were reported in the last year (2006–7), as they relate to anti-authority forms of online social networking postings by high school students. Before I move on to addressing the legal frameworks and tensions between student free expression and school supervision in the upcoming chapter, it would be helpful to deconstruct a couple of these media excerpts. This deconstruction is followed by brief mention of the media impact on society as it relates to larger political issues. I raise these broader issues here to illustrate how society models attitudes to young people. When these attitudes are reflected in the discriminatory comments that teenagers post online, society reacts negatively and with surprise, without recognizing that the postings simply reflect and mirror adult attitudes in society that surround young people. I have modified some of Edwards' (2005) headings to analyse the way in which specific words are used in media reports to convey a particular type of message.

Cyber-victims – good students who get caught

One of the patterns that emerged in many of the news media articles about kids who were suspended from school for their online postings is that they were all generally good students. Each one ran astray and paid too heavy a price for his/her teenage horseplay. For example, Brad Parsons is described as a 'teen who "likes hanging out and chilling" with his friends'; that 'he and his friends have long had problems with [a vice-principal]'; and that their group was singled out because they hung around in the back of the school where 'other students created problems'. He is then by implication described as a model student:

> whose favourite classes are English and drama, says he was getting good grades and was finishing an essay on MacBeth when he was expelled. . . . 'I'm losing out on my education because of this and it's going to set me back', he said.
>
> (Chung, 2007)

As Edwards would argue, all this emphasis on the fact that Brad is a good student who likes English and drama; who had ongoing problems with the assistant principal; and will now likely lose out on his education; together with his mother's comments to the effect that we all said mean things about teachers, have the combined effect of trivializing the content of the online expression that got him into trouble in the first place. Nor do we hear the side of the assistant principal as to the nature of the ongoing 'trouble' this particular group of kids who hung out in the back of the school had with her (or she had with them). Moreover, the article states conflicting facts as to whether he was expelled or not. Earlier on, the article says Brad had been told he was going to be expelled but wasn't, and the same article later states, that as a fact, he was expelled. The school superintendent is reported to confirm in a different, later and better balanced report that he was not in fact expelled, although he claimed to reporters that he had been expelled (Girard and Nguyen, 2007).

Even though I am strongly against suspensions for this form of cyber-bullying, and while I do believe these youngsters when they say that they did not realize the seriousness of the demeaning words they use online, it does bother me that, in presenting Brad as a squeaky clean student who wouldn't think of doing wrong, the media trivializes the fact that the expression possibly crossed a fine line. It is important that students are shown that some of their comments could render them liable for a legal offence such as cyber-libel, which I will discuss in Chapter 7. Moreover, even though the students maintain their belief that this was a private conversation, as Edwards (2005) would argue, the media angle taken in this case shifted the focus away from the importance of engaging with the teens to discuss the issues they were having with their assistant principal. Clearly there were conflicts. The article also precluded an explanation from her perspective. It is highly likely that she was having as much trouble with the teens as they were having with her when they 'hung out' in the back of the school.

Hence, although I do not believe these tensions should be conceptualized as a battle, and nor do I necessarily agree with the formal and rather harsh initiatives that are emerging internationally to address this form of cyber-bullying, I certainly do not absolve the students of responsibility. What I would like to see are increased efforts to *guide them to take responsibility for their actions*. We ought to help them understand the impact their expression has on the overall climate and learning within the school, and also find out whether their comments are the result of a poisoned environment that exists within the school.

Another media account discussed above presents Julia Wilson's experience (discussed earlier) in a similar way. Julia is described as a teenager from a well-to-do suburb. The article implies that someone who has hearts on her knapsack could do nothing wrong. As I pointed out, the impact of Julia's online threat was minimized because of her racial background and the economic status of her parents. The following excerpts make her appear completely innocent, which takes the focus off the fact that she *did* write the words 'Kill Bush', and, regardless of how much she did not agree with the Iraq war, this was not the way to express her views:

'I wasn't dangerous. I mean, look at what's (stenciled) on my backpack – it's a heart . . . I'm a very peace-loving person', said Wilson, an honor student who describes herself as politically passionate. 'I'm against the war in Iraq. I'm not going to kill the president'.

Moreover, presenting her as a clueless teenager is equally effective:

'Are you serious!?!? Omg. Am I in a lot of trouble?' her daughter wrote back, using code for 'Oh, my God.'

(Yahoo, 2006)

Quite clearly, her decision to organize a protest against the war in Iraq and the fact that she is an honours student suggest she is bright enough to realize that when she posted the expression it would definitely draw a reaction. My point in deconstructing this media article is to show that, although the teen clearly made a mistake and may not have realized the implications of her actions, it is important to acknowledge that teens ought to take some responsibility for her actions. In Julia's case, her parents took the positive steps of guiding her towards positive ways to engage in a form of activism on an issue she felt strongly about. Organizing a protest against the Iraq war gave her the agency she had sought online and a feeling that she could contribute to solving the problem. In other cases where students have made negative comments about their teachers, they too are using the Internet as a tool for agency – where they feel empowered to do something about a poisoned environment at their school or trouble with one teacher. Regrettably, they quickly find out that this form of agency is not as effective, and this is where a non-reactive but educational approach would provide them with alternative avenues to express their feelings and contribute to changing their learning environment.

Cyber-criminals: police as hero

In contrast to the report of Brad Parsons as a model student, two other reports on the same story focused on the student protest and the 'clash' between students and police. One of them in *The Toronto Star* (Girard and Nguyen, 2007), read as follows:

> Four teenagers have been arrested after a protest over the punishment of a fellow high school student turned violent when police, trying to divert traffic, were pelted by objects including a bottle and a skateboard.
>
> The ugly incident outside Birchmount Park Collegiate Institute in the Danforth Avenue and Birchmount Road area yesterday followed the suspension earlier this week of five students after school administrators discovered derogatory comments about Birchmount Park staff . . .
>
> 'Everyone was on the road and then things started flying and the cops started flipping out,' said Ryan Duffy, 16, a Grade 11 student who saw the melee in which angry protesters yelled at police and chased officers as the young men were arrested, handcuffed and pinned on the ground, then thrown into cruisers . . .

The use of words such as 'ugly', 'pelted', 'pinned on the ground, then thrown into cruisers' highlights the power of the state in winning the battle. In the same article are comments by the superintendent noting that 'bullying using a new information technology . . . gives kids way more power than they've had'.

It comes through quite clearly in many similar media reports that the battle is about power between schools and students – and if the students are getting too much power using new 'technology', then the police will heed the call to order and put them back in their place, using force if necessary.

Although the students in this case are also reported as having provoked police officers – apparently they threw bottles and skateboards – nonetheless, it is the way that this media report presents the sequence of events that is suggestive of who wins the battle when the heroes are brought in. Moreover, note the singular use of the word 'technology' rather than 'technologies' by the superintendent. This is an example of the adult mindset towards technologies that Lankshear and Knobel (2006) have drawn to our attention. It implies that technology as a singular entity – just like 'digital literacy' – can be controlled and managed, suggesting a lack of appreciation of its plurality and fluidity.

I want to emphasize again that I do not believe the students involved are absolved of responsibility for their words and actions. I have already illustrated this, using examples of the media reports that make the perpetrators look like victims. This is the elusive fine line that always comes up between free expression and authority.

Media framing of global issues

Before moving to a discussion of the legal considerations, I believe it is in order to highlight a few examples of how, in greater society, aside from issues relating to cyber-bullying, the media also play a significant role in shaping public perceptions. These ultimately play themselves out as value conflicts or discrimination in schools.

For example, post-11 September media reports have had a tremendous influence in formulating people's perspectives about certain groups in society by essentializing the characteristics of all members of that group. Take Muslims as an example again, because it is this group that has suffered the most from contemporary political media framing and stereotyping. For example, by referring to 'Muslim terrorist' but not 'Christian bomber' (such as, Timothy McVeigh, who bombed a high-rise building killing approximately 160 people), the media create a fear of all Muslims in the minds of the public. Martin and Phelan (2002) argue that the association of terrorism with the broader culture from which it emerges creates stereotypes that are propagated through the repetition of identifying labels. Said (1997) reminds us that this construction of non-Western cultures as alien and irrational is part of a much larger system of hegemonic colonial forces that have traditionally essentialized and diminished the heterogeneity and diversity of Islam.

The mass media have largely neglected to depict the everyday lives of Muslims in favour of a more sensationalized image (Shaheen, 2003). This is evidenced by the ubiquity of clichés that characterize Muslims and Arabs as fundamentalists and terrorists (Martin and Phelan, 2002; Nacos and Torres-Reyna, 2002; J. Shaheen, 2003). Such clichés have informed the world-views of powerful stakeholders in public institutions such as schools. Consequently, educational decisions are often rooted in hegemonic ideologies rather than a genuine understanding of minority religions and cultures. In the United Kingdom and Canada, the courts have intervened to adjudicate cases that involve the banning of religious clothing such as the hijab, or symbols in schools, such as the Sikh kirpan, a ceremonial dagger to be worn by Khalsa Sikh males at all times (Shariff, 2006; Shariff and Johnny, 2007a). The attitudes perpetuated by news reports have a substantial influence on shaping teacher and school principal attitudes and, ultimately, those of our children.

Even prior to 11 September, Dolmage (2000), in his article entitled 'lies damned lies!', laid out the facts clearly that the news media often publish headlines relating to one news item (such as gang violence) next to unrelated photographs (such as a black teen), so that the image and association sticks in the readers' minds. Moreover, Dolmage provides evidence of the inaccurate and exaggerated statistics that are sometimes presented by reporters who may not be as diligent in their research as they ought to be. Thus the news media censors by making deliberate decisions on what should be presented to the public and what should be withheld. This filters into the school system and the consciousness of stakeholders who buy into the media messages and especially the stereotypes. Consequently, the news media have a powerful influence on shaping what children learn in schools.

Media framing perpetuated racial stereotypes in North America as early as the late 1800s, when newspapers were largely anti-Chinese (Anderson, as cited in Mahtani, 2001). There was a general absence of women of colour for a thirty-year period in prominent Canadian magazines such as *MacLean's* (MacGregor, as cited in Mahtani, 2001). It is regrettable to note that this has not changed significantly. More recently, in the United States, major networks such as CBS have refused to air political advertisements that are critical of President Bush, and children's shows that show families with same-sex parents have also been refused by stations such as PBS (Sanders, 2005). Whether one labels these acts of exclusion as discrimination or ideological dominance (Lorimer, 1999), the main point is that both conscious and unconscious forms of censorship are rampant in the mass media. It is not surprising then that students reiterate discriminatory and disrespectful attitudes and perspectives when they find the freedom of cyberspace, absent of the need to conform to adult rules.

Courts as censors

Courts have significant impact in shaping public policy. Judiciaries internationally will have a role in ultimately shaping the way that schools respond to cyber-bullying and Internet use by children and young people. In the upcoming chapter, I highlight several court decisions that have relevance to cyber-bullying and that determine appropriate remedies for educational policy and practice. Recent court cases define and describe cyber-bullying and determine appropriate remedies. Rulings not only address the case at hand, but also set precedents, which influence future legal and policy decisions. In so doing, courts define, monitor and maintain the limits of persons and activities.

Judges make their rulings based on the facts of each case, but, in doing so, often accepting social constructs that I have talked about, which are already embedded in the language. In this regard, the courts are merely another arm of the influential power base that governs public institutions such as schools. When these constructs go unquestioned, courts tacitly legitimate them, including taken-for-granted assumptions about children, school, free speech and authority. Existing power relationships thereby continue, reinforced by the courts. Law, therefore, wields power — both in terms of the decisions courts render and the constructs they subtly endorse. To understand legal power, it is important to look at the language of law, for, in law, language is power. Hence, the perspectives of critical theorists and pedagogues such as Giroux (2003), Kincheloe (2005), Apple (1990; 2000) and McLaren (1998) draw attention to the way in which the courts 'talk about' cyber-bullying and how, in legal terms, it could become defined and embedded in legal precedent. Through the lens of critical theory and cultural studies of law, it is essential to examine the assumptions that judges make about educator authority and the fiduciary relationships of trust between teachers and their students, and to examine how these relationships impinge upon and restrict free speech and learning. Once a landmark court decision in an emerging area such as cyber-bullying is handed down, the doctrine of *stare decisis* (adherence to precedent) ensures that most future decisions adhere to the landmark precedent, unless the court can 'distinguish' a case as sufficiently different to move away from precedent. In this regard, the courts have a powerful influence on shaping governmental policy and practice. Schools, as government agents, must adhere to the standards set out by the courts.

Having set the context of power hierarchies among stakeholders, I now move to discussion of the legal frameworks that apply to the tension between student free expression, privacy, safety and supervision in cyberspace in Chapter 7.

Chapter 7

Balancing free expression
Privacy and safety in cyberspace

The landscape upon which the line where the balance tips from protected speech for students to permissible punitive power for school administrators has changed dramatically. The Internet marks that landscape change as dramatically as the Front Range marks the end of the Great Plains.

(Beidler vs North Thurston Sch. Dist., No. 99-2-00236-6
Thurston Cty. Super. Ct., July 18, 2000)

Introduction

Unlike in Golding's (Golding, 1954) time, today's young people do not have to go to a remote island to find a changed landscape. It is as close as the cellphone or the family microcomputer. Cyberspace has become a real locale without clearly established rules on cyber-civility. On the Internet, no one has yet found an acceptable and workable way to create and enforce the modicum of culture that allows people to get along with each other. Nowhere on the Internet is this more true than in the virtual space frequented by children, who often have the technological capacity and skill to run electronic circles around their elders, but who lack the internal psychological and sociological controls to moderate their behaviour.

Maintaining civil behaviour is difficult enough in organized society, even where the rule of law is supposed to prevail, and where order and authority exist to protect innocent citizens. But what happens – as in dystopian fiction – when the rules and the authority are removed or are perceived by young people as inapplicable in cyberspace? This is the dilemma that schools confront as they attempt to navigate the legal and moral challenges around responding to cyber-bullying and, ultimately, as they attempt to develop in students appropriate moral compasses for an electronic age.

This chapter joins a body of emerging work on the legal issues relating to cyber-bullying and its impact on student safety and learning in the school context. Most of the cases are from the United States and Canada (Balfour, 2005; Servance, 2003; Willard, 2003). At this stage, my legal research in other countries is just beginning. It builds on my own previous work that examines the legal considerations relating to freedom of expression and safety under the Canadian Charter of Rights and Freedoms; Canadian human rights law and American civil rights law (Title IX): Internet sexual harassment; potential school liability under Canadian and American tort law; and finally, international conventions relating to children's rights (Shariff, 2004; Shariff and Gouin, 2005; Shariff and Strong-Wilson, 2005).

North American laws are largely derived from British common law, which continues to be applied in most post-colonial countries across the globe. Therefore, although I rely for the most part on the North American jurisprudence and legislation in this chapter, the policy guidelines that I develop to inform solutions to these issues are pertinent to the international context. Countries such as India, Japan, United Kingdom, Australia, South Korea and New Zealand work within similar legal frameworks and can also benefit from an appreciation of applicable legal frameworks and judicial trends. As the preliminary data presented in Chapter 3 on the emerging international profile of cyber-bullying indicate, many countries are just awakening to an awareness of cyber-bullying. As already noted, scholarship in many countries is not yet established and is currently beginning to get underway. Research projects are emerging worldwide to examine how young citizens in various countries are adapting to, and using, technology. The way in which schools, as institutional agents of the political and social orders of each country, respond has also yet to be assessed. As far as my own international research project on cyber-bullying is concerned (www.cyberbullying.co.nr/) I will, subsequent to publication of this book, be working with international collaborators to compile a separate and updated publication. Our publication, to be launched in 2008–9, will contain focused chapters on the profile, extent and responses taking place in each country involved in our project. Our edited publication will include academic papers to be delivered at an international conference to be held jointly with NetSafe, a non-profit organization in New Zealand, in July 2008.

In the meantime, it is nonetheless important to consider how North American and British courts have addressed the complexities of free expression, privacy, cyber-libel and responses to student expression, especially in terms of the legal obligations to supervise expression on and off campus.

My doctoral research on bullying and general research in education law issues confirm that courts have always deferred to educational expertise, being reluctant to infringe on the authority of those in charge of providing public education (Case, 1997). Courts are further reluctant to unleash the floodgates to litigation in cases of bullying, because of the potential for millions of claims that might clog the judicial system. Because of the number of people who can access technology and run into some form of abuse, it is not surprising that most claims of bullying or cyber-bullying are settled out of court. I mentioned a number of such cases in Chapters 2–4.[1] With respect to general bullying and educational malpractice cases mentioned here, the courts have unequivocally stated that 'as a matter of public policy' they cannot get involved in educational decisions, unless there is clear evidence of constitutional infringement or issues of gross negligence or libel (Jafaar, 2002).

I begin with a review of relevant established and emerging areas of law through analysis of judicial decisions, to identify a set of educational and legally defensible policy standards. My purpose is to guide educators and parents in knowing the extent of their responsibilities to intervene when students engage in cyber-bullying (whether it is peer-to-peer or anti-authoritarian cyber-discourse). Put another way, I highlight limits on the extent to which educators are obliged to intervene and discipline students when communications in cyberspace take on abusive dimensions. Based on legal decisions pertaining to certain forms of bullying or cyber-bullying, such as sexual harassment, homophobia, institutional responsibilities, libel and cyber-libel, negligence in supervision of students – all of which have clarified institutional or personal obligations (even in matters that do not relate specifically to cyber-bullying) – we can develop a set of standards that are educational, non-arbitrary and 'legally defensible'. The term 'legally defensible' means that, if challenged in a court of law, school administrators or teachers could defend their actions by establishing that they were aware of, and understood, the extent or limits of their responsibilities to intervene, and did so within the parameters of the boundaries established by the courts.

Given that most cases on traditional bullying have been settled out of court without going to trial, even fewer precedents on cyber-bullying exist at the time this book is written. Murphy's Law might dictate that, as soon as this book hits the presses, a landmark case on cyber-bullying will surface and set a legal precedent. If that happens, the new decision will be reported in journals or book chapters that follow and will add to the foundation that I provide here. For now, it is possible to seek guidance from thousands of cases involving negligence in supervision on school playgrounds and field trips and cyber-libel cases involving adults and Internet use (tort law); sexual and homophobic harassment and other forms of discrimination under civil and human rights law; and freedom of expression and privacy considerations under constitutional law, particularly where the fostering of a positive school environment is concerned. These court rulings under established and emerging law make it possible to extrapolate and gauge the legal boundaries (or extent of authority and responsibilities) that can be expected of educational stakeholders when dealing with cyber-bullying. If we can find consistencies or trends in judicial decisions regarding the institutional and professional responsibilities of adults in school contexts, and detect shifts in judicial approaches to assessing on- and off-campus technology use and supervision, we can inform the development of a framework of standards to address the existing policy vacuum. This, however, is only the first step in developing a set of guidelines for educators.

As I will explain in Chapter 8, having some knowledge of the legal boundaries will not be sufficient for schools. Once identified, these legal standards need to be applied to a larger educational framework. In Chapter 8, I establish that the standards extrapolated here are also compatible with comprehensive educational theories in critical pedagogy, social justice, leadership and substantive law. In other words, Chapter 7 will take readers through analysis of various legal interpretations that are applicable to cyber-bullying among peers and anti-authority forms of expression, and develop a framework of standards (see Table 7.1, p. 224) to highlight the key legal responsibilities of schools. Those standards will then be applied, in Chapter 8, to an educational framework that facilitates an understanding of how they can inform the core educational philosophy of teachers and school administrators, and how this in turn can inform ethical, educational and legally defensible policies and practices in schools. Applied together, the legal and educational components show greater promise of fostering school environments (physical and virtual) that are inclusive and conducive to improved learning. Ultimately, these ought to be the goals of education.

Legal frameworks

In presenting the legal frameworks, I focus on the two quite separate forms of cyber-bullying:

1   peer-to-peer cyber-bullying; and
2   anti-authority cyber-insubordination.

Each of these forms requires application of different but overlapping areas of law, because of the nature and content of the expression; the private or public nature; the on- or off-campus considerations, and the nexus to school or home. As I have mentioned, the jury is still out as to whether anti-authority online comments on social networking sites constitute cyber-bullying.

Although many aspects of cyber-bullying are clearly criminal in nature (such as threats of violence, criminal coercion, terrorist threats, stalking, hate crimes, child pornography and sexual exploitation, all of which would most likely be subject to prosecution if brought before the courts), I focus greater attention on the institutional responsibilities of schools, as opposed to the criminal liability of students, although I will touch upon the need to educate students about the fine line at which their forms of expression can breach criminal laws.

Tort law

The first of the legal frameworks is tort law (or the law to correct 'wrongs' committed intentionally or unintentionally) (Linden and Klar, 1994). There are two areas of tort law relevant to cyber-bullying of peers and authority figures: libel and negligence. Given that there is so much concern expressed by school authorities about the anti-authority version of cyber-bullying on social communication networks, we may as well begin our review by taking a look at the issue of libel as a tort – or wrong committed intentionally or unintentionally, and the impact of libellous comments on targets of such expression (teachers and school authorities).

As we have seen from the student comments in Chapters 4–6, students who post such comments insist that they have no intention of hurting or directly communicating with the teachers and school officials they discuss online. They insist that these comments were not meant to be read by school officials – and that these were simply private conversations between friends. In that context, students do not consider their actions to be cyber-bullying because the teachers are not the direct targets of harassment. Unlike peer-to-peer cyber-bullying, where web sites are intentionally set up for the purpose of drawing the victim's attention to his or her flaws, the expression posted about teachers are not directed to them – and therefore any harm done is unintentional. It is plausible to argue under tort law, however, that depending on a variety of circumstances, a wrong can be done to someone unintentionally (negligently), and that this can lead to liability – or a claim for compensation for the harm done. Clearly, most young people are not aware that they risk legal liability in this way, which suggests the need to educate them about how the law of torts can be applied. Few adults, with the exception of those who work in law-related fields, are aware of the liability issues involved in tort law. Therefore, I believe a short introduction is necessary. I begin with the Canadian context because Canadian tort law is derived largely from British common law, hence there are many similarities.

Cyber-libel: Canadian context

Bernstein and Hanna explain that cyber-libel comprises defamation and/or libellous written comments:

> Simply defined, defamation is the making of a derogatory statement to a third party that discredits or impugns the reputation of a person, where the statement is not defensible on the grounds that it is true, fair comment or protected on some ground of privilege.
>
> (Bernstein and Hanna, 2005)[2]

Bernstein and Hanna confirm that, generally, libel is defamation in a fixed medium (written or permanent form), whereas slander is oral defamation (spoken words not recorded or fixed in any medium). In this regard, most defamation on the Internet is properly characterized as libel, whereas verbal comments, insults and threats made over cellphones might be considered to be slander, because they are made over electronic airwaves. Text-messaging via cellphones would constitute libel. Bernstein and Hanna explain that, although cyber-libel is not a new cause of action or an independent tort, it has several distinguishing features and complexities. I suggest that these features are pertinent to cyber-bullying among adolescent peers.

First, as I have already observed, defamatory comments that are posted on the Internet can be read by a vast audience. Consider, for example, Ghislain Reza, known as the Star Wars kid, and David Knight, both of whom were defamed in front of millions of people. This raises serious legal considerations of whether existing defamation law can sufficiently remedy or vindicate victims of cyber-bullying. Second, defamed material on the Internet can be republished quickly and easily and reproduced infinitely. This makes it difficult to identify the original perpetrator and the extent to which that person was responsible for the libel. For example, 106 clones were made of the Star Wars kid video. Although the original was made by Ghislain Reza himself, the video was stolen and posted on the Internet by known perpetrators, whom he sued. The extent to which those perpetrators could be held responsible for the clones of the video that were made from the Internet version is questionable (Bernstein and Hanna, 2005). Given that there are few established precedents on distribution of liability in Internet cases, this might have been a consideration in Reza's out of court settlement. Moreover, as the earlier profiles of cyber-bullying indicate, the information can be posted anonymously on the Internet, and perpetrators can hide behind screen names, making it almost impossible for victims to identify them.

Finally, as Bernstein and Hanna point out, information on the Internet travels through several computer systems between the author and recipients (a variety of intermediaries such as bulletin board messages, social networking sites, blogs, web pages, emails), all of which can be stored on various servers. The information can be easily and repeatedly recalled. This, they note, gives rise to many Internet intermediary liability issues (ibid., p. 7). They quote L.B. Lidsky, who describes the difference between defamation in a physical setting and Internet defamation in the virtual realm:

> Although Internet communications may have the ephemeral qualities of gossip with regard to accuracy, they are communicated through a medium more pervasive than print, and for this reason they have tremendous power to harm reputation. Once a message enters cyberspace, millions of people worldwide can gain access to it. Even if the message is posted in a discussion forum frequented by only a handful of people, any one of them can republish the message by printing it or, as is more likely by forwarding it instantly to a different discussion forum. And if the message is sufficiently provocative, it may be republished again and again. The extraordinary capacity of the Internet to replicate endlessly almost any defamatory message lends credence to the notion that 'the truth rarely catches up with a lie.' The problem for libel law, then, is how to protect

reputation without squelching the potential of the Internet as a medium of public discourse.

(Lidsky, 2000, as quoted in Bernstein and Hanna, 2005, p. 7)

Bernstein and Hanna (p. 9) explain that, for plaintiffs to succeed in a defamation action, they must prove:

1   that the statement that the plaintiff is complaining about is 'defamatory';
2   that the defamatory statement refers to the plaintiff; and
3   that the impugned statement was published, or made known, to a third person.

Hence, David Knight could argue that the statements posted on a web site, next to his photograph, labelling him a homosexual and a paedophile are defamatory; that they refer to him, as evidenced by his photograph; and that these statements were clearly published and made known to millions of third persons – anyone with Internet access. Similarly, the angry teachers who have been described as paedophiles, or as masturbating in the classroom, could potentially sue the students who posted those comments for cyber-libel.

What would their chances of success be in Canada under a defamation suit? According to Bernstein and Hanna, Canadian courts, unlike those in the United States, have been more willing to aggressively vindicate reputation attacks committed over the Internet, with substantial damage awards (ibid., p. 8). The Ontario Court of Appeal has articulated the defamatory test as follows:

A defamatory statement is one which has a tendency to injure the reputation of the person to whom it refers (which tends, that is to say, to lower him [or her] in the estimation of right thinking members of society generally and in particular to cause him [or her] to be regarded with feelings of hatred, contempt, ridicule, fear, dislike or disesteem). The statement is judged by the standard of an ordinary, right thinking member of society. Hence the test is an objective one . . . The standard of what constitutes a reasonable or ordinary member of the public is difficult to articulate. It should not be so low as to stifle free expression unduly nor so high as to imperil the ability to protect the integrity of a person's reputation. The impressions about the content of any broadcast, or written statement, should be assessed from the perspective of someone reasonable, that is, *a person who is reasonably thoughtful and informed*, rather than *someone who has an overly fragile sensibility*. A degree of common sense must be attributed to viewers [emphasis added].

(*Colour Your World Corp. vs Canadian Broadcasting Corp.* (1998) 38 O.R. (3d) 97)

The objective test is whether, in the eyes of a reasonably thoughtful person, rather than someone with overly fragile sensibilities, it would lower, discredit or negatively impact the reputation of the plaintiff and expose them to hatred or ridicule.

Bram wrote about his teacher masturbating in the back of the class, a fact vehemently denied by the teacher. Bram's comments are not significantly different from the range of transnational cases of students making negative postings about their teachers that I briefly described in Chapter 3.

Although most adults who knew the teachers or school administrators involved would see the expression for what it is and not take it seriously, a significant concern of late, as explained in Chapter 2, is that prospective employers are now surfing Facebook and other similar social networks to check the backgrounds of prospective applicants. Moreover, postings that discuss a teacher's hygiene, or a vice-principal's appearance, weight, or accent can all create significant embarrassment that might cause some people to withdraw from their workplace altogether.

An unsuspecting school principal, who may not know about online comments about him or her, could in good faith apply for a new employment position and be denied it, because the jokes posted by his or her students may create a doubt in the minds of his or her prospective employers, that he or she really might be a sexual paedophile. The question that arises is whether even 'reasonable' employers, especially in professions such as education, child care, social work or health care, will take the risk of hiring people into positions of fiduciary authority once their reputations have been marred. If there had been no cases involving teachers and school administrators who have been criminally charged and convicted of engaging in paedophilia and sexual abuse of their charges, then perhaps the matter would be moot, as no one would believe the student comments. However, given hundreds of sexual abuse cases in Catholic boarding schools and native residential schools (Stonebanks, in press), as well as teacher misconduct and sexual abuse (Piddocke *et al.*, 1997), the 'ordinary-reasonable-person' test may be difficult to apply.

As a number of legal academics have commented (Jafaar, 2002; MacKay and Dickinson, 1998), teachers, like doctors, are held to a higher standard of moral conduct and sometimes pay too heavy a price for the actions they take in their private lives. People work hard to earn a reputation, and losing it because of a frivolous joke online cannot be easy. In many cases, the psychological impact has caused teachers to have nervous breakdowns or go on stress leave. This might explain the immense pressure on local and national teachers' unions to do something to stop it.

In peer-to-peer bullying, the impact of this form of cyber-bullying is no less devastating. Consider again the case of David Knight. In David's situation, being labelled as a paedophile internationally might have exposed him to the contempt of most reasonable persons. He had career aspirations to become an air cadet and then an airline pilot. His determination and support from family helped him to achieve these career goals. However, his abuse came a few years ago, prior to the popularity of Facebook, MySpace, and YouTube. There is no telling whether he would have been accepted into the Canadian air cadets or into pilot training if the military or the airline company he applied to were to do a Google search and find online profiles of David described as a sexual predator and paedophile.

Hence, the question at hand is whether most reasonable adults would see the web site and be sufficiently informed or thoughtful to dismiss the statement, on the basis that it was most likely made by kids as a joke. In defining what constitutes a 'reasonable, informed and thoughtful person', we might also consider whether adolescents, within the context of peer pressure, are sufficiently mature to interpret the statements as true or as defamatory. Some key Canadian decisions relating to cyber-libel may shed some light on these questions. Although the cases below are not in the school context, they contain similarities to the online postings by students.

In the first case (*Vaquero Energy Ltd vs Weir* (2004) ABQB 68), Vaquero became aware that anonymous postings on a financial bulletin board, operated by Stockhouse Media Corporation, contained messages that called the president of Vaquero insane, and a moron and equated him to Hitler, Saddam Hussein and Osama bin Laden. The court ruled that these statements would have a significant impact on the reputation of the company and its president and awarded $10,000 for loss of reputation, $40,000 to the president and CEO and an additional $25,000 as punitive damages to the president.

The courts made similar findings in another case (*Barrick Gold Corp. vs Lopehandia* (2004) O.J. No. 2329), which began with a dispute between a large gold-producing company and a mining company as to rights over certain gold reserves in Chile. Lopehandia conducted an Internet campaign over seven months where he posted false and defamatory material against Barrick to people interested in the gold mining industry. The accusations included 'fraud, tax evasion, money laundering, manipulating world gold prices, misrepresentation, obstruction of justice and crimes against humanity' (as quoted in Bernstein and Hanna, 2005, p. 29). Barrick was successful in obtaining a motion for default judgement but received only $15,000 in damages because the lower court judge believed that the comments would not be taken seriously by a reasonable reader. The Ontario Court of Appeal overruled this decision and increased the award for general damages to $75,000 plus punitive damages of $50,000. Finally, the court granted a restraining order preventing any further defamatory statements from being made against Barrick or any of its personnel. Relying on an earlier case (*Ross vs Holly*, 2004, as cited in Bernstein and Hanna, 2005),[3] the court in Barrick observed that web site postings are far more powerful than email because of their potential to reach a substantially wider audience. Moreover, the court stated:

> While it is always important to balance freedom of expression and the interests of individuals and corporations in preserving their reputations, and while it is important not to inhibit the free exchange of information

and ideas on the Internet by damages awards that are overly stifling, defendants such as Mr Lopehandia must know that courts will not countenance the use of the Internet (or any other medium) for purposes of a defamatory campaign of the type engaged in here.

(*Barrick Gold vs Lopehandia*, as quoted in Bernstein and Hanna, 2005, p. 30)

The Supreme Court of Canada also made clear (*Hill vs Church of Scientology of Toronto* [1995] 2 S.C.R. 1130 at 1175) that a good reputation is as important as freedom of speech, which is not an unfettered right:

A good reputation is closely related to the innate worthiness and dignity of the individual. It is an attribute that must, just as much as freedom of expression, be protected by society's law . . . Democracy has always recognized and cherished the fundamental importance of an individual . . . The reputation tarnished by libel can seldom regain its former luster. A democratic society therefore, has an interest in ensuring that its members can enjoy and protect their good reputation so long as it is merited.

(*Hill vs Church of Scientology of Toronto* [1995] 2 S.C.R. 1130 at 1175)

In a case that is more similar to the situation involving instructors or teachers in positions of authority, the findings in an Australian case (*Cullen vs White* (2003), WASC, 153) are relevant. This case involved an educational setting at a university. Cullen was a professor at Divine Word University. One of his former students, William White, created a web site disputing Cullen's doctoral credentials, posting lewd insinuations that he was a paedophile and inviting others to write defamatory comments. The Australian court stated:

In the present case, I am satisfied that the defamatory publications are likely to have a very harmful effect upon the plaintiff's reputation and his standing as an academic. I also accept that the plaintiff has suffered a great deal of personal distress and anguish as a result of the publications and that they have caused him very considerable annoyance. It is likely that they will make it more difficult for him to obtain appropriate employment in the future. The damages award must compensate him in respect of those matters and be sufficient to signal to the public the vindication of his reputation . . . [para.19]

The plaintiff also seeks exemplary damages. Exemplary damages are awarded where the defendant has been guilty of conscious, high-handed behaviour in contumelious disregard of the plaintiff's rights: *Uren v John Fairfax and Sons* (supra) at 138, 154; *Todd v Swan Television and Radio Broadcasters Pty Ltd* [2001] WASC 334 at [139]. The objects of exemplary

damages are to punish the defendant and deter others from similar conduct. They also achieve the appeasement of the victim's sense of grievance:
Cotogno v Lamb (No 3) (1986) 5 NSWLR 559.

(*Cullen vs White* [2003] WASC 153)

The court awarded damages of AU$75,000 and AU$25,000 in exemplary
damages.

You may recall the Chinese case from Chapter 3, where Xiaorong modified
his teacher's photographs into all kinds of bestial forms and posted them
online. The student admitted that he downloaded the teacher's pictures from
the school's web site, searched pornography and animal pictures online and
used Photoshop software to combine those pictures into seven photos. He
claimed that he did not know he had broken the law and insisted he thought
what he had done was simply a joke. It was not to meant to harm the teacher
at all. He reported doing it to draw attention to himself. At the time, I asked
readers to make a mental note about this student's perspective because, when
it comes to posting defamatory and libellous anti-authority materials online,
there is a definite pattern that emerges globally. One aspect is the students'
desire to draw attention to themselves. When they are seeking attention from
peers, they want to prove that they can be sillier or crazier than everyone else.
However, when the same young people are trying to attract adult attention,
or the attention of someone they respect, they might be just as keen to show
they are productive and focus on using online tools in very intelligent ways.

Generally, students use these tools appropriately, although, as the UK
survey in Chapter 3 showed, not all of the students are using it efficiently
because they don't have the coaching or confidence. It is ironical that we only
pay attention to the ways in which young people are using the technology
when they get into trouble – and then we realize that tools such as Facebook
and YouTube exist. As Lankshear and Knobel's (2006) adult mindset theory
affirms, it is only when we can apply legal answers to enhance control that we
begin to address the problems. We ought to be looking at how young people
are using these tools and other technology all the time and work with them
so that they can be proud of how they are using them – and display their
productive work worldwide now that we have the platform.

As far as the legalities were concerned in Xiaorong's case, although the
police felt that he should be punished, they took into consideration that he
had no motivation to insult others subjectively, and, as he is still a high school
student, they gave him a caution and fines of 500 Yuan. According to Chinese
criminal law, those behaviours that harm society but do not belong to criminal
activities are penalized by the public security organ based on Regulations of
the People's Republic of China on Administrative Penalties for Public
Security.[4] This case was judged according to Article 42.[5] There was no report
as to how the school responded to these actions – whether educationally or in
any disciplinary forms.

Australian and Canadian cyber-libel decisions are promising for victims of cyber-bullying who may want to commence cyber-libel proceedings. However, it is important to emphasize, as Bernstein and Hanna (2005) do, that defamation law, especially in cyberspace, is complex. Therefore, success would largely depend upon a range of facts and circumstances specific to each case (see also Lidsky (2000) for other discussions on cyber-libel).

In light of the tendency by Canadian courts to value reputation over freedom of expression (based on the reasonable person test), we might ask what our courts are saying about the responsibility of ISP providers to monitor and close down bulletin boards, email address and web sites once they have been notified that cyber-bullying and, as part of it, defamation and libel have occurred. This aspect of defamation law is far more complex and better explained by defamation law experts such as Lidsky (2000) and Bernstein and Hanna (2005). Litigation would entail the launching of a 'John' or 'Jane Doe' proceeding for defamation. As part of such an action, it would be necessary to obtain a court order to compel the ISP or bulletin board operator to disclose the identification information. Furthermore, a determination would need to be made by the courts as to whether the online defamation constituted 'broadcasting'.

It is worth mentioning a Canadian defamation case (*Newman et al. vs Halstead et al.* [2006] BCSC 65) that involved online libel (or cyber-libel) of teachers by an adult, not one of their students. The case involved numerous plaintiffs (mostly school teachers) who filed a lawsuit for defamation against the adult defendant by the name of Halstead. Halstead was a 'community activist' and heavily involved in matters related to the education system through parent organizations and school bodies.

Halstead used email and web sites to make numerous defamatory statements against the plaintiff teachers, accusing them of violence, bullying and other inappropriate behaviour, both in and out of school. She also implied that some of the plaintiffs were the subject of criminal investigation.

The court found her fully liable for making defamatory statements against the plaintiffs. The court also found that no defences to defamation were applicable to the case. The court awarded significant damages to the plaintiffs in the amount of $626,000, including compensatory, aggravated and punitive damages, in addition to injunctive relief. Halstead was prohibited from making further defamatory comments of the type found in the plaintiffs' pleadings, whether by the Internet or otherwise. Moreover, she was required to seek leave from the court before publishing any further statements about the plaintiffs. Although the judgement did not use terms such as cyber-bullying, it did consider Halstead's behaviour to be significantly problematic. The intent of the cyber-bullying was to lower the reputations of the teachers involved and achieve the removal of these teachers from their teaching positions, through pervasive and consistent character assassinations via use of emails, web site postings and Internet chat sites, as well as the filing of criminal allegations against certain teachers. Some of the teachers bore the brunt of Halstead's attacks more than others. The extent of the harm was varied but severely impacted on many of the teachers, both personally and professionally. It impacted on their ability to have a rapport with their students as well as parents, some of who might believe Halstead's stories. Furthermore, the public and widely distributed nature of the comments online reduced the possibility of seeking employment elsewhere at other schools.

The American context relating to cyber-libel and ISP responsibilities is quite interesting, and a number of cases are relevant to our discussion.

Cyber-libel: American context

In the United States, according to David A. Myers (2006), one American piece of legislation that is relevant to cyber-bullying is the Communications Decency Act (CDA) (United States Congress, 1996). This Act grants broad immunity to ISPs. The legislation leaves no one legally accountable for cyber-targeting (which includes cyber-bullying, harassment, stalking, defamation, threats and so on). Section 230 of this Act provides in part:

(c) Protection for 'Good Samaritan' blocking and screening of offensive material.

(1) Treatment of publisher or speaker. No provider or user of an interactive computer service shall be treated as the publisher or speaker of any information provided by another information content provider.

(2) Civil Liability. No provider or user of an interactive computer service shall be held liable on account of – (A) Any action voluntarily taken in good faith to restrict access to or availability of material that the provider or user considers to be obscene, lewd, lascivious, filthy, excessively violent, harassing, or otherwise objectionable, whether or not such material is constitutionally protect; or (B) any action taken to enable or make available to information content providers or others the technical means to restrict access to material described in paragraph (1).

(Ibid.)

Myers (2006) explains that one landmark case (*Zeran vs America Online, Inc.*, 958 F. Supp. 1124, 1134 (E.D. Va) aff'd, 129 F.3d 327 (4th Cir. 1997)) is the general precedent used by American courts to rule on Internet abuse. This case resulted in leaving no legal accountability for injuries caused by anonymous postings on the Internet. It involved a series of anonymous postings on America Online's (AOL) message board following the Oklahoma City bombings in April, 1995. The messages claimed to advertise 'naughty Oklahoma t-shirts'. The captions on the T-shirts included 'Visit Oklahoma . . . It's a Blast!!!' And 'Finally a Day Care Center That Keeps Kids Quiet – Oklahoma 1995'. The individual who posted the messages identified himself as Ken Z and provided Zeran's phone number as the person to call to order the offensive T-shirts. Zeran received abusive telephone calls and even death threats as a result and notified AOL, which in turn terminated the contract from which the messages originated. However, the perpetrator continued to set up new accounts with false names and credit cards. Zeran finally sued AOL, claiming negligence. The court ruled that section 230 of the CDA provided absolute immunity to AOL, regardless of its awareness of the defamatory material.

The Zeran ruling, Myers notes (2006), maintains the status of Internet providers as 'distributors' rather than 'publishers'. Publishers (e.g. book publishers) are liable for defamation by third parties using their services, especially if they are made aware of it and fail to act to prevent the behaviour. The Zeran decision followed a case in which an Internet provider was elevated to the status of 'publisher' (*Stratton Oakmont, Inc. vs Prodigy Services Co.*, 1995 WL 323710 (N.Y. Sup. Ct., 1995)). Prodigy had decided to regulate the content of its bulletin boards (in part, to market itself as a 'family orientated' computer service). By taking on an editorial role, Prodigy opened itself up to greater liability than computer networks that do not edit content. Thus, service providers argued that, if they agree to monitor and edit online content, they in fact subject themselves to greater liability. This is why most Internet providers ignore reports of abuse. Most are confident that they will not be held liable subsequent to Zeran. The irony of this, as Myers (2006) points out, is that the title of S.230 reads 'Protection for "Good Samaritan" blocking and screening of offensive material'. The objective of the CDA was to protect proactive online service providers and preserve competition between ISPs on the Internet.

Myers makes the point that, if David Knight were bringing his lawsuit in the United States, S.230 might make it too difficult for him to argue that the Internet provider was aware of, and, therefore, responsible for, the web site with his picture, labelling him as a homosexual paedophile and drug pusher. Nonetheless, he believes 'the winds of change are stirring' for S.230 immunity. At the state level, he cites common law case (*Bryson vs News America Publ'ns, Inc.*, 672 N.E. 2d 1207 (Ill. 1996)). The case involved a fictional story entitled 'Bryson' written by Lucy Logsdon. Lucy wrote about being bullied at school by Bryson, whom she referred to as a 'slut'. The real Bryson read the story and remembered living in the same town as Lucy Lodgson. She sued News America for libel and won. The court stated that, even though the story was labelled as fictional, it portrayed realistic characters, responding in a realistic manner to realistic events, and that a reasonable reader might logically conclude that the author of the story had drawn upon her teenage experiences to write it. Myers suggests that, if the courts rely on this case, David Knight's lawyers might well argue that the web site with David's picture (labelling him as a paedophile), could reasonably be interpreted as true by those who visited the web site, resulting in negligence and liability against the Internet provider.

Furthermore, in another case (*Doe vs GTE Corp.*, 347 F.3d 655, 660 (7th Cir. 2003) involving the secret filming of athletes showering in a changing room that was posted and sold on a web site, the Seventh Circuit Court of Appeals upheld S.230 immunity relying on Zeran, in favour of GTE corporation. However, Judge Easterbrook questioned the reasoning in Zeran, noting that S.230 is supposed to be the 'Good Samaritan', blocking and screening offensive material, but, in fact, by eliminating liability for ISP's, it ends up defending abusers and defeating legitimate claims by victims of tortuous abuse on the Internet. It is for these reasons that the Lori Drew case mentioned on p. 89 would likely be unsuccessful if MySpace was prosecuted.

Negligence, supervision and malpractice

Moving from whether students can be held responsible for tort law by engaging in cyber-libel, there is a second aspect of tort law that applies. This involves the potential for schools to be held liable in an actionable claim for negligence if they do not act quickly to protect student victims of peer-to-peer cyber-bullying. Moreover, it is also worth determining whether teachers, as government agents, can be held legally liable if they fail to educate adolescents to engage in socially responsible discourse.

In 'real' space, victims who are injured while at school can bring claims for compensation against teachers and schools for injuries at school or on field trips (MacKay and Dickinson, 1998). British and North American law historically places on educators a 'duty of care *in loco parentis*'. This means that educators have a duty to care for their students as if they were standing in place of their parents. Not only that, a late nineteenth century case (*Williams vs Eady* [1893] 10 TLR 41) established that teachers must act as 'careful and prudent parents' when it comes to protecting students.

The key question here is whether this duty of care extends to the responsibility of teachers to *educate* students to be respectful to each other. The 'careful parent' legal doctrine does not address teachers' professional responsibilities as educators. Although claims for educational malpractice have been made, American courts categorically have denied that schools can be held liable for failing to educate. This implies that teachers cannot be held legally liable when students engage in covert forms of verbal and psychological bullying. The courts maintain that education is a matter of public policy and does not fall into the professional realm as do medical and legal malpractice, and that teachers are not considered to be 'professionals' in the same sense that lawyers and doctors are professionals. This might be because teachers are generally autonomous in carrying out their teaching duties. As long as they stay within curriculum guidelines, they have the discretion to select educational resources that meet those guidelines.

Jafaar (2002), however, advances a strong argument that public policy is the very aspect of educational malpractice that can work to support victims' claims that are brought against schools. Her arguments are important for victims of bullying. She believes the courts fail to recognize that public education has evolved to develop professional standards of conduct that are no longer confusing and unambiguous. Professional expectations in the school context are now standardized and easily recognized and should therefore be enforceable at law as a matter of sound public policy.

Jafaar's arguments build on similar positions advanced by Hines (1991) and Parker (1993). She argues that, over the last twenty years, as the public school system grew to incorporate the needs of society, the teaching profession has become more standardized. She asserts that, even though legislation on schooling might not provide clear standards for teachers as professionals, there are other important sources of public policy that clearly define and establish the professional standards expected from teachers and other education professionals. For example, although the Ontario Education Act provides ambiguous wording with respect to the duty of teachers regarding instruction, 'to teach diligently and faithfully the classes or subjects assigned to the teacher by the principal' (s. 264 (1) (a)), in November 1999, the OCT approved and published the Standards of Practice for the Teaching Profession that clarify the scope of this legislated duty. Jafaar (2002) further explains that the very fact that the OCT and similar bodies such as the British Columbia College of Teachers (BCCOT) have established standards for teacher certification confirms that school teaching is now a profession, with established standards of professional practice. She argues that the policy directives of teacher certification bodies undermine, if not nullify outright, the argument by courts that no duty of care exists owing to the lack of clearly defined standards.

If Jafaar's reasoning is applied to cyber-bullying, a claim might include, for example, a teacher's failure to adhere to British Columbia performance standards guidelines on social responsibility (1997). Under these standards, *teachers must monitor the social development of students at different grade levels*. The broader objectives of teaching social responsibility are described as follows:

> Human and Social Development is one of the goals of the BC school system. This broad goal further specifies that students are expected '*to develop a sense of social responsibility, and a tolerance and respect for the ideas and beliefs of others*' [emphasis added].
>
> (British Columbia Ministry of Education, 1997)

The British Columbia standards provide a framework for monitoring and evaluating a variety of school and classroom programmes intended to promote, among other things, student responsibility. Although the standards are discretionary guidelines, they might be useful to courts in determining educational malpractice. However, a better alternative might be to mandate that school educators receive professional development education regarding bullying in schools as well as knowledge of the relevant legal standards.

In an earlier American case (*Hunter vs Board of Education of Montgomery County*, 439 A. 2d 582 (Md. 1982), the dissenting opinion of Judge Davidson provides an anomaly in terms of acknowledging an actionable tort of educational malpractice. In this case, the sixteen-year-old plaintiff claimed that he had negligently been required to repeat first grade and this had social consequences resulting in bullying. It led to embarrassment, learning deficiencies and 'loss of ego strength' (ibid., p. 582). Justice Davidson stated his opinion as follows:

> In my view, public educators are professionals. They have special training and state certification is a prerequisite to their employment. They hold themselves out as possessing certain skills and knowledge not shared by non-educators. As a result, people who utilize their services have a right to expect them to use that skill and knowledge with some minimum degree of competence.
>
> (Ibid., p. 589)

Judge Davidson argued that he would have articulated the applicable pedagogical standard as one 'based upon customary conduct' (Hines, 1991, p. 158), the standard applied in medical malpractice claims, and rejected the commonly held judicial assumption that acceptance of such a claim would result in a flood of litigation:

> In recognizing a cause of action for educational malpractice, this Court would do nothing more than what courts have traditionally done from time immemorial—namely provide a remedy to a person harmed by the negligent act of another. Our children deserve no less.
>
> (Ibid., p. 590)

I have mentioned earlier that if students are not receiving reciprocal respect from teachers, if they sense that their teachers are not engaged in promoting their well-being and education, if they are tacitly condoning peer-to-peer bullying by turning a blind eye, then all of these might in effect contribute to the anti-authority forms of expression that emerge online. Because most students are not well equipped to raise formal protests regarding a lack of attention to their overall education, the anti-authority forms of cyber-bullying could, in fact, represent expressions of the lack of attention to students' social development.

My point is that, if teachers are neglecting to provide guidance on civil and social responsibility, if they are modelling forms of bullying themselves and know that the courts will not hold them responsible for educational malpractice in the same way as doctors are held responsible for medical malpractice, they are bound to make less of an effort to develop social responsibility in young people. Hence, as educational professionals, it seems ironical that teachers who might in fact ignore a central part of their mandate are not held accountable for it, but in turn call loudly for accountability by the very students they have failed to educate in social responsibility. This is where I argue very strongly in support of Jafaar (2002), that teachers ought to be held accountable to certain standards to educate for social responsibility in schools. I believe, if this were the case, we would witness a lot less of the negative online postings by students about their teachers. It boils down to issues of mutual trust and respect, which my own research suggests are almost absent in many schools.

I believe it is essential to pay more attention to the fact that negligence to educate children for social responsibility can result in egregious psychological harm. A Canadian decision (*Gould vs Regina (East) School Division No. 77 (1996) [1997] 3 WWR 117 (Sask.)*) left the door slightly ajar to the possibility that teachers might be held liable in cases of egregious (but unspecified) psychological harm to students. In this case, seven-year-old Jacklynne and her parents brought an action against the board of education and its employee, teacher Karen Zarowny. Their claim included a claim in negligence and breach of the Education Act as well as educational malpractice. The plaintiffs alleged that Jacklynne was subjected to 'unsatisfactory, inappropriate and objectionable behaviour' (para. 8) by Ms Zarowny; that she failed to perform the duties of a teacher in accordance with the Education Act and that she 'bullied' the infant plaintiff while she was in her grade 1 class.

The suit alleged that Ms Zarowny spoke too loudly in class, bullied, ridiculed and intimidated her pupils, failed to 'fulfill the learning needs of the infant plaintiff' and modelled intolerance to her students (para. 45). The judge stated that, given the right set of circumstances, conduct that was 'sufficiently egregious and offensive to community standards of acceptable fair play' (p. 18) might support a cause of action for educational malpractice. Although this suggests that egregious forms of bullying and particularly cyber-bullying might indeed qualify, the court did not clarify what circumstances and behaviours might qualify as 'sufficiently egregious and offensive'. In considering the allegation of bullying by the teacher, Judge Matheson considered how courts should deal with such ambiguity:

> But what standard will the court utilize to judge the appropriateness of the complained of activities? When does speaking in a sufficiently loud enough manner to be heard by all students become unacceptably loud? What one person may perceive as in inappropriately loud and intimidating voice, another person may envision as necessary as an attention getter. And while one student may consider the curriculum as inadequate for his or her needs, the majority of students may reach an opposite conclusion.

> It is surely not the function of the courts to establish standards of conduct for teachers in their classrooms, and to supervise the maintenance of such standards. Only if the conduct is *sufficiently egregious and offensive*

to community standards of acceptable fair play should the courts even consider entertaining any type of claim in the nature of educational malpractice [emphasis added].

(Ibid., p. 18)

Incidentally, this opinion highlights the same difficulties related to recognizing the differences between innocent teasing by peers and bullying. Nonetheless, it would be interesting to determine whether a court would find verbal and cyber-bullying as 'sufficiently egregious and offensive' and serious enough to result in psychological harm, whether it is instigated by peers against peers, or even if it involves 'private' discussions containing libellous comments about teachers. Given the devastating psychological impact on teachers and students, it is plausible that such expression does constitute 'egregious psychological harm'.

Although peer-to-peer cyber-bullying, with its anonymous and nebulous nature, ought to be considered offensive to most 'community standards of acceptable fair play', it is the anti-authority online postings that have, as observed in Chapters 4 and 5, resulted in the most attention from teachers, their unions, and school and government officials. Thus it would be in order to conclude that the latter form is deemed to be far more offensive to 'community standards of acceptable fair play'. The law is slow to change, especially when judges are well aware of the flood of litigation that might be unleashed if Internet providers are held liable.

Tort law, supervision and risk

The law of torts and negligence has another area that is applicable to the issue of cyber-bullying. I have dealt with this issue in great detail elsewhere (Shariff, 2003); however, I briefly highlight some of the key legal standards that are applicable to cyber-bullying.

First, under the British common law of torts, which continues to be applied in most post-colonial countries, including North America, schools have a legal duty of care to supervise students. Under this duty of care, teachers and principals are to act as 'careful and prudent parents'. This doctrine was developed over 100 years ago, when schools were smaller and mainly residential schools. The difficulty is that applying this doctrine, especially in an era of digital literacies, is less practical. Nonetheless, a failure properly to supervise students can result in an actionable tort of negligence (unintentional tort). The onus is on the student who brings the claim, say they were a victim of bullying or cyber-bullying, to establish four criteria:

1   that there was a duty of care;
2   that they experienced a tangible injury (psychological injury is harder to establish compared with physical injury);

3   that the injury was foreseeable by the supervisor and could have been
     prevented;
4   that the injury was caused by the actions or omissions of the supervisor.

Hence, in a case of peer-to-peer cyber-bullying, a victim might report the
bullying to the school several times, and the teacher may wave it away as
nothing serious, or tell the student it is a parental responsibility. If the student
attempts to commit suicide and fails, and then brings an action for negligence
in supervision, it can be argued that there was sufficient tangible psychological
harm to cause the student to want to commit suicide; that repeated cyber-
bullying was foreseeable; and that it continued because of the failure (omission)
by the teacher to prevent it. There are no legal precedents on school negligence
in supervision cases relating to cyberspace to date. David Knight's case would
have been exemplary had it gone ahead, because it would have required the
court to consider defamatory web sites and their role in tort law, both from a
supervision and a cyber-libel perspective. However, this case is now on the
way to being settled, so we will not know unless another action is brought
before the courts.

Finally, relating to the anti-authority web sites, it is possible that, under
tort law, a student could be assessed for liability for negligence, even if he claims
that he did not intend to harm the teacher with his demeaning words. If the
teacher can establish that there was sufficient embarrassment and psychological
harm that might cause her to suffer mental illness or prevent her from finding
employment; and if the teacher can establish that the harm from the student
expression was 'foreseeable' and that the actions – the expression of the student
'caused' her to become mentally ill, then there is the possibility of liability
under tort law. It would be difficult, however, to establish that the student had
a duty of care towards the teacher, other than under a student code of conduct.
In addition, not realizing that the Internet is public space may not hold
out as an excuse. There is the legal doctrine of *volenti non fit injuria* that might
come to play. This doctrine works on the principle that, if an action carries a
certain level of risk and if that risk is known, but if he or she undertakes the
action nonetheless, then he or she can be held partially liable for any injury
resulting from their act. In the case of cyber-bullying, the court might hold
that the student knew full well that the Internet is a public space and that
he or she ought to be held liable for their actions. As few actions have been
brought under this aspect of tort law, the possibility of an actionable tort is at
this point mere speculation. How the courts might bring some of the principles
of tort law, which are rooted in doctrines developed over 100 years ago, to bear
in an information age is yet to be seen.

In the meantime, schools need guidelines that provide reasonable boundaries
and direction as to the extent of their responsibility. This would alleviate their
reluctance to breach freedom of expression guarantees or student privacy
rights. Although, as Roher (2007) observes, web providers are increasingly

willing to take down offensive expression, there is often a delay while the complaints are checked out. If there is a backlog, the expression may stay online for many days, which allows time for it to be downloaded and saved so that it can resurface even after the originating site is blocked. This is further complicated by the highly public debates and protests I highlight in earlier chapters, on the boundaries between freedom of expression, privacy and safety. The debate has its heart in constitutional principles of equality, freedom of expression, privacy and safety. These legal principles and areas of law are separate from the tort law issues we have considered above.

Constitutional law: freedom of expression versus safety and privacy

My research to date has not disclosed any known cases specifically relating to cyber-bullying in the school context in the United Kingdom, or in other parts of the world. The courts in the United States, being a highly litigious country, have already heard cases on cyber-bullying and have applied a triumvirate of well-established US judicial decisions relating to student freedom of expression, in the absence of legal precedents relating to cyberspace.

There have been mixed court rulings on the extent of school responsibilities or expectations to interfere when students engage in forms of cyber-bullying from home computers. In one case, the 'Phlashlyte' underground newspaper was critical of school policy. Given that this expression might not have been as offensive as some of the sexual and demeaning commentaries posted online, the court noted: 'School officials may not judge a student's behaviour while he is in his home with his family nor does it seem . . . they should have jurisdiction over his acts on a public street corner' (*Sullivan vs Houston Independent School District*, 307 F. Supp. 1328 1340 (S.D. Tex. 1969); 1969 U.S. Dist. LEXIS 13342; 13 Fed. R. Serv. 2d (Callaghan) 519).

Similarly, in a Missouri case, a seventeen-year-old student was suspended for ten days for creating a web site from home that included vulgar language and making critical comments about the school's home page. He was ordered to take down the web-page, an injunction was granted, and the suspension was cancelled on the following basis:

> Disliking or being upset by the content of a student's speech is not an acceptable justification for limiting student speech . . . Speech within the school that substantially interferes with school discipline may be limited. Individual student speech which is unpopular but does not substantially interfere with school discipline is entitled to protection.
> (*Beussink vs Woodland R-IV School District*, 30 F. Supp. 2d 1175 (E.D. Mo. 1988))

The court went on to say that fear of disruption to the school environment must be a *reasonable fear* – not an 'undifferentiated fear'. The court had a point regarding the 'undifferentiated' and 'reasonable' fear. As I have discussed in the preceding chapters, the fear created by media reports, harsh school policies and concern about reputation could result in a 'chilled environment', and, in some schools, the reaction to student expression might be the result of an already 'poisoned' environment, causing irrational fears in the minds of teachers that the Internet is helping students get out of control. As the court said in a late 1960s case (*Tinker vs Des Moines Independent Community School District*, 3930 U.S. 503 (1969)), 'students do not leave their rights to free expression at the school house gates', and it is important to make an informed assessment, that where online comments posted about teachers are honest and close to the truth, they ought not to be reacted to with such force. Where the comments are clearly libellous, it is worth talking to the students to determine the source of their anger. Is the anger rooted in a poisoned school environment? Are the resulting cyber-comments the only outlet of expression for students? The following case is an example of a school's overreaction to student online discourse.

In a Washington state case, a tongue-in-cheek web site, the 'Unofficial Kentlake High Home Page' was created by Emmett, a high school senior, co-captain of the basketball team, with a 3.95 grade point average. In North America, a 3.95 grade point average out of 4.0 means that Emmett was a straight 'A' student. The web site included positive and negative disclaimers and joke obituaries. The purpose of the joke obituaries was to release some of the tension of exams and assignments, where students wrote their own obituaries for a laugh. Based on the joke obituaries, an online voting system began on the web site about 'who should die next' and become the subject of the mock obituaries. Someone reported the web site to the media, who reported the site as including a 'hit-list' of people Emmett was planning to kill. The web site was immediately taken down, and Emmett was expelled for 'intimidation, harassment, disruption to the educational process, and violation of Kent School District copyright'. A restraining order was also granted. Emmett sued the school, and the court stated the following:

> The School District argues, persuasively, that school administrators are in an acutely difficult position after recent school shootings . . . Web sites can be an early indication of a student's violent inclinations . . . The defendant, however, has presented no evidence that the mock obituaries and voting were intended to threaten anyone, did actually threaten anyone, or manifested any violent tendencies whatsoever.
>
> (*Emmett vs Kent School District No 413*, 92F.
> Supp. 2d 1088 (WD Wash. 2000))

The court drew attention to the overreaction by the school, which was out of context of the online joke about people being killed. In this case, the court ruled that the fact that the web page was created outside school grounds, without school supervision, was relevant to the school's ability to discipline, even if the intended audience was school-based.

This case is important for students such as Brad and Bram, who were suspended for their online expressions. These boys, who felt that their comments were outside school jurisdiction, as well as some of their parents, would support the Emmett decision as being fair. However, other judicial decisions have made it clear that, if there is a nexus (or connection) to the school (peers, teacher, school property), then there is an absolute right to intervene.

For example, the court handed down a different ruling in a Pennsylvania case. J.S. was a student in the eighth grade at Nitschmann Middle School during 1997–98. Kathleen Fulmer had taught there for twenty-six years as a maths teacher. J.S. informed a fellow student that he had created a 'Teacher Sux' web site that included on it:

> Why Fulmer should be fired
> She shows of her fat f—— legs
> She's a bitch
> Why should she die?
> Give me $20 to help pay for the hitman
> Diagram of Mrs Fulmer with her head cut off

> (*J.S., a minor, vs Bethlehem Area School District*,
> 757 A.2d 412, 422. (Pa. Cmwlth. 2000))

After viewing the Fulmer site, the principal informed Mrs Fulmer, as he took the threats seriously. Mrs Fulmer was frightened, fearing someone would try to kill her. Mrs Fulmer had lasting effects, including stress, anxiety, loss of appetite, loss of sleep, loss of weight and sense of lost well-being. The court stated that schools must teach by example the shared values of a civilized society. It is not socially acceptable to threaten or harass those who are charged with educating our young people. The student's web site materially disrupted the learning environment. The principal was embarrassed by the student's allegations, and Mrs Fulmer felt threatened. Teachers and students were aware of the student's disdain for school officials. They discussed the web site at school. This behaviour presented a substantial interference with the educational process.

The school board voted to permanently expel the student from its schools. The student appealed, and the decision went to trial. The trial judge supported the decision. On appeal to the Commonwealth Court of Pennsylvania, the court upheld the expulsion, because the contents of the web site constituted threats that were criminal in nature and not constitutionally protected (*J.S., a minor, vs Bethlehem Area School District*, 757 A.2d 412, 422. (Pa. Cmwlth. 2000)).

This decision was similar to a Canadian case of telephone bullying, where fourteen-year-old Dawn Marie Wesley hanged herself after one of her classmates uttered the words 'You're f——g dead!' over the phone after ten days of intense bullying (*R. vs D.W. and K.P.D.* [2002] BCPC 0096). Dawn Marie's perpetrator was charged with criminal harassment because the 'perceived intent to harm' was taken seriously by the victim as actual intent to harm, resulting in her suicide. Although this was a lower court ruling, it may have opened the door to future claims, including those involving cyber-bullying, where perceived intent of harm is very real. Biber *et al.* (2002, as cited in Glaser and Kahn, 2005) found that unwanted sexual comments and harassment online were found to be most threatening. They suggest that the online medium may be more frightening than face-to-face harassment, especially because the perpetrator can take refuge in his or her virtual identity.

Fourteen-year-old D.W.H., the teenager who said the words, was held criminally liable but maintained throughout that she had no intention of killing Dawn-Marie. D.W.H. was invited on talk-show celebrity Oprah Winfrey's television show and on another talk show was asked to apologize publicly for Dawn-Marie's death – something that I felt was too harsh a punishment for a teenager who uttered words that young people often use in uncontrolled anger, but rarely mean literally.

To make matters worse, D.W.H. was an aboriginal Canadian. The Caucasian girls who had joined her in bullying Dawn-Marie were let off with no criminal liability or court sentence. What was even more unfair, in my opinion, was a lecture delivered to D.W.H.'s aboriginal community on bullying by American 'bullying' expert Barbara Coloroso (It's a girl's world: A documentary about social bullying (video), 2004).[6] It seemed ironical that an aboriginal community that had sustained generations of bullying and abuse from North American settlers; a community that had its children torn away from its families and placed in Catholic residential schools to be beaten and sexually abused by priests; a community that bears the scars of generations of displaced families and cultural traditions because of colonization, was subjected to a lecture on why bullying is not acceptable. The First Nations people in Canada were subjected to terrible abuses by European colonists who wanted to 'civilize' them. Hence, I would argue that we are never justified as a society to take 'bullying' at face value. There is always a larger context that also needs attention. This is why I seriously caution against being too quick to lay blame on children and the Internet, without critically questioning our own institutional systems and power hierarchies.

There are landmark school cases from both Canada and the United States, however, that do provide some direction as to where the courts stand under existing law, and how they might rule in cases of cyber-bullying that require censorship of student expression by schools. In each of these cases involving free speech in schools, one of the key considerations is *space* – or where the expression occurs. Questions of where the speech originated (on or off campus), who instigated it, how it impacted others and how it was addressed, inform the deliberations of this issue by the courts. As we attempt to apply these deliberations to the contemporary context, we must remind ourselves that even though cyber-bullying takes place in the electronic airwaves, it creates unwelcome physical school environments, where equal opportunities to learn are greatly reduced (Shariff, 2003). Cyber-bullying, regardless of where it originates, is an *educational* issue. However, as I have stressed earlier in this book, responses to it cannot be addressed and accommodated to fit a convenient package of interventions to be blueprinted. The legal considerations discussed below support my view that a conceptual appreciation of the censorship issues that emerge as a result of cyber-bullying is far more complex.

Constitutional considerations

In most democratic nations, freedom of expression is guaranteed to its citizens. In the Canadian context, section 2 of the Charter (*Canadian Charter of Rights and Freedoms*, Schedule B, Constitution Act, 1982, Canada Act, c. 11 (UK)) provides that everyone is entitled to freedom of 'thought, belief, opinion and expression'. These freedoms are only limited by section 1 of the Charter, which helps the courts weigh and balance individual rights with the collective rights of the greater good in a democracy. Accordingly, section 1 of the Charter states that the rights set out in it are subject 'only to such reasonable limits prescribed by law as can be demonstrably justified in a free and democratic society'. Any school policy that infringes individual rights must therefore be justified by the policymaker as having *a pressing and substantial objective* to protect the greater good of society. The onus also rests with policymakers to establish that the rights in question will be infringed *as minimally as possible* (see *R. vs Oakes* [1986] 1 S.C.R. 103).

According to Mackay and Burt-Gerrans (2005), the section 1 analysis has generally been applied to justify protecting the widest possible definition of freedom of expression. These scholars explain that expression is constitutionally protected as long as it is not violent (*Irwin Toy Ltd vs Québec (Attorney General)* [1989] 1 S.C.R. 927). This means that *any expression that intends to convey non-violent meaning* is normally safeguarded by the courts. This wording is critical when we consider the student postings online. Depending on the exact content of the expression – if students are simply joking about their teachers and *intends to convey non-violent meaning,* it should be safeguarded by the courts.

This interpretation has been extended to the school setting. For instance, one of the best known cases of protected freedom of expression in schools involved a rap song that contained a message to students to reduce promiscuity. Chris Lutes sang a song by Queen Latifah, entitled 'Let's talk about sex', in school, even though the song had been banned by the school district. He was suspended and sought judicial review. The court (*Lutes vs Board of Education of Prairie View School Division No. 74* (1992) 101 Sask. R. 232 (Q.B.)) found that his freedom of expression rights under section 2(b) of the Canadian Charter of Rights and Freedoms had been violated, and that the policy banning the song did not reasonably justify the infringement of those rights. In fact, the court stated that this was an overreaction to an educational song about sexual abstention because an assistant superintendent was visiting the school at the time when Lutes, knowing who he was, continued to sing it in his presence.

Expression as 'material and substantive disruption'

The decision rendered in Lutes supports a standard for free speech in schools established in American cases – that unless student expression *materially and substantially* disrupts the learning process, it cannot be censored or suppressed. For instance, in a landmark 1969 case, John and Mary Tinker and Christopher Eckhardt were suspended because they wore black armbands to school as a silent form of political protest against the Vietnam war (*Tinker vs Des Moines Independent Community School District*, 3930 U.S. 503 (1969)). They had ignored school administrators' warnings not to wear them. They sued the school district under the freedom of expression provisions of the First Amendment. The court ruled in favour of the students, stating the famous dictum that '[i]t can hardly be argued that either students or teachers shed their constitutional rights to freedom of speech or expression at the schoolhouse gate' (p. 506).

Servance (2003) explains that the key to the Tinker holding is that, unless schools can show a valid reason for restricting free speech, students should be allowed to express their right to free speech. The court acknowledged, however, that this is not an unfettered right. Students have a right to regular speech unless that speech either materially disrupts a school's ability to carry out its mission in an orderly fashion or infringes upon the rights of others to be free from harassment. It is the *material and substantial* standard created in Tinker that courts continue to apply in contemporary cases. As noted by Justice Fortas:

> The principle of these cases is not confined to the supervised and ordained discussion which takes place in the classroom. The principal use to which the schools are dedicated is to accommodate students during prescribed hours for the purpose of certain types of activities. Among those activities is personal intercommunication among the students . . . This is not only an inevitable part of the process of attending school; it is also an important part of the educational process. A student's rights, therefore, do not embrace merely the classroom hours. When he is in the cafeteria, or on the playing field, or on the campus during the authorized hours, he may express his opinions, even on controversial subjects like the conflict in Vietnam, if he does so without 'materially and substantially interfere[ing] with the requirements of appropriate discipline in the operation of the school' and without colliding with the rights of others . . . *but conduct*

by the student, in class or out of it, which for any reason – whether it stems from time to time, place, or type of behaviour – materially disrupts classwork or involves substantial disorder or invasion of the rights of others is, of course, not immunized by the constitutional guarantee of freedom of speech [emphasis added].

(*Tinker vs Des Moines Independent Community School District*, 3930 U.S. 503 (1969))

There is no question that Justice Fortas was referring to the school environment as it was then, but, if this standard continues to apply in contemporary cases of free expression and supervision, it is arguable that the prescribed hours of school work have changed as students are increasingly expected to work on computers and access the Internet for their school-based assignments outside school hours. Furthermore, a key point in this statement is that personal communication among students 'is not only an inevitable part of the process of attending school; it is also an important part of the educational process' (ibid.). It can be argued that, if intercommunication among students is an integral aspect of the educational process and if such communication 'materially or substantially' disrupts the learning of others (thereby affecting their rights of equal access and opportunities to learn without harassment or discrimination), schools have the authority to censor it. The learning environment in schools is no longer restricted to the campus. It is fluid. Interaction in the physical school setting continues in cyberspace. Students (and teachers), through email, continue their inter-communications in cyberspace. Thus the on-campus/off-campus distinction is not easily defined. It is much more realistic to consider the educational environment in terms of physical and virtual contexts in which learning and student communication take place.

When the nature of student intercommunication crosses the invisible but very real line from regular horse-play and teasing to bullying, there exists a responsibility for an educational response by schools, especially when there is a nexus – or connection to the school (Mitchell and Kendall, 2007; Roher, 2007). When the bullying moves into the virtual school environment, without any supervision or attention from educators, it can have devastating consequences, not only on student learning, but on student health (Shariff, 2004).

Clearly, cyber-bullying has a profound impact on the learning of all students, both on and off school property. Justice Fortas' comments regarding student conduct in class or out of it are applicable in this regard: '[w]hether it stems from time to time, place, or type of behaviour – materially disrupts class work or involves substantial disorder or invasion of the rights of others is, of course, not immunized by the constitutional guarantee of freedom of speech' (*Tinker vs Des Moines Independent Community School District*, 3930 U.S. 503 (1969), p. 513). Accordingly, it makes sense that, if the courts are to continue relying on Tinker, that it is this aspect of the case that applies to restrictions on freedom of speech in the cyber-bullying context. That is not to say that I do not agree with the decision in the context of the silent, political protest that was made by the students concerned in the case. I wholeheartedly agree that students do not leave their rights to free speech at the school-house gate. I stress, however, that when such speech comprises harassment and abuse of other students and embarrassment of teachers and school officials, without being addressed through some form of dialogue and communication with the students involved, it creates a hostile and unwelcome environment for students (both on campus and in cyberspace), as it disrupts the educational objectives of schools.

Expression as 'disruption of basic educational mission'

In the American context, a new standard on student speech was set in 1986. The Supreme Court held in Fraser (*Bethel School District No. 403 et al. vs Fraser, a minor, et al.* 478 U.S. 675 (1986)) that schools may prohibit speech that undermines their 'basic educational mission' (p. 504). The case involved a campaign speech made by student Matthew Fraser that contained insinuations about sexual and political prowess:

> I know a man who is firm – he's firm in his pants . . . [He] takes his pants and pounds it in . . . He doesn't attached things in spurts – he drives hard, pushing and pushing until finally – he succeeds . . . [He] is a man who will go to the very end – even the climax for each and every one of you.
>
> (*Bethel School District No. 403 et al. vs Fraser,*
> *a minor, et al.* 478 U.S. 675 (1986))

The school suspended Fraser noting that his speech distressed some students at assembly. He was not allowed to speak at graduation and sued the school under his First Amendment rights to free speech. Responding to the dissenting opinions in Tinker, the court voiced its concerns about the need for schools to retain control over student behaviour and noted that schools are not the type of arena for the type of vulgar expression in Fraser's speech. The court noted that schools should not have to tolerate speech that is inconsistent with school values. Although the court acknowledged that it is crucial to allow unpopular speech, it emphasized that schools have a vital role in preparing students to participate in democratic society, by teaching students the 'appropriate form of civil discourse' necessary in civil society' (p. 511).

Of significant relevance to censorship of online student expression today, this ruling also stated that schools must teach students the boundaries of socially acceptable behaviour (Servance, 2003). The court stated that threatening or offensive speech has little value in a school setting and cannot be ignored by schools. Moreover, the court noted that the speech infringed the rights of others (although it did not specifically state it, the rights of females in the audience). The sexual insinuations to rape were clearly offensive and threatening to students.

The Fraser decision extends Tinker, and is also, in my view, applicable to censorship of student freedom of expression in the cyber-bullying context. As I have explained in Chapters 2–4, a substantial amount of the emerging research on Internet communications discloses sexual harassment, sexual solicitation and threats against women or female students. Not only does this form of cyber-bullying materially disrupt learning and impede educational objectives, it creates power imbalances within the school environment and distracts female students from equal opportunities to learn. Consistent with the Fraser ruling, expression of this infringes their constitutional rights in an educational context and creates a hostile and negative school environment (physical and virtual).

Most recently, in an Indianapolis case where a teenager was placed on probation for posting an expletive-laden entry on MySpace criticizing her school principal, the Indiana Court of Appeals ruled against the school and lifted a lower court ruling that had allowed her probation. The three-judge panel ordered the Putnam Circuit Court to set aside its penalty against the girl, referred to as A.B.: 'While we have little regard for A.B.'s use of vulgar epithets, we conclude that her overall message constitutes political free speech' (Wilson, J. in *A.B. vs State of Indiana*, 2007). Although it is not clear what political message the student had posted, the appeal court did not see her comments as disruptive to learning or the school's educational mission.

Nexus: computers as school property

Under Section 8 of the Canadian Charter of Rights and Freedoms, everyone has the right to be free from unreasonable search and seizure. Hence, protection of privacy is guaranteed within reasonable limits in a free and democratic society. Furthermore, section 7 of the Charter states that 'everyone one has the right to life, liberty and security of the person'. In the cyber-bullying context, both these sections are relevant. The boundaries with respect to the obligations on schools to override search and seizure rights to protect others must be balanced with the right to life, liberty and security of the person. Furthermore, victims might argue that their rights to life, liberty and security of the person are infringed under section 7 when schools fail to intervene and protect them from cyber-bullying.

Based on section 1 considerations, the courts generally give priority to the safety of the greater number of stakeholders as justification for overriding privacy rights. For example, the Supreme Court of Canada (*R. vs M.R.M.* [1998] 3 S.C.R. 393) has ruled that, as long as a school principal is not acting as an agent of the police, he or she can search student lockers if there is a suspicion of hidden weapons or drugs. The high court held that school lockers are the property of schools. When there is a danger to safety and learning of the students, the infringement on student privacy rights can be reasonably justified under section 1 of the Charter. Given the devastating psychological consequences of cyber-bullying on victims and the entire school environment, it is quite possible that, with a Charter interpretation that requires a balancing of the victim's right to safety under s. 7 and the perpetrators' right to computer privacy under s. 8 and free expression under s. 2(b), the court might rule in favour of the victim.

For example, Mackay and Burt-Gerrans (2005) explain that the rationale used by the Supreme Court in *R. vs M.R.M.* was that students should already have a lowered expectation of privacy because they know that their school principals or administrators may need to conduct searches in schools, and that safety ought to be the overriding concern to protect students. The high court explained its interpretation of a safe and ordered school environment:

> Teachers and principals are placed in a position of trust that carries with it onerous responsibilities. When children attend school or school functions, it is they who must care for the children's safety and well-being. It is they who must carry out the fundamentally important task of teaching children so that they can function in our society and fulfill their potential. In order to teach, school officials must provide an atmosphere that encourages learning. During the school day, they must protect and teach our children.
>
> (*R. vs M.R.M.* [1998] 3 S.C.R. 393)

This statement by the court is also highly significant to indirect or unintentional cyber-bullying of teachers. The statement places a high responsibility on teachers and the protectors of children and disseminators of education.

The court's rationale is along the line of US cases that have also confirmed school lockers as the property of schools. Therefore, it is not an infringement of constitutional rights to search and seize the contents, if they breach school policies (*Singleton vs Board of Education USD 500* 894 F. Supp. 386 (D. Kan. 1995)). For example, the courts noted (*People vs Carlos Overton* 20 N.Y. 2d 360 at 596 (1967)) that schools can issue policies regarding what may be stored in school lockers. Correspondingly, educators are entitled to conduct spot checks or involuntary searches of lockers to ensure that students comply with these regulations. In fact, the courts regard the inspection of student lockers not only as a right but also as a *duty* of schools when it is believed that a student is using school property to harbour illegal materials. This logic could certainly be applied to the cyber-bulling context, if schools have a censorship policy regulating the type of content that may be sent or received from school computers. For instance, it could be argued that, similarly to lockers, emails are owned by the school because they are transmitted using school property. Therefore, if a student is suspected of sending harassing comments via email or has found such comments while browsing on school computers, the school should consider it their responsibility to monitor and discipline this activity.

This point might be further justified by other cases (including *Garrity vs John Hancock Mut. Life Ins. Co.* 18 IER Cases 981 (D. Mass. 2002)), which find that employers have a right to inspect employee email accounts when employees are notified that messages are accessible to a third party. With regards to school searches, we can also consider cases such as *New Jersey vs T.L.O.* In this ruling, it was held that, although students have a legitimate expectation of privacy within the school setting, schools also have a right to search student property, without a warrant, if there are reasonable grounds for suspecting that the student is violating either the law or the regulations of a school (*New Jersey vs T.L.O.* 469 U.S. 325 (1985)). If this is expanded to cyberspace and the virtual school environment, it could be argued that the nexus to school is no longer limited to physical space. Therefore, although students have a legitimate expectation of privacy for their online conversations, if there is some connection to the school, especially to teachers as authority figures, it follows that something needs to be done about it. *The larger question for me is what ought we do abut it. The key to resolving these issues is the manner in which we respond.* Again, it would seem reasonable for schools to apply this rationale, if there is reason to believe that students are using school computers or school web sites to conduct illegal activity such as the harassment of others.

Student expression off-campus

Canadian and US courts have shown the importance of restricting lewd and indecent forms of expression in the school environment and also provided teachers with the power to search school property in order to maintain order and safety in the school. Although the cases I have discussed are applicable to censorship in schools, they do not address whether schools can censor student expression that occurs among classmates about school authorities from home computers on weekends.

Human and civil rights jurisprudence: school environment

At present, there are more US constitutional precedents that relate to free expression, safety and equality in cyberspace than there are Canadian Charter rulings. It may be some time before the Supreme Court of Canada rules on the censorship issues involved in cyber-bullying, because such cases are generally brought under tort law for negligence and under human rights law. This does not suggest, however, that constitutional considerations are not implied or expected. A number of Canadian human rights cases on sexual harassment (for example, *Robichaud vs Canada (Treasury Board)* [1987] 2 S.C.R 84) have ruled that institutions are responsible for providing safe environments for their employees, even if the sexual harassment by a co-worker occurs outside the workplace. The fact that the victims must face their tormentors in the workplace imposes an obligation on the employer to address the problem effectively. This case is very relevant to censorship of online student expression, because school officials often maintain they are not responsible for harassment by schoolmates that occurs virtually and outside school hours. Yet, as the high court confirmed in Robichaud, if the victim has to face the perpetrator within the institution, the institution is responsible for correcting the problem, no matter where the harassment actually takes place. The high court reiterated that, in order to meet the broader objectives of human rights law (namely, to eradicate antisocial conditions in society), human rights law must be consistent with Charter principles. Therefore, institutions must ensure that individuals have equal opportunities to learn and work without fear of harassment. In this case, equal opportunity to work or learn was at issue. Section 15 (1) of the Charter reads as follows:

> Every individual is equal before and under the law and has the right to the equal protection and equal benefit of the law without discrimination and, in particular, without discrimination based on race, national or ethnic origin, colour, religion, sex, age or mental or physical disability.
> (Canadian Charter of Rights and Freedoms, Schedule B,
> Constitution Act, 1982, Canada Act, c. 11 (UK))

The high court also established (in *Ross vs New Brunswick School District No. 15* [1996] 1 S.C.R. 825) that schools must provide conditions that are conducive to learning. Although the Ross case involved the free speech of a teacher who distributed anti-Semitic publications outside of school, the following statement from the ruling has been quoted in almost every Charter argument for a positive school environment:

> [S]chools are an arena for the exchange of ideas and must, therefore, be premised upon principles of tolerance and impartiality so that all persons within the school environment feel equally free to participate. As the board of inquiry stated, a school board has a duty to maintain a positive school environment for all persons served by it.
> (*Ross vs New Brunswick School District No. 15* [1996]
> 1 S.C.R. 825, para. 42)

Even though Ross' anti-Semitic publications were distributed outside the school context, the court noted that he poisoned the school and classroom environment for his Jewish students within the classroom. They knew about his publications and felt threatened, fearful and uncomfortable. Hence, if we are to draw upon the rationale used in the Ross case, it would seem that the on-campus/off-campus (physical versus virtual space) distinction is moot. It is the *effect* of the harassment, bullying and threats – despite the fact that they are made outside the physical school setting – that is important. If they prevent students from learning in the physical school setting, if they create a poisoned environment for any student, then it is the school's responsibility to step in and censor them.

School environment and a 'deliberately dangerous school environment' were also the subject of a controversial landmark decision in 1998. The American Supreme Court broke tradition with avoiding the floodgates in the case of *Davis vs Munroe County Bd. of Ed.* The case involved persistent sexual harassment of a grade 5 female student, Lashonda Davis, whose parents informed the teachers and the school principal numerous times, but nothing was done. Lashonda's grades dropped, and her health was negatively affected. In a majority 5:4 decision, the Supreme Court ruled that, in failing to act to protect Lashonda, the school had created a 'deliberately dangerous environment' which prevented 'equal opportunities for learning' (*Davis vs Munroe County Bd. of Ed.* 526 U.S. 629 (1999)). It could plausibly be argued that cyber-bullying (peer-to-peer and anti-authority) creates a similarly dangerous environment for victims in the physical school setting.

Summary: legal standards for schools

As I have established in the above discussion, there are a number of legal standards that are clearly applicable to censorship involving student expression as it relates to online harassment or cyber-bullying. First, based on the US cases on free expression, schools must ensure there is no *material and substantive disruption to learning* (*Tinker vs Des Moines Independent Community School District*, 3930 U.S. 503 (1969)). Second, there should be *minimal disruption of the basic educational mission* (*Bethel School District No. 403 et al. vs Fraser, a minor, et al.* 478 U.S. 675 (1986)). Third, and drawing on Canadian Charter cases, schools are required to ensure that they create a *school environment that provides equal opportunities to learn without fear of harassment or bullying (of any kind – physical, verbal, virtual)* (*Chamberlain vs Surrey School District No. 36* [2002] 4 S.C.R. 710, 2002 SCC 86; *Davis vs Munroe County Bd. of Ed.* 526 U.S. 629 (1999); *Jubran vs North Vancouver School Distr. No. 44* [2002] B.C.H.R.T.D. No. 10 (Q.L.) 221; *R. vs M.R.M.* [1998] 3 S.C.R. 393; *Robichaud vs Canada (Treasury Board)* [1987] 2 S.C.R 84; *Ross vs New Brunswick School District No. 15* [1996] 1 S.C.R. 825). As we know, cyber-bullying impacts learning and social conditions in the physical school setting. Therefore, if schools fail to address the situation, they will be creating a *deliberately dangerous environment* (*Davis vs Munroe County Bd. of Ed.* 526 U.S. 629 (1999)) for their students, and also for their faculty and support staff. Moreover, in cases of online postings, there should be a *nexus to the school* – some kind of connection where the expression must either come from a school computer, or involve

Table 7.1 Applicable legal standards: emerging and established (Shariff, 2007)

Legal framework	Standards for administrators	Standard for teachers	Standard for parents	Standard for students
Tort law (cyber-libel)	Can intervene if nexus to school. Expression must involve 'unfair comment'.	How the libel is interpreted by a person who is reasonably *thoughtful and informed*, rather than someone who has an overly *fragile sensibility*.	Need to explain the line at which 'joking' in the public realm of cyber-space can cross the line to become libel and result in liability. Need basic understanding of libel laws.	Learn that cyber-space is rarely private space. Learn limitations on free speech. Engage in responsible use and accountability. Inform others who cross the line.
Tort law (supervision)	Duty of Care 'in loco parentis'. Must be aware of: • Tangible harm • Foreseeable harm • Cause of injury (related to action or omission by administrator).	Obligation to act as 'Careful and Prudent parent'. Duty of Care 'in loco parentis'. Must be aware of: • Tangible harm • Foreseeable harm • Cause of injury (related to action or omission by teacher).	Equally responsible for supervising and being aware of their children's online postings and discourse.	Legal doctrine of *volenti non fit jura* says claimants can be held responsible for their actions if they know the risk involved and still undertake it – this could relate to anti-authority expression and cyber-bullying.
Human or civil rights law (institutional responsibility)	Duty to avoid 'deliberately dangerous environment' or 'poisoned environment'. Provision, protection and participation by students in learning and developing codes of conduct.	Teachers must be trained and sensitive to on- and off-campus bullying (virtual & physical settings). Protection, provision and encourage participation of students.	Must be aware of their children's rights to learn in an environment free of discrimination, conducive to learning.	Learn that when they harass or cyber-bully they create a poisoned school environment (virtual & physical) – impacts learning. Participate in developing codes of conduct.
Constitutional principles	Must justify infringement of rights to protect greater good and minimally impair stakeholder rights. Can intervene if student speech 'materially & substantially disrupts learning' or 'interferes with learning or educational mission'.	Must be aware 'students do not leave expression rights at the schoolhouse gate' but know limits of such expression.	Teach their children that freedom of speech is a right, but not an 'unfettered right'. It is not unlimited and there are boundaries.	Know their rights to free expression. Know the limits on those rights. Can be held accountable for overstepping limits.
Criminal law	Perceived intent = Real threat. Possibility of fraud charges for wire fraud for taking on new identities in cyber-space that might cause victims to fear or perceive threat.	Need awareness of where cyber-bullying crosses the line to become criminal threat, e.g. pornographic, racist, homophobic.	Need awareness of where cyber-expression can cross the line to become perceived as 'threats' that are criminal and teach their children.	Learn that unintended threats can be perceived as real threats resulting in criminal liability.

schoolmates, teachers or school authorities, or a school web site. This, again, depends upon the nature of the speech, as we saw in the Indiana ruling that stated that, even though students' speech can be vulgar, students still have the right to free speech if it constitutes political speech under the US First Amendment and civil liberties provisions.

Under the Canadian Charter, it might be argued by victims or their parents that failure to protect them infringed their section 7 rights to life, liberty and security of the person. The *effect* of the expression, its *real* and *perceived impact*, is also critical in any justification by schools to intervene (*R. vs D.W. and K.P.D.* [2002] BCPC 0096). Finally, it can be argued that, if cyber-bullying is undertaken by classmates from school computers, schools are bound to a lesser extent by the Charter or the First Amendment obligation to protect student free speech or privacy (*R. vs M.R.M.* [1998] 3 S.C.R. 393). They have the authority to intervene when that speech is instigated on school property (the computers).

To help readers remember these standards, I have summarized them in Table 7.1.

However, simply laying out a set of legal standards for educators and policymakers, many of whom have minimal background in law, is not sufficient. In Chapter 8, I propose a formula for teacher education and professional development that incorporates these standards into a model that combines legal literacy and educational theories. Together, these will better prepare educational professionals to develop informed, thoughtful, non-arbitrary, ethical and legally responsible solutions and policy responses to cyber-bullying, without having to engage in a zero-tolerance battle with kids or technologies. The solutions I propose are collaborative. They are grounded in democratic principles and comprehensive educational pedagogies. We have at our disposal many options that replace the need to wage a war on kids. When these situations appear to get out of hand, and when school administrators find that they are in the midst of a crisis where they are required to listen to angry teachers and their supporting unions, upset parents and students who insist they did no wrong; when they see headlines in the media that completely distort what really took place at the school, out of context, it is easy to feel overwhelmed by the 'horns of the dilemma'. It is to addressing these 'horns' that I now turn in my final chapter.

Chapter 8

Harmonious solutions

"Horns" of the dilemma

Figure 8.1 'Horns' of the dilemma

Source: Hanif Shariff, 1999, age 10

Introduction

I concluded the last chapter with a reference to the 'horns of the dilemma' and introduce my final chapter with a related cartoon. When I first sent this cartoon to my editor, he was concerned that the image might trivialize the issues addressed in this book. Indeed, at first glance, it is easy to appreciate his concerns. The final chapter, in particular, is of critical importance, because it is here that I provide 'solutions' to the horns of the dilemma, to the battles in cyberspace, to calm the concerns of upset parents, teachers and students. Regrettably, I do not bring a packaged solution. There are no blueprints or rubrics, but there are guidelines. The above depiction brings the fresh insight of a ten-year-old child. It simplifies a very complex situation by showing how it can so easily be resolved. As adults, we become so engrossed in the complexities of certain challenges that we fail to recognize the most straightforward solutions are staring us in the face.

Ten years ago, I sought to depict the 'horns of the dilemma' as I prepared to defend my Masters thesis on competing rights and interests in the Surrey school board book ban. The case is referred to in Chapter 6, under the school board as stakeholder section. My son Hanif (whose name ironically means 'seeker of the truth') was already a thriving musician at age ten. I asked him to find me some 'horns' on the Internet, expecting him to come up with depictions of animal horns. Incredibly, his depiction illustrated some key challenges that schools confront in handling censorship and cyber-bullying controversies of the day. At the same time, this simple cartoon also provides straightforward solutions.

The cartoon depicts school authorities in the centre, with the various 'horns' or stakeholder voices demanding their attention. The school authorities are very much aware that the situation is potentially explosive. Suppose the dilemma is caused by a highly publicized incident of cyber-bullying, where one of the medium-sized horns represents students who have voiced insulting and unflattering opinions about their teachers and school officials online. The larger horns might represent the angry voices of the teachers, supported by their teachers' unions; other large horns represent parents who might be angry at their children or, more likely, angry at school officials and teachers for suspending their children and overreacting. Each 'horn' is blowing loudly – but not cohesively. Each stakeholder is looking for a different solution. The students want their own space and, at a deeper level, may have unresolved issues with the teachers they demean so publicly. The teachers have their own issues – with the administration, with each other, with the parents and with the students. They might feel the administration bows down to the wishes of parents, undermining the respect they receive from students. They might also feel that the administration is paying lip-service to taking action against cyber-bullying, and that the school has done little more than develop anti-bullying policies that are largely ineffective. The teachers want stronger action. The administration is trapped in the middle, attempting to please everyone. In the midst of this, another loud horn – the media. The media catch wind of a sensational controversy, blow all the wrong things out of proportion, and frames the story out of context. What transpires is a 'squeak and squawk' concert, with all the horns being out of sync. The noise is deafening – as battles usually are – and many participants are injured. What are the solutions?

This is where the cartoon is insightful and not in the least trivial. Look at the potential of the various horns. Just as these instruments can make a lot of disjointed and unbearable noise, so too can these very instruments – the stakeholder voices – come together with a powerful, harmonious and beautiful sound when orchestrated, nurtured or conducted in a thoughtful and careful manner. It takes a knowledgeable and experienced conductor to bring these voices together in harmony. When each instrument is given a chance to be heard, to bring out the beauty of its strings and chords, when thoughtful attention is paid to orchestrate, listen and conduct a piece of music with patience and collaboration, then harmony among the instruments can make beautiful music. Although not everyone is born a musician, practice can bring great results. It takes work, together with constant and critical questioning of our own assumptions and those of others, to make a concerted effort and listen to the voices of *all* stakeholders in a pluralistic school system. The ability to hear, interact and empower on an intellectual and pluralistic level is central to addressing the horns of the dilemma in making policy decisions. My point in using this metaphor is that it is essential to *talk* about the dilemmas in an *intelligent, respectful* and *trusting* manner. Adult educators ought to model these responsibilities at all times.

As schools attempt to deal with cyber-bullying, expertise and patience, the ingredients necessary for collaborative and cohesive learning, have been largely absent. Reactive anti-bullying programmes and zero-tolerance suspension policies do nothing but add anger and frustration to an already disjointed 'orchestra' of stakeholder claims. I have presented sufficient research evidence in earlier chapters to show that these initiatives are largely superficial and do not address the heart of the issues. Little progress can be expected, unless competing stakeholder rights and interests are addressed through critical and pedagogically informed programmes and policies. Teachers and school administrators need to be better equipped to address contemporary dilemmas. Teacher education and professional development programmes have, to date, done a poor job of equipping educators to navigate stakeholder claims. The Internet and digital literacies have complicated matters.

Pragmatic and comprehensive solutions

In order to develop a cohesive and collaborative stakeholder approach to addressing the dilemmas of cyber-bullying, a pragmatic shift is necessary. Such a shift ought to inform the way we conceptualize issues of censorship and cyber-bullying. Three key gaps come through in cyber-bullying controversies:

1   The need for informed and improved teacher education and professional development of school officials and policymakers.
2   The need to level the power hierarchies among stakeholders to reconceptualize schooling through collaborative and non-restrictive learning approaches. It is important that these are grounded in a comprehensive

foundation of digital literacies, critical pedagogies, leadership and substantive law, such that we learn *together* with children and take advantage of the enormous fluidity, capacity and communicative and learning potential that contemporary technologies provide.

3   In the absence of the above two options, it will be difficult to foster and sustain school environments that are inclusive and conducive to learning, that prepare students for democratic engagement in civil society – whether it takes place in physical or virtual settings.

To address these gaps, I introduce two models and a concept map that were developed as part of my pre-service teacher education and professional development at McGill University over the last four years. I believe these models not only contribute significantly to meeting the legal responsibilities outlined in Chapter 7 (Table 7.1), but also inform the development of proactive and collaborative policies on cyber-bullying at international levels.

My critical legal literacy model is grounded in a conceptual understanding of substantive legal principles and legal pluralism. These are not the same as the positivist or punitive aspects of law that educators tend to rely upon. Such reliance leads to assumptions among teachers and school administrators that the law has no place in pedagogy or educational policy.

Legal literacy

Legal literacy for educators prepares them to apply substantive legal principles that inform the fundamental principles of democracy and civil behaviour towards others. Through discussion and analysis of case law that provides various educational, programmatic and policy challenges, the model includes competing rights and stakeholder conflicts such as the free-expression and privacy debate in cyberspace. Teachers learn to apply practical exercises and knowledge to an improved understanding of the legal standards included in Table 7.1. More specifically, teachers gain a practical understanding of what we mean when we talk about equality, freedom of expression, freedom of religion and conscience, the right to life, liberty and security, the right to be free from unreasonable search and seizure and so on, in a constitutional sense. They learn the extent of their responsibilities of supervision under tort law as *in loco parentis* and their obligations as 'careful and prudent parents'. My approach gives teachers an opportunity to learn how courts balance and weigh competing rights and how this balancing of rights and responsibilities is an integral aspect of running a democratic school system.

I find it disturbing that so few teachers and school officials have a minimal grounding in substantive law. This limits their understanding of law as an instrument of control – which requires them to handle every situation through adversarial, punitive and positivist solutions. As I explained in Chapter 5, censorship and didactic control of what children learn in schools contribute to the discriminatory and demeaning attitudes that rear their ugly heads in the content of student expression (cyber-bullying) against peers and teachers. Elsewhere (S. Shariff and Johnny, 2007a) I have written that many of the comprehensive perspectives and forms of knowledge omitted from our school system are censored either behind closed doors or in such a skilful way that it is not always obvious. For example, Apple and Christian-Smith (1991), in their discussion of learning materials, remind us that textbooks are the product of a selective tradition – 'someone's selection, someone's visions of legitimate knowledge and culture, one that in the process of enfranchising one group's cultural capital disenfranchises another's' (ibid., p. 4). Although these scholars concede that some modern texts have aimed to incorporate multicultural perspectives, they argue many of these perspectives are only mentioned in passing rather than discussed in any great depth. Moreover, Charles Taylor argues that, when the reality of another is not adequately represented, it can lead to a sort of social oppression. He states:

> Equal recognition is not just the appropriate mode for a healthy demo-cratic society. Its refusal can inflict damage on those who are denied it. The projection of an inferior or demeaning image on another can actually distort and oppress, to the extent that the image is internalized . . . Race relations and discussions of multiculturalism are under-girded by the premise that the withholding of recognition can be a form of oppression.
>
> (Taylor, as cited in McDougall and Philips Valentine, 1999, p. 335)

The manner in which knowledge is constructed for our school system is undoubtedly an important consideration for how we understand and define student expression and acceptable forms of communication. Take, for instance, the work of scholars such as Montgomery (2005). He found in his explora-tion of racism in schools that, although Canadian history textbooks seem to acknowledge examples of racism, they are presented as isolated occurrences that take place only among exceptionally flawed individuals. He argues that 'this depiction of Canada as a space of vanquished and managed racism . . . perpetuates mythologies of white settler benevolence while it at once obscures the banal racisms upon and through which the nation state is built and rebuilt' (ibid., p. 439). Such examples remind us that censorship is not only about what is banned from our schools but also *how information is presented*. Obscur-ing the reality of marginalized groups in official textbooks can certainly have significant ramifications for society because, as Inglis (1985) notes, 'a curriculum is no less than the knowledge system of a society and therefore not only an ontology but also the metaphysics and ideology which that society has agreed to recognize as legitimate and truthful; it sets the canons of truthfulness' (ibid., p. 22).

As I reported on censorship studies elsewhere (Shariff and Manley-Casimir, 1999), much of the time, principals, teachers, secretaries, clerks and other school employees take it upon themselves to self-censor all kinds of books and educational resources. Sometimes 'offending' pages are torn out of books or blacked out. Hence, it is not surprising, as Lankshear and Knobel (2006) observe, that educators transport this mindset to online learning and expression. To address these uses of agency and discretion and begin to incorporate elements of trust and student empowerment, the type of professional development and teacher education model I recommend below is grounded in legal literacy and legal pluralism. This combination takes into account 'cultural specificity' (MacDonald, 2006). When applied, the model draws upon a range of educational theories that are largely informed by a critical perspective.

Prospective teachers, graduate students and school administrators learn critically to assess their own agency and leadership approaches, question their own assumptions about student differences and apply them to the legal literacy framework. This exercise helps them determine whether they, in fact, bring a hegemonic perspective to their teaching, supervision and administrative duties, including discipline and punishment for the forms of expression that underpin bullying and cyber-bullying.

Practical solutions: online limitations

Teacher education and professional development programmes need to integrate and apply the foregoing approaches with more practical attention to digital literacies. Developing familiarity and confidence with digital literacies ought to be a key element of these courses. Media literacy experts can be called in to support such programmes on an ongoing basis and work with prospective teachers and school administrators to identify online resources in a range of teaching subjects. Hands-on Internet research strategies and links to useful resources; blogs that discuss civil liberties, freedom of expression and its limitations; digital definitions that can be found on sites such as Wikipedia.com; legislation and policy information; educational web sites ranging from geography to arts and architectures, to writing competitions and good journalism; links to case law, to scientific and medical journals; links that provide information about NASA and the space programme; links that connect to cultural information; music web sites; literature, poetry – the list is endless. Experts in digital literacies need to be invited to engage in hands-on practice with prospective teachers to guide them on how to develop resources of databases of useful web sites, so that slowly they can overcome the restrictive mindset and integrate digital literacies as a normal part of their everyday teaching.

In Canada, the Media Awareness Network (see www.mediawareness.com, 'MNet') has developed teacher education programmes that they license out to school boards. These programmes include introductions to constitutional and human rights law, and criminal justice issues relating to young people, all of which interactively utilize the Internet, so that teachers develop proficiency in its use. This non-profit organization has also developed excellent interactive online resources that help young people critically assess their social relationships and attitudes online. For younger students, they have created an interactive game called 'Privacy Playground: The First Adventure of the Three CyberPigs' and 'CyberSense and Nonsense: The Second Adventure of the Three CyberPigs' (Media Awareness Network, no date).

For older students, they have also developed an interactive educational programme that addresses online hate, which has been licensed to approximately eighty school districts across Canada (Steeves and Wing, 2005). I am working with MNet to develop in-depth lesson plans for prospective teachers and high school students on children's rights; ethical online communication and moral codes of social communication; tort law and cyber-libel; tort law and negligence in supervision; criminal law as it relates to online threats and harassment; constitutional and international human rights provisions. The organization is also developing networks with the Canadian Girl Guides Association and the Canadian Red Cross on anti-bullying education, focusing on respect. In this regard, they are launching an enormous public awareness campaign. MNet works with kids' help phone lines in various provinces across Canada and is a member in PREVNet, an academic networking organization that brings together researchers interested in young people's social relationships nationally and internationally. Other initiatives under consideration include online mediation among youth groups, and youth experts who work with adults to show them how to navigate the Internet.

Similarly, in the United Kingdom, the Teacher Resource Exchange web site (British Educational Communications and Technology Agency, no date, b) allows for exchange of online resources developed by teachers, as does the Becta online resource directory for teachers (British Educational Communications and Technology Agency, 2007). Awards are given out to schools that incorporate and raise awareness of ways to integrate digital literacies in schools (British Educational Communications and Technology Agency, no date, a).

Moreover, the examples from the ALA in response to the proposed DOPA bill in the United States, in Chapter 7, suggest that libraries can be instrumental in developing adult online proficiency. This expertise can, in turn, support children's use of online tools. The range of online educational resource guides is expanding everyday, as IT experts join with educational pedagogues, librarians and academics to develop improved access and proficiency in digital literacies.

It is not within the scope of this book to list them all, however, it is in order to cite one important study by library scientists who engaged children in the development of a web portal for peers. Large *et al.* (2006) embarked upon a research study that investigated three challenges to developing Internet resources for classroom use. They wanted to determine how elementary school students use web portals to find information in support of class-based projects. They also examined what constitutes an effective web portal design for elementary school students; and, finally, they wanted to know whether inter-generational design techniques can be used to design such a web portal. The study used two inter-generational teams (one team comprising three researchers and eight grade 6 students; the other team the same three researchers and six grade 3 students). Each team designed a low-tech web portal prototype. The research was conducted in an elementary school located in a middle-class suburb of Montreal.

Subsequently, the two low-tech portals were converted into working prototypes to search the web for sites in English or French relating to Canadian history. The portals were evaluated by single-sex focus groups comprising children in grades 6 and 3. The researchers report that, overall, these users responded very positively to both portals and said they would choose to use them over other well-known portals such as Google or MSN if seeking information for a project on Canadian history. Drawing from a literature review of web portal design that incorporated user-centred design method-ologies, contextual design approaches and learner-centred approaches, the designers developed a new methodological framework that they called 'bonded design', because they believed that this term encapsulated the essence of what was experienced by all members of the design team. These experiences are best explained in their own words from the following excerpts:

> The team comprised 11 individuals in one case and eight in the other, but these individuals can be divided into two groups: the children and the adult designers. Each group had its special and unique expertise that was essential to the successful completion of the team's task. The children were experts in thinking like children; they represented the user com-munity for which the two portals were being designed. Adults all too frequently cling to the illusion that they understand children and can conjure how children think and behave. They nurture this illusion from one of two misconceptions: that they were themselves once children and can return at will through time to recapture that lost youth; or that they have children of their own through whose observation they can generate a child's view of the world. Alas, with few exceptions, adults are deluding themselves. Their emergence from childhood is irreversible. *If adults wish to understand children, they must work alongside them as collaborators* [emphasis added].
>
> (Large *et al.*, 2006, p. 78)

The inter-generational web design project also reflected my metaphor of the 'horns' working together, regardless of their different strengths and contributions. For example, the researchers explain:

> While the children were involved alongside adults as team members, each with an equal voice, not every voice sang the same song. The children were novice users. Of course they had a critical expertise – they understood how children think and behave – but they knew little about web portals or the design process. In contrast, the adults had expertise in portal design and functionality but could not think like children. Furthermore, there can be no denying that it was the adults who set the agenda, designed the initial research plan, and determined such important details as the length, content, and organization of sessions. Although the atmosphere in the design sessions was relaxed and informal, when required, it was the adults and not the children who brought things to order.
>
> (Ibid.)

If considered in terms of adults' fear of losing control, this model illustrates that children need direction from adults even in situations where the adults may not necessarily have a great deal of expertise. Nonetheless, the learning took place both ways:

> From the perspective of all team members – adults as well as children – the design process was evolutionary. By the final sessions, the adults had a better understanding of the children's perspectives, and likewise the children were much better informed about portal functionality, design, and working as a team. This introduces an irony: The children are involved in the process because they think as children and not as designers, but gradually as they acquire more knowledge they become potentially less representative of their peer group.
>
> Neither the children nor the adult designers alone, then, could have accomplished the design task facing them – to design two web portals appropriate for young information seekers. But when these two disparate groups were bonded in the design teams, *they were able to draw upon their relative strengths and achieve something neither could do in isolation* [emphasis added].
>
> (Ibid.)

These are the kinds of initiative that I believe need to be considered. The strengths that each inter-generational team bring to the collaboration develop a strong sense of bonding and mutual respect.

Hence, the essence of the bonded design brought together by Large and his research team is a means of bringing together inter-generational members of a team that unites despite the diversity of its members. The team includes adult experts in design and children who are 'experts' in the sense of knowing what online requirements children might have. The adults and children work together throughout the design process. The authors note that, like co-operative enquiry, bonded design emphasizes an inter-generational partnership in working towards a common goal. It also ensures that children play an active role in the web design, giving them a sense of agency and confidence that they would not experience if they were merely evaluators or testers at the end of the design process.

The researchers explain that bonding design also shares aspects of learner-centred design in that it provides a learning environment for all team members – children and adults alike. Learner-centred design assumes that everyone is a learner, whether a professional or a student. In designing web portals for children, the team's objective was to make sure that the design incorporated the interests, knowledge and styles of the child users it was built for.

Although they shared reservations about the true equality of children alongside adults in a design team, they concluded that co-operative enquiry was the central focus in the involvement of children from the beginning to completion of the design process.

They explain that, essentially, bonded design is situated between co-operative enquiry and informant design. It is dependant on the belief in the ability of children to work as partners in all aspects of the design process; however, it retains reservations about the extent to which full and equal co-operation can occur across the generational divide, and, therefore, in these respects, some informant or instructive aspects are necessary from the adults involved in the design team. The researchers also report that the web portals were created in a significantly short period of time and that both were converted into working web portals that can be used by children. In this sense, they note the efficiency of bonding design. Ultimately, the researchers note that the strength of bonding design resides in the fact that it unites children and adults, novices and experts in a shared experience, but retains their individual strengths and weaknesses, their different expertise in a co-operative venture. Figure 8.2 illustrates how the bonding design works to bring stakeholders together.

This example of engaging both adults and children in developing online educational resources is in keeping with constitutional principles of equality and freedom of expression, as well as in line with international conventions of the rights of the child. It allows children the opportunity to engage and participate in developing online tools. Such empowerment gives them ownership, and with ownership comes responsibility, where each one of the children involved in the project would not want to see it used for cyber-bullying or defamatory statements. This is one of many important initiatives. Teachers should get used to engaging with students in the development and creation of web portals, online blogs and discussion groups, so that they no longer feel excluded, and so that young people no longer perceive cyberspace

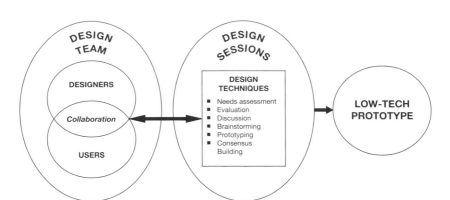

Figure 8.2 The bonded design model
Source: Large *et al.*, 2006, p. 80

as their own private space. Teenagers will show much more respect to their teachers if they recognize their knowledge of IT, their willingness to engage in online discussions and their proficiency in helping them find resources. When students perceive that their teachers lack expertise and are afraid of the Internet, they will more likely be tempted to take advantage of the situation. If a conscientious effort is made by more adults to accept and actively to use technology as a primary source of learning, with texts and books that complement such use, students will gradually gain confidence in their teachers' expertise and demonstrate greater respect.

Building proficiency at home

It is also important that this engagement begins at home and continues at school. To that end, the recommendations of the UK study 'UK children go online' (UKCGO) (Livingstone and Bober, 2005) are worth taking into consideration.

On regulating the Internet at home, the UKCGO stresses that parents face difficult challenges as they seek to manage their children's use of technologies. As the following quotes suggest, parents are concerned and aware about their responsibilities to monitor what their children are doing online:

> I think parents should also try and educate themselves. You can say 'my children know' and leave them . . . [but those] parents are going wrong. So you leave the child alone to sit down on the net for two, three hours? No! Sit in with the child . . . It's not wrong to learn from your children . . . You have to be interested in what your child is doing.
>
> (Mother of Anisah, 15, from London,
> ibid., p. 24)

Well, we've had long talks with them and they are fully aware of the dangers of chat rooms and things. And I do trust them to a certain extent. I do sort of. If they are on there, I just sort of look over their shoulder or something, but I do trust them not to. I think they're quite aware of the dangers that are lurking there.

(Mother of Eve, 12, and Clarissa, 12,
from Surrey, ibid.)

The UK study makes two policy recommendations as far as Internet use in the home is concerned:

First, it encourages parents to share in children's Internet use. This means that parents need to increase their supportive activities when children are online. Simple questions such as what they are doing online, keeping an eye on the screen, helping them find resources, staying in the same room even if it is on another computer, and going online together. The study found that this increases young people's online skills and opportunities. Although the findings suggest this may not reduce online risks, they suggest it could improve parental awareness of the risks their children encounter. Obviously, the extent to which parents can engage with their children online will depend upon their own Internet skills. Therefore, some parents will be in a better position to participate than others. Nonetheless, this recommendation of the study ought to be considered seriously by all parents, and not only those concerned that their children are engaging in unhealthy or antisocial online activities.

Second, the study suggests that parents respect their children's online privacy in the home. Although this sounds like a contradiction to the first suggestion, the study argues for a sensitive balance. If parents are too pushy about monitoring, restricting and controlling their children's online activities, this could encourage evasion rather than co-operation with attempts at Internet regulation in the home. As the study notes, teenagers can be fiercely protective of their privacy when parents are perceived to interfere. At the same time, parents need more information, confidence and guidance; hence, it requires a sensitive negotiation of space, within the home and in cyberspace. Ultimately, parents need to build an element of trust such that children are comfortable having them around at all times that they are online.

The overall policy guidelines from the UKCGO study stress that care must be taken *not to reduce young people's online opportunities*. The report observes that, as many of the children interviewed expressed anxieties about online risks, or restrictive parental (and school) practices as limiting their online opportunities, the researchers recommend care in designing literacy and safety initiatives. Although the report acknowledges that, at present, increasing online opportunities go hand in hand with increasing risks, their findings hint that carefully targeting parental regulation may protect children from risks by increasing their online expertise.

The researchers believe that target guidance and regulation can be directed more carefully at different groups of children. The researchers explain that children and young people adopt different styles of engagement with the Internet. This depends not only on demographic factors but also on skills and interests, which leads them to balance opportunities and risks in different ways. Thus, they suggest that guidance and regulation should be more carefully targeted for those who are risk averse (or whose parents are risk averse), through increased encouragement from experts. The advanced explorers would benefit from advanced critical and safety guidance.

Finally, the report recommends improvements in designing web sites that encourage Internet literacy. They note that, as children's and young people's level of online skills has a direct influence on the breadth of online opportunities, multiple routes to improving Internet literacy are recommended. As an example, they explain that some web sites ask for personal information that young people are trained not to give out. However, this prevents them from linking into other good sites. The messages sent to children are thus confusing – either you do want them to access these sites or you don't. Accordingly, the UK researchers recommend the development of increased and better child and youth portals, similar to the Web portal built by Large *et al.* (2006) in their inter-generational bonding exercise. The UKGCO researchers propose that as even the most skilled children and young people cannot avoid online risks, more attention needs to be paid to structuring the online environment itself, so as to make it safer for them and all users. Thus, they suggest a two-pronged approach that addresses the skills and competence of children and young people, and the nature and organization of the online environment in which they are engaged (ibid., p. 27).

To that end, there are a number of connective ethnographies being undertaking with respect to online/offline literacies. One excellent source is an article by Kevin Leander (in press). The UKCGO report, emerging ethnographies on new online and offline literacies, the work of Lankshear and Knobel (2006); and that of boyd and Jenkins (Wright, 2006) all represent the desired mindset and approach to accessing and engaging in a knowledge society that is no longer in the future, it is here and now. This is the alternative mindset that ought to inform the work of educators who continue to administer and teach children and young people in our public and private educational institutions. The controversies, power hierarchies and arbitrary responses to young people's adaptation to their new lived realities need to be shelved in favour of a genuine effort to engage with the educational tools of the twenty-first century. Removing or banning these tools is not an option, just as removing children from their rightful place in educational institutions through suspensions and expulsion seriously impairs their international human rights to participation. Suspensions should not be an option. These responses are as outdated as corporal punishment, which was so prevalently used within the last thirty years. Just as there is a fine line between acceptable and unacceptable online expressions, so is there a fine line between restricting access to the virtual world or supporting it. As I have noted, censorship of what students read, access, debate and express has been an integral aspect of schooling.

Raising student awareness of censorship

I would like to stress that working with children to develop civic virtue and social responsibility is not limited to cyberspace. Lisa K. Winkler (2004) is a New York educator who agrees that we ought to ensure students can become responsible citizens, capable of meeting the complex challenges in society. She believes that, in addition to teaching reading, writing, speaking, listening and viewing, it is important that students also become aware of censorship in all its forms Winkler uses mock trials and readings where students are given permission to choose their own books, as well as short writing assignments to bring the issue of censorship into the classroom. Ken Petress (2004) agrees that, in class, discussions about the motivations that lie behind censorship to encourage critical analysis by students are essential. Leslie Keene (2004) in fact provides activities that go with the classroom discussions suggested in her book, *Who said I can't read this?* Keene has developed units that feed off the resources provided by the ALA. The Book and Periodical Council of Canada launches an annual 'Freedom to Read' week every February (Book and Periodical Council, 2004), where they publish lists of challenged and banned books, with synopses of the book. Discussions about censorship can begin with a currently controversial issue that makes students aware of all sides of the problem, such as discussion of banned music, books, controversial web sites and movies, and the reasons for the controversy from all sides. Teachers can facilitate discussion and recommend readings that provide alternative or a range of perspectives on the issue.

As Foerstel (1994) noticed, as long as there are authors who have meaningful things to say, the horns of censorship will be raised, creating an enormous dilemma for schools, although I certainly realize that, in some cases, censorship might serve useful purposes, such as when material that is harmful to society is restricted from use in the public education system, especially child pornography and hate crimes, which we have noted proliferate on the Internet.

However, there is much written about the health and educational benefits of introducing students to a range of opinions or sensitive and controversial issues (Bettelheim, 1989; Elbaz-Luwisch, 2004; Katch, 2001; Shariff, 2004). For instance, when children gain exposure to more than one perspective, they garner the knowledge they need to make informed decisions about their lives and, ultimately, how they express their views and attitudes towards others. Avoidance can merely generate conflict, as suppressed concerns fester and surface through explosive disputes (Elbaz-Luwisch, 2004; Herzog, 1995;

Larson, 1997; Shariff, 1999; Shariff *et al.*, 2000, 2001). In other words, the educational growth of children and the promotion of tolerance in society, benefit from a school system that includes a wide-ranging curriculum, one that adequately acknowledges the realities, values and culture of a number of different social groups. The lived realities, oral traditions, cultures and religion, and gendered perspectives ought to be at the heart of development education if the educational beneficiaries are to be empowered towards self-sufficiency, democracy, health and peace.

In discussing the censorship aspects as they play out in cyber-bullying controversies, I have conceptualized censorship as an act of power in an educational system that excludes certain groups. In the preceding chapters, I developed this understanding even further by considering how censorship plays a key role in cultural hegemony and control of student spaces and what they are exposed to and allowed to learn in those spaces. To that end, I have drawn upon scholarly perspectives on pluralism and civil society that provide guidance on valuing and validating the histories, contributions and cultures of students from diverse backgrounds.

I have also alerted educators to the fact that censorship is a legal issue that ought to be grounded more in substantive human rights and legal pluralism than in positivist policy approaches that can result in costly ramifications for school boards. I agree with the observation that we currently seem to be building 'an architecture that unleashes 60 percent of brain [and] a legal system that closes down that part of the brain' (Lessing, 2004, as cited in Lankshear and Knobel, 2006, p. 21). Lankshear and Knobel (2006) argue that closing down 60 per cent of the brain is exactly the impact of current policy directions in education generally, as well as of official versions of 'digital literacy' (p. 21). This is certainly true when zero-tolerance policy approaches and reactive censorship (withdrawing computer privileges, book banning, firewalls etc.) are arbitrarily applied under pressure from some teachers and parents. A positivistic approach most often erupts in hotly debated controversies that divert the focus away from student concerns.

On the contrary, with the help of substantive, critical and legally pluralistic doctrines, my book demonstrates that substantive law is an essential component of knowledge construction and education that cater to a pluralistic global society.

Critical legal literacy model for teacher education

I present and analyse the issues within the broader socio-cultural context, using models and a guiding concept map that show greater promise of being ethical, educational and legally defensible when censorship controversies erupt.

Figure 8.3 illustrates how the model can inform the core educational philosophy of educators in navigating difficult cyber-bullying and censorship dilemmas.

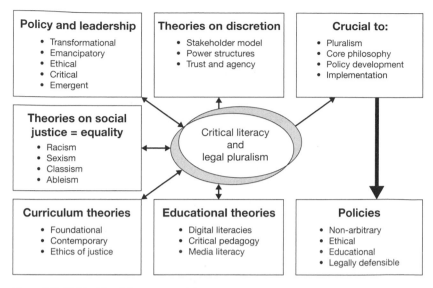

Figure 8.3 Critical legal literacy model

Source: Shariff (2006)

Using the critical legal literacy model, which could incorporate, for example, classroom approaches advocated by critical pedagogues (Apple, 2000; Kincheloe, 2005), prospective educators can begin to remove the layers of prejudicial attitudes that have developed as a result of years of censorship and reconstruct knowledge that is grounded in comprehensive legal, digital literacy and critical perspectives. There is now a substantial amount of excellent literature on digital literacies, as well as a range of studies that review ways in which technology is used by children and adults (Leander, in press; Mazzarella, 2005; Lankshear and Knobel, 2006).

My critical legal literacy approach provides fewer opportunities for conflict and allows for incorporation of educational resources, hard copy and digital curricular approaches that engage and validate the diversity and ethical and cultural frameworks of their students. Although I do not suggest that use of this model would bring the desired results instantly, it will, over time, facilitate the process to break down hegemonic barriers. The model also addresses the fact that educational decision-makers use *agency* when they select, censor and punish students. In that connection, it will also help educators critically assess the forms of agency and knowledge construction they bring to their decisions about whether to discuss negative online or face-to-face discourse with their students. Regardless of whether the content of a student's offensive expression included sexual connotations about the teacher, this could be a teachable opportunity. For example, if I were the teacher about whom Bram wrote on

Facebook, I would have students research the etymology of bullying, the history of bullying and school censorship controversies involving freedom of expression and supervision – and ask them to come to decisions about where the lines crossed over to become cyber-libel and criminal expression.

Moreover, I would attempt to find out what fuelled the anger that resulted in the comments made online. Was the student unhappy with his grade? Did he perceive unfair treatment? Was he having problems at home and taking out his frustrations this way? There is always fire where there is smoke, and it is the source of that fire that needs to be addressed.

Given the litigious nature of school controversies between educators, students and parents over free expression, supervision, privacy and safety, it is imperative that teachers' knowledge construction is grounded in legal literacy, critical pedagogy and critical media literacy, as well as theories of leadership, ethics and social justice. Currently, I believe that many university teacher education and professional development programmes lack coherent models that provide educators with the conceptual grounding they need for a wired and litigious world. Such grounding would facilitate recognition of the common elements and congruence between substantive legal principles, critical pedagogies and ethical frameworks that incorporate the cultural and paradigmatic perspectives of a broad range of stakeholders.

As explained in Chapter 6, it is of significant importance that school curricula not only include a comparative historical perspective of world civilizations, but that they also engage stakeholders and students in presenting their own ethical perspectives (whether grounded in religion or secularism) to inform their contributions (both historical and current). These foundational forms of knowledge, I believe, would go much further in the long term to reducing bullying and cyber-bullying than suspensions and expulsions, which have already been proven to be ineffective. Most importantly, exposure to the background, histories and struggles of people from all walks of life would contribute to an environment that is more accepting of differences, as it should be in schools.

A concept map: positive school environments

One of the legal standards identified in Chapter 7 (see Table 7.1) is the obligation on schools to avoid tacit condoning of bullying and harassment such that they create a 'deliberately dangerous environment' for students and teachers. There is a clear legal expectation, based on human rights and civil law decisions in North America[1] that schools are required to foster and sustain positive school environments.

Moreover, throughout this book, I have emphasized that the school environment plays an important role in knowledge production and learning in the school context. I have explained that, when the lived realities and educational resources of some stakeholders are ignored, there is an impact on the school environment, whether it is physical or virtual (involving classmates' cyber-bullying). Hence, what is learned from the critical legal literacy model can be transported into a concept map that informs the objectives of fostering and sustaining school environments that are welcoming and inclusive, thereby empowering all students to engage confidently in their learning. This could mean allowing them to explore the Internet, but preparing them through discussion and dialogue to know when to avoid predators; when to avoid joining peers in joking that crosses the line to cyber-bullying and cyber-libel; and to speak up against cyber-bullying or discriminatory forms of expression.

One example of students who spoke up against cyber-bullying took place in the aftermath of the mass college shootings in Virginia, United States, in April 2007. Facebook was used by young people in two ways. The first was that thousands of young people reached out to the students of Virginia Tech University with their condolences. The exchanges helped them develop bonds and feel as though they were contributing to a helpless situation. Others, however, began to attack an Asian student because the killer had been South Korean. This was quickly abated by the influx of responses from young people who protested against the singling out and stereotyping of Asian youth on Facebook (Agence France Presse, 2007).

Cyber-bullying is reduced in an environment where selection of what is taught, discussed and validated as learning is informed by a proactive educational approach that incorporates critical pedagogies, digital and media literacy, legal literacy and relevant ethical frameworks. Such an approach is not built on assumptions, but incorporated through dialogue and engagement of students from all backgrounds. This is where social networking tools, as Jenkins and boyd (Wright, 2006) both observe, can have significant positive value. The research presented earlier confirms that the more involved students are in establishing the parameters and content of their own education, the more likely they are to engage critically in their learning.

I have discussed some of the common patterns that emerge when school environments are 'poisoned' and where relationships among administration, teachers, parents and students are not cohesive. I present a concept map that incorporates the critical legal literacy approached described above (see Figure 8.4). The concept map informs teacher education on bullying and cyber-bullying and illustrates the benefits of more proactive, rather than reactive, responses. The approach educators adopt ultimately determines whether the school environment will be positive and conducive to learning or poisoned and detrimental to learning.

The model illustrates that a reactive approach that underpins suspensions, expulsions, censorship of student expression, and use of technologies results in tacit condoning of discriminatory attitudes through blanket policies that ignore difference. Moreover, a reactive approach generally reduces student safety because it encourages racism, sexism, homophobia and other forms of discrimination. A reactive approach can also be rooted in historically negative and fractured relations between administration and staff, and a lack of common educational goals. There is no question that student learning in such an

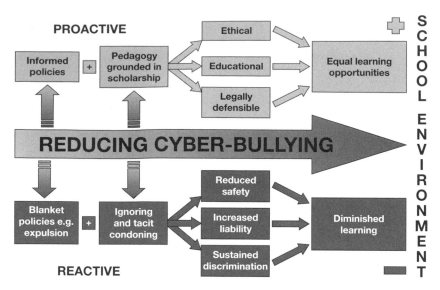

Figure 8.4 Concept map incorporating critical legal literacy

Source: © 2007 Shaheen Shariff, Ph.D., McGill University

environment is impeded, because students are distracted by the negative, hostile and exclusionary messages they receive.

Zero tolerance provides no opportunity for dialogue, analysis of demeaning forms of expression, or consideration of all stakeholder perspectives. Students can be shown the impact of their expression on the teachers they decide to pick on, their ability to work or find other employment; their feelings of frustration at not being validated as good teachers, which ultimately affect their spouses and families. When school environments are more nurturing than hostile, teenagers such as Brad, Bram, Julia and others discussed in Chapters 5 and 6 might think more carefully before they post negative comments about teachers and administrators online. This is where the stakeholder model I have developed as part of the critical legal literacy model is also useful.

Levelling stakeholder hierarchies of power

Figure 8.3 includes a stakeholder model within the critical legal literacy approach. It is in the same box as 'trust and agency'. This is an important component of the critical legal literacy approach. During my ten years or so of studying legal issues in education, I have developed a very simple test for non-arbitrary balancing of competing rights in the school context. The test is modelled on the adjudication process that Canadian courts use in weighing and balancing stakeholder rights to rule on questions of equality, freedom of expression, freedom of religion and conscience, and so on. This is how the stakeholder model works.

The stakeholder model

The stakeholder model can be applied to a range of specific democratic challenges in schools that involve stakeholder conflicts. Although the model may appear to be somewhat mechanistic, I suggest it is a first step in helping educators navigate stakeholder concerns regarding cyber-bullying and student expression.

Drawing from a combination of legal tests derived from US and Canadian jurisprudence on constitutional challenges, the stakeholder model guides an understanding and appreciation of the perspectives that each stakeholder brings to the issue. In Chapters 5 and 6 I mentioned several high schools that had experienced a significant number of anti-authority postings about teachers and school administrators by students at the schools.

Poisoned environment

In one high school (high school X), over 100 students had joined a Facebook forum under the school name. Approximately twenty students were caught discussing teachers, and, out of those, four were narrowed down as posting the most negative comments about teachers. When I met with administrators, what struck me was the history of deep divisions among staff within departments, some of whom did not even speak to each other. There was resentment towards the administration because it had changed so often, and resentment and mistrust towards the school board. Parents were competitive and demanding, as this school has a highly competitive academic programme; and the approach of older teachers was didactic. Moreover, the new administrators informed us that young teachers who joined the school very quickly became part of, and were influenced by, the cynical culture at the school.

Cyber-bullying was a symptom of this poisoned environment, where students put into words the negative feelings their teachers conveyed and modelled. I was invited to attend the school to give workshops for teachers and students on cyber-bullying. I realized this would make no difference unless I was able to address the deeper issues and the divided school culture at the school. How could I address the 'horns of the dilemma'? This was a perfect time to draw upon the stakeholder model for help.

Step 1: Identify the stakeholders

As I have emphasized throughout this book, although the media would have people believe that cyber-bullying is limited to a battle between teachers and students, or among students themselves, this assessment is inaccurate. If we take the case of high school X, we realize antagonism between teachers at the school and the administration goes back many years, to when the school ceased being a private school and was taken over several times by different school boards. Each time a new school board took over, administrative changes were made. Promises made by the previous board were rarely carried out by the next school board. However, teachers remained at the school because it of its reputation as an institution of high academic stature. This fact made the school attractive to teachers and gave them a high stake in remaining at the school. Administrators came and went, in some cases because they could not handle the hostility of the teachers. Students were of a high calibre, as a significant number of them were in an International Baccalaureate programme. This made the school attractive to competitive parents who wanted their children to succeed academically. Using Step 1 of the Stakeholder model, we can identify several stakeholders:

1   the current school board – elected trustees;
2   new administrators;
3   parents who support student free expression off-campus and those who do not; parents who support suspensions as discipline and those who oppose it;
4   teachers who:

- endorse use of social networking tools online and those who do not understand or use the Internet;
- engage in didactic teaching methods and support punitive measures such as suspensions and expulsions;
- prefer interactive teaching in which students are empowered and have a voice.

5   students ranging from those who use social networking tools solely for personal purposes and those who use them as a discussion forum to express their views.

When student online comments were discovered at high school X, the teachers signed a petition demanding that the offending students be asked to leave the school. The teachers' union endorsed their petition. Parents, on the other hand, felt their children were being unfairly punished and argued that teachers were overreacting. The administration was caught in the middle. The media became involved when information was leaked out, resulting in dissonance and conflict. This is where step 2 of the model comes in useful. The key claims set out below have emerged from the scholarship on media framing; my review of the range of media reports on cyber-bullying; case studies discussed in Chapters 5–7; interviews with school administrators and teachers under my research grants; and anonymous student surveys under my two research projects funded by the SSHRC, reported in Chapter 4. Some claims emerge from personal communication with teachers, administrators, and school board members from a range of schools as part of my ongoing research and consulting activities. They are also exemplified in high school X, where the problems appear to have existed for many years, and where sensitivities are described as running deep. Table 8.1 shows what stakeholder claims at school X might look like.

Step 2: Validate their claims

See Table 8.1.

Step 3: Critically weigh each claim against the others

It is always easier to weigh the rights and interests of stakeholders once they have been identified and their claims heard. It is the first two steps that most reactive policy responses overlook.

School board claims

In their haste to 'control' the students, appease teachers or parents and preserve the good reputations of their schools, school board officials often override the first two steps of the stakeholder model and focus only on the students. When the claims of other stakeholders are not heard or validated, the process is doomed to failure. Teachers and parents begin to lack confidence in the school board because their concerns are ignored. I have been contacted so often by frustrated parents of children who are victims of bullying and cyber-bullying. In every case, parents have come up against the 'wall of defence' described in Chapter 6. Having anti-bullying policies and task forces in place is not enough. Similarly, teachers and school administrators who attend my graduate courses at McGill express frustration at the fact that often their school board policies are not supported with adequate training or time to implement initiatives to address bullying. If school board claims are applied to Step 2 of the stakeholder model, we find that, from an administrative perspective, maintaining reasonable control and managing a crisis are justified priorities. The question that challenges this justification is whether prioritizing control of the situation ought to trump the educational concerns of stakeholders such as the students and their parents. That is the question that will determine how much weight the school board justifications carry.

School administrator claims

School administrators are often, as depicted in the 'horns of the dilemma' cartoon that opened this chapter, caught in the middle. The school board wants head teachers and principals to maintain the school reputation and keep things under control. They want to avoid media attention at all costs. They need to

Table 8.1 Validating stakeholder claims

	Media	School board	School administrators	Teachers[a]	Parents	Students
Claim 1	Wants a sensational story that can be framed a certain way – the 'battle'	Concerned about reputation and regaining control of the situation	Trying to balance demands of all stakeholders – parents, teachers, students, school board	Angry with students for hitting home with some comments, and for sexually charged statements	Concerned about disruption to their children's learning	Need positive learning environment to succeed academically
Claim 2	Wants a story that supports the teachers because they are angry	Has to meet parent expectations – doesn't want to reduce popularity or standards	Concerned about reputation, but also overwhelmed with work – no time to meet everyone's needs	Concerned about their marred reputation and the possibility of finding employment elsewhere	Concerned about fair treatment for their children	Pressured by parents to achieve academically
Claim 3	Wants a story with scapegoats – the students, technology, school administration	Wants teachers to know that the school board is listening and doing something	Concerned about gaining the trust of teachers and developing a cohesive, collaborative school climate	Already mistrust school board – cynical and angry about board response and promises to do something	Concerned about their children's and their own reputations if publicized	Need avenues to express their feelings about the tensions within the school
Claim 4	Wants a story about disruption to a bright student's academic achievement	Has policies on bullying and cyber-bullying – due diligence	Want to ensure fairness in disciplining students, especially those graduating	Already mistrust administration – cynical and angry that they don't care	Concerned that teachers will mistreat their children if they stay	Need privacy unsupervised – away from adults = cyberspace. Made mistakes – 'just joking' – need another chance
Claim 5	Wants to focus on the most negative comments – the behaviour without looking at the motivations	Has created task force on cyber-bullying – due diligence	Want to retain trust of parents	Determined to get revenge and be vindicated – looking for 'blood' according to one administrator	Do not particularly want to uproot their children from school – especially if they are graduating	Not receiving enough attention from teachers – sense that teachers don't care because they are too busy fighting among themselves

a These claims relate to disgruntled teachers who have been strongly impacted by anti-authority cyber-bullying and who call for punishment of students rather than seek educational alternatives. The author acknowledges that many committed teachers might seek alternate, educational and proactive solutions.

keep parents happy. In cases where academically proficient students are caught cyber-bullying, school administrators are required to make tough choices about how to discipline them. Should they support teachers who want the students suspended or expelled? Should they listen to parents who insist their child remain in school and be allowed to graduate? In all the chaos, do administrators create opportunities or have the time to hear the students' side of things? How school administrators react can have an enormous influence on a negative or positive school climate. School administrators need to remember that, over and above the logistics of juggling stakeholder demands, they are the school heads or principals of institutions of *learning*. Their priorities ought to be the *students*. Students watch the reactions of their school administrators. Based on the legal standards identified in Chapter 7, it is arguable that cyber-bullying disrupts *learning*, and also disrupts the *educational mission* of the school. When classmates or teachers are the subjects of cyber-bullying, there is also a nexus to the school. Administrators should always be cognizant of the fact that one clearly established legal responsibility of educators is to ensure schools do not create a hostile or 'deliberately dangerous' school environment. The obligation resides in the responsibility to ensure the school climates (physical or virtual) are conducive to learning. It is at this point that the administrative claims lose legitimacy. Zero-tolerance suspensions convey a sense of intolerance; a lack of caring; a lack of responsibility. Removing the 'problem' child from the school appears to absolve schools of responsibility to do more. However, this action in and of itself creates a hostile and chilled school climate. This is especially true when students notice that very little action is taken to address peer-to-peer bullying or cyber-bullying. In this context then, it is reasonable to ask whether suspension is a justifiable claim on the part of school principals and head teachers.

I have always argued that the only educational value of suspensions is that they teach and model *intolerance*. Educators argue that students need consequences. There are many other ways in which students can experience the consequences of their actions, some of which I will address later in this chapter. The lack of creativity within school systems globally to find other alternatives never ceases to amaze me. I would argue that, if weighed on a scale against educational alternatives, school suspensions do not carry significant weight on the scale of legitimate claims

Teacher claims

When teachers who discover they have been defamed, demeaned and libelled in the highly public forum of cyberspace demand consequences, it is reasonable to agree that their claims are highly justified. Their claim for *revenge* in the form of suspensions and expulsions against students, however, is *not* justified and carries little weight. Such claims might be informed by dissatisfaction and disillusion with the school board and administrative support in the past, and a lack of confidence or trust in the way things are run at the school. Nonetheless, unless teachers refocus their attention on *why they are there*, unless they reconceptualize their role as educators, protectors, caregivers and student mentors, I would strongly argue that they are not justified in demanding harsh discipline. Suspensions are rooted in military models and boot camps. They are not grounded in educational pedagogies. Those responsible for the education and nurturing of future generations ought to remember this. Instead of demanding a ban on YouTube, or calling for 'forceful' action, educators could be searching for ways to address these issues by utilizing the infinite educational resources that technologies now provide. If teachers were able to overcome the mindsets that Lankshear and Knobel (2006) argue hold them back, the possibilities for creative collaboration with bored and cynical students are infinite. If teachers can engage with students and empower students to guide them in becoming familiar with new technologies, they have a greater chance of succeeding. The resolution I present in Chapter 6, drafted by the CTF begins to do this. The resolution is sufficiently comprehensive and seeks to learn more about how young people are using the technologies.

The predominant teacher responses, as evidenced in interviews with teachers (Shariff, 2007b) suggest that, when weighed on a scale against the types of online educational opportunity described above, teachers' demands instead for suspension or expulsion and their general lack of attention to peer-to-peer bullying among students carry little weight on the scale of legitimate claims. If we consider this from the perspective of UK common law and Canadian obligations under tort law, the duty of care on teachers to be 'careful and prudent parents' and stand in place of parents (*in loco parentis*) holds that there is an ethic of care and responsibility to exhibit concern, nurturance and guidance of students. If teachers only hold out for punishment and revenge, it would seem that their claims fall widely short of a legal duty of care to their students.

Table 8.1 shows how important it is to communicate. If the school board is really intent on hearing the teachers, school trustees need to demonstrate it in ways that go beyond simply having anti-bullying and anti-cyber-bullying policies in place. Moreover, the teachers need to allow new administrators time to catch up and make a difference. They need to foster opportunities to develop relationships of trust. As educators, their claims for vindication are less valid than student claims for a learning environment that is less poisoned and more conducive to learning. This requirement, as established by law, is detailed in Chapter 7, and, if teacher responsibilities are placed under the legal 'duty of care' and 'careful and prudent parent' doctrine, how many careful parents would not give their children a second chance once they had made a mistake? Yet again, claims made by students carry greater validity than the hostile responses by teachers. Moreover, according to the courts, the test for cyber-libel is whether *an ordinary person who is not unduly sensitive* would interpret the expression as truth. The reality is that some teachers may be unduly sensitive, and this sensitivity may also be reflected in the OCT's survey (2007), which suggests 84 per cent of teachers report being cyber-bullied. This is perhaps why the cases of comments that were made by students that were close to the truth received such strong reactions.

For example, in one case, the teacher had openly declared she was a lesbian, and yet she was extremely offended when the students described her online as a lesbian. Another teacher was chided for her accent. She was extremely annoyed by this but, in reality, she had a strong accent. Rather than seeking revenge through suspensions, teachers ought to focus on how they can explain the impact of the online statements to students. As educators, it is their responsibility to communicate and engage in dialogue with students about *why* those statements, no matter how close to home they might be, are hurtful. By dialogue, I mean *engaging their respect and trust*, listening to and *hearing* student perspectives. A teacher's first priority should be to determine whether it was the poisoned environment at the school that led to the online comments. If so, the next step would be to seek student input as to how the learning environment might be improved for them. Find out *what is missing*, what *teachers might be doing that upsets students*, and *how* they can change some of their teaching approaches. Are students receiving opportunities to provide opinions? Are these opinions being validated?

The participation rights of children and adolescents are protected under the United Nations *International Convention of the Rights of the Child* (1989). Canada and a range of European and Asian countries have signed a treaty that requires attention to *provision, protection* and *participation* of students in their learning. If this is not happening adequately, teachers should inform students that they have this right and work with them to develop ways to ensure their participation in classroom discussions, in developing codes of conduct and so on. The problem is that few teachers have any knowledge of human rights or their implications for educational policy and practice (Shariff and Sarkar, 2004). Once students come to realize that teachers are genuinely interested in their well-being and learning experiences, they will be significantly more open to hearing why their online expressions should not cross the line to cyber-libel or defamation. As the Media Awareness Network has shown (Media Awareness Network, no date) when children and teenagers take leadership in addressing peer behaviour, they can be very effective.

Moreover, if teachers were to pay more attention to peer-to-peer bullying and cyber-bullying and critically evaluate their own modelling of attitudes to kids, some of them might realize that they have not been listening to the kids – and that their students need avenues to discuss concerns that are bothering them.

I recall, for example, my own son who was frustrated with his maths teacher in grade 7. He was the only student in the class who was taking advanced Grade 8 maths and the teacher saw marking his assignments as a chore. This was a co-taught classroom with two teachers, in a middle school. As a result, one of the teachers was always late returning his marked assignments. She rarely paid him any attention in class, other than to ask him to teach students who had difficulty in maths. One day, after asking for his marked test back several times, he received a curt response from the teacher saying she had not marked his test. In frustration, he uttered the words 'f— you' under his breath. The other teacher heard him, and he was suspended. The school administration in this case handled the issue very well. Although he still had to serve his in-school suspension, after being made aware of the issue, they invited him to meet with a visiting delegation of government officials from the ministry of education, as an ambassador or leader in the school to show them around, answer questions and ask them about certain policy changes they were planning to make. This showed that the school had confidence in his ability and provided him with an opportunity to take leadership. While I do not suggest that he should not have received any consequences for uttering the 'F' word clearly against his teacher, I wonder what would have happened if the Internet had been available and he had had a chance to unleash his frustrations with more words about her.

Moreover, if I had not taken the time as a parent to find out what this unusual behaviour on his part was all about, would he have received the leadership opportunity the school gave him? I wonder how many students do fall through the cracks when they are bored, disengaged or frustrated with teachers in schools and cannot turn to parents. Accordingly, I suggest that, when young people engage in this kind of expression online, it is definitely worth hearing their point of view *before* deciding on the consequences. Of course, there is the teacher's perspective that she had a heavy workload and this was extra work – but when we weigh and validate each claim we can argue that *students are at school to learn* and, when the teacher is not doing an adequate job of teaching, then her claim is less valid than that of the student who is doing his best to learn.

In the same example, if we consider how the school administrators turned a negative into a positive learning opportunity, while also preserving the school reputation with the ministry officials, they fostered, at least at the school level, a proactive environment. It might be argued that there are other children who do not use this kind of language. We all believe our children are not capable of using this kind of language occasionally, but we know in the back of our minds that they all use it, as do most adults under frustrating circumstances. What my son learned that day was that he has support at home and at the school, and that when he is bored or having difficulty with the teacher, he can always turn to someone instead of stewing about it himself. He also learned that using the 'F' word has consequences, but that the conse-quences he received were very fair and thoughtful.

Parental claims

In most of the cyber-bullying cases discussed earlier and studied elsewhere (Shariff, 2004; 2005; Shariff and Johnny, 2007b), parents reported two general responses from schools:

1   if their child was a victim, then the schools put up a wall of defence, assuming parents were overprotective; or

2   if their child was found to be a perpetrator of peer-to-peer or teacher cyberbullying, then often they found the punishment too harsh.

Parents cannot be blamed for being anxious about the academic and social implications for their children's progress when they receive suspensions or school transfers. Their primary concerns of safety, protection and participation, as well as free expression rights of their children, are legitimate. These concerns attain a high rating along the spectrum of stakeholder claims, because all of them are constitutionally protected. Alternatively, parents should not be absolved of their responsibility to engage with children and instil in them values of respect, inclusive and non-discriminatory or demeaning discourse, and the reasonable limits on their expression. This is especially true for parents of students who make sexually libellous comments about teachers or peers. There is an incumbent responsibility on parents to ensure they collaborate with the school administration and teachers to help their children appreciate how far they have crossed the line towards becoming criminally and legally liable for their words and actions. Hence, parental claims that place the entire responsibility of educating children on schools carry minimal weight.

Media priorities

Media reporters should be repeatedly reminded that the framing of their stories has substantial impact on creating and sustaining an unhealthy level of fear among teachers, parents and school administrators. The media should be made to realize that the framing of their stories (especially their carefully contrived headlines) contributes to an unconscious fear and a poisoned environment in some schools. School boards and administrators ought to communicate with media reporters in their area and ensure that they also publish positive reports about the student energy, commitment, loyalties, volunteer activities and community service at their schools. There are many young people who participate in important community work – fundraising, organizing concerts and sports events, working with the elderly and those with special needs, and we rarely see large newspaper headlines announcing these achievements. Schools and media might work collaboratively on joint projects involving students, the media, the Internet and communications. This would empower and engage students in making important contributions to knowledge construction in society – in positive and 'constructive' ways. These solutions would go much further in shifting the way that the media present young people in contemporary society. It is time to focus the public attention on all those young people who are intelligent, ethical, resourceful and creative.

I walked through some of the considerations that are useful in applying the stakeholder model and took readers through the process of weighing and juxtaposing competing stakeholder claims to assess their respective validity. This non-arbitrary process has no room for reactive responses or band-aid solutions. Although I appreciate that, at times when all stakeholders are making demands at the same time, a reactive response appears to be the only choice, I would urge educational policymakers to remember the cartoon on dealing with the horns of the dilemma. The process is worth undertaking to hear and capture the important claims (in musical terms, the notes and their tone), and to bring these voices together collaboratively and cohesively to create harmony. Although arguably, this sounds far too Utopian, I am not describing a panacea. Judges adjudicate complex cases using this process all the time. Although I agree that the outcomes of some judicial decisions are not always satisfactory, I proffer that at least the stakeholder model allows for a thoughtful and ethical assessment of the issues, bearing in mind the legal standards and responsibilities identified in Chapter 7 and the educational and ethical considerations that impact all stakeholders. There is one final step in the stakeholder model.

Step 4: Minimal impairment of rights

Once stakeholder claims have been weighed against each other, it is important for the decision-makers involved to ensure that whatever policy decision is most validated, that decision or policy does *not substantially infringe* on the rights of certain stakeholders. For example, if the school decides to stay with a zero-tolerance policy and suspend only the students who make sexually libellous comments about teachers, this policy is justifiable. Why? Because it protects the interests of the larger number of teachers. However, the policy-makers must then ensure that they consider whether any of the offending students are graduating shortly; the extent to which the suspensions will affect their grades and chances of acceptance at college or university, and so on. In cases where a straight-A student receives a suspension of this sort, it may be worthwhile to consider an alternative consequence that does not have an impact on the student's entire academic future. Although the defamatory expression can certainly impact a teacher's reputation, it is important to remember that we are still dealing with an immature young person who needs to be educated as to why he or she should not behave this way. Young people deserve a second chance. Let me clarify this in more legal terms

In the case of students' online expression that demeans teachers and school officials on Facebook, most school responses have been to suspend the students involved. Some of these students, like Brad Parsons, have protested infringement of their rights to free expression. Many parents agree. They believe that their school has no right to interfere with comments made from home computers in a private, online conversation. The school might have a policy calling for zero-tolerance suspension. This might be supported by government legislation. Nonetheless, school officials have important decisions to make.

They must consider whether the student comments were so harmful that they negatively impacted the entire *school environment and learning of all students* at the school or in the classroom. As the freedom of expression cases have ruled, schools do have the authority to intervene if the expression *materially or substantially* impacts learning, or if it interferes with the school's educational mission. In the case of sexually charged comments about teachers being paedophiles or masturbating in class, I would argue that such comments pose a risk to the greater good in several ways. They undermine the authority of the teachers or school officials in question. When students read the comments, they are likely to gossip and giggle in class. This disrupts their focus and learning and upsets the teacher. When the teacher finds out, his or her anger also has a significant impact that poisons the entire school environment.

Although I agree that schools have a responsibility to ensure that blatantly insulting or abusive postings are removed, and that students are aware of the consequences for such postings, I do not agree with the *means* that schools and some governments adopt, such as suspension policies, banning of technologies from the classroom, withdrawing computer privileges or, as they have in some cases, suspending students from school field trips they were eagerly looking forward to. Students should be engaged in developing codes of conduct and policies. Consequences should include an educational component, such as making offenders aware of their impact on the lives, confidence and self-esteem of their victims, whether they are peers, teachers or administrators. Zero tolerance does not teach students to take responsibility or be accountable for their actions. Instead, it attempts to muzzle them. This in my view does not *minimally impair* student free expression rights. It attempts to muzzle them completely. This is why the minimal impairment test is a crucial fourth step in the stakeholder model. It is incumbent on school officials to determine educational options to help students realize the impact of their statements. I would argue for introduction of the circle sentencing approaches, for example, that are used by many aboriginal communities. Using that method, perpetrator(s) are brought to face their victims and hear their reactions and pain. Not only that, instigators must hear how their actions negatively affected the lives of victims' families and loved ones. In the case of anti-authority online defamation, they should hear from the teachers, their families and other students who want to learn but find it distracting when these controversies take place. Similarly when peer-to-peer cyber-bullying is involved, the perpetrators should be made to face the victims' parents, their siblings and anyone else who is impacted.

Conclusion

While I have argued in the previous chapter that schools have a legal basis for extending their reach into cyberspace, I reiterate that censoring student web sites or searching emails, for example, is *not* the most effective means of preventing cyber-bullying. On the contrary, I recognize that school discipline policies are least successful when they merely serve as a reactionary mechanism to unwanted behaviour. Although I believe that schools have an obligation to monitor inflammatory student speech, it is equally important to recognize that educators have a duty to cultivate an educational atmosphere that is consistent with the moral and political principles essential to expanding democratic values. In other words, when cyber-bullying becomes pervasive within a school, we cannot simply place the blame on students. Instead, we must look at the values and beliefs that our schools and constitutional principles impart and select educational measures to ensure that these values promote acceptance, respect and decency among students.

As noted by scholars such as Giroux (2003), school discipline is best achieved when it incorporates an element that aims to educate students about both moral and political principles. Giroux argues that:

> schools should provide forms of critical education in which ethics and values are used to teach students to keep the spirit of justice alive in them- selves, embrace the need to be compassionate, respect the rights of others, and be self-conscious about the consequences of their actions.
>
> (Ibid., p. 94)

I have also observed that adults need to become proficient and participate with young people in learning how to use the technologies that form such an important and prominent part of their lives. If adults do not take the initiative to do this, they will eventually be shut out – or, it could be argued, censored, from the virtual worlds of their children and students. As I have already mentioned, students are increasingly forging social relationships and learning much of what they know through new technologies. It is incumbent on educators to engage with these technologies to develop interactive curriculum programmes that are not restricted to class time. As I explained earlier, the potential for learning in the digital age is enormous. Consider, for example, some of the pedagogical suggestions recommended by Lankshear and Knobel (2006). They comment that the 'digit' or 'skill teaching' aspect of digital literacies is far less important than allowing room for social relationships to 'emerge organically' (p. 20) through immersion in new technologies. They recommend the kinds of knowledge producing school that are being developed on a school-by-school basis by Chris Bigum, Leonie Rowen and Associates (Knowledge Producing Schools web site, 2005; Lankshear and Knobel, 2003). They also recommend James Gee's celebrated study, *What video games have to teach us about learning and literacy* (2003), in which Gee explores game playing as a sociocultural practice (where he tests what drives people to learn and keep learning, and how they achieve and grow in their learning).

In this book, I have attempted to provide an adjusted lens through which we ought to view the highly publicized issue of cyber-bullying. I introduced the following metaphor in Chapter 1 and believe it is in order to recall it now: An artist has to take time away from his painting when the colours he is using become so blurred that he can no longer see them clearly. He takes time out to visit an optometrist. During his eye exam, the focus is no longer on *what* he sees, but *how* he sees. It is the adjustment to the lens through which he sees and interprets his surroundings that is the focus during that short visit to the optometrist (Esmail, 2007). Similarly, this book was written to help educators and policymakers to stop briefly and consider readjusting the lenses that seem to have blurred their policy and practice alternatives to such an extent, that they need to refocus and reconceptualize the issues. Instead of seeing cyber-bullying as a problem and a battle that needs to be controlled and squelched, an adjusted lens will refocus our attention on what these symptoms are telling us, and how we can address the root causes that drive such expression.

I hope I have succeeded in my quest to inform educators about the importance of addressing the rights and interests of an increasingly broad range of stakeholders. I have explained that, when issues that are important to some members of the school community are simply ignored, forms of bullying and cyber-bullying, censorship controversies and court challenges are most likely to rear their noisy heads. As school landscapes evolve to keep up with changes in technology and society, it is important to consider the simple alternatives provided in this book, ones that are less costly than the calls for 'battle', loss of children's lives through suicide, and positivist rules that attempt to force conformity. Although I have provided a number of models and a concept map, which I believe show greater promise of addressing the policy vacuum and the enormous challenges that technologies bring, I reiterate that this book is not a 'how to' text. Rather, I hope it has provided readers with an adjusted lens that discloses rich context for discussion and dialogue about the definitional complexities and the biological, environmental and systemic influences that shape and perpetuate the content of student expression in cyberspace. Furthermore, I hope it motivates readers to engage in a responsible process of analysis that avoids reliance on reactive decisions, which lead to the kinds of 'battle' that the media are always eager to write about.

Ultimately, the approach I advocate suggests greater promise of addressing the 'horns of the technology dilemma' that challenge educators in contemporary schools, than do reactive and insidious forms of selection and censorship that sustain orthodoxy, manage student expression and promote a culture of conformity. In keeping with Hamed Nastoh's plea to *educate* rather than punish young people who push the boundaries of social discourse and cyberspace, I hope this book has convinced readers that cyber-bullying, as currently defined, is not a battle, but a plea for improved and increased attention to education, dialogue, bonding and engagement with our young people. In that regard, it is an *opportunity* with infinite potential to address ignorance, overcome orthodoxy and undertake the challenges of our shared knowledge society, through ethical, educational, digital-bonding and legally defensible policies and practices. Our children and society, as a whole, deserve no less.

Notes

1 Cyberspace: battleground or opportunity?

1 Most of the studies I report on traditional bullying in Chapter 2 are drawn from my doctoral dissertation on research from 1999 to 2001. Although they are not as current as studies on cyber-bullying, they are important for a comprehensive understanding of bullying overall.

2 Profile of traditional and cyber-bullying

1 Suicide note, published with the kind permission of Nasimah Nastoh, Hamed's mother.
2 Eight to 9 per cent of elementary school children are bullied frequently (once or more a week) and 2 to 5 per cent of students bully others frequently (Bentley and Li, 1995). Surveys cited by the National Crime Prevention Council (NCPC) disclose similar results (Boulton and Underwood, 1992). Roher (1997) reports that, out of 457 students surveyed, 20 per cent reported more than one incident; 8 per cent of the students questioned are bullied weekly or more often. In a recent US survey of over 15,000 young people in grades 6 to 10, Nansel *et al.* (2001) found that 9 per cent of students reported being bullied frequently, and over 8 per cent of students admitted to frequent bullying. In a recent study of junior secondary school students, Henderson *et al.* (2002) found, out of 490 students from grades 8–10 (50 per cent female, 50 per cent male) 64 per cent of the respondents indicated they had been bullied, 12 per cent reported being victimized regularly (once or more a week), and another 13 per cent admitted to participating in bullying regularly (once or more a week). The majority of respondents reported observing bullying at the school, but only 40 per cent said they tried to intervene. See also DiGiulio (2001).
3 A bully was described as 'a tyrannical coward who makes himself a terror to the weak', '[A] low-minded unscrupulous bully, notorious for his pro-Slavery sympathies', or a '[R]uffian hired for purposes of violence or intimidation' (Dicey, 1863, p. 646).
4 Mooney *et al.* (1991) found that 96 per cent of the 308 seven- to eleven-year-olds reported teasing as the most frequent form of bullying they experienced. See also Boulton and Hawker (1997). Seventy-four per cent of girls spend time on chat rooms and instant messaging (Berson *et al.*, 2002); 14 per cent of Canadian youths are harassed electronically, and 15 per cent admitted harassing others electronically (Leishman, 2002).
5 Olweus (1993) first highlighted the difference between direct (open, physical attacks) and indirect (social isolation and exclusion of victims) bullying. Björqvist *et al.* (1992) went further to distinguish between physical aggression (hitting, pushing, kicking),

direct verbal aggression (name calling, threatening), and indirect aggression (e.g. telling tales, spreading rumours, deliberately excluding a person from activities).

6 Artz and Riecken (1997), Lanctot (2001) and Moretti (2002) reported violent acts as prevalent in males, but on the rise in females. Schissel's (1993) analysis of trends in official Canadian youth crime rates disclosed a steady increase in the number of violent offences committed by females from 1970–90. Tanner (1996) cites a 21 per cent increase in the number of female youths charged between 1986 and 1990, cautioning, however, that this still only represented 18 per cent of all youths charged during this time. Moretti (2002) reports that the gender gap, in terms of the seriousness and physical nature of bullying and violence between boys and girls, is narrowing.

7 This discrepancy in the research is now recognized by scholars in the field, resulting in a conference that specifically focused on girls and violence. The conference objective was to gain a more accurate profile of girls and violence through a joint review of research by psychologists, sociologists and criminologists who specifically study this perspective (Vancouver Conference on Aggressive and Violent Girls, 2002).

8 See also Katch (2001), Chamberlain and Houston (1999) and Henderson and Hymel (2002).

9 Although the research on prevalence of bullying is reported under a separate heading in this chapter, these statistics are important here because they relate to sexual harassment as a primary form of bullying in schools. See also Louis Harris and Associates (1993); Chamberlain and Houston (1999); Tolman et al. (2001). Watkinson (1999) and Bowlby and Regan (1998) provide Canadian statistics that corroborate American findings.

10 O'Connell and colleagues (1999) videotaped 185 bullying episodes by students in grades 1–6, and observed that just over half (54 per cent) contained a bully, a victim and two or more peers. An average of four students was present during the episodes. Significantly, they found that the duration of the bullying increased as the number of peers watching the episode increased. In 54 per cent of the cases, peers simply observed the episode. In nearly 21 per cent of the cases, peers physically or verbally joined in the bullying.

11 Hamed Nastoh, Dawn-Marie Wesley, Emmett Fralick suicides; murder of Reena Virk; shootings at Columbine and Mayo, Alberta.

12 The Dufour litigation was abandoned by the parents after filing a Statement of Claim in the Vancouver Supreme Court Registry.

13 Seventy-five per cent of Americans interviewed thought school shootings were likely to happen in their community.

14 These authors also agree that most young people who engage in crime are not dangerous. They engage in petty thefts, break and enter or play truant from school.

15 Providing American statistics, he notes that, in 1992 and 1993, a total of seventy-six students were murdered or committed suicide at school – an average of about thirty-eight a year. Six years later, a total of sixty-nine students suffered school-associated, violent deaths (murder and suicide) in a two-year period. The number also decreased 40 per cent from 1998 to 1999, from forty-three to twenty-six. DiGiulio argues that, when compared with the rate of youth murders occurring outside the school context, in 1992–1993 young persons between the ages of five and nineteen were over 100 times more likely to be murdered away from school than in school according to a report from the Office of Juvenile Justice and Delinquency Prevention.

16 This is a result of the baby-boomers having children.

17 Doob et al. (1995) observe, for example, that, whereas previously schoolyard fights were simply reported to school administrators, they are now more frequently reported to police.

3 A transnational snapshot

1 Article 2: A person who disturbs public order, endangers public safety, infringes on the rights of person and property or hampers social administration, which is harmful to the society and which, according to the provisions of the Criminal Law of the People's Republic of China, constitutes a crime, shall be investigated for criminal responsibility according to law; and if such an act is not serious enough for criminal punishment, the public security organ shall impose on him a penalty for administration of public security according to this Law.

2 Article 42: A person who commits one of the following acts shall be detained for not more than 5 days or be fined not more than 500 Yuan; and if the circumstances are relatively serious, he shall be detained for not less than 5 days but not more than 10 days and may, in addition, be fined not more than 500 Yuan:

  1 writing letters of intimidation or threatening the personal safety of another person by other means;
  2 openly humiliating another person or slandering another person by fabricating stories;
  3 framing-up another person by fabricating stories in an attempt to make the person subject to criminal investigation or to penalty for administration of public security;
  4 threatening, humiliating or beating up a witness or his close relative or retaliating against either of them;
  5 repeatedly dispatching pornographic, humiliating, intimidating or other information to disturb the normal life of another person; or
  6 peeping, secretly taking photos, eavesdropping, or spreading the privacy of another person.

3 Article 246: Those openly insulting others or using force or other methods or those fabricating stories to slander others, if the case is serious, are to be sentenced to three years or fewer in prison, put under criminal detention or surveillance, or deprived of their political rights.

4 The role of gender: biological and environmental influences

1 Salkind (1990, p. 361) defines personality as 'the pattern of behaviours and thought that characterizes individuals, distinguishes them from others and remains relatively stable throughout their lives'. A longitudinal study supports these findings (DiGiulio, 2001). Researchers discovered that half of the children with behaviour problems in the fourth grade (including fighting, stealing or lying) were arrested by age fourteen. Of those, 75 per cent were repeatedly arrested at least three times by the time they were eighteen years of age.

2 He found that 35 to 40 per cent of children who were described as being bullies in grades 6 to 9 were convicted of at least three officially registered crimes by age twenty-four. Only 10 per cent who were not described as bullies ended up with convictions later in life.

3 Hall (1999) cites research that provided some evidence to suggest human aggression is biologically determined (Thiessen, 1976). Smith (1995) summarized a large body of literature examining genetic influences and concluded they have little impact and that most aggression is shaped by environmental factors.

4 Cesare Lombroso in the latter part of the nineteenth century was known for measuring the skulls and ears of notorious male criminals but failed to establish a clear link. William Sheldon, an American criminologist known as the father of somatotyping,

was more successful in linking aggression to physique and temperament. There have also been numerous studies on the linkage between violence and the presence of the extra Y chromosome in men, but these again are not conclusive. Studies of identical twins provide more concrete evidence that genetics is a potent predictor of aggression.

5 Hall (1999) cites a number of studies on the impact of hormones on aggression, including Berkowitz (1993), Mazur (1983), Thiessen (1976) and Renfrew (1997), all of which find a link between hormones and environmental influences that result in aggressive behaviour. Renfrew reports evidence that suggests a mediating connection between the male hormone testosterone and aggressive behaviour.

6 Lanctot (2001) reports a correlation of the increase in aggressive tendencies in girls with the onset of early puberty, particularly as this plays out in their interactions with older boys. Moretti (2002) reports increased conduct disorder in girls around the age of sixteen.

7 Reena Virk, Jamie Dufour and Dawn Marie Wesley studies (Artz, 1998b).

8 Prinsloo and DuPlessi (1998, p. 11) described this as 'awakening a positive attitude to fellow human beings and awakening a sense of . . . social conscience' (as cited in DiGiulio, 2001). South African studies have found that, for girls especially, the family is a formidable shaper of self-concept (Marjoribanks and Mboya, 1998).

9 Cited in Hall (1999), Glueck and Glueck's (1962) well-known study on the relationship between family environment and criminal or violent tendencies identifies a range of socio-cultural influences that include hostile treatment and erratic punishment. Numerous others have found a correlation between child abuse, poor parenting, neglect and aggression in children. James (1995) identifies three familial characteristics that consistently distinguish the development of violent tendencies in young people, especially those from low socio-economic groups:

  1 severe and erratic punishment bordering on abuse;
  2 marital discord, including frequent observing of spousal abuse; and
  3 a high level of parental irritability.

James suggests a causal relationship between a hostile caregiver and aggression in children in later life.

10 This was true in the case of Reena Virk, Jamie Dufour, Dawn-Marie Wesley and studies of girls who engaged in extreme violence by 1997.

5 Controlling kids' spaces

1 The NCH (2005) survey found that nearly 30 per cent of cyber-bullied students told no-one. Seventy per cent of the children in grades 6–8 surveyed under my own research in Quebec (Shariff, SSHRC project, 2007b), said they did not believe it was the school's responsibility to intervene in bullying outside of the physical school property.

2 Although most of these case examples are taken from media reports that frame stories in a certain way, what is indisputable in all of them is the way in which young people perceive and use their online space. I deconstruct some of these cases later on, to analyse ways in which the media put a certain twist in our understanding of these cases. In the meantime, the facts regarding the positions generally adopted by various stakeholders – students, parents, politicians and educators – are consistent across news reports.

3 The end of the article says he was expelled, whereas he was in fact only suspended by school authorities.

4 Happy slapping is explained in Chapter 2.

5 For more information, contact P.Tsatsou@lse.ac.uk.

6 Available at www.legifrance.gouv.fr/WAspad/UnTexteDeJorf?numjo=INTX0600091L.

7 While this book was in press, OFSTED launched a report on bullying/cyber-bullying on 14 February 2008, at www.ofsted.gov.uk.

8 Mitchell *et al.* (2003); O'Connell *et al.* (2002); Wolak *et al.* (2006).

9 Girodo *et al.* (2002); Mitchell *et al.* (2005); Mota (2002); Volokh (1997).

10 Cao and Maume (1993); Cohen and Cantor (1980); Collins *et al.* (1987); Cook (1987); Gaetz (2004); Garofalo *et al.* (1987); Lasley (1989); Lynch (1987); Madriz (1996); Moriarty and Williams (1996); Mustaine and Tewksbury (1997, 2000); Roncek and Bell (1981); Roncek and Maier (1991); Sampson and Wooldredge (1987); Spano and Nagy (2005); Tseloni *et al.* (2004); Woolredge *et al.* (1992).

11 Available at www.okhouse.gov/Committees/CommitteeReports/7017.doc.

12 Available at www.ilga.gov/legislation/billstatus.asp?DocNum=1682andGAID=9and GA=95andDocTypeID=SBandLegID=29749andSessionID=51.

13 Popular web sites fitting this definition include MySpace (www.myspace.com/), Friendster (www.friendster.com/) and LiveJournal (/www.livejournal.com/). This definition, however, could potentially cover a much broader range of web sites. Many news web sites such as Slashdot (http://slashdot.org/) and blogs such as RedState (www.redstate.com/) permit both public profiles and personal journals. Amazon.com (www.amazon.com/) allows personal profiles including photos, interests and contact information. In addition, many media companies such as News.com (http://news.com. com/) and publisher CNET Networks (www.cnetnetworks.com/) permit users to create profiles displaying photos and other personal information, as well as sending email to other members. Some popular chat services include ICQ (www.icq.com/), AOL Instant Messenger (www.aol.com/) and Yahoo! Chat (http://messenger.yahoo.com/chat.php).

6 Stakeholder power

1 I wish to acknowledge and thank Myles Ellis, Director, Economic and Member Service, of the Canadian Teachers' Federation for permission to publish this resolution.

2 The complainants include the Dufour family, who commenced civil litigation on behalf of their daughter Jamie Dufour but abandoned the case; Azmi Jubran's human rights case; the decision was appealed twice, with the final British Columbia Court of Appeal ruling in favour of Azmi Jubran. Jane Forin who joins Leanne Dufour and Nasimah Nastoh in raising awareness of the issues; twelve parents in Teulon, Manitoba, who made their children's experiences with the school public through the CBC National News; and Emmett Fralick's parents (Emmett also committed suicide). Similar sentiments have been verbally raised by many concerned parents at public forums on bullying which I attended, including a parent workshop held during the annual conference of the British Columbia Parent Advisory Council on 3 May 2002.

3 Personal communications received by parents Jane Forin, Nasim Nastoh, Jamie Dufour's mother and Nancy Knight are among those that confirm a 'wall of defence' – a term coined by Jane Forin of Courtney, British Columbia, Canada. The pattern of denial is also evident in court documents filed in several actions against schools for failing to protect victims of bullying.

4 All information provided here with respect to the named cases of bullying (whether taken from publicly available court documents or cited with parental permission) is based on public information – either from the media or from the victims and/or their families. No information has been used here without their permission. Neither the author nor publisher accepts liability for information that might have been inaccurately reported by the media or for any false accusations contained in filed court documents.

5 Andrew Forin, who was not involved in bullying but filmed a bullying incident and was manipulated into selling it to the media, was suspended for making the school look bad. Azmi Jubran put up with three years of bullying before punching a

perpetrator in the stomach. He was suspended; his perpetrators were not disciplined. In one case, an Ontario boy was jailed for four months without bail for writing a story entitled Twisted about retaliating against his perpetrators.

6 For example, in the wake of well-publicized cases of bullying in the last six years, blanket zero-tolerance policies have been widely adopted in schools as seemingly sensible and efficient ways to curb bullying. In Chapter 7, I will explain why these policies are not as sensible or effective as they appear.

7 The sources of these personal communications with school administrators cannot be disclosed because of ongoing consultation to resolve some of the heated and sensitive issues currently underway at the school.

7   Balancing free expression: privacy and safety in cyberspace

1 Ghislain Reza, the 'Star Wars kid', David Knight – under settlement negotiation; Jamie Dufour – court case abandoned.

2 See also Takach (1999).

3 In this case, Pat Holly, a member of the First Nations, sent thirty emails accusing the plaintiff of grave robbing and committing crimes against his people during the course of her archaeology digs.

4 Article 2: A person who disturbs public order, endangers public safety, infringes on the rights of person and property or hampers social administrations, which is harmful to the society and which, according to the provisions of the Criminal Law of the People's Republic of China, constitutes a crime, shall be investigated for criminal responsibility according to law; and if such an act is not serious enough for criminal punishment, the public security organ shall impose on him a penalty for administration of public security according to this Law.

5 Article 42: A person who commits one of the following acts shall be detained for not more than 5 days or be fined not more than 500 Yuan; and if the circumstances are relatively serious, he shall be detained for not less than 5 days but not more than 10 days and may, in addition, be fined not more than 500 Yuan:

   1 writing letters of intimidation or threatening the personal safety of another person by any other means;
   2 openly humiliating another person or slandering another person by fabricating stories
   3 framing-up another person by fabricating stories in an attempt to make the person subject to criminal investigation or penalty for administration of public security;
   4 threatening, humiliating or beating up a witness or his close relative or retaliating against either of them;
   5 repeatedly dispatching pornographic, humiliating, intimidating or other information to disturb the normal life of another person; or
   6 peeping, secretly taking photos, eavesdropping, or spreading the privacy of another person.

6 See also Stonebanks (in press) on the impact of residential schools on Canadian aboriginal peoples.

8   Harmonious solutions

1 I have presented some of this research in Chapter 6 and also at conferences at the University of Oxford in the United Kingdom, at the University of Grenada in Spain, and at the American Education Research Association Conferences in San Francisco (2006) and Chicago (2007).

References

Adam, A. (2001). Cyberstalking: Gender and computer ethics. In E. Green and A. Adam (eds), *Virtual gender: Technology, consumption and identity*. New York: Routledge, pp. 209–24.

Adam, A. (2002). Cyberstalking and internet pornography: Gender and the gaze. *Ethics and Information Technology*, 4: 133–42.

Advertiser, The (2003). Girls lured via Internet. 27 September [electronic version]: 42.

Agence France Presse (2007). Foreign students don't fear backlash. *The Gazette*: A4.

Akiba, M. (2004). Nature and correlates of ijime – Bullying in Japanese middle school. *International Journal of Educational Research*, 41(3): 216–36.

American Library Association (2006). Challenged or banned books [electronic version]. Retrieved 1 December 2006 from www.ala.org/ala/oif/bannedbooksweek/challenged banned/challengedbanned.htm.

Anand, S. S. (1999). Preventing youth crime: What works, what doesn't and what it all means for Canadian juvenile justice. *Queen's Law Journal*, 25(1): 177–249.

Apple, M. W. (1990). *Ideology and curriculum*, 2nd edn. New York: Routledge.

Apple, M. W. (2000). *Official knowledge: Democratic education in a conservative age*, 2nd edn. New York: Routledge.

Apple, M. W. and Christian-Smith, L. K. (1991). The politics of the textbook. In M. W. Apple and L. K. Christian-Smith (eds), *The politics of the textbook*. New York: Routledge, pp. 1–21.

Arons, S. (1986). *Compelling belief*. Amherst, MA: University of Massachusetts Press.

Artz, S. (1998a). *Sex, power and the violent school girl*. Toronto, ON: Trifolium Books.

Artz, S. (1998b). Where have all the school girls gone? Violent girls in the school yard. *Child and Youth Care Forum*, 27(2).

Artz, S. and Riecken, T. (1997). What, so what, then what? The gender gap in school-based violence and its implications for child and youth care practice. *Child and Youth Care Forum*, 26(4): 291–303.

Ashford, M. W. (1996). *Boredom as a neglected issue in violence prevention programs in schools*. Vancouver: Simon Fraser University.

Askew, S. (1989). Aggressive behaviour in boys: To what extent is it institutionalized? In D. Tattum and D. Lane (eds), *Bullying in schools*. Stoke-on-Trent: Trentham.

Associated Press (2004). Japanese girl fatally stabs a classmate. *The New York Times*, 2 June: 12.

Associated Press (2006). Indiana students outraged over schools' blog crackdowns [electronic version]. *foxnews.com*, 2 October. Retrieved 5 October 2006 from www.foxnews.com/story/0,2933,217121,00.html.

Asthana, A. (2006). Discipline to go beyond school gate [electronic version]. *Guardian Unlimited*, 5 February. Retrieved 22 July 2007 from http://education.guardian.co.uk/pupilbehaviour/story/0,,1703314,00.html.

Asthana, A. (2007). School war against the bullies brings academic success [electronic version]. *Guardian Unlimited*, 3 June. Retrieved 13 August 2007 from http://education.guardian.co.uk/pupilbehaviour/story/0,,2094886,00.html

Asthana, A. and Smith, D. (2007). Teachers call for YouTube ban over 'cyber-bullying' [electronic version]. *Guardian Unlimited*, 29 July. Retrieved 22 August 2007 from http://observer.guardian.co.uk/uk_news/story/0,,2137177,00.html.

Australian Bureau of Statistics (2005). Household use of information technology, Australia, 2004–5 [electronic version]. *Australian Bureau of Statistics*. Retrieved 15 August 2007 from www.ausstats.abs.gov.au/Ausstats/subscriber.nsf/0/CA78A4186873588CCA2570 D8001B8C56/$File/81460_2004-05.pdf.

Bakan, J. (1999). Beyond censorship: An essay on free speech and law. In K. Petersen and A. C. Hutchinson (eds), *Interpreting censorship in Canada*. Toronto, ON: University of Toronto Press, pp. 80–100.

Balfour, C. (2005). *A journey of social change: Turning government digital strategy into cybersafe local school practices*. Paper presented at 'Safety and security in a networked world: Balancing cyber-rights and responsibilities', Oxford Internet Institute, University of Oxford. Retrieved 10 August 2007 from www.oii.ox.ac.uk/microsites/cybersafety/?view=papers.

Barak, A. (2005). Sexual harrasment on the Internet. *Social Science Computer Review*, 23(1): 77–92.

Bartlett, L. (2007). Cyber bully concern grows [electronic version]. *cooltech iafrica.com*, 29 March. Retrieved 29 March 2007 from http://cooltech.iafrica.com/features/729468.htm.

BBC (2005). Mother rages at 'slap attackers' [electronic version, 19 May 2005]. *BBC News Online*. Retrieved 14 August 2007 from http://news.bbc.co.uk/2/hi/uk_news/england/manchester/4563419.stm.

Beckerman, L. and Nocero, J. (2002). You've got hate mail. *Principal Leadership (High School Ed.)*, 3(4): 38–41.

Becta. (2007). What is an acceptable use policy? Web page. Retrieved 23 August 2007 from http://schools.becta.org.uk/index.php?section=is&catcode=ss_to_es_pp_aup_03&rid=11087.

Belew, B. (2007). Cyberbullying in China – Students record video while physically belittling teacher [electronic version]. *The biz of knowledge*. Retrieved 12 August 2007 from www.thebizofknowledge.com/2007/05/cyberbullying_in_china_student.html #more.

Belsey, B. (2005). Internet usage: Facts and news. Web page. Retrieved 8 July 2005 from www.cyberbullying.ca/facts_st.html.

Bentley, K. M. and Li, A. K. F. (1995). Bully and victim problems in elementary schools and students' beliefs about aggression. *Canadian Journal of School Psychology*, 11: 153–65.

Berkowitz, L. (1993). *Aggression: Its causes, consequences, and control*. Philadelphia, PA: Temple University Press.

Bernstein, A. and Hanna, B. W. (2005). *Cyberlibel: Defamation proofing your online world*. Paper presented at the the Ninth Annual Canadian IT Law Association Conference, Montreal, Quebec, Canada.

Berson, I. R., Berson, M. J. and Ferron, J. M. (2002). Emerging risks of violence in the digital age: Lessons for educators from an online study of adolescent girls in the United States. *Journal of School Violence*, 1(2): 51–71.

Besag, V. E. (1989). *Bullies and victims in schools: A guide to understanding and management.* Milton Keynes: Open University Press.

Bettelheim, B. (1989). *The uses of enchantment: The meaning and importance of fairy tales.* New York: Vintage Books.

Björqvist, K., Lagerspetz, K. M. J. and Kaukiainen, A. (1992). Do girls manipulate and boys fight? Development trends in regard to direct and indirect aggression. *Aggressive Behavior*, 18: 117–27.

Bohn, G. (2006). Curb 'cyberbullies' prof urges. *The Vancouver Sun*, 22 February: A9.

Book and Periodical Council (2004). Freedom to read week. Web page. Retrieved 26 August 2007 from www.freedomtoread.ca/freedom_to_read_week/index.asp.

Booth, D. W. (1992). *Censorship goes to school.* Markham, ON: Pembroke.

Boulton, M. (1993). A comparison of adults' and children's abilities to distinguish between aggressive and playful fighting in middle school pupils. Implications for playground supervision and behavior management. *Educational Studies*, 19(3): 193–203.

Boulton, M. and Hawker, D. (1997). Verbal bullying: The myth of 'sticks and stones'. In D. Tattum and G. Herbert (eds), *Bullying: Home, school and community.* London: David Fulton, pp. 53–63.

Boulton, M. and Underwood, K. (1992). Bully/victim problems among middle school children. *British Journal of Educational Psychology*, 62: 73–87.

Bowlby, B. L. and Regan, J. W. (1998). *An educator's guide to human rights.* Aurora, ON: Aurora Professional Press.

boyd, d. and Jenkins, H. (2006). MySpace and Deleting Online Predators Act (DOPA) [electronic version]. *MIT Tech Talk*, 26 May. Retrieved 13 August 2007 from www.danah.org/papers/MySpaceDOPA.html.

Boyd, N. (2000). *The beast within: Why men are violent.* Vancouver, BC: Greystone Books.

Brail, S. (1996). The price of admission: Harassment and free speech in the wild, wild west. In L. Cherny and E. R. Weise (eds), *Wired_women: Gender and new realities in cyberspace.* Toronto, ON: Seal Press.

Brantingham, P. and Brantingham, P. (1995). Criminality of place: Crime generators and crime attractors. *European Journal on Criminal Policy and Research*, 3: 5–26.

Brecher, E. J. (1994). Crossing 'confidence gap' poses high hurdle for girls [electronic version]. *The Miami Herald*, 30 September, 1F. Retrieved 19 August 2007.

Bringelson, C. (2005). On intellectual freedom [electronic version]. *Intellectual Freedom and Social Responsibility*, 24. Retrieved 22 November 2006 from www.scholibraries.ca/articles/154.aspx.

British Columbia Ministry of Education (1997). Policy circular number 97-04, pp. 9–10.

British Educational Communications and Technology Agency (2007). Becta Home Page, August. Web site. Retrieved 26 August 2007 from www.becta.org.uk/.

British Educational Communications and Technology Agency (no date, a). School improvement professionals event. Presentation. Awareness of ICT in schools for school improvement professionals. Retrieved 26 August 2007 from http://events.becta.org.uk/display.cfm?cfid=662527&cftoken=63d05f972705–4b7df789-c05d-eae1–98481165ea7bbc6b&resID=29602.

British Educational Communications and Technology Agency (no date, b). Teacher exchange resource. Web site. Retrieved 26 August 2007 from http://tre.ngfl.gov.uk/.

Brotherhood of the Lamb web site (no date). Retrieved 10 August 2006 from www.brotherhoodofthelamb.com.

Brown, L. (2007). Teachers declare war on cyber-bullying [electronic version]. *TheStar.com*, 13 July. Retrieved 13 August 2007 from www.thestar.com/article/235675.

Bukowksi, W. and Sippola, L. (2001). Groups, individuals, and victimization: A view of the peer system. In J. Juvonen and S. Graham (eds), *Peer harrassment in school: The plight of the vulnerable and victimized*. New York, London: Guilford Press.

Butler-Kisber, L. and Portelli, J. P. (2003). The challenge of student engagement: Beyond mainstream conceptions and practices. *McGill Journal of Education*, *38*(2): 207.

Campbell, M. (2005). Cyberbullying: An old problem in a new guise? *Australian Journal of Guidance and Counseling*, *15*(1): 68–76.

Canadian Charter of Rights and Freedoms (1982). Schedule B, Constitution Act, 1982, Canada Act, c. 11 (UK).

Canadian Press (2007). Ontario takes aim at bullying [electronic version]. *TheStar.com*, 16 April. Retrieved 16 April 2007 from www.thestar.com/News/article/203714.

Cao, L. and Maume, D. J. (1993). Urbanization, inequality, lifestyles and robbery: A comprehensive model. *Sociological Focus*, *26*(1): 11–26.

Case, R. (1997). *Understanding judicial reasoning: controversies, concepts and cases*. Toronto, ON: Thompson Educational Publishing.

CBC News (2006). Regina bylaw to target cyber-bullies [electronic version]. *cbc.ca*, 25 April. Retrieved 13 August 2007 from www.cbc.ca/canada/saskatchewan/story/2006/04/25/bullying-regina060425.html.

Chamberlain, E. and Houston, B. (1999). School sexual harassment policies: The need for both justice and care. In M. S. Katz, N. Noddings and K. A. Strike (eds), *Justice and caring: The search for common ground in education*. New York: Teachers College Press, pp. vi, 186.

Chomsky, N. (2007). Preface to *The myth of the liberal media*. In D. Macedo and S. R. Steinberg (eds), *Media literacy: A reader*. New York: Peter Lang, pp. 24–6.

Chu, J. (2005). You wanna take this online? Cyberspace is the 21st century bully's playground where girls play rougher than boys. *Time, Canadian Edition*, 8 August: 42–3.

Chung, M. (2007). Online comments were 'inside joke'. Posts meant for friends only, teen says [electronic version]. *TheStar.com*, 25 March. Retrieved 15 August 2007 from www.thestar.com/article/195823.

Churchill, A. (2007). Experience being 'cyberbullied'. Unpublished research conducted as part of a three year research project on cyber-bullying, funded by Social Science and Humanities Research Council of Canada (SSHRC). Shaheen Shariff, McGill University, Principal Investigator.

Cohen, L. and Cantor, D. (1980). The determinants of larceny: An empirical and theoretical study. *Journal of Research in Crime and Delinquency*, *17*(2): 140–59.

Collins, J., Cox, B. G. and Langan, P. A. (1987). Job activities and personal crime victimization: Implications for theory. *Social Science Research*, *16*(4): 345–60.

Cook, P. J. (1987). Robbery violence. *The Journal of Criminal Law and Criminology*, *78*(2): 357–76.

Crick, N. R., Grotpeter, J. K. and Bigbee, M. A. (2002). Relationally and physically aggressive children's intent attributions and feelings of distress for relational and instrumental peer provocations. *Child Development*, *73*(4): 1134–42.

Darwin, C. (2003). *The Origin of Species*. New York: Signet Classics.

Davidson, J. (2004). Teens and technology: Where they get lost on line. *Australian Financial Review*, 14 February 14: 14.

Dedman, B. (2000). Schools may miss mark on preventing violence [electronic version]. *Chicago Sun-Times*, 16 October. Retrieved 12 August 2007 from www.ustreas.gov/usss/ntac/chicago_sun/shoot16.htm.

Dei, G. S. (1997). Race and the production of identity in the schooling experiences of African-Canadian youth. *Discourse studies in the cultural politics of education, 18*(2): 241–57.

d'Eon, J. and Senoo, Y. (2007). Cyber bullies in Japan: A cultural perspective. Study material, 10 February. Paper presented at the initial team meeting of the International Cyberbullying Research Project, McGill University, Montreal, funded by the Social Science and Humanities Research Council of Canada (SSHRC). Shaheen Shariff, Principal Investigator.

Department for Children, Schools and Families (DfCSF) (2007). Don't suffer in silence. Web site. Retrieved 23 August 2007 from www.dfes.gov.uk/bullying/.

Devlin, A. (1997). Offenders at school: Links between school failure and aggressive behaviour. In D. Tattum and H. Graham (eds), *Bullying: Home, school and community*. London: David Fulton Publishers, pp. 149–58.

Dibbell, J. (1993). A rape in cyberspace or how an evil clown, a Haitian trickster spirit, two wizards, and a cast of dozens turned a database into a society. *Village Voice, 21* December, *38*: 36–42.

Dicey, E. (1863). *Six months in the federal states*. London/ Cambridge: Macmillan.

Dick, J. and Canadian Library Association (1982). *Not in our schools?!!!: School book censorship in Canada: A discussion guide*. Ottawa: Canadian Library Association.

DiGiulio, R. C. (2001). *Educate, mediate, or litigate? What teachers, parents,and administrators must do about student behavior*. Thousand Oaks, CA: Corwin Press.

Dolmage, W. R. (2000). Lies, damned lies and statistics: The media's treatment of youth violence. *Education and Law Journal, 10*: 1–46.

Doob, A. N., Marinos, V., Varma, K. N. and University of Toronto, Centre of Criminology (1995). *Youth crime and the youth justice system in Canada: A research perspective*. Toronto, ON: Centre of Criminology, University of Toronto.

Eck, J. (2002). Preventing crime at places. In L. Sherman, D. Farrington, B. Welsh and D. MacKenzie (eds), *Evidence-based crime prevention*. New York: Routledge, pp. 241–94.

Education Act (1990) R.S.O., c. E. 2.

Edwards, L. Y. (2005). Victims, villains, and vixens. In S. R. Mazzarella (ed.), *Girl wide web*. New York: Peter Lang, pp. 13–30.

Egan, K. (1997). *The educated mind: How cognitive tools shape our understanding*. Chicago, IL: University of Chicago Press.

Eicher, D. (1994). Perils of puberty girls 'crash and burn' in adolescence. *The Denver Post*, 4 July: E01.

Elbaz-Luwisch, F. (2004). How is education possible when there's a body in the middle of the room? *Curriculum Inquiry, 34*(1): 9–27.

Epp, J. R. (1996). Schools, complicity, and sources of violence. In J. R. Epp and A. M. Watkinson (eds), *Systemic violence: How schools hurt children*. London: Falmer Press, pp. 1–25.

Esmail, A. (2007). *Untitled lecture*. Paper presented at the Institute of Ismaili Studies, McGill University, Montreal, Quebec, August.

European Commission (2007a). EU kids online, 7 June. Web site. Retrieved 23 August 2007 from www.eukidsonline.net/.

European Commission. (2007b). Safer Internet *plus* Programme, 31 July. Web site. Retrieved 22 August 2007 from http://ec.europa.eu/information_society/activities/sip/programme/index_en.htm.

European Commission (2007c). Making the Internet a safer place: The Safer Internet fact sheet [electronic version], 2 February. Retrieved 22 August 2007 from http://ec.europa.eu/information_society/doc/factsheets/018-saferinternetplus.pdf.

European Committee on Crime Problems (2001). Draft convention on cyber-crime [electronic version], 29 June. Retrieved 29 June from www.privacyinternational.org/issues/cybercrime/coe/cybercrime-final.html.

Findlay, G. (2007). Facebook: Student and parent [electronic version]. *The Current*, 2 May. Retrieved 2 May 2007 from www.cbc.ca/thecurrent/2007/200705/20070502.html.

Finkelhor, D., Mitchell, K. and Wolak, J. (2000). *Online victimization: A report on the nation's youth*. Retrieved 12 August 2007 from www.unh.edu/ccrc/pdf/Victimization_Online_Survey.pdf.

Finn, J. (2004). A survey of online harassment at a university campus. *Journal of Interpersonal Violence, 19*: 468–83.

Finn, J. and Banach, M. (2000). Victimization online: The downside of seeking human services for women on the Internet. *Cyberpsychology and behavior, 3*(5): 785–96.

Flynn, R. (2007). Private communication: Interpretation of changes to Bill 212, 27 July 2007 email to S. Shariff.

Foerstel, H. N. (1994). *Banned in the USA: A reference guide to book censorship in schools and public libraries*. Westport, CT: Greenwood Press.

Forss, P. (2006). 14% of students experience cyber bullying through SMS: survey [electronic version]. *Channel News Asia*, 19 June. Retrieved 20 June 2006 from www.channelnewsasia.com/stories/singaporelocalnews/view/214481/1/.html.

Forss, P. (2007). Educators concerned about increasing trend of cyber-bullying [electronic version]. *Channel News Asia*, 18 June. Retrieved 14 August 2007 from www.channelnewsasia.com/stories/singaporelocalnews/view/282978/1/.html.

Franek, M. (2006). Foiling cyberbullies in the new wild west. *Educational Leadership, 63*(4): 39–43.

Fratina, S. (2007). India's Internet censorship policy. Unpublished report produced as part of the International Cyberbullying Research Project, McGill University, Montreal, funded by the SSHRC. Shaheen Shariff, Principal Investigator.

Gaetz, S. (2004). Safe streets for whom? Homeless youth, social exclusion, and criminal victimization. *Canadian Journal of Criminology and Criminal Justice/La Revue canadienne de criminologie et de justice pénale, 46*(4): 423–56.

Gamson, W. A. and Modigliani, A. (1989). Media discourse and public opinion on nuclear power: A constructionist approach. *The American Journal of Sociology, 95*(1): 1–37.

Garbarino, J. (1999). *Lost boys: Why our sons turn violent and how we can save them*. New York: The Free Press.

Garofalo, J., Siegel, L. and Laub, J. (1987). School-related vicitimizations among adolescents: An analysis of national crime survey narratives. *Journal of Quantitative Criminology, 3*(4): 321–38.

Gáti, A., Tényi, T., Túry, F. and Wildmann, M. (2002). Anorexia nervosa following sexual harassment on the Internet: A case report. *The International Journal of Eating Disorders, 31*(4): 474–7.

Gee, J. P. (2003). *What video games have to teach us about learning and literacy*. New York: Palgrave/Macmillan.

Genta, M. L., Menesini, E., Fonzi, A., Costabile, A. and Smith, P. K. (1996). Bullies and victims in schools in central and southern Italy. *European Journal of Psychology of Education*, *11*: 97–110.

Gerstenfeld, P., Grant, D. and Chiang, C. (2003). Hate online: A content analysis of extremist Internet sites. *Analysis of Social Issues and Public Policy*, *3*(1): 29–44.

Gibson, C. (2006). Standing up to cyber bullies [electronic version]. *Adelaidean: News from the University of Adelaide*, August. Retrieved 28 November 2006 from www.adelaide. edu.au/adelaidean/issues/13601/news13683.html.

Girard, D. and Nguyen, L. (2007). Students, police clash [electronic version]. *TheStar.com*, March 24. Retrieved 1 April 2007 from www.thestar.com/article/195604.

Girodo, M., Deck, T. and Morrison, M. (2002). Dissociative-type identity disturbances in undercover agents: Socio-cognitive factors behind false-identity appearances and reenactments. *Social Behavior and Personality*, *30*(7): 631–44.

Giroux, H. A. (2002). Democracy, freedom, and justice after September 11th: Rethinking the role of educators and the politics of schooling. *Teachers College Record*, *104*(6): 1138–62.

Giroux, H. (2003). *The abandoned generation: Democracy beyond the culture of fear*. New York: Palgrave/Macmillan.

Glover, D., Cartwright, N. and Gleeson, D. (1998). *Towards bully-free schools*. Buckingham, Philadelphia, PA: Open University Press.

Glueck, S. and Glueck, E. T. (1962). *Family environment and delinquency*. Boston, MA: Houghton Mifflin.

Goff, H. (2007). Websites urged to act on bullies [electronic version]. *BBC News Online*, 16 April. Retrieved 13 August 2007 from http://news.bbc.co.uk/2/hi/uk_news/ education/6539989.stm.

Golding, W. (1954). *Lord of the flies*. New York: Penguin Putnam.

Gramsci, A. (1971). *Selections from the prison notebooks of Antonio Gramsci*. London: Lawrence Wishart.

Gramsci, A. (1975). *Letters from prison* (L. Lawner, trans.). London: Jonathan Cape.

Gregson, K. S. (2005). What if the lead character looks like me? Girl fans of *Shoujo* anime and their web sites. In S. R. Mazzarella (ed.), *Girl wide web: Girls, the Internet and the negotiation of identity*. New York: Peter Lang.

Hall, M. T. (1999). Administrative discretion and youth violence in schools: An analysis. Unpublished doctoral dissertation. Burnaby, BC: Simon Fraser University.

Handa, S. (1997). Caught between omissions: Exploring 'culture conflict' among second generation South Asian women in Canada. Unpublished doctoral dissertation. Toronto, ON: University of Toronto.

Harmon, A. (2004). Internet gives teenage bullies weapons to wound from afar [electronic version]. *New York Times*, 24 August. Retrieved 26 August 2004 from www.nytimes. com./2004/08/26/education.

Harris, M. (2007). Facebook is for 'good' kids – MySpace is for freaks. *The Gazette*, 29 June.

Harris, S. and Petrie, G. (2002). A study of bullying in the middle school. *National Association of Secondary School Principals (NASSP) Bulletin*, *86*(633): 42–53.

Hasegawa, M., Iwasaki, K. and Nakata, H. (2006). Junior high and high school students' real knowledge and the assessment of risk in using the Internet. *The Bulletin of Liberal Arts and Social Science Studies in Kinjo Gakuin University*, 1–12.

Hasegawa, M., Iwasaki, K. and Nakata, H. (2007). Junior high and high school students' actual knowledge and the assessment of risk in using Internet. Interim report. Paper presented at the initial team meeting of the International Cyberbullying Research Project, McGill University, Montreal, funded by the Social Science and Humanities Research Council of Canada (SSHRC). Shaheen Shariff, Principal Investigator. Translation by Yasuko Senoo.

Haynie, D. L., Nansel, T. R., Eitel, P., Crump, A. D., Saylor, K., Yu, K. *et al.* (2001). Bullies, victims, and bully/victims: Distinct groups of at-risk youth. *Journal of Early Adolescence, 21*: 29–49.

Henderson, N. R. and Hymel, S. (2002). *Peer contributions to bullying in schools: Examining student response strategies.* Paper presented at the National Association of School Psychologists (NASP) Annual Convention (Poster session), Chicago, Illinois.

Henderson, N. R., Hymel, S., Bonanno, R. A. and Davidson, K. (2002). *Bullying as a normal part of school life: Early adolescents' perspectives on bullying and peer harassment.* Paper presented at the Safe Schools Safe Communities Conference (Poster session), Vancouver, British Columbia.

Herring, S. C. (2002). Cyberviolence: Recognizing and resisting abuse in online environments. *Asian Women, 14*: 187–212.

Herzog, M. J. R. (1995). School censorship experiences of teachers in southern Appalachia. *International Journal of Qualitative Studies in Education, 8*(2): 137–48.

Higginbottom, N. and Packham, B. (2007). Student cracks government's 85M porn filter [electronic version]. *The Herald Sun,* 26 August. Retrieved 26 August 2007 from www.news.com.au/story/0,23599,22304224-421,00.html.

Hinduja, S. and Patchin, J. (in press). Cyberbullying: An exploratory analysis of factors related to offending and victimization. *Deviant Behavior.*

Hindustan Times (2008). Retrieved 13 January 2008 from www.hindustantimes.com/StoryPage.

Hines, M. A. (1991). Malpractice in education. In W. F. Foster and F. Peters (eds), *Education and law: Strengthening the partnership.* Georgetown, ON: CAPSLE, pp. 154–62.

Hodges, E. V. E. and Perry, D. G. (1996). Victims of peer abuse: An overview. *Reclaiming Children and Youth: Journal of Emotional and Behavioral Problems, 5*(1): 23–8.

Hogg, C. (2006). Japan's deadly bullying problem [electronic version]. *BBC News Online,* 6 December. Retrieved 14 August 2007 from http://news.bbc.co.uk/2/hi/asia-pacific/6213716.stm.

Hoover, J. H. and Olsen, G. W. (2001). *Teasing and harassment: The frames and scripts approach for teachers and parents.* Bloomington, IN: National Educational Service.

Howe, R. B. and Covell, K. (2000). Schools and the participation rights of the child. *Education and Law Journal, 10*: 107–23.

Inglis, F. (1985). *The management of ignorance.* Oxford: Blackwell.

Itoh, M. (1999). Iwaki-shi 'ijime' jisatsu jiken hanketsu nit suite [electronic version]. *IO.* Retrieved 18 March 2007 from www.itoh.org/io/parent/iwaki.htm.

Ivengar, S. (1991). *Is anyone responsible? How television frames political issues.* Chicago, IL: University of Chicago Press.

Jackson, P. W. (1986). *The practice of teaching.* New York: Teachers College Press.

Jafaar, S. B. (2002). Fertile ground: instructional negligence and the tort of educational malpractice. *Education and Law Journal, 12*(1): 131–22.

Jaishankar, K. and Shariff, S. (in press). Cyber bullying: A transnational perspective. In F. Schmallager and M. Pittaro (eds), *Crimes of the Internet.* Upper Saddle River, NJ: Prentice Hall.

Jalongo, M. R. and Creany, A. D. (1991). Censorship in children's literature: What every educator should know. *Childhood Education,* 67(3): 143–8.

James, O. (1995). *Juvenile violence in a winner-loser culture: Socio-economic and familial origins of the rise in violence against the person.* London, New York: Free Association Books.

Janoviček, N. (2001). *Reducing crime and victimization: A service provider's report.* Prepared for the Feminist Research, Education, Development and Action Centre; Burnaby, BC: Simon Fraser University.

Jenkins, H. and boyd, d. (2006). Discussion: MySpace and Deleting Online Predators Act (DOPA) [electronic version]. *Digital Divide Network,* 30 May. Retrieved 12 June 2006 from www.digitaldivide.net/articles/view.php?ArticleID=592.

Jiwani, Y. (1997). *Reena Virk: The erasure of race? Kinesis.* Vancouver, BC: FREDA Centre for Research on Violence Against Immigrant and Refugee Girls and Women; Burnaby, BC: Simon Fraser University.

Jiwani, Y. (2001). *Mapping violence: A work in progress.* Vancouver, BC: Feminist Research, Education, Development and Action Centre; Burnaby, BC: Simon Fraser University.

Juvonen, J. and Graham, S. (2001). *Peer harassment in school: The plight of the vulnerable and victimized.* New York, London: Guilford Press.

Kapoor, G. (2003). School spats: Fights, squabbles and school rivalries take a nasty turn online [electronic version]. *Rediff India Abroad,* 26 May. Retrieved 12 August 2007 from www.rediff.com/netguide/2003/may/26bully.htm.

Katch, J. (2001). *Under deadman's skin: Discovering the meaning of children's violent play.* Boston, MA: Beacon Press.

Keene, L. (2004). Who said I can't read this? *School Library Media Activities Monthly,* 21(2): 29–32.

Kincheloe, J. L. (2004). Introduction. In J. L. Kincheloe and S. R. Steinberg (eds), *The miseducation of the West: How schools and the media distort our understanding of the Islamic world.* Westport, CT, London: Praeger Publishers, pp. 1–23.

Kincheloe, J. L. (2005). *Classroom teaching: An introduction.* New York: Peter Lang.

Knowledge Producing Schools web site (2005). October 22. Retrieved 19 August 2007 from deakin.edu.au/education/lit/kps/.

Kochenderfer-Ladd, B. and Wardrop, J. L. (2001). Chronicity and instability of children's peer victimization experiences as predictors of loneliness and social satisfaction trajectories. *Child Development,* 72(1): 134–51.

Kozol, J. (2005). *The shame of the nation: The restoration of apartheid schooling in America.* New York: Crown.

Kumpulainen, K., Rasanen, E. and Henttonen, I. (1999). Children involved in bullying: psychological disturbances and the persistence of the involvement. *Child Abuse and Neglect: The International Journal,* 23(12): 1253–62.

Kumpulainen, K., Rasanen, E., Henttonen, I., Almqvist, F., Kresanov, K. *et al.* (1998). Bullying and psychiatric symptoms among elementary school-age children. *Child Abuse and Neglect: The International Journal,* 22(7): 705–17.

Lampert, A. (2006). Prof raises alarm about cyber-bullying [electronic version]. *The Gazette,* 21 February. Retrieved 13 August 2007 from www.canada.com/montrealgazette/news/montreal/story.html?id=51354824–385b-4fd6–971e-27ece9185803&k=62517.

Lanctot, N. (2001). *Violence among females from adolescence to adulthood: Results from a longitudinal study.* Paper presented at the Vancouver Conference on Aggressive and Violent Girls. Simon Fraser University, Vancouver, British Columbia.

Land, J. (2006). Bullies inflicting 'extreme misery' on UK school pupils [electronic version]. *24dash.com*, 6 November. Retrieved 10 November 2006 from www.24dash.com/printNews/48/12656.htm.

Lankshear, C. and Knobel, M. (2003). *New literacies: Changing knowledge and classroom learning.* Buckingham: Open University Press.

Lankshear, C. and Knobel, M. (2005). *Digital literacies: Policy, pedagogy and research considerations for education.* Opening plenary address. Paper presented at the ITU Conference, Oslo, Norway. Retrieved 9 August 2007 from www.geocities.com/c.lankshear/Oslo.pdf.

Lankshear, C. and Knobel, M. (2006). *New literacies: Everyday practices and classroom learning*, 2nd edn. Maidenhead, New York: Open University Press.

Large, A., Nesset, V., Beheshti, J. and Bowler, L. (2006). 'Bonded design': A novel approach to intergenerational information technology design. *Library and Information Science Research*, 28(1): 64–82.

Larson, C. L. (1997). Is the land of Oz an alien nation? A sociopolitical study of school community conflict. *Educational Administration Quarterly*, 33(3): 312–50.

Lasley, J. (1989). Drinking routines/lifestyles and predatory victimization: A causal analysis. *Justice Quarterly*, 6(4): 529–42.

Leander, K. (in press). Toward a connective ethnography of online/offline literacy networks. In J. Coiro, M. Knobel, C. Lankshear and D. Lou (eds), *Handbook of research on new literacies*. Mahwah, NJ: Lawrence Erlbaum.

Lee, J. (2005). Teens with mobiles to steal thunder from 3G revolution [electronic version]. *The Sydney Morning Herald*, 17 February. Retrieved 12 August 2007 from http://smh.com.au/articles/2005/02/16/1108500153501.html.

Leishman, J. (2002). Cyber-bullying: The Internet is the latest weapon in a bully's arsenal [electronic version]. *CBC News. The National*, 10 October. Retrieved 27 January 2003 from http://cbc.ca/news/national/news/cyberbullying/index.html.

Lenhart, A. (2007). Data memo [electronic version]. *PEW Internet and American Life Project*, 27 June. Retrieved 14 August 2007 from www.pewinternet.org/pdfs/PIP%20Cyberbullying%20Memo.pdf.

Li, Q. (2005). Cyber-bullying in schools: The nature and extent of adolescents' experience. Paper presented at the American Education Research Association (AERA) Conference, Montreal.

Lidsky, L. B. (2000). Silencing John Doe: Defamation and discourse in cyberspace. *Duke Law Journal*, 49(855): 862–5.

Limber, S. P. and Small, M. A. (2003). State laws and policies to address bullying in schools. *School Psychology Review*, 32(3): 445–55.

Linden, A. M. and Klar, L. N. (eds) (1994). *Canadian tort law: Cases, notes and materials*, 10th edn. Markam, ON, Vancouver, BC: Butterworths Canada.

Livingstone, S. and Bober, M. (2005a). *UK children go online: Final report of key project finding*, April. Retrieved 14 August 2007 from www.lse.ac.uk/collections/children-go-online/UKCGO_Final_report.pdf.

Livingstone, S. and Bober, M. (2005b). *UK children go online: Final report of key project findings*, April. London: Economic and Social Research Council.

Lorimer, R. (1999). The market and professional censorship of Canadian school textbooks. In K. Petersen and A. C. Hutchinson (eds), *Interpreting censorship in Canada*. Toronto, ON: University of Toronto Press, pp. 367–85.

Louis Harris and Associates (1993). *Hostile hallways: The AAUW survey on sexual harassment in America's schools*. Washington, DC: American Association of University Women.

Lynch, J. (1987). Routine activity and victimization at work. *Journal of Quantitative Criminology*, *3*(4): 283–300.

Ma, X. (2001). Bullying and being bullied: To what extent are bullies also victims? *American Educational Research Journal*, *38*(2): 351–70.

Maag, C. (2007). Retrieved 13 January 2008 from www.nytimes.com/2007/11/28/us/28hoax.html.

McCarthy, P., Rylance, J., Bennet, R. and Zimmermann, H. (2001). *Bullying from The Backyard to Boardroom*, 2nd edn. Leichhardt: The Federation Press.

McCormick, N. and Leonard, J. (1996). Gender and sexuality in the cyberspace frontier. *Women and Therapy*, *19*(4): 109–19.

MacDonald, R. A. (2006). *Pluralistic human rights: Universal human wrongs*, 1 November. Paper presented at the Dialogues on human rights and legal pluralism workshop. Centre for Human Rights and Legal Pluralism, Faculty of Law, McGill University, Montreal.

McDougall, A. and Philips Valentine, L. (1999). Selective marginalization of Aboriginal voices: Censorship in public performance. In K. Petersen and A. C. Hutchinson (eds), *Interpreting censorship in Canada*. Toronto, ON: University of Toronto Press, pp. 334–50.

Macedo, D. and Steinberg, S. R. (2007). *Media literacy: A reader*. New York: Peter Lang Publishing.

Mackay, A. W. and Burt-Gerrans, J. (2005). Student freedom of expression: Violent content and the safe school balance. [Special issue: Schools and courts: Competing rights in the new millennium]. *McGill Journal of Education*, *40*(3), 423–44.

MacKay, A. W. and Dickinson, G. M. (1998). *Beyond the 'Careful Parent': Tort liability in education*. Toronto, ON: Emond Montgomery Publications.

MacKay, A. W. and Flood, S. (2001). Negligence principles in the school context: New challenges for the 'careful parent'. *Education and Law Journal*, *10*(3): 371–92.

Mackey-Kallis, S. and Hahn, D. (1994). Who's to blame for America's drug problem?: The search for scapegoats in the 'war on drugs.' *Communication Quarterly*, *42*(1): 1–20.

MacKinnon, R. (2001). Virtual rape. *Journal of Computer Mediated Communication*, *2*(4): n.p.

McLaren, P. (1991). Schooling the postmodern body: critical pedagogy and the politics of enfleshment. In H. A. Giroux (ed.), *Postmodernism, feminism, and cultural politics: redrawing educational boundaries*. Albany, NY: State University of New York Press, pp. 144–73.

McLaren, P. (1998). *Life in schools: An introduction to critical pedagogy in the foundations of education*, 3rd edn. New York: Longman.

MacLean, S. (2006). Survey reveals cyber bullying [electronic version]. *Australian IT*, 20 April. Retrieved 20 April 2006 from http://australianit.news.com.au/.

McLuhan, M. (1964). *Understanding media: The extensions of man*. New York: Mentor.

McMillin, D. C. (2005). Teen crossings: Emerging cyberpublics in India. In S. R. Mazzarella (ed.), *Girl wide web: Girls, the Internet, and the negotiation of identity*. New York: Peter Lang, pp. 161–78.

McNeil, L. M. (1988). *Contradictions of control: School structure and school knowledge.* New York: Routledge.

McVeigh, B. J. (2003). Individualization, individuality, inferiority, and the Internet: Japanese university students and e-mail. In N. Gottlieb and M. McLelland (eds), *Japanese Cybercultures.* London: Routledge.

Madriz, E. (1996). The perception of risk in the workplace: A test of routine activity theory. *Journal of Criminal Justice, 24*(5).

Mahtani, M. (2001). Representing minorities: Canadian media and minority identities. *Canadian Ethnic Studies, 33*(3): 99–133.

Mainchi Daily News (2007). Prime minister backs harsher punishment for school bullies [electronic version, 22 January]. *MSN-Mainichi Daily News.* Retrieved 22 January 2007 from http://mdn.mainichi-msn.co.jp/national/news/20070122p2a00m0na016000c.html.

Mann, J. (1997). A perilous age for girls. *The Washington Post*, October 10: E03.

Marjoribanks, K. and Mboya, M. M. (1998). Factors affecting the self-concepts of South African Students. *Journal of Social Psychology, 138*(5): 572–80.

Martin, M. and Phelan, S. (2002). Representing Islam in the wake of September 11: A comparison of US television and CNN online messageboard discourses. *Prometheus, 20*(3): 263–9.

Mazur, A. (1983). Physiology, dominance and aggression in humans. In A. P. Goldstein and Syracuse University Center for Research on Aggression (eds.), *Prevention and control of aggression.* New York: Pergamon Press, pp. 145–55.

Mazzarella, S. R. (ed.) (2005). *Girl wide web. Girls, the Internet, and the negotiation of identity.* New York: Peter Lang.

Mazzarella, S. R. and Pecora, N. (2002). *Girls in crisis: Newspaper coverage of adolescent girls.* Paper presented at the meeting of the National Communication Association, New Orleans, LA.

Media Awareness Network (2005). Kids' online activites: Key findings [electronic version]. *Young Canadians in a wired world: Key findings.* Retrieved 10 January 2006 from www.media-awareness.ca/english/resources/special_initiatives/survey_resources/students_survey/key_findings/kids_online_key_findings.cfm.

Media Awareness Network (no date). Media Awareness Network web site. Retrieved 10 December 2006 from www.mediawareness.com

Medical News Today (2007). Survey identifies teen online behaviors associated with online interpersonal victimization [electronic version, 7 February]. *Medical News Today.* Retrieved 14 August 2007 from www.medicalnewstoday.com/articles/62418.php.

Mitchell, A. (2004). Bullied by the click of a mouse [electronic version]. *The Globe and Mail*, 24 January. Retrieved 10 August 2007 from www.theglobeandmail.com/servlet/story/RTGAM.20040124.wbully0124/BNStory/Front/?query=bullying.

Mitchell, K. J., Finkelhor, D. and Wolak, J. (2003). The exposure of youth to unwanted sexual material on the Internet: A national survey of risk, impact, and prevention. *Youth and Society, 34*(3): 330–58.

Mitchell, K. J., Finkelhor, D. and Wolak, J. (2005). Protecting youth online: Family use of filtering and blocking software. *Child Abuse and Neglect: The International Journal, 29*(7): 753–65.

Montgomery, K. (2005). Imagining the antiracist state: Representations of racism in Canadian history textbooks. *Discourse: studies in the cultural politics of education, 26*(4): 427–42.

Mooney, A., Creeser, R. and Blatchford, P. (1991). Children's views on teasing and fighting in junior schools. *Educational Research*, *33*: 103–12.

Moretti, M. (2002). Aggressive and violent behaviour in girls: Rates, risk factors and relevance for adjustment. Paper presented at the Vancouver Conference on Aggressive and Violent Girls, Simon Fraser University, Vancouver, British Columbia.

Moriarty, L. J. and Williams, J. E. (1996). Examining the relationship between routine activities theory and social disorganization; An analysis of property crime victimization. *American Journal of Criminal Justice*, *21*(1): 43–59.

Morita, Y. and Kiyonaga, K. (1994). *Ijime: Kyôshitsu no yamai (Bullying: Pathology in classrooms*, 2nd edn. Tokyo: Kanedo-shobô.

Mota, S. (2002). The U.S. Supreme Court addresses the Child Pornography Prevention Act and Child Online Protection Act in *Ashcroft v. Free Speech Coalition* and *Ashcroft v. American Civil Liberties Union*. *Federal Communications Law Journal*, *55*: 85–98.

MSN. (2006). MSN cyberbullying report: Blogging, instant messaging and email bullying amongst today's teens [electronic version]. Retrieved 12 August 2007 from www.msn.co.uk/img/specials/portal/cyberbullying/cyberbullying_tall_revised3.pdf.

Mustaine, E. E. and Tewksbury, R. (1997). The risk of victimization in the workplace for men and women: An analysis using routine activities/lifestyle theory. *Humanity and Society*, *21*(1): 17–38.

Mustaine, E. E. and Tewksbury, R. (2000). Comparing the lifestyles of victims, offenders, and victim-offenders :A routine activity theory assessment of similarities and differences for criminal incident participants *Sociological Focus*, *33*(3): 339–62.

Myers, D. A. (2006). Defamation and the quiescent anarchy of the Internet: A case study of cyber-targeting. *Penn State Law Review*, *110*(3): 667–86.

Mynard, H., Joseph, S. and Alexander, J. (2000). Peer victimisation and post traumatic stress in adolescents. *Personality and Individual Differences*, *29*: 815–21.

Nacos, B. and Torres-Reyna, O. (2002). Muslim Americans in the news before and after 9–11. Paper presented at the Symposium: Restless searchlight: terrorism, the media and public life, cosponsored by the APSA Communication Section and the Shorenstein Center at the John F. Kennedy School, Harvard University.

Nansel, T., Overpeck, M., Pilla, R. S., Simons-Morton, B. and Scheidt, P. (2001). Bullying behaviors among US youth: Prevalence and association with psychosocial adjustment. *Journal of the American Medical Association*, *285*: 2094–2100.

National Crime Prevention Council (1997). *Report on Bullying*. Retrieved 24 July 2005 from www.crime-prevention.org.

NCH. (2005). *Putting U in the picture. Mobile Bullying Survey 2005*. Retrieved 5 December 2006 from www.nch.org.uk/uploads/documents/Mobile_bullying_%20report.pdf.

Neuman, W. R., Just, M. R. and Crigler, A. N. (1992). *Common knowledge: News and the construction of political meaning*. Chicago, IL: The University of Chicago Press.

Noll, E. (1994). The ripple effect of censorship: Silencing in the classroom. *English Journal*, *83*(8): 59–64.

O'Connell, P., Pepler, D. and Craig, W. (1999). Peer involvement in bullying: Insights and challenges for intervention. *Journal of Adolescence*, *22*: 437–52.

O'Connell, R., Barrow, C. and Sange, S. (2002). *Young peoples' use of chat rooms: Implications for policy strategies and programs of education*. London: Home Office.

Olweus, D. (1978). *Aggression in the schools: Bullies and whipping boys*. Washington. DC, New York: Hemisphere, distributed solely by Halsted Press.

Olweus, D. (1991). Bully/victim problems among school children. Basic facts and effects of a school based intervention program. In D. J. Pepler and K. H. Rubin (eds), *The development and treatment of childhood aggression*. Hillsdale, NJ: Erlbaum.

Olweus, D. (1993). *Bullying at school: What we know and what we can do*. Oxford, Cambridge MA: Blackwell.

Olweus, D. (2001). Peer harassment: A critical analysis and some important issues (introduction). In J. Juvonen and S. Graham (eds), *Peer harassment in school: The plight of the vulnerable and vicitmized*. New York: Guildford Press, pp. 3–20.

Ontario College of Teachers (2007). COMPAS State of the Teaching Profession [electronic version]. *Professionally Speaking, The Magazine of the Ontario College of Teachers*. Retrieved 28 August 2007 from www.oct.ca/publications/PDF/survey07_e.pdf.

Out-Law News (2006) Europe investigates dangers of mobiles to children [electronic version, 27 July]. *Out-Law News*. Retrieved 22 August 2007 from www.out-law.com/page-7141.

Parker, J. C. (1993). Educational malpractice: A tort is born. *Education and Law Journal*, 4: 163–87.

Patchin, J. and Hinduja, S. (2006). Bullies move beyond the schoolyard: A preliminary look at cyberbullying. *Youth Violence and Juvenile Justice*, 4(2): 148–69.

Payne, S. (2007). Cyber-bullying: It's not 'cool', it's cruel [electronic version]. *Bangkok Post Learning Post*, 1 May. Retrieved 12 August 2007 from www.bangkokpost.net/education/index.htm.

Pellegrini, A. D. and Bartini, M. (2000). A longitudinal study of bullying, victimization, and peer affiliation during the transition from primary school to middle school. *American Educational Research Journal*, 37(3): 699–725.

PEN Canada (2006). Challenging books [electronic version]. *PEN Canada Spring Bulletin*. Retrieved 4 December 2006 from www.pencanada.ca/media/NewsletterSpring06.pdf.

Pepler, D. and Craig, W. (1997). *Bullying: Research and interventions. Youth Update*. A publication of the Institute for the Study of Antisocial Youth.

Perkins, C. (1997). Any more colorful we'd have to censor it. In S. deCastell and M. Bryson (eds), *Radical in-ter-ventions: Identity, politics and differences in educational praxis*. Albany, NY: SUNY, pp. 247–68.

Perry, D. G., Williard, J. C. and Perry, L. C. (1990). Peers' perceptions of the consequences that victimized children provide aggressors. *Child Development*, 61: 1310–25.

Petress, K. (2004). The role of censorship in school. *Journal of Instructional Psychology*, 32(3): 248–52.

Phipher, M. (1994). *Reviving Ophelia: Saving the selves of adolescent girls*. New York: Ballentine Books.

Piddocke, S., Magsino, R. and Manley-Casimir, M. (1997). *Teachers in trouble: An exploration of the normative character of teaching*. Toronto, ON: University of Toronto Press.

Plato. (1987). *The republic* (D. Lee, trans.). London: Penguin Books.

Pollack, W. (1998). *Real boys*. Markham, ON: Fitzhenry & Whiteside.

Portsmouth Herald Editorial Board (2005). Internet age brings new form of harassment: Cyber-bullying [electronic version]. *Portsmouth Herald*, 30 March. Retrieved 12 August 2005 from http://archive.seacoastonline.com/2005news/03302005/editoria/72651.htm.

Press Association (2006). Teachers to be given powers outside school [electronic version]. *Guardian Unlimited*, 8 February. Retrieved 22 July 2007 from http://education.guardian.co.uk/pupilbehaviour/story/0,,1705138,00.html.

PREVNet (2006). Cyber-bullying Meeting. PREVNet, Promoting relationships and eliminating violence. A national network funded by Canadian Centres for Excellence, Toronto, 15 December.

Prinsloo, E. and Du Plessis, S. (1998). *Socio-education 1*. Pretoria: University of South Africa, Department of Educational Studies.

Rahul. (2007). Orkut: The sex hub! [electronic version]. *Merinews*, 21 March. Retrieved 12 August 2007 from www.merinews.com/catFull.jsp?articleID=124543.

Rauste-Von Wright, M. (1992). The function of aggression in the life process of adolescents. In A. Fraczek and H. Zumkley (eds), *Socialization and aggression*. Berlin: Springer-Verlag. pp. 185–99.

Razack, S. (1998). *Looking white people in the eye: Gender, race, and culture in courtrooms and classrooms*. Toronto, ON: University of Toronto Press.

Reading Evening Post (2006). Cyber bullying blighting our lives [electronic version]. *getreading*, 1 June. Retrieved 13 August 2007 from www.getreading.co.uk/news/2001/2001939/cyber_bullying_blighting_our_lives.

Reichman, H. (1993). *Censorship and selection: Issues and answers for schools*, rev. edn. London, Chicago, IL: American Library Association.

Reiss, A. J., Roth, J. A. and National Research Council (US), Panel on the Understanding and Control of Violent Behavior (1993). *Understanding and preventing violence*. Washington, DC: National Academy Press.

Renfrew, J. W. (1997). *Aggression and its causes: A biopsychosocial approach*. New York: Oxford University Press.

Research committee for protection of children against negative influences in the virtual community in the National Police Agency (2006). Baacharu shakai no motarasu heigai kara kodomo o mamoru tameni, final report [electronic version], December. Retrieved 19 March 2007 from www.npa.go.jp/safetylife/syonen29/finalreport.pdf.

Riga, A. (2007). Cyberbullying: Schools are fighting back. *The Gazette*, 5 August: A1, A4.

Rigby, K. (1997). Reflections on *Tom Brown's Schooldays* and the problem of bullying today. *Australian Journal of Social Science*, 4(1): 85–96.

Rigby, K. (2001). Health consequences of bullying and its prevention in schools. In J. Juvonen and S. Graham (eds), *Peer harassment in school: The plight of the vulnerable and victimized*. New York, London: Guilford Press, pp. 310–31.

Rigby, K. (2002). How successful are anti-bullying programs for schools? Paper presented at the Australian Institute of Criminology (invited) in conjunction with the Department of Education, Employment and Training, Victoria and Crime Prevention, Victoria, Melbourne.

Rios-Ellis, B., Bellamy, L. and Shoji, J. (2000). An examination of specific types of ijime within Japanese schools. *School Psychology International*, 21(3): 227–41.

Rivers, I. (2003). *Bullying: Implications for mental health*. Paper presented at the Child Mental Health Research Networking Day, Postgraduate Medical Education Centre, York, UK, January.

Robertson, H.-J. (1998). *No more teachers, no more books: The commercialization of Canada's schools*. Toronto, ON: McClelland & Stewart.

Roher, E. (1997). *An Educator's Guide to Violence in Schools*. Toronto, ON: Canada Law Books.

Roher, E. (2007). Intimidation.com: Dealing with cyberbullying. Paper presented at the CAPSLE Conference, Vancouver, British Columbia.

Roncek, D. and Maier, P. (1991). Bars, blocks, and crimes revisited: Linking the theory of routine activities to the empiricism of 'hot spots'. *Criminology*, 29(4): 725–53.

Roncek, D. W. and Bell, R. (1981). Bars, blocks, and crimes. *Journal of Environmental Systems*, *11*: 35–47.

Rusk, J. (2007). High school suspends 19 for bullying principal on website [electronic version]. *The Globe and Mail*, 13 February. Retrieved 13 February 2007 from www.theglobeandmail.com/servlet/story/RTGAM.20070213.wxfacebook13/BNStory/.

Sacco, M. (1994). The censorship of young adult literature. In J. E. Brown (ed.), *Preserving intellectual freedom: Fighting censorship in our schools*. Urbana, IL: National Council of Teachers of English, pp. 63–72.

Sadria, M. (2007). Islamic arts and architectures. Paper presented at the Summer Institute on Islam, McGill University, Montreal, Quebec, 13 August.

Said, E. (1997). *Covering Islam: How the media and the experts determine how we see the rest of the world*. New York: Vintage Books.

Salkind, N. (1990). *Child development*. Chicago, IL: Holt, Rinehart & Winston.

Salmivalli, C. (1999). Participant role approach to school bullying: Implications for intervention. *Journal of Adolescence*, *22*: 453–9.

Salmivalli, C. (2001). Group view on victimization: empirical findings and their implications. In J. Juvonen and S. Graham (eds), *Peer harassment in school: The plight of the vulnerable and victimized*. New York, London: Guilford Press, pp. 398–419.

Salmivalli, C., Lagerspetz, K., Björqvist, K., Österman, K. and Kaukiainen, A. (1996). Bullying as a group process: Participant roles and their relations to social status within the group. *Aggressive Behavior*, *22*(1): 1–15.

Sampson, R. and Wooldredge, J. (1987). Linking the micro- and macro-dimension of lifestyle – routine activity and opportunity models of predatory victimization. *Journal of Quantitative Criminology*, *3*: 371–93.

Sanders, B. (2005). Censorship of the media creating insidious chill on free expression of our airwaves [electronic version]. *CommonDreams.org News Center Website*, 17 February. Retrieved 9 November 2006 from www.commondreams.org/views05/0217-32.htm.

Sankey, D. (2007). Beware: Your prospective boss could see you naked on the Net. *The Gazette*, 18 July: B6.

Schissel, B. (1993). *Social dimensions of Canadian youth justice*. Don Mills, ON: Oxford University Press Canada.

Schmidt, S. (2006). Web ensnares teens up to eight hours a day. Instant messages average 40 a day. *The Gazette*, 15 November: A14.

Schuster, B. (2001). Rejection and victimization by peers: Social perception and social behavior mechanisms. In J. Juvonen and S. Graham (eds), *Peer harassment in school: The plight of the vulnerable and victimized*. New York, London: Guilford Press.

Schwartz, D., Dodge, K. and Coie, J. (1993). The emergence of chronic peer victimization. *Child Development*, *64*: 1755–72.

Schwartz, D., Dodge, K., Pettit, G. S. and Bates, J. E. (1997). The early socialization of aggressive victims of bullying. *Child Development*, *68*(4): 665–75.

Sears, J. T. (1993). Responding to the sexual diversity of faculty and students: Sexual praxis and the critically reflective administrator. In C. A. Capper (ed.), *Educational administration in a pluralistic society*. Albany, NY: State University of New York Press, pp. xiv, 323.

Sefa-Dei, G. (1997). Race and production of identity in the schooling experiences of African-Canadian youth. *Discourse: Studies in the cultural politics of education*, *18*(2): 241–56.

Séguin, R. (2002). Quebec youth face extortion from peers, survey finds. *The Globe and Mail*, 21 November: A8.

Sengupta, S. (2006). Orkut: The new danger [electronic version]. *Merinews*, 16 November. Retrieved 12 August 2007 from www.merinews.com/catFull.jsp?articleID=123746& category=Technology&catID=4.

Senoo, Y. (2007). Netto-ijime (cyber-bullying): Bullying moves to cyberspace. Unpublished term paper for EDEM 609 Issues in Education Masters course. Prof. Shaheen Shariff. Department of Integrated Studies in Education, Faculty of Education, McGill University.

Servance, R. L. (2003). Cyber-bullying, cyber-harassment and the conflict between schools and the First Amendment. *Wisconsin Law Review* (6), 1213–15.

Shaheen, J. (2003). Reel bad Arabs: How Hollywood vilifies a people. *The Annals of the American Academy of Political Social Science*, 588: 171–93.

Shaheen, J. G. (2000). Hollywood's Muslim Arabs. *Muslim World* (90), 22–42.

Shariff, S. (1999). Managing the dilemma of competing rights: The case of the three books. Unpublished Master of Arts thesis, Simon Fraser University, Vancouver, British Columbia.

Shariff, S. (2000). Identifying successful school and community programs for youth: An evaluation rubric and compendium of sources. A research project of Youth Justice Education Partnerships supported by Justice Canada [electronic version], May. Retrieved 23 July 2005 from www.acjnet.ca.

Shariff, S. (2001). Email from 'Raveger, Raveger'. In *Legal Context of Education, EDUC 445. Course Study Guide*. Burnaby, BC: Centre for Distance Education, Simon Fraser University.

Shariff, S. (2003). A system on trial: Identifying legal standards for educational, ethical and legally defensible approaches to bullying in schools. Unpublished doctoral dissertation. Burnaby, BC: Simon Fraser University.

Shariff, S. (2004). Keeping schools out of court: Legally defensible models of leadership to reduce cyber-bullying. Educational Forum. *Delta Kappa Pi*, 68(3): 222–3.

Shariff, S. (2005). Cyber-dilemmas in the new millenium: Balancing free expression and student safety in cyber-space. Special issue: School and courts: Competing rights in the new millennium. *McGill Journal of Education*, 40(3): 467–87.

Shariff, S. (2006a). Balancing competing rights: A stakeholder model for democratic schools. *Canadian Journal of Education*, 29(2): 476–96.

Shariff, S. (2006b). Cyber-dilemmas: Balancing free expression and learning in a virtual school environment. *International Journal of Learning*, 12(4): 269–78.

Shariff, S. (2006c). Cyber-hierarchies: A new arsenal of weapons for gendered violence in schools. In C. Mitchell and F. Leech (eds), *Combatting Gender Violence in and around schools*. London: Trentham Books, pp. 33–41.

Shariff, S. (2007a). Adult perceptions of cyber-bullying. Compiled by research assistant Julie d'Eon. Unpublished research conducted as part of a three year research project on cyber-bullying, funded by SSHRC. Shaheen Shariff, McGill University, Principal Investigator.

Shariff, S. (2007b). Unpublished research conducted as part of a three year research project on cyber-bullying, funded by SSHRC. Shaheen Shariff, McGill University, Principal Investigator; Margaret Jackson and Wanda Cassidy, Simon Fraser University, Co-Investigators.

Shariff, S. (2007c). 'What's the school's role? What about rights? and Would you report it?'. Data compiled by research assistants, Andrew Churchill, Julie d'Eon and Tomoya Tsutsumi. Tables and figures prepared by Andrew Churchill. Unpublished research conducted as part of a three year research project on cyber-bullying, funded by SSHRC. Shaheen Shariff, McGill University, Principal Investigator.

Shariff, S. (in press). *Cyberbullying: What schools need to know to control misconduct and avoid legal consequences*. New York: Cambridge University Press.

Shariff, S. and Manley-Casimir, M. E. (1999). Censorship in schools: Orthodoxy, diversity and cultural coherence. In K. Petersen and A. C. Hutchinson (eds), *Interpreting censorship in Canada*. Toronto, ON: University of Toronto Press, pp. 157–81.

Shariff, S. and LaRocque, L. (2001). Unpublished report on violence in schools and school anti-violence policies for British Columbia Ministry of Education. Simon Fraser University, Vancouver, British Columbia.

Shariff, S. and Sarkar, M. (2004). Investigating inclusion: From educational policies to practice. A project funded by the SSHRC. Unpublished research findings. Department of Integrated Studies in Education, Faculty of Education, McGill University.

Shariff, S. and Gouin, R. (2005). Cyber-dilemmas: Gendered hierarchies, free expression and cyber-safety in schools. Paper presented at the Safety and security in a networked world: Balancing cyber-rights and responsibilities, Oxford Internet Institute, University of Oxford, UK. Retrieved 9 August 2007 from www.oii.ox.ac.uk/microsites/cybersafety/ ?view=papers.

Shariff, S. and Strong-Wilson, T. (2005). Bullying and new technologies: What can teachers do to foster socially responsible discourse in the physical and virtual school environments? In J. Kincheloe (ed.), *Classroom teaching: An introduction*. New York: Peter Lang Publishers, pp. 219–40.

Shariff, S. and Hoff, D. L. (2007). Cyber-bullying: Clarifying legal boundaries for school supervision in cyberspace [electronic version]. *International Journal of Cyber Criminology*. Retrieved 9 August 2007 from www40.brinkster.com/ccjournal/Shaheen&Hoffjcc.htm.

Shariff, S. and Johnny, L. (2007a). *Censorship! . . . or Selection?: Confronting a curriculum of orthodoxy through pluralistic models*. Rotterdam: Sense Publishers.

Shariff, S. and Johnny, L. (2007b). Cyber-libel and cyber-bullying: Can schools protect student reputations and free expression in virtual environments? Paper presented at the American Educational Research Association (AERA) Conference. Chicago, Illinois.

Shariff, S., Case, R. and Manley-Casimir, M. (2000). Balancing competing rights in education: Surrey School Board's book ban. *Education and Law Journal*, *10*(1): 47–105.

Shariff, S., Case, R. and LaRocque, L. (2001). Begging the questions: The court of appeal decision in the Surrey school board controversy. *Education and Law Journal*, *11*(1): 85–111.

Shriever, B. (2007). Cyberbullying: Students have always gossiped and complained about their teachers. But in cyberspace such behaviour can take a life of its own [electronic version]. *Professionally Speaking, The Magazine of the Ontario College of Teachers*. Retrieved 28 August 2007 from www.oct.ca/publications/professionally_speaking/September_ 2007/cyberbullying.asp.

Simmons, D. (2006). Cyber bullying rises in S Korea [electronic version]. *BBC Click Online*, 3 November. Retrieved 30 March 2007 from http://news.bbc.co.uk/2/hi/programmes/ click_online/6112754.stm.

Simpson, J. A. and Weiner, E. S. C. (eds) (1989). *The Oxford English dictionary* (Vol. 2). Oxford: Clarendon Press/Oxford University Press.

Skiba, R. and Peterson, R. (1999). The dark side of zero tolerance: Can punishment lead to safe schools? *Phi Delta Kappan, 80*(5): 372–6, 381–3.

Slee, P. T. (1995). Peer victimization and its relationship to depression among Australian primary school students. *Personality and Individual Differences, 18*: 57–62.

Slee, P. T. and Rigby, K. (1993). Australian school children's self-appraisal of interpersonal relations: the bullying experience. *Child Psychiatry and Human Development, 23*: 272–83.

Smith, D. J. (1995). Youth crime and conduct disorders: Trends, patterns and causal explanations. In M. Rutter and D. J. Smith (eds), *Psychosocial disorders in young people: Time trends and their causes*. Chichester, and New York: Published for Academia Europaea by J. Wiley, pp. 389–489.

Smith, W. J. (2004). Balancing security and human rights: Quebec schools between past and future. *Education and Law Journal, 14*(1): 99–136.

Smith, P. K. and Sharp, S. (1994). *School bullying: Insights and perspectives*. London, and New York: Routledge.

Smith, P. K. and Shu, S. (2000). What good schools can do about bullying: Findings from a survey in English schools after a decade of research and action. *Childhood, 7*: 193–212.

Smorti, A., Menesini, E. and Smith, P. K. (2003). Parents' definitions of children's bullying in a five-country comparison. *Journal of Cross-Cultural Psychology, 34*(4): 417–32.

Snider, M. (2004). Stalked by a cyberbully. *Maclean's, 24* May, *117*: 76.

Soloyon, C. (2005). A gift from the devil: Worry about on-line activities. *The Gazette*, 2 February: A2.

Song, W. (2006). Ijime ga jisatsu ni tsunagaru nihon no 'kuuki' [electronic version]. *Nikkei Business Online*, 2 November. Retrieved 18 March 2007 from http://business.nikkeibp. co.jp/article/manage/20061031/112784/.

Spano, R. and Nagy, S. (2005). Social guardianship and social isolation: An application and extension of lifestyle/routine activities theory to rural adolescents. *Rural Sociology, 70*(3): 414–37.

Spitzberg, B. and Hoobler, G. (2002). Cyberstalking and the technologies of interpersonal terrorism. *New Media and Society, 4*: 71–92.

State of Illinois (2007). Illinois Social Networking Prohibition Act, SB1682.

State of Oklahoma (2007). House Bill No. 1715.

Steeves, V. and Wing, C. (2005). Young Canadians in a wired world. Media Awareness Network web site. Retrieved 4 December 2006 from www.media-awareness.ca/english/ research/YCWW/phaseII/.

Stein, N. (1991). It happens here, too: Sexual harassment in the school. *Education Week, 11*(13): 32.

Stein, N. (1995). Sexual harassment in K-12 schools: The public performance of gendered violence. *Harvard Educational Review: Special Issue: Violence and Youth, 65*(2): 145–62.

Stein, N. (1999). *Classrooms and courtrooms: Facing sexual harassment in K-12 schools*. New York: Teachers College Press.

Stonebanks, C. (in press). *The James Bay Cree*. Rotterdam: Sense Publishers.

Suler, J. R. and Philips, W. L. (1998). The bad boys of cyberspace: Deviant behavior in a multimedia chat community. *Cyberpsychology and Behavior, 1*(3): 275–94.

Swartz, J. (2005). Schoolyard bullies get nastier online [electronic version]. *USA Today*, 7 March. Retrieved 12 August 2007 from www.usatoday.com/tech/news/2005-03-06-cover-cyberbullies_x.htm.

Takach, G. S. (1999). Internet law: Dynamics, themes and skill sets. *Canadian Business Law Journal, 32*(1): 1–83.

Tanaka, T. (2001). The identity and formation of the victim of 'shunning'. *School Psychology International*, 22(4): 463–76.

Tanner, J. (1996). *Teenage troubles: Youth and deviance in Canada*. Toronto, ON: Nelson Canada.

Tattum, D. P. (1997). Developing a programme to reduce bullying in young offenders' institutions. In D. Tattum and H. Graham (eds), *Bullying: Home, school and community*. London: David Fulton Publishers, pp. 159–72.

Tattum, D. P. and Herbert, G. (1993). *Countering bullying: Initiatives by schools and local authorities*. Staffordshire: Trentham Books.

Tavani, H. and Grodzinsky, F. (2002). Cyberstalking, personal privacy, and moral responsibility. *Ethics and Information Technology*, 4: 123–32.

Thiessen, D. D. (1976). *The evolution and chemistry of aggression*. Springfield, IL: Thomas.

Thomas, C. and Canadian Press (2007). Discipline over student postings on Facebook highlight need for education: Ont [electronic version]. *Redorbit breaking news*, 1 May. Retrieved 15 August 2007 from www.redorbit.com/news/education/919877/discipline_over_student_postings_on_facebook_highlight_need_for_education/index.html.

Tolman, D. L., Spencer, R., Rosen-Reynoso, M. and Porches, M. (2001). 'He's the man!' Gender ideologies and early adolescents' experiences with sexual harassment. Paper presented at the American Educational Researchers Association (AERA) Conference, Seattle, Washington.

Tremblay, R. E. (1991). Aggression, pro-social behaviour and gender: Three magic words but no magic wand. In D. L. Pepler and H. K. Rubin (eds), *The development and treatment of childhood aggression*. Hillsdale, NJ: Lawrence Erlbaum Associates, pp. 71–7.

Tseloni, T., Wittebrood, K., Farrell, G. and Pease, K. (2004). Burglary victimization in England and Wales, the United States and the Netherlands. *The British Journal of Criminology*, 44(1): 66–91.

United Nations (1989). Convention on the rights of the child. New York: United Nations.

United Nations (2001). World conference against racism web site. Retrieved 9 August 2007 from www.un.org/WCAR/.

United States Congress (1996). Communications Decency Act.

Volokh, E. (1997). Freedom of speech, shielding children, and transcending balancing [electronic version]. *Supreme Court Review*, 141: 141–97. Retrieved 20 August 2007 from www.law.ucla.edu/faculty/volokh/shield.htm.

Wallechinsky, D., Wallace, A., Basen, I. and Farrow, J. (2005). *The book of lists*. Toronto, ON: Alfred A. Knopf Canada.

Wason-Ellam, L. (1996). Voices from the shadows. In J. R. Epp and A. M. Watkinson (eds), *Systemic violence: How schools hurt children*. London: Falmer Press, pp. 93–104.

Watkinson, A. M. (1999). *Education, student rights, and the Charter*. Saskatoon, SK: Purich.

Welsh, D. M. (1998). Limiting liability through education: Do school districts have a responsibility to teach students about peer sexual harassment? *Journal of Gender and the Law*, 6: 165–97.

Whitney, I. and Smith, P. K. (1993). A survey of the nature and extent of bullying in junior/middle and secondary schools. *Educational Research*, 35: 3–25.

Wikipedia (2007a). Description of cyber-bullying. Retrieved 10 May 2007 from http://en.wikipedia.org/wiki/Cyberbullying.

Wikipedia (2007b). Description of Kuso. Retrieved 14 August 2007 from http://en.wikipedia.org/wiki/Kuso.

Wikipedia (2007c). Description of happy slapping. Retrieved 23 August 2007 from http://en.wikipedia.org/wiki/Happy_slapping#_note-9.

Wikipedia (2007d). Description of the Deleting Online Predators Act of 2006. Retrieved 23 August 2007 from http://en.wikipedia.org/wiki/Deleting_Online_Predators_Act_of_2006(#_note-thomas#_note-thomas).

Wikipedia (2007e). Description of the Communications Act of 1934. Retrieved 23 August 2007 from http://en.wikipedia.org/wiki/Communications_Act_of_1934.

Wikipedia (2007f). Description of the Children's Internet Protection Act. Retrieved 23 August 2007 from http://en.wikipedia.org/wiki/Children%27s_Internet_Protection_Act.

Willard, N. (2003). Off-campus, harmful online student speech. *Journal of School Violence*, *1*(2): 65–93.

Willard, N. (2005). Educator's guide to cyber bullying: Addressing the harm caused by online social cruelty [electronic version]. Retrieved 10 December 2005 from www.cyberbully.org.

Willard, N. (2007). Educator's guide to cyberbullying and cyberthreats [electronic version], April. Retrieved 12 August 2007 from www.cyberbully.org/cyberbully/docs/cbct educator.pdf.

Winkler, L. K. (2004). Celebrate democracy! Teach about censorship. *English Journal*, *94*(5): 48–51.

WiredSafety (n.d.). Cyberstalking and harassment. Web page. Retrieved 23 August 2007 from http://wiredsafety.org/gb/stalking/index.html.

Wolak, J., Mitchell, K. J. and Finkelhor, D. (2003). Escaping or connecting? Characteristics of youth who form close online relationships. *Journal of Adolescence*, *26*(1): 105–19.

Wolak, J., Mitchell, K. J. and Finkelhor, D. (2006). *Online victimization of children: Five years later*. Washington, DC: National Center for Missing and Exploited Children.

Wooldredge, J. D., Cullen, F. T. and Latessa, E. J. (1992). Research note victimization in the workplace: A test of routine activities theory. *Justice Quarterly*, *9*(2), 325–35.

Wright, P. (1986). Schemer schema: Consumers' intuitive theories about marketers' influence tactics. *Advances in Consumer Research*, *13*: 1–3.

Wright, S. (2006). MySpace and Deleting Online Predators Act (DOPA) [electronic version]. *MIT Tech Talk*. Retrieved 13 August 2007 from www.danah.org/papers/MySpaceDOPA.pdf.

Wyman, M. (2000a). Rowling thunder. *The Vancouver Sun*, 21 October: B1, B5.

Wyman, M. (2000b). You can lead a fool to a book but you can't make them think. *The Vancouver Sun*, 26 October: A1, A4.

Yahoo (2006) California Grade 9 girl questioned about threats to Bush on MySpace [electronic version]. *Yahoo! News Canada*, 13 October. Retrieved 16 October 2006 from http://ca.news.yahoo.com/s/capress/061013/ztechnology/myspace_bush_threat.

Ybarra, M. L. and Mitchell, K. J. K. (2004a). Online aggressor/targets, aggressors and targets: A comparison of associated youth characteristics. *Journal of Child Psychology and Psychiatry*, *45*: 1308–16.

Ybarra, M. L. and Mitchell, K. J. K. (2004b). Youth engaging in online harassment: Associations with caregiver-child relationships, Internet use, and personal characteristics. *Journal of Adolescence*, *27*(3): 319–36.

Ybarra, M. L., Mitchell, K. J. K., Finkelhor, D. and Wolak, J. (2007). Internet prevention messages: Targeting the right online behaviors. *Archives of Pediatric and Adolescent Medicine*, *161*(2): 138–45.

Yoneyama, S. and Naito, A. (2003). Problems with the paradigm: The school as a factor in understanding bullying (with special reference to Japan). *British Journal of Sociology of Education*, 24(3): 315–30.

Zhang, W. and Wei, J.-Y. (2007a). Internet use in China. Paper presented at the initial team meeting of the International Cyberbullying Research Project, McGill University, Montreal, funded by the Social Science and Humanities Research Council of Canada (SSHRC). Shaheen Shariff, Principal Investigator.

Zhang, W. and Wei, J.-Y. (2007b). The cyber-bullying research (China II). Hangzhou, China: Zhejiang University, funded by the SSHRC. Shaheen Shariff, Principal Investigator, McGill University, Montreal, 22 July.

Zubrick, S. R., Silburn, S. R., Teoh, H. J., Carlton, J., Shepherd, C. and Lawrence, D. (1997). *Western Australian child health survey: Education, health and competency catalogue 4305.5*. Perth: Australian Bureau of Statistics.

Cases

R. vs M.R.M. [1998] 3 S.C.R. 393

R. vs Oakes [1986] 1 S.C.R. 103

Robichaud vs Canada (Treasury Board) [1987] 2 S.C.R. 84

Ross vs New Brunswick School District No. 15 [1996] 1 S.C.R. 825

Ross vs Holly (2004), cited in Bernstein and Hanna (2005)

Singleton vs Board of Education USD 500 894 F. Supp. 386 (D. Kan. 1995)

Stratton Oakmont, Inc. vs Prodigy Services Co., 1995 WL 323710 (N.Y. Sup. Ct., 1995)

Sullivan vs Houston Independent School District, 307 F. Supp. 1328, 1340 (S.D. Tex. 1969)

The People vs B. F. Jones, 62 Mich. 304 (1886)

Tinker vs Des Moines Independent Community School District, 3930 U.S. 503 (1969)

United States of America vs Jake Baker, 890 F. Supp. 1375 (E. D. Mich. 1995)

Vaquero Energy Ltd vs Weir (2004) ABQB 68

Williams vs Eady [1893] 10 TLR 41

Zeran vs America Online, Inc., 958 F. Supp. 1124, 1134 (E.D. Va) aff'd, 129 F.3d 327 (4th Cir. 1997)

Index